Studies in

Macroeconomics and Welfare

The Editors

BB BHATTACHARYA is Director, Institute of Economic Growth (IEG), Delhi. He specialises in macroeconomics and econometric modelling and forecasting. A former President of the Indian Econometric Society, Professor Bhattacharya is currently the President of the Indian Association for Research in National Income and Wealth.

ARUP MITRA is Professor of Economics at the Institute of Economic Growth, Delhi. His research interests include: labour and welfare, urban development, industry, infrastructure and gender.

Studies in

Macroeconomics and Welfare

Editors

BB Bhattacharya
Arup Mitra

Published by Academic Foundation
in association with
THE INDIAN ECONOMETRIC SOCIETY

ACADEMIC FOUNDATION
NEW DELHI

First published in 2005
by

ACADEMIC FOUNDATION

4772-73 / 23 Bharat Ram Road, (23 Ansari Road),
Darya Ganj, New Delhi - 110 002 (India).
Phones : 23245001 / 02 / 03 / 04.
Fax : +91-11-23245005.
E-mail : academic@vsnl.com
www : academicfoundation.com

in association with

THE INDIAN ECONOMETRIC SOCIETY

Studies in Macroeconomics and Welfare
Editors: B.B. Bhattacharya, Arup Mitra
ISBN 81-7188-461-X

Designed and typeset by Italics India, New Delhi.
Printed and bound in India.

Contents

...CONTD. ..

...CONTD. ..

Section II

Welfare

List of Boxes, Figures and Tables

BOXES

FIGURES

...CONTD. ..

TABLES

...CONTD. ..

...CONTD. ..

...Contd. ..

Preface

Economic growth and welfare have been the matter of prime concern in economic reforms in India during last one decade and a half. While there have been a number of studies on these issues in general, not much attention, however, has been paid to their empirical verification. This volume presents selected papers on macro economic policies and welfare in India, using econometric techniques. The papers were originally presented in the 40th Annual Conference of the Indian Econometric Society held at the Institute of Social and Economic Change (ISEC), Bangalore in February 2004, and subsequently revised in the light of the discussion in the conference. These papers are not only interesting in terms of econometric methodology but also relevant for planning and public policy.

Section 1 of the volume focuses on money demand, interest rate, exchange rate, inflation, and the effects of monetary and fiscal policies on the Indian economy. This section also includes papers dealing with some of the theoretical issues like growth-equity trade-off, environmental concerns relating to air pollution in the mega cities and aspects of production behaviour in the agricultural sector, as they have wide applicability and bear significant implications for macro-economic policies.

Section 2 revolves around issues relating to poverty, human development, health care and public policy and the effectiveness of micro-finance in improving the standard of living. These are some of the issues, which are of critical importance in the context of economic reforms with a human face. The role of public policy in providing the essential links between growth and welfare would then be understood in a more meaningful way.

We are grateful to the Indian Econometric Society for sponsoring the conference, and to ISEC for hosting the conference. Special thanks to Dr. G. Ananthapadmanabhan, Secretary and Dr. K.R. Shanmugam, Treasurer of the Indian Econometric Society for organising the conference and helping publish this volume.

— **B.B. Bhattacharya**
Arup Mitra

Editors/Contributors

Editors:

B.B. Bhattacharya is currently Director of the Institute of Economic Growth, Delhi. He specialises in macroeconomics and econometric modelling and forecasting. A former President of the Indian Econometric Society, Professor Bhattacharya is currently the President of the Indian Association for Research in National Income and Wealth.

Arup Mitra is Professor of Economics at the Institute of Economic Growth, Delhi. His research interests include labour and welfare, urban development, industry, infrastructure and gender.

Contributors:

Sangeeta Chakravarty .... *Lecturer, Institute of Economic Growth, Delhi.*

Mahua Paul .... *Lecturer, Institute for Social and Industrial Development, New Delhi*

Pami Dua .... *Professor, Department of Economics, Delhi School of Economics, Delhi.*

Nishita Raje .... *Asstt. Adviser, Department of Economic Analysis and Policy, Reserve Bank of India, Mumbai.*

Satyananda Sahoo .... *Research Officer, Department of Economic Analysis and Policy, Reserve Bank of India, Mumbai.*

A. Soumya .... *Research Scholar, Central University, Hyderabad.*

K.N. Murty .... *Professor and Head, Department of Economics, Central University, Hyderabad.*

Srivydya Subramaniam .... *Lecturer, Department of Economics, SGTB Khalsa College, Delhi.*

A.K. Giri .... *Asstt. Professor, Economics and Finance Group, Birla Institute of Technology and Science, Pilani.*

B. Kamaiah .... *Professor, Department of Economics, University of Hyderabad, Hyderabad.*

Balwant Singh .... *Adviser, NIPD, Reserve Bank of India, Mumbai*

Sushila Augustine .... *Asstt. Adviser, Department of Statistical Analysis and Computer Services, Reserve Bank of India, Mumbai*

Ajit R. Joshi .... *Director, Department of Statistical Analysis and Computer Services, Reserve Bank of India, Mumbai*

Rajashree Rajpathak .... *Research Officer, Department of Statistical Analysis and Computer Services, Reserve Bank of India, Mumbai*

Satya P. Das .... *Professor, Indian Statistical Institute, New Delhi.*

Chetan Ghate .... *Asstt. Professor, Indian Statistical Institute, New Delhi.*

M.N. Murty .... *Professor, Institute of Economic Growth, Delhi.*

S.C. Gulati .... *Professor, Institute of Economic Growth, Delhi.*

Avishek Banerjee .... *Consultant, Institute of Economic Growth, Delhi.*

K.P. Mani .... *Faculty, College of Co-operation Banking and Management, Kerala Agricultural University, Thrissur, Kerala.*

Siddhartha Mitra .... *Reader, Gokhale Institute of Politics and Economics, Pune.*

S.D. Brahmankar .... *Senior Statistician, National Council of Applied Economic Research, Delhi.*

Vishal Handa .... *Research Assistant, National Council of Applied Economic Research, Delhi.*

Lekha S. Chakraborty .... *Fellow, National Institute of Public Finance and Policy, New Delhi.*

Anindita Chakrabarti........ *Lecturer, Unit for Child and Youth Research, Tata Institute of Social Sciences, Mumbai.*

Subrata Mukherjee.......... *Research Scholar, Centre for Development Studies; Thiruvananthapuram.*

D. Rajasekhar .... *Professor and Head, Decentralistion and Development Unit, Institute of Social and Economic Change, Bangalore.*

S. Madheswaran............ *Associate Professor, Institute of Social and Economic Change, Bangalore.*

Samapti Guha .... *Research Associate, MFMI Chair Unit, Institute of Rural Management, Anand.*

Gautam Gupta............. *Professor, Department of Economics, Jadavpur University, Kolkata.*

Section I

Macroeconomics

1

Forecasting the Exchange Rate with a Bayesian Vector Auto Regression (BVAR) Model: The Indian Experience

B.B. BHATTACHARYA
SANGEETA CHAKRAVARTY
MAHUA PAUL

1. Introduction

Ever since the statistical time series models were developed by Box and Jenkins (1970), they were used extensively for forecasting of economic variables. The Box and Jenkins type time-series models are very easy to compute and therefore became very popular as a forecasting method. In general these models give reasonably good short-term forecasts, provided there is no structural change during the beyond-sample forecast period. The main draw back of these models is that because these are based on univariate approach they ignore the causal relationship between forecasted variable with other economic variables.

A more sophisticated time series model for forecasting is Vector-Auto-regression (VAR) model propounded by Sims (1980) and later refined by Litterman (1984). VAR, like univariate Box and Jenkins, is also a theoretic in principle, but unlike Box and Jenkins model, it incorporates inter-relationships among variables. The choice of variables included in a VAR set, lag length and order of variables in terms of causality etc. are decided partly on a priori reasoning, but mainly on statistical criteria. VAR models can therefore be used for much more sophisticated analysis, such as impact of shocks, direction of causality and lead-lag etc.

A major limitation of VAR model is that it suffers from over parameterisation. A proper VAR estimation requires a large number of observations, and because of this it is generally estimated with monthly or higher frequency data. Forecasts from VAR are therefore robust over a short period. A survey of forecasting performance of several models, including VAR, done by Fair (1979) has highlighted this problem. To solve the problem of over parameterisation Litterman (1984) developed Bayesian Vector Auto Regression (BVAR) model, in which some restrictions are imposed on parameters. The restrictions can be imposed which are based on either economic theory or statistical considerations.

BVAR forecasting models have been used successfully to forecast economic variables. Litterman (1986) suggested that BVAR model forecast better than the best commercial structural model for the US economy. Amirizadeh and Todd (1984) showed that BVAR forecasting model perform as well as structural model and univariate model. Dua and Ray (1995) found BVAR model appropriate for forecast of non-agricultural employment and unemployment in the state economy of Connecticut, USA. Sen and Maru (1997) used BVAR model to provide quarterly forecasts of GDP and inflation for Indian economy.

In this paper we build a BVAR model for forecasting monthly exchange rate in India. This is the first step to eventually build an early warning model, based on both objective and subjective shocks. Since exchange rate is subject to wide shocks caused by both domestic and external factors, including speculation, we thought it fit to build a BVAR model for it. In this model the Rupee-US Dollar is related to foreign exchange reserves, exports, imports and inflation. The plan of the paper is as follows. In section 2 we describe the Bayesian Statistics and the methodology of BVAR model. Section 3 describes the data and the variables. Section 4 presents the empirical results and Section 5 presents the conclusions.

2. Bayesian Statistics

The Bayesian approach to statistics is a procedure where modeller combines his beliefs with the evidence contained in the data. In classical approach we estimate a set of parameters but in Bayesian approach a set of prior probabilities about the parameters are to be estimated.

As an illustration, let us consider an AR(p) model for a variable y_t, which is written as follows:

$$y_t = \alpha+\beta_1 y_{t-1}+\beta_1 y_{t-2}+....+\beta_p y_{t-p}+u_t \tag{2.1}$$

where u_t is a white noise disturbance term.

If a modeller has a strong prior that the first order autoregressive coefficient in an AR(p) model is equal to 1 and all other coefficients are zero, such prior would be consistent with a view that the concerned variable follows a random walk.

In Bayesian approach the prior information about the parameters $\beta_1, \beta_2, ..., \beta_p$ can be expressed mathematically using univariate prior density function $g(\beta_1)$, $g(\beta_2)$, ..., $g(\beta_p)$. Suppose to estimate the above model (2.1), consider the random walk prior, then the mean of β_1 must be equal to 1, whereas the mean of all other parameter are zero. This prior assumes that the coefficients on higher order lags are more likely to be zero than the lower order lags. This tightening of the prior for higher order lag could be achieved by making the prior variance decrease with increasing lag length.

In the Bayesian estimation, the coefficient estimate is obtained by the combination of the evidence from the sample data with the prior information. The information contained in the sample data is the sample probability density function $g(y_t|\beta)$, which can also be stated as the density of the random variable y_t conditional on the value of the parameter.

The posterior density function $g(\beta|y_t)$ is obtained by using the Bayes theorem.

$$g(\beta|y_t) = g(y_t|\beta)\ g(\beta)/g(y_t) \tag{2.2}$$

where $g(y_t)$ is the unconditional density of the variable y_t, which for a given sample data is a normalisation which ensures that $g(\beta|y_t)$ is a probability density function.

2.1 Comparison of VAR and BVAR Model

The VAR model introduced by Sims (1980) can be expressed as follows:

$$Y_t = c + A(L)Y_t + u_t$$

where c is a (nx1) vector of constant, A(L) is a (nxn) matrix of polynomials in the backward-shift operator L with lag length p, Y_t is a (nx1) vector of endogenous variables and u_t is a (nx1) vector of error terms. The draw back of this model is that many parameters would have to be estimated, and some of which may be statistically insignificant. The problem of over parameterisation is acute in small sample size because of loss of degrees of freedom. Over parameterisation generally leads to large out of sample forecasting errors.

Such problems with the unrestricted VAR led to the development of the BVAR, which tried to overcome the problem of over parameterisation by retaining the theoretical structure. Litterman suggested the application of Bayesian procedure in estimating the parameters of the system. He suggested that instead of eliminating the longer lags or eliminating the less important variable, he imposes restrictions on the coefficients through Bayesian approach. Litterman's prior restriction is based on the consideration that, many economic variables behave like random walk, therefore systematic variation is relatively small compared with the random variation, so the prior distribution of the parameters should closely confirm to the random walk model. Instead of dropping a variable or a lag which forces its coefficients to be zero, Bayesian approach make the coefficients of the longer lags to be non-zero but regards them as more likely close to zero than shorter lag. Thus in BVAR model parameter assumes the distribution with mean zero except the first lag of the own variable in each equation. The standard deviations of the prior distribution will decrease as the lag length increases and tighten the distribution around the prior mean of zero at longer lags.

The Bayesian prior provides an alternative way of inducing stationarity in the data. If a series is non-stationary then one cannot expect to get a stable relationship from the data, as in the case when trend component is stochastic. For example in random walk forecast at level form will have uncertainty that increase as forecast horizon increases because of random change. In such a situation first differencing the data may achieve stationarity, but in the process some information would be lost. Litterman's random walk prior gives an alternative way to induce stationarity in the data characterised by stochastic trend without first differencing them. The presence of unit root and co-integration in the data is a key issue in estimating vector autoregression. The problem of unit root can be get rid of by differencing the data. If the co-integrating vector was found to exist between some linear combination of the variables then relative error correction terms have to be included. Otherwise the model will be mis-specified.

The advantage of Bayesian method is that it does not need any special care for non-stationarity and co-integration. The reason behind this is that the Bayesian approach is based on the likelihood function, which has the same Gaussian shape regardless of the presence of unit root in the data. Sims (1988) and Sims, Stock and Watson (1990) therefore recommend that specification of variables in the BVAR model should be in levels. In this case the loss of information through differencing can be avoided and yet the basic characteristics can be retained.

2.2 *Choice of Prior*

The prior distributions for all coefficients are assumed to be independent normal. Thus the two parameters to be specified are the mean and standard deviation for each coefficient. All coefficients assume a prior mean of zero except for the first lag coefficient of the dependent variable in each equation, which is set equal to unity.

The standard deviation of the prior distribution for lag m of variable j in equation i for all i, j and m - S(i, j, m) is specified as follows:

$$S(i, j, m) = [\omega\, g(m)\, f(i, j)]\, Si/Sj \qquad (2.2.1)$$

$$f(i, j) = 1 \text{ if } i=j$$

$$=kij \text{ otherwise } 0 \leq kij \leq 1$$

$$g(m) = m^{-d},\ d > 0$$

The scalar ω is the overall tightness of the prior. A tighter prior can be produced by the value of ω. f(i, j) sets the tightness of the prior for the jth variable in the ith equation. By reducing the value of k_{ij} we can decrease the interaction, tightness of the prior. If we increase k_{ij}, we get less tight prior and in that case vector part of BVAR model is more important. Similarly if we decrease ω means Bayesian part becomes more important. If f(i,j)=0.5 it implies that relative to variable i, the variable j has a weight of 50 per cent.

The parameter g(m) gives the tightness on lag m relative to lag 1. The shrinkage of the standard deviation as lag length increases is determined by g(m), given by a decay parameter d, which imposes either harmonic decay $g(m) = m^{-d}$ or geometric decay $g(m) = m^{d-1}$.

The key issue of BVAR model is the choice of the hyper parameters ω, k_{ij} and decay parameter d. The search of all the parameters is not possible and according to Litterman longer lags with d=0 is not suitable. If one has to tighten up the prior with increasing lag a harmonic decay d=1 or 2 may do well, but geometric decay tends to get too tight too fast. For overall tightness reasonable procedure is to set the hyper parameters ω=.1 or .2. One can tighten up the prior by giving less weights to the other variable in the system. Tightness controls directly the important own lag. Setting it too small values will force the own lags too close to the prior mean. The ratio Si/Sj is a scalar factor, where Si is the standard error of a univariate autoregression for variable i. The ratio scales the variables to account for differences in units of measurement and allows the specification of the prior without taking into consideration of the magnitudes of the variables. The parameters of the prior are said to be hyper-parameter in order to distinguish them from the estimated coefficient, which are parameters of the model itself.

Prior values on ω or f(i,j) can be used to specify the BVAR for forecasting. The accuracy of the forecasts generated by using different combination of hyper parameter ω along with the lag length m and decay parameter d can be evaluated by using Theil's U statistic and RMSE (root mean square error).

3. Data and Variables

The choice of variable included in the BVAR model is by economic reasoning. For this study the variables included in the model are exchange rate, foreign exchange reserves export, import and inflation. The monthly data for these variables are taken from the Reserve Bank of India (RBI) Bulletin for the time period April 1991 to 2003 October.

The rational for choosing these variables are as follows. The exchange rate of rupee affects both exports and imports. In turn the trade balance – exports minus imports – affects exchange rate. The exchange rate is also influenced by inflation. Given inflation in the world economy (more appropriately in the trading partner countries), a rise in the domestic inflation would reduce purchasing power of rupee and hence exchange rate is expected to depreciate. Finally, the existing stock of foreign exchange reserves provides a stabilising factor in the exchange rate: more supply of foreign exchange reserves more stable would be exchange rate and vice-versa. The foreign exchange reserves also influence speculation on the exchange rate. A diminishing foreign exchange reserves can fuel negative speculation leading to depreciation. Most foreign exchange crisis are caused by sharp fall in foreign exchange reserves, and as a consequence the exchange rate depreciates heavily.

4. Empirical Results

In order to analyse the robustness of the BVAR approach, we have estimated the parameters of the models and the forecast performance statistics in level forms. BVAR is estimated for different values of hyper parameters. VAR is estimated in logs, levels and in difference form.

As argued earlier, the choice of hyper parameter is the key issue of BVAR. A complete search for all possible hyper parameter is not possible. However the sensitivity of each model's forecasting performance to overall tightness and the relative tightness on cross lags was examined. The choice of lag length for VAR is six, which is determined by Akaike Information Criteria. In order to see the clear evidence on the choice of lag length, we estimate BVAR with lag m=5,6,7, with various combination of hyper parameters (ω, k). The best model with lag length six gives us the least RMSE and Theil's U statistic. Several BVAR models are estimated with various values of hyper parameter ω, k and d. Doan (1992) recommended d=1, k=.5 and ω=.2, to see how much BVAR forecast are sensitive to hyper parameters. The various values chosen in the neighbourhood points mentioned by Doan are considered for this analysis. They are as follows: (ω, k)=(.2,.5); (.2,.7);(.1,.5); (.4,.3);(.4,.8) and (.3,.3) Since our lag length of the model is six, so we have tried for higher values of decay d=2 apart from d=1 to see how sensitive is our forecast performance. The choice of the prior is determined on the basis of out of sample forecast performance statistic. Tight prior as well as loose priors are obtained by increasing and decreasing the interaction parameter k. The results of RMSE and Theil's statistic for out of sample forecast are reported in Table 1.1 and Table 1.2 (given at the end of the text) for all the models From the Table 1.1, it is very clear that as the value of the interaction parameter k is increasing keeping the overall tightness parameter ω fixed, the value of RMSE increased for one step ahead forecast. It is further noticed that for higher values of k=.7 and .8, the RMSE is more in comparison to smaller value of k. For d=1, (ω, k)=(.1,.5) and (.3,.3), the value of RMSE is almost same as 0.253 and 0.252. But the Theil's U statistic is least for (.3,.3). So our preferred BVAR model is with prior ω=.3, k=.3 and d=1. Out of sample forecast statistic at various horizons (1,2,3 and 4) are given in Table 1.2 for VAR at levels, logs and BVAR with priors (.3,.3) and (.1,.5). For all the BVAR models for one step ahead forecast, U statistic <1 and the difference is also very negligible, so it is very difficult to choose the hyper parameters which will give accurate forecast.

We also compare the forecasting performance of the best BVAR model (.3,.3) with VAR models in all forms: levels and log levels. Bayesian VAR seems to perform better than VAR. From the Table 1.1 it seems that the forecast performance is less sensitive to an increase in the overall tightness on the prior. When the values of the interaction parameters are lowered, then the forecast performance statistics seems to improve. It can be concluded from this that the tighter restriction on interaction parameter increases the forecasting performance of the model. From the best BVAR (d=1,ω=.3,k=.3), the conditional forecasts are obtained assuming a 5 per cent appreciation or depreciation in the exchange rate. Both BVAR and VAR model follows the same trend.

The graphical representation of all the results can be seen from the appendix given at the end of the study.

The overall inference that may be drawn from this study is that the forecasting performance of BVAR model depends crucially on fixation of hyperparameters. Thus the prior distribution plays an important role in BVAR forecasting. It is therefore necessary that the priors should be determined after carefully examining results from alternative BVAR models. The results also confirm that in comparison to BVAR, the performance of VAR cannot be ruled out.

5. Conclusions

The objective of this paper is to focus on the forecast performance of BVAR model in comparison to the VAR model. For this we have estimated both VAR and BVAR models for forecasting monthly exchange rate in India. The simple Bayesian VAR structure with five variables give very encouraging out of sample forecasts to actual values. The evidence suggests that prior beliefs can improve forecasting performance.

The BVAR model selection procedure specially the specification of hyper parameter is little complicated, but its superior forecasting ability raises hopes of more effective use of it in future. With proper estimation of prior it can not only be an effective alternative to simple VAR, but its superior properties can be very useful in developing an appropriate model for forecasting macro variables sensitive to wide-spread subjective speculation. The present exercise may be repeated to other variables to test the robustness of the BVAR as an effective model of forecasting under uncertainties.

APPENDIX

Table 1.1

Forecast Statistics for Exchange Rate (One Step Ahead)

Model			*RMSE*	*Theil*
VAR (Levels)			.326	.012
LVAR (Logs)			.078	.0012
VAR (Growth)			.344	.015
Bayesian VAR (BVAR)				
d=1	ω=.2	k=.5	.256	.0041
d=1	ω=.2	k=.7	.265	.0053
d=1	ω=.1	k=.5	.253	.0047
d=1	ω=.3	k=.3	.252	.0045
d=1	ω=.3	k=.5	.263	.0055
d=1	ω=.4	k=.3	.257	.0049
d=1	ω=.4	k=.8	.278	.0068
d=2	ω=.2	k=.5	.257	.0049
d=2	ω=.1	k=.5	.249	.0044
d=2	ω=.3	k=.3	.256	.0048
LBVAR (Logs)				
d=1	ω=.3	k=.3	.025	.0005

Table 1.2

Forecast Statistic for Exchange Rate at Various Horizons

Model	*Horizon*	*RMSE*	*Theil*
VAR (Levels)	1	0.326	0.0120
	2	0.325	0.0121
	3	0.320	0.0124
	4	0.320	0.0127
VAR (Logs)	1	0.078	0.0012
	2	0.030	2.79E-05
	3	0.029	2.72E-05
	4	0.029	2.65E-05
Bayesian VAR (BVAR)			
d=1, ω=.1,k=.5	1	0.253	0.0047
	2	0.255	0.0048
	3	0.254	0.0049
	4	0.253	0.0049
d=2, ω=.1,k=.5	1	0.249	0.0044
	2	0.248	0.0044
	3	0.248	0.0045
	4	0.247	0.0045
d=1, ω=.3,k=.3	1	0.252	0.0045
	2	0.252	0.0044
	3	0.251	0.0043
	4	0.248	0.0043
d=2, ω=.3,k=.3	1	0.256	0.0048
	2	0.256	0.0049
	3	0.255	0.0050
	4	0.254	0.0050

Figure 1.1

Actual and One Step Ahead Forecast of VAR in Levels

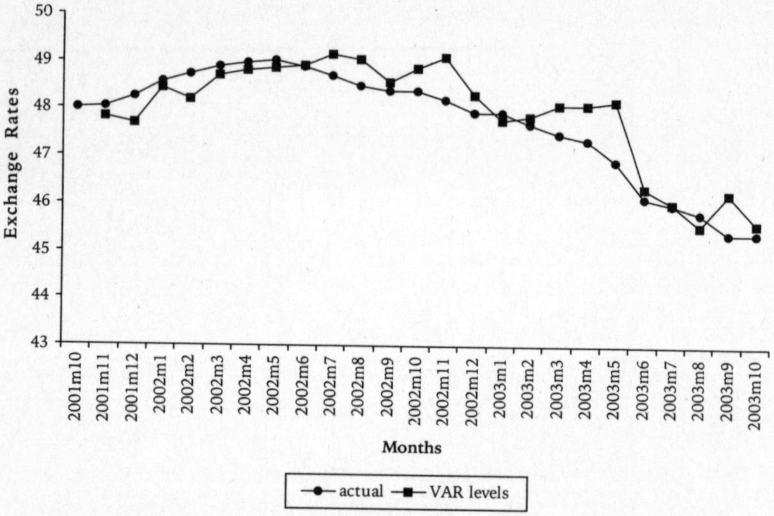

Figure 1.2

Actual and Out of Sample Forecasts of Prior (.3,.3)

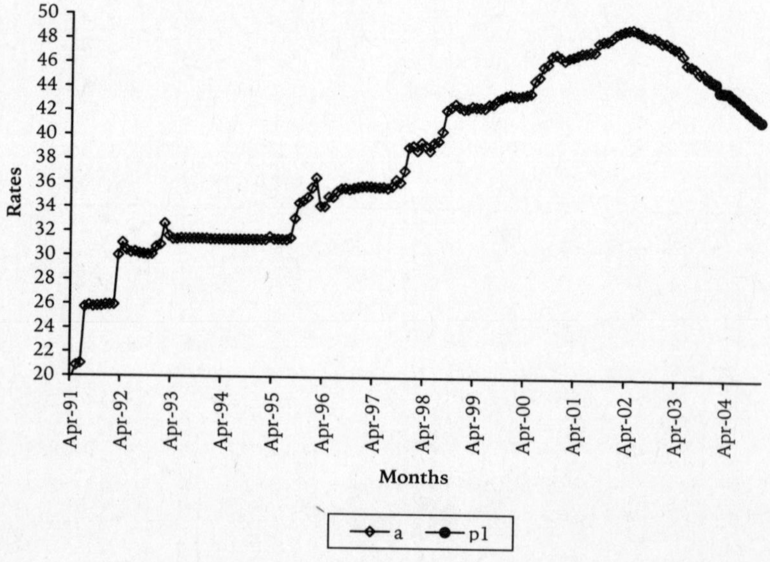

Figure 1.3

Actual, .3,.3 and .1,.5 1step Ahead in Sample Forecast

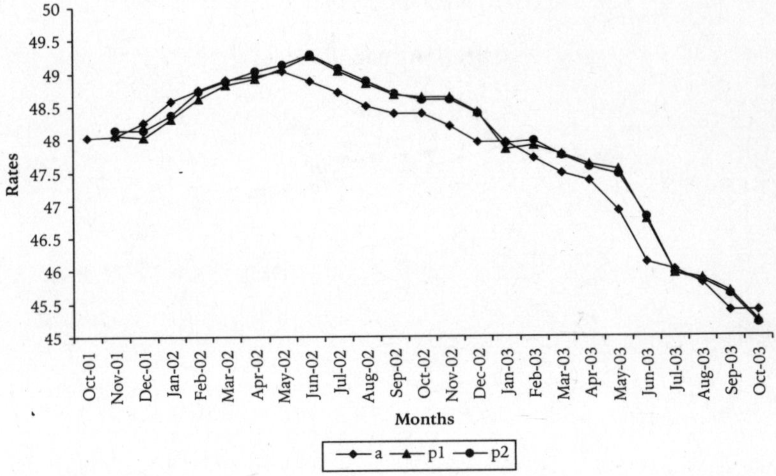

Figure 1.4

Actual and Forecasts of VAR and BVAR (.3,.3) in Logs (in sample)

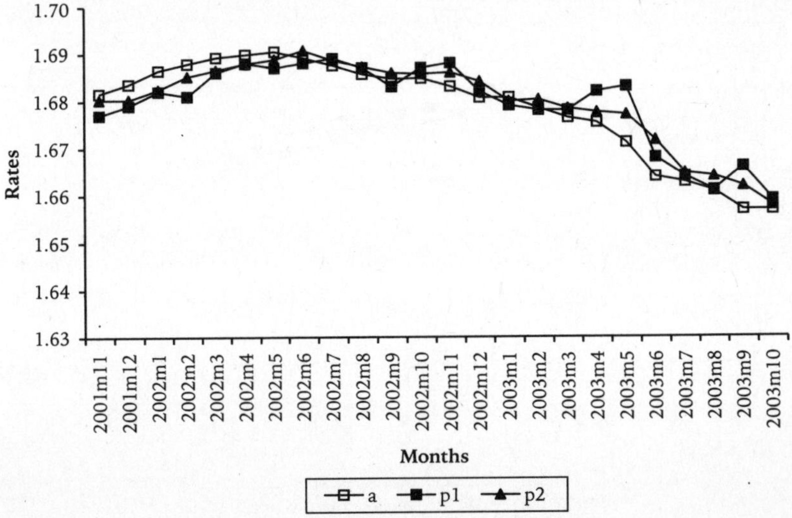

Figure 1.5

BVAR Model with Prior (.3,.3) at Various Horizons with Actual Values of Exchange Rates

1st Step Ahead Forecast

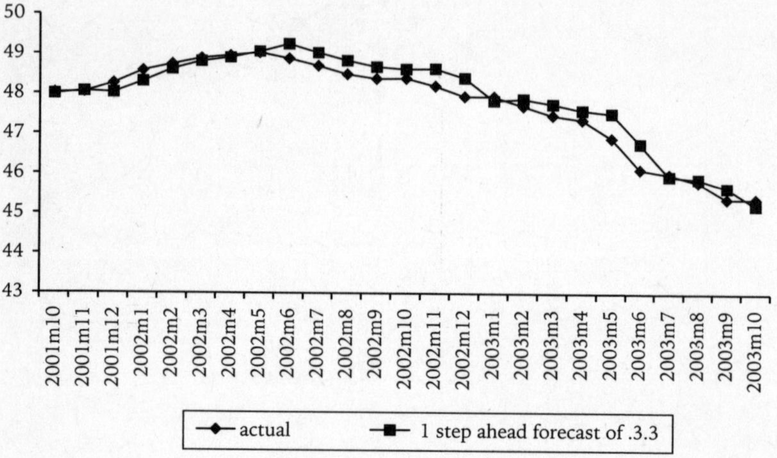

2nd Step Ahead Forecast

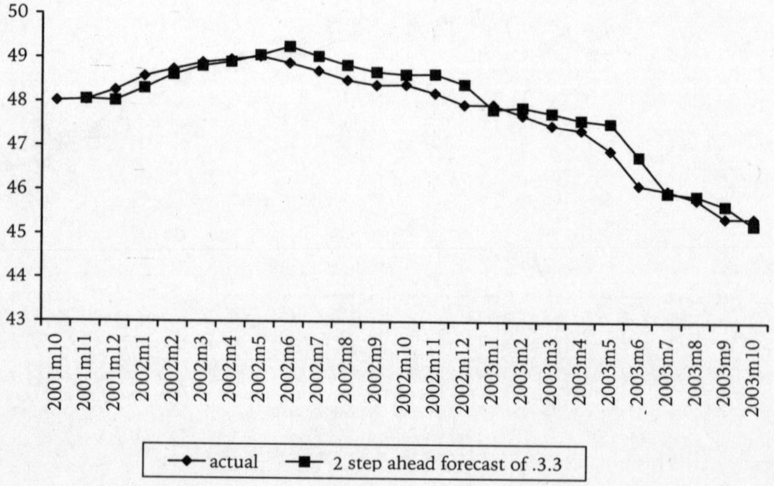

3rd Step Ahead Forecast

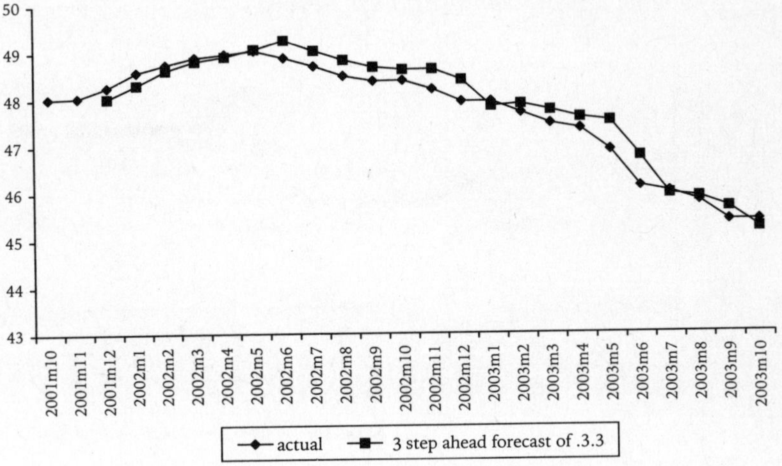

4th Step Ahead Forecast

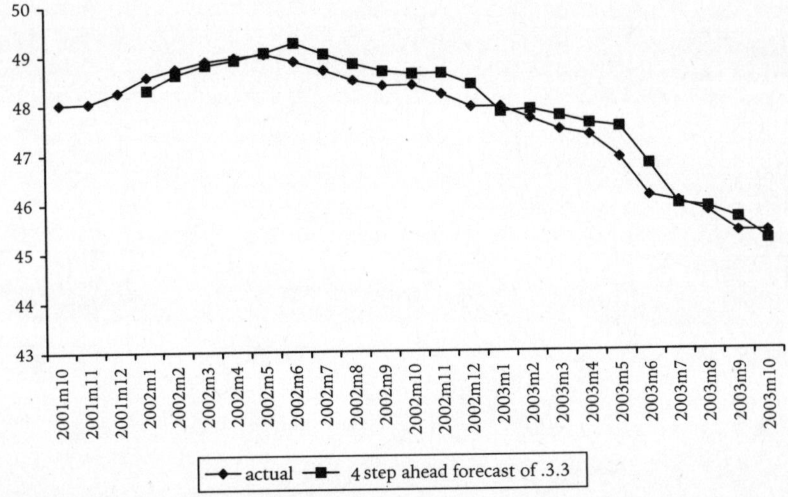

Figure 1.6

Conditional BVAR and VAR in Logs Forecast of Out-of Sample

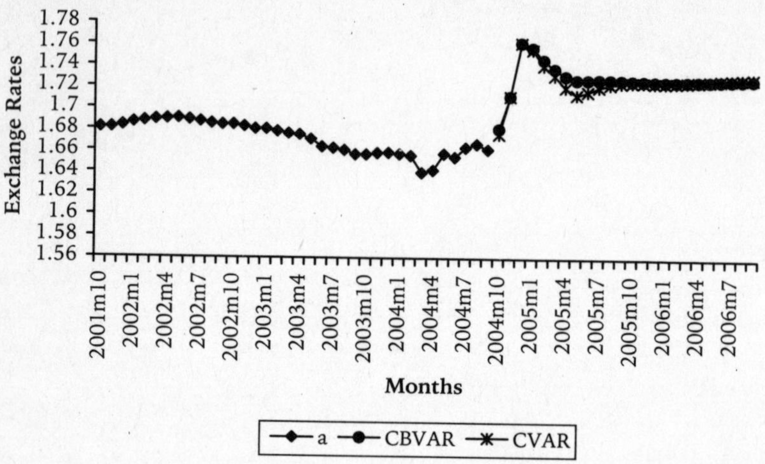

References

Amirizadeh, H. and R.M. Todd (1984). "More Growth Ahead for Ninth District States", *Quarterly Review*, 8, Federal Reserve Bank of Minneapolis, Fall, 8-17.

Fair, Ray (1979). "An Analysis of the Accuracy of the Four Macro Econometric Models", *Journal of Political Economy*, 87(4).

Litterman, R.B. (1986). "Forecasting with Bayesian Vector Autoregression—Five Years of Experience", *Journal of Business and Economic Statistics*, 4, 25-38.

Litterman R.B. (1984). "Forecasting and Policy Analysis with Bayesian Vector Autoregression Models". *Quarterly Review*, 8, Federal Reserve Bank of Minneapolis, Fall, 30-41.

Sims, Stock and Watson (1990). "Inference in Linear Time Series Models with Some Unit Roots", *Econometrica*, Vol. 58, 113-144.

Sims, C.A. (1980). "Macroeconomics and Reality", *Econometrica*, 48, 1-48.

Box, G.E.P. and G.M. Jenkins (1970). *Time Series Analysis, Forecasting and Control* (Holden –Dary, San Francisco).

Dua, P. and S.C. Ray. (1995). "A BVAR Model for Connecticut Economy", *Journal of Forecasting*, 14, 217-227.

Sen, K. and Niral Maru (1997). "A Bayesian Vector Autoregression Forecasting Model for the Indian Economy". *Journal of Quantitative Economics*, Vol 13, No.1 January 97, 1-15.

Doan, T.A. (1990). *RATS User's Manual.*

Doan, T.A., Litterman and C. Sims (1984). "Forecasting and Conditional Projection Using Realistic Prior Distributions", *Econometric Reviews*, 3, 1-100.

McNees, S.K. (1986). "Forecasting Accuracy of Alternative Techniques: A Comparison of US Macroeconomic Forecasts", *Journal of Business and Economic Statistics*, 4, 5-15.

Spencer, David, E. (1993). "Developing a Bayesian Vector Autoregression Forecasting Model", *International Journal of Forecasting*, 9, 407-421.

2

Forecasting Indian Interest Rates Using Univariate and Multivariate Models

PAMI DUA, NISHITA RAJE
SATYANANDA SAHOO

1. Introduction

The interest rate is a key financial variable that affects decisions of consumers, businesses, financial institutions, professional investors and policymakers. Movements in interest rates have important implications for the economy's business cycle and are crucial to understanding financial developments and changes in economic policy. Timely forecasts of interest rates can therefore provide valuable information to financial market participants and policymakers. Forecasts of interest rates can also help to reduce interest rate risk faced by individuals and firms. Forecasting interest rates is very useful to central banks in assessing the overall impact (including feedback and expectation effects) of its policy changes and taking appropriate corrective action, if necessary.

An important constituent of the package of structural reforms initiated in India in the early 1990s, was the progressive deregulation of interest rates across the broad spectrum of financial markets. As part of this process, the central bank (Reserve Bank of India) has taken a number of initiatives in developing financial markets, particularly in the context of ensuring efficient transmission of monetary policy. An important consideration in this regard is the signalling role of monetary policy and its implications for equilibrium interest rates. Furthermore, the use of a 'multiple indicator approach' to monetary policy formulation has underscored the information content of rate variables to optimise management goals. Besides, with the progressive integration of financial markets, 'shocks' to one market can have quick 'spill-over' effects on other markets. In particular, with the liberalisation of the external sector, the vicissitudes of capital flows can have implications for the orderly movement of domestic interest rates. Moreover, given the extant large volume of government's market borrowings and the role of the Reserve Bank in managing the internal debt of the Government, an explicit understanding of the determinants of various interest rates and their expected trajectories over the future can facilitate proper coordination of monetary/interest rate policy, exchange rate policy and fiscal policy.

Against this backdrop, the objective of this paper is to develop models to forecast short-term and long-term rates: call money rate, 15-91 days Treasury bill rate and rates on 1-year, 5-years and 10-years government securities. Univariate as well as multivariate models are estimated for each interest rate. Univariate models include autoregressive integrated moving average (ARIMA) models, and ARIMA models with autoregressive conditional heteroscedasticity (ARCH) and generalised autoregressive conditional heteroscedasiticity (GARCH) effects. Multivariate models include vector autoregressive (VAR) models specified in levels, vector error correction models (VECM), and Bayesian vector autoregressive (BVAR) models. In the multivariate models, factors such as liquidity, bank rate, repo rate, yield spread, inflation, credit, foreign interest rates and forward premium are considered. The random walk model is used as the benchmark for evaluating the forecast performance of each model.

For each interest rate, a search for the "best" forecasting model, *i.e.*, one that yields the most accurate forecasts is conducted. This search encompasses the evaluation of the performance of the aforementioned alternative forecasting models. Each model is estimated using weekly data from April 1997 through December 2001 and out-of-sample forecasts up to 36-weeks-ahead are made from January through September 2002. The starting period April 1997 corresponds to the diffusion of interest rate deregulation to various markets.

The format of the study is as follows. Section 2 gives a brief backdrop to the ensuing discussion and presents some stylised facts on interest rates in the context of financial sector reforms and the changes in the monetary policy environment in India. Section 3 describes the conceptual underpinnings of the different models considered. It also reviews the tests for non-stationarity and describes the methodology for comparing the out-of-sample forecast performance of the models. Section 4 presents the empirical results of the alternative models and Section 5 concludes.

2. Interest Rates and Monetary Policy in India: Some Stylised Facts

The role of interest rates in the monetary policy framework has assumed increasing significance with the initiation of financial sector reforms in the Indian economy in the early 1990s and the progressive liberalisation and integration of financial markets. While the objectives of monetary policy in India have, over the years, primarily been that of maintaining price stability and ensuring adequate availability of credit for productive activities in the economy, the monetary policy environment, instruments and operating procedures have undergone significant changes. In fact, the Reserve Bank's Working Group on Money Supply (1998) observed that the emergence of rate variables in a liberalised environment has adversely impacted the predictive stability of the money demand function (although the function continues to exhibit parametric stability) and concluded that monetary policy based solely on monetary targets can lack precision. The Group also underscored the significance of the interest rate channel of monetary transmission in a deregulated environment. This was, in fact, the underlying principle of the multiple indicator approach that was adopted by the Reserve Bank during 1998-99, whereby a set of economic variables (including interest rates) were to be monitored along with the growth in broad money, for monetary policy purposes. Monetary Policy Statements of the Reserve Bank in recent years have also emphasised the preference for a soft and flexible interest rate environment within the framework of macroeconomic stability.

In the regulated and controlled era, *i.e.*, the pre-reform period prior to 1991, monetary policy operations were largely conditional on the government budgetary operations. The interest rates were mostly administered, which kept the yield on government securities at sub market rates and hindered the development of a vibrant secondary market. In the post-reform period, monetary policy operating procedures used for management of short-term liquidity have been largely based on indirect or market-based operations. Interest rates across various financial markets have been progressively rationalised and deregulated. The reforms have generally aimed towards the easing of quantitative restrictions, removal of barriers to entry, wider participation, increase in the number of instruments and improvements in trading, clearing and settlement practices as well as informational flows. Furthermore, the elimination of automatic monetisation of government budget deficit, the progressive reduction in statutory reserve requirements and the shift from direct to indirect instruments of monetary control, have impacted the structure of financial markets and enhanced the role of interest rates in the system.

There have been distinct steps to improve the policy framework and the operating procedures of monetary policy. Currently, both the actual monetary policy and the operating procedures compare favourably with those of major developed countries. While the targeting framework has technically changed from that of monetary targeting to the multiple indicator approach at the operational level, the monetary aggregates and bank credit are still important information and indicator variables. There has been greater stress on the use of interest rates although there is no target announced for these rates. Consistent with international practice, "the use of Cash Reserve Ratio (CRR) as an instrument of monetary control has been de-emphasised and the liquidity management in India is increasingly undertaken through open market operations (OMOs), both outright and repos" (Reddy, 1999).

The Reserve Bank influences liquidity and in turn, short-term interest rates via changes in CRR, OMOs, changes in the Bank rate[1], modulating the refinance limits and the Liquidity Adjustment Facility (LAF)[2] [Figure 2.1]. The LAF was introduced in June 2000 to modulate short-term liquidity in the system on a daily basis through repo and

1. The Bank rate is the discount rate or the rate at which the central bank lends to the commercial banks. Earlier, the central bank also provided refinance to the commercial banks at this rate although more recently the central bank has linked its refinance rate to the reverse repo rate.
2. The Interim Liquidity Adjustment Facility (ILAF) was introduced in April 1999. The ILAF was a precursor to the present day Liquidity Adjustment Facility (LAF). The ILAF provided a mechanism for liquidity management through a combination of repo (absorption), export credit refinance and collateralised lending facilities (CLF) supported by open market operations at set rates of interest. After gauging the success at the ILAF, a full-fledged LAF was initiated on June 5, 2000. Repo (absorption)/reverse repo (injection) auctions were conducted on a daily basis except Saturdays, with a tenor of one day except on Fridays and days preceding the holidays. Interest rate in respect of both repo and reverse repos were decided through cut-off rates emerging from auctions conducted by the Reserve Bank on uniform price basis. Since August 2000, repo auctions of tenors ranging between three to seven days were introduced. Note that the definition of a repo in the Indian context refers to an absorption unlike the international usage where the repo is an injection.

Figure 2.1

Determinants of Short-Term Interest Rates in India

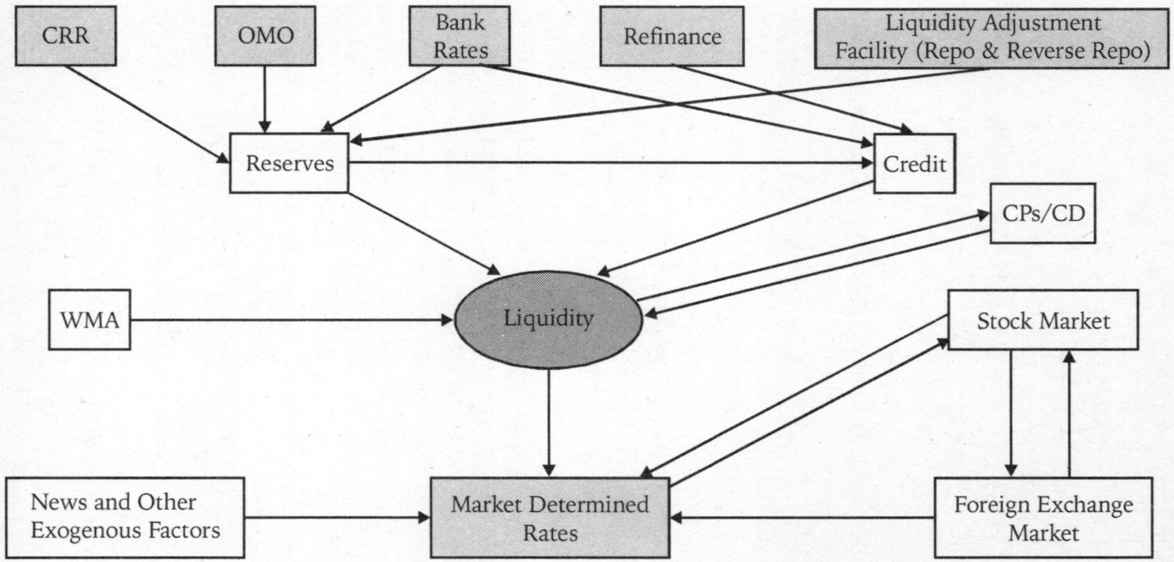

CRR: Cash Reserve Ratio (CRR); OMO: Open Market Operations; WMA[3]: Ways and Means Advances; CD: Certificates of Deposits; CP: Commercial Paper.

3. Ways and Means Advances are the accommodation provided to Governments (State and Central) to meet their temporary budget mismatches.

reverse repo auctions, and in effect, providing an informal corridor for the call money rate. The LAF sets a corridor for the short-term interest rates consistent with policy objectives. The Reserve Bank also uses the private placement route in combination with open market operations to modulate the market-borrowing programme of the Government. In the post 1997 period, the Bank rate has emerged as a reference rate as also a signalling mechanism for monetary policy actions while the LAF rate has been effective both as a tool for liquidity management as well as a signal for interest rates in the overnight market.

The liquidity in the system is also influenced by 'autonomous' factors like the Ways and Means Advances[4] (WMA) to the Government, developments in the foreign exchange market and stock market and 'news'.

Period of the Study

The period of the study begins in April 1997 for several reasons. First, the April 1997 Monetary and Credit policy was in many ways "the big bang" in monetary policymaking. It was the year by which almost the entire process of interest rate liberalisation and rationalisation had been completed. Most of the deregulation in terms of lending and deposit rates took place between 1990-1997. Currently, banks have the freedom to offer different interest rates for various maturities and the minimum maturity for term deposits has been reduced to 15 days. Second, in 1997 the Bank rate was reinstated and all lending by the RBI such as the refinance rates were linked to the Bank rate. The interest rate on savings deposits is, however, prescribed by the RBI. Third, 1997 also saw the progressive reduction in CRR and SLR, and increase in liquidity of the banking sector. Fourth, banking norms were also successively upgraded towards the Basel standards. The policy of transparent interest rates was stressed and banks were required to declare their PLRs and spreads over these PLRs for all advances except for consumer credit. In February 1997, banks were given the freedom to announce separate PLRs for the cash credit component and loan system component, provided they announced the maximum spread in both cases.

---

4. The automatic monetisation facility was replaced in April 1997, by limit based Ways and Means Advances (WMA) to meet temporary mismatches in government receipts and expenditure. WMA have short-term liquidity impact on a day-to-day basis, but are strictly governed by limits.

The changes in the financial sector environment affected the structure and movement of interest rates during the period under consideration (1997-2002). First, the trends in different interest rates (call money, treasury bills and government securities of residual maturities of one, five and ten years or more) are indicative of a general downward movement particularly from 2000 onwards (Figures 2.2A and 2.2B), reflecting the liquidity impact of capital inflows and deft liquidity and debt management in the face of large government borrowings. There were, however, two distinct aberrations in the general trend during this period, which essentially reflected the impact of monetary policy and other regulatory actions taken to quell exchange market pressures. The first occurred in January 1998 in the wake of the financial crisis in South-East Asia while the second occurred around May-August 2000 due to excess demand conditions in the foreign exchange market. At the time, the central bank used monetary and other regulatory measures along with repo auctions to serve as circuit breakers of arbitrage running from money to foreign exchange segments. This tightening of market conditions affected the credit market and had a visible impact on all market determined rates.

Figure 2.2A

Trends in Interest Rates (1997-1998)

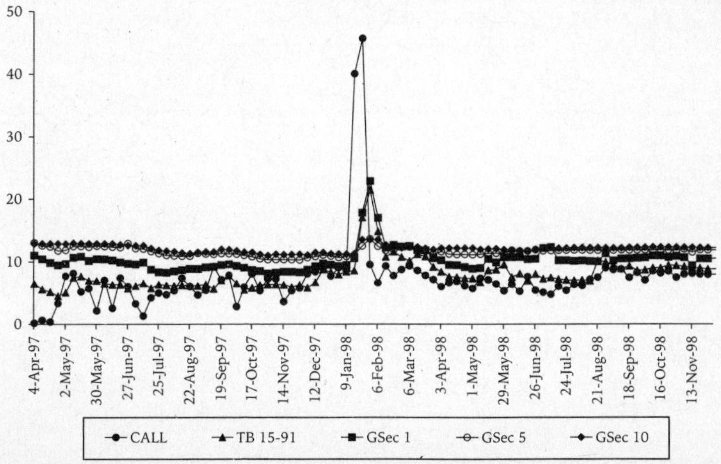

Figure 2.2B

Trends in Interest Rates (1998-2002)

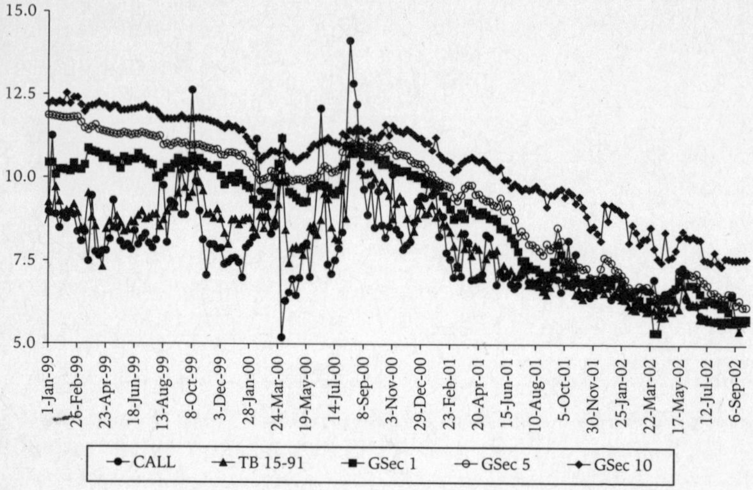

Second, increases in residual maturities have been associated with higher average levels of interest rates (reflecting an upward sloping yield curve) but lower volatility in interest rates (Table 2.1).

Table 2.1

Interest Rates – Summary Statistics
(4th April 1997 – 27th September 2002)

Interest Rates	*Mean*	*Max*	*Min*	*Standard Deviation*
Call	7.67	45.67 (23rd Jan 1998)	0.18 (4th Apr 1997)	3.46
TB15-91	7.97	21.44 (30th Jan 1998)	4.49 (25th Apr 1997)	1.76
Gsec1	9.34	22.86 (30th Jan 1998)	5.37 (22nd Mar 2002)	1.90
Gsec5	10.14	13.61 (30th Jan 1998)	6.14 (20th Sep 2002)	1.82
Gsec10	10.95	13.50 (23rd Jan 1998)	7.38 (9th Aug 2002)	1.50

3. Alternative Forecasting Models: A Brief Overview

Predicting the interest rate is a difficult task since the forecasts depend on the model used to generate them. Hence, it is important to study the properties of forecasts generated from different models and select the "best" on the basis of an objective criterion. The aim of this study is to select the "best" model for each interest rate from a number of alternative models estimated[5].

3.1 Univariate Models

The benchmark model for each interest rate is a naïve model that implies that the projection for the next period is simply the actual value of the variable in the current period. Other univariate models are the ARIMA model and the ARIMA model extended to include ARCH/GARCH effects.

The advantage of using the ARIMA model along with the ARCH/GARCH effects is that it accommodates relaxation of the assumption of constant variance of the innovation process as described in Engle's (1982) seminal paper and its extension by Bollerslev (1986) on modelling the conditional variance of the error process. One possibility is to model the conditional variance as an AR(q) process using the square of the estimated residuals, i.e., the autoregressive conditional heteroscedasticity (ARCH) model. The conditional variance thus follows an MA process, while in its generalised version – GARCH – it follows an ARMA process. Adding this information can improve the performance of the ARIMA model due to the presence of the volatility clustering effect characteristic of financial series. In other words, the stochastic errors, ε_t although serially uncorrelated through the white noise assumption, are not independent since they are related through their second moments. Hence, large values of ε_t are likely to be followed by large values of ε_{t+1} of either sign. Consequently, a realisation of ε_t

---

5. Fauvel, Paquet and Zimmermann (1999) provide a survey of major methods used to forecast interest rates as well as a review of interest rate modelling. Examples of studies that examine forecasting of interest rates are as follows: Ang and Bekaert (1998); Barkoulas and Baum (1997); Bidarkota (1998); Campbell and Shiller (1991); Chiang and Kahl (1991); Cole and Reichenstein (1994); Craine and Havenner.(1988); Deaves (1996); Dua (1988); Froot (1989); Gosnell and Kolb (1997); Gray (1996); Hafer, Hein and MacDonald (1992); Holden and Thompson (1996); Iyer and Andrews (1999); Jondeau and Sedillot (1999); Jorion and Mishkin (1991); Kolb and Stekler (1996); Park and Switzer (1997); Pesando (1981); Prell (1973); Roley (1982); Sola and Driffil (1994); and Throop (1981).

exhibits behaviour in which clusters of large observations are followed by clusters of small ones. To model extended persistence, higher order ARCH models or generalised ARCH (GARCH) models can be used.

Clearly, univariate models are not ideal since these do not use information on the relationships between different economic variables. These are, however, a good starting point since predictions from these models can be compared with those from multivariate models. We now consider multivariate forecasting models that rely on the interrelationships between different variables.

3.2 VAR and BVAR Modelling

As a prelude to the discussion on multivariate models, it is apposite to note that according to RBI's Statement on Monetary and Credit Policy for 2002-03, short-term forecasts of interest rates need to take cognisance of possible movements in all other macreconomic variables including investment, output and inflation, which are, in turn, susceptible to unanticipated changes emanating from unforeseen domestic or international developments. Multivariate forecasting models address such concerns and are often formulated as simultaneous equations structural models. In these models, economic theory not only dictates what variables to include in the model, but also postulates which explanatory variables to use to explain any given independent variable. This can, however, be problematic when economic theory is ambiguous. Further, structural models are generally poorly suited for forecasting. This is because projections of the exogenous variables are required to forecast the endogenous variables Another problem in such models is that proper identification of individual equations in the system requires the correct number of excluded variables from an equation in the model.

A vector autoregressive (VAR) model offers an alternative approach, particularly useful for forecasting purposes. This method is multivariate and does not require specification of the projected values of the exogenous variables. Economic theory is used only to determine the variables to include in the model.

Although the approach is "atheoretical," a VAR model approximates the reduced form of a structural system of simultaneous equations. As shown by Zellner (1979), and Zellner and Palm (1974), any linear structural model theoretically reduces to a VAR moving average (VARMA) model, whose coefficients combine the structural coefficients. Under some conditions, a VARMA model can be expressed as a VAR model and as a Vector Moving Average (VMA) model. A VAR model can also approximate the reduced form of a simultaneous structural model. Thus, a VAR model does not totally differ from a large-scale structural model. Rather, given the correct restrictions on the parameters of the VAR model, they reflect mirror images of each other.

The VAR technique uses regularities in the historical data on the forecasted variables. Economic theory only selects the economic variables to include in the model. An unrestricted VAR model (Sims 1980) is written as follows:

y_t = $C + A(L)y_t + e_t$, where

y = an (nx1) vector of variables being forecast;

A(L) = an (nxn) polynomial matrix in the back-shift operator L with lag length p, = $A_1L + A_2L^2 + \ldots\ldots\ldots + A_pL^p$;

C = an (nx1) vector of constant terms; and

e = an (nx1) vector of white noise error terms.

The model uses the same lag length for all variables. One serious drawback exists — overparameterisation produces multicollinearity and loss of degrees of freedom that can lead to inefficient estimates and large out-of-sample forecasting errors. One solution excludes insignificant variables/lags based on statistical tests.

An alternative approach to overcome overparameterisation uses a Bayesian VAR model as described in Litterman (1981), Doan, Litterman and Sims (1984), Todd (1984), Litterman (1986), and Spencer (1993). Instead of eliminating longer lags and/or less important variables, the Bayesian technique imposes restrictions on these coefficients on the assumption that these are more likely to be near zero than the coefficients on shorter lags and/or more important variables. If, however, strong effects do occur from longer lags and/or less important variables, the data can override this assumption. Thus the Bayesian model imposes prior beliefs on the relationships between different variables as well as between own lags of a particular variable. If these beliefs (restrictions) are appropriate, the forecasting ability of the model should improve. The Bayesian approach to forecasting therefore provides a scientific way of imposing prior or judgmental beliefs on a statistical model. Several prior beliefs can be imposed so that the set of beliefs that produces the best forecasts is selected for making forecasts. The selection of the Bayesian prior, of course, depends on the expertise of the forecaster.

The restrictions on the coefficients specify normal prior distributions with means zero and small standard deviations for all coefficients with decreasing standard deviations on increasing lags, except for the coefficient on the first own lag of a variable that is given a mean of unity. This so-called "Minnesota prior" was developed at the Federal Reserve Bank of Minneapolis and the University of Minnesota.

The standard deviation of the prior distribution for lag m of variable j in equation i for all i, j, and m — $S(i, j, m)$ — is specified as follows:

$$S(i, j, m) = \{wg(m)f(i, j)\}si/sj;$$

$$f(i, j) = 1, \quad \text{if } i = j;$$

$$= k \quad \text{otherwise } (0 < k < 1); \text{ and}$$

$$g(m) = m^{-d}, \; d > 0.$$

The term s_i equals the standard error of a univariate autoregression for variable i. The ratio s_i/s_j scales the variables to account for differences in units of measurement and allows the specification of the prior without consideration of the magnitudes of the variables. The parameter w measures the standard deviation on the first own lag and describes the overall tightness of the prior. The tightness on lag m relative to lag 1 equals the function $g(m)$, assumed to have a harmonic shape with decay factor d. The tightness of variable j relative to variable i in equation i equals the function $f(i, j)$.

To illustrate, assume the following hyperparameters: $w = 0.2$; $d = 2.0$; and $f(i, j) = 0.5$. When $w = 0.2$, the standard deviation of the first own lag in each equation is 0.2, since $g(1) = f(i, j) = s_i/s_j = 1.0$. The standard deviation of all other lags equals $0.2[s_i/s_j\{g(m)f(i, j)\}]$. For $m = 1, 2, 3, 4$, and $d = 2.0$, $g(m) = 1.0, 0.25, 0.11, 0.06$, respectively, showing the decreasing influence of longer lags. The value of $f(i, j)$ determines the importance of variable j relative to variable i in the equation for variable i, higher values implying greater interaction. For instance, $f(i, j) = 0.5$ implies that relative to variable i, variable j has a weight of 50 per cent. A tighter prior occurs by decreasing w, increasing *d*, and/or decreasing *k*. Examples of selection of hyperparameters are given in Dua and Ray (1995), Dua and Smyth (1995), Dua and Miller (1996) and Dua, Miller and Smyth (1999).

The BVAR method uses Theil's (1971) mixed estimation technique that supplements data with prior information on the distributions of the coefficients. With each restriction, the number of observations and degrees of freedom artificially increase by one. Thus, the loss of degrees of freedom due to overparameterisation does not affect the BVAR model as severely.

Another advantage of the BVAR model is that empirical evidence on comparative out-of-sample forecasting performance generally shows that the BVAR model outperforms the unrestricted VAR model. A few examples are Holden and Broomhead (1990), Artis and Zhang (1990), Dua and Ray (1995), Dua and Miller (1996), Dua, Miller and Smyth (1999).

The above description of the VAR and BVAR models assumes that the variables are stationary. If the variables are non-stationary, they can continue to be specified in levels in a BVAR model because as pointed out by Sims *et al.* (1990, p.136) '......the Bayesian approach is entirely based on the likelihood function, which has the same Gaussian shape regardless of the presence of non-stationarity, [hence] Bayesian inference need take no special account of non-stationarity'. Furthermore, Dua and Ray (1995) show that the Minnesota prior is appropriate even when the variables are co-integrated.

In the case of a VAR, Sims (1980) and others, e.g. Doan (1992), recommend estimating the VAR in levels even if the variables contain a unit root. The argument against differencing is that it discards information relating to co-movements between the variables such as co-integrating relationships. The standard practice in the presence of a co-integrating relaionship between the variables in a VAR is to estimate the VAR in levels or to estimate its error correction representation, the vector error correction model, VECM. If the variables are non-stationary but not co-integrated, the VAR can be estimated in first differences.

The possibility of a co-integrating relationship between the variables is tested using the Johansen and Juselius (1990, 92) methodology. They suggest the LR test based on the maximum eigenvalue (λ_{max}) to determine the number of the co-integrating vectors. Since λ_{max} test has a sharper alternative hypothesis as compared to λ_{trace} test, it is used to select the number of co-integrating vectors.

If the presence of co-integration is established, the concept of Granger causality can also be tested in the VECM framework. For example, if two variables are co-integrated, i.e. they have a common stochastic trend, causality in the Granger (temporal) sense must exist in at least one direction (Granger, 1986; 1988). Since Granger causality is also a test of whether one variable can improve the forecasting performance of another, it is important to test for it to evaluate the predictive ability of a model.

Granger-causality can be tested by (i) the statistical significance of the lagged error correction term by a standard t-test; and (ii) a joint test applied to the significance of the sum of the lags of each explanatory variables, by a joint F or Wald χ^2 test. Alternatively, a joint test of all the set of terms described in (i) and (ii) can be conducted by a joint F or a Wald χ^2 test. The third option is used in this paper.

3.3 *Testing for Non-stationarity*

Before estimating any of the above models, the first econometric step is to test if the series are non-stationary or contain a unit root. Several tests have been developed to test for the presence of a unit root. In this study, we focus on the augmented Dickey-Fuller (1979, 1981) test, the Phillips Perron (1988) test and the KPSS test proposed by Kwiatkowski *et al.* (1992).

We follow Doldado, Jenkinson and Sosvilla-Rivero's (1990) procedure for the ADF and PP test. A sequential procedure is used to test for the presence of a unit root when the form of the data-generating process is unknown. Such a procedure is necessary since including the intercept and trend term reduces the degrees of freedom and the power of the test implying that we may conclude that a unit root is present when, in fact, this is not true. Further, additional regressors increase the absolute value of the critical value making it harder to reject the null hypothesis. On the other hand, inappropriately omitting the deterministic terms can cause the power of the test to go to zero (Campbell and Perron, 1991).

We conduct the Phillips-Perron (1988) test for a unit root mainly because the Dickey-Fuller tests require that the error term be serially uncorrelated and homogeneous while the Phillips-Perron test is valid even if the disturbances are serially correlated and heterogeneous. In both the ADF and the PP test, the unit root is the null hypothesis. A problem with classical hypothesis testing is that it ensures that the null hypothesis is not rejected unless there is strong evidence against it. Therefore these tests tend to have low power, that is, these tests will often indicate that a series contains a unit root. Kwiatkowski *et al.* (1992), therefore suggest that based on classical methods, it may be useful to perform tests of the null hypothesis of stationarity in addition to tests of the null hypothesis of a unit root. Tests based on stationarity as the null can then be used for confirmatory analysis, that is, to confirm conclusions about unit roots. Of course, if tests with stationarity as the null as well as tests with unit root as the null, both reject or fail to reject the respective nulls, there is no confirmation of stationarity or non-stationarity.

Thus, three tests, augmented Dickey-Fuller, Phillips Perron and KPSS tests, are used to test for the presence of a unit root. The KPSS test, with the null of stationarity, helps to resolve conflicts between ADF and PP tests. If two of these three tests indicate non-stationarity for any series, we conclude that the series has a unit root.

In sum, the study proceeds as follows. First, the series are tested for the presence of a unit root using the augmented Dickey-Fuller, Phillips Perron and KPSS tests. If the interest rate series are non-stationary, univariate models, i.e. ARIMA without and with ARCH-GARCH effects, are fitted to differenced, stationary series.

Multivariate models include VAR, VECM, and BVAR models. To estimate VAR models, if all the variables are non-stationary and integrated of the same order, the Johansen test is conducted for the presence of co-integration. If a co-integrating relationship exists, the VAR model can be estimated in levels. Tests for Granger causality are also conducted in the VECM framework to evaluate the forecasting ability of the model. Lastly, Bayesian vector autoregressive models are estimated that impose prior beliefs on the relationships between different variables as well as between own lags of a particular variable. If these beliefs (restrictions) are appropriate, the forecasting ability of the model should improve.

The forecasting ability of each model is evaluated by examining the performance of out-of-sample forecasts and the "best" forecasting model is selected.

3.4 Evaluation of Forecasting Models

The "best" forecasting model is one that produces the most accurate forecasts. This means that the predicted levels should be close to the actual realised values. Furthermore, the predicted variables should move in the same direction as the actual series. In other words, if a series is rising (falling), the forecasts should reflect the same direction of change. If a series is changing direction, the forecasts should identify this.

To select the best model, the alternative models are initially estimated using weekly data over the period April 1997 to December 2001 and tested for out-of-sample forecast accuracy from January 2002 to September 2002. In other words, by continuously updating and re-estimating, we conduct a real world forecasting exercise to see how the models perform. The model that produces the most accurate one- through thirty-six-week-ahead forecasts is designated the "best" model for a particular interest rate.

To test for accuracy, the Theil coefficient (Theil, 1966), is used that implicitly incorporates the naïve forecasts as the benchmark. If A_{t+n} denotes the actual value of a variable in period (t+n), and ${}_tF_{t+n}$ the forecast made in period t for (t+n), then for T observations, the Theil U-statistic is defined as follows:

$$U = \left[\sum (A_{t+n} - {}_tF_{t+n})^2 / \sum (A_{t+n} - A_t)^2\right]^{0.5}$$

The U-statistic measures the ratio of the root mean square error (RMSE) of the model forecasts to the RMSE of naive, no-change forecasts (forecasts such that ${}_tF_{t+n} = A_t$). The RMSE is given by the following formula:

A comparison with the naïve model is, therefore, implicit in the U-statistic. A U-statistic of 1 indicates that the model forecasts match the performance of naïve, no-change forecasts. A U-statistic > 1 shows that the naïve forecasts outperform the model forecasts. If U is < 1, the forecasts from the model outperform the naïve forecasts. The U-statistic is, therefore, a relative measure of accuracy and is unit-free.

Since the U-statistic is a relative measure, it is affected by the accuracy of the naïve forecasts. Extremely inaccurate naïve forecasts can yield U <1, falsely implying that the model forecasts are accurate. This problem is especially applicable to series with trend. The RMSE, therefore, provides a check on the U-statistic and is also reported.

To evaluate the forecast performance, the models are continually updated and reestimated. The models are estimated for the initial period April 1997 through December 2001. Forecasts for up to 36-weeks-ahead are computed. One more observation is added to the sample and forecasts up to 36-weeks-ahead are again generated, and so on. Based on the out-of-sample forecasts for the period January through September 2002, the Theil U-statistics and RMSE are computed for one- to 36-weeks-ahead forecasts and the average of successive four U-statistics and RMSE are also computed. The overall average of the U statistic and the RMSE for up to 36-weeks-ahead forecasts is also calculated to gauge the accuracy of a model.

4. Estimation of Alternative Forecasting Models

4.1 Tests for Non-stationarity

The first step in the estimation of the alternative models is to test for non-stationarity. Three alternative tests are used, i.e., the augmented Dickey-Fuller (ADF) test, Phillips Perron (PP) test and the KPSS test. If there is a conflict between the ADF and PP tests, this is resolved using the KPSS test. If at least two of the three tests show the existence of a unit root, the series is considered as non-stationary. The tests for non-stationarity use weekly data from April 1997 to September 2002. Unit root tests are also conducted for a longer time span using monthly data from early 1990s onwards since Shiller and Perron (1985) and Perron (1989) note that when testing for unit roots, the total span of the time period is more important than the frequency of observations. In the same vein, Hakkio and Rush (1991) show that co-integration is a long-run concept and hence requires long spans of data rather than more frequently sampled observations to yield tests for co-integration with higher power. The inferences from monthly data conform to those from weekly data and show that except for the week-to-week inflation rate, all the variables can be treated as non-stationary. Testing for differences of each variable confirms that all the variables are integrated of order one[6].

---

6. Details of unit root tests are available in Dua *et al.* (2003).

4.2 *Estimation of Univariate and Multivariate Models*

The univariate best-fit models for the first-differenced interest rates are estimated as follows for the period April 1997 to December 2002:

Call Money Rate:	ARMA (2,2); ARMA(2,2)-GARCH(1,1)
Treasury Bill Rate – 15-91 days	ARMA(3,0); ARMA(3,0)-ARCH(1)
Government Securities – 1-year	ARMA(1,0); ARMA(1,0)-GARCH(1,1)
Government Securities – 5-years	ARMA(2,0); ARMA(2,0)-ARCH(2)
Government Securities – 10-years	ARMA(1,0); ARMA(1,0)-ARCH(1)

These models are used to generate out-of-sample forecasts from January through September 2002.

Three kinds of multivariate models are estimated – vector autoregressive (VAR) models, vector error correction models (VECM), and Bayesian vector autoregressive (BVAR) models. First, a VAR model is estimated. Second, its error correction representation is derived. Finally, alternative BVAR models are estimated using the optimal lag length determined for an unrestricted VAR.

To estimate a VAR, it is important to first determine if the variables included in a VAR are also co-integrated. If the variables are indeed co-integrated, the VAR model can be estimated in level-form. Accordingly, we first test for co-integration between the variables for each of the interest rates. The optimal lag length for each VAR system is determined by the Akaike Information Criterion, Schwartz Bayesian Criterion and the likelihood ratio test.

4.3 *Selection of Variables and Estimation of Multivariate Models*

To estimate the multivariate models, the variables are selected for each model on the basis of economic theory and out-of-sample forecast accuracy. Several factors can impact interest rates. Furthermore, their impacts may differ depending upon the maturity spectrum of the interest rates. For instance, for short-term/medium-term rates, factors that might impact interest rates include monetary policy; liquidity, demand and supply of credit, actual and expected inflation, external factors such as foreign interest rates and change in foreign exchange reserves, and the level of economic activity. For long-term interest rates, demand and supply of funds and expectations about government policy might be relatively more important.

Some of these factors also emerge from the stylised model developed by Dua and Pandit (2002) under covered interest parity condition. The equation for the real interest rate derived from their model can be expressed as a function of expected inflation, foreign interest rate, forward premium, and variables to denote fiscal and monetary effects. Based on this model, the inflation rate, foreign interest rate, forward premium and a variable to gauge monetary policy are included in the forecasting model. In addition to these variables, the following are also included: yield spread[7]; liquidity in the monetary system[8]; and a variable to measure credit conditions. Other variables such as CRR, foreign exchange reserves, exchange rate, stock prices, advance, turnover, 3- and 6-months US TB rate (secondary market) and reserve money, were also tried. Since these did not improve the forecast accuracy in any of the equations, these results are not reported. The repo rate[9] is also considered.

There are, of course, other variables that might impact interest rates such as current and future economic activity and expectations of government policy as mentioned above. However, since the models reported in this study are estimated using weekly data, the selection of variables was obviously circumscribed and, therefore, all of these effects could not be incorporated.

Nevertheless, some of these effects are captured in financial spreads that are measured by differences in the yields on financial

7. The yield spread is defined as the difference between the Government of India dated securities on residual maturity of 10-years and above and the 91-days Treasury Bills rate. It may be mentioned that the empirical models reported in this study use the Government of India Treasury Bills on residual maturity of 15-91 days based on the secondary market outright transactions in Government Securities (face value). Since data on exact 91-days are not available for the secondary market instruments, the 91-days Treasury Bills rate (primary market) has been used while calculating the yield spread.

8. The liquidity variable, as an indicator of market liquidity is estimated from bank reserves. Most of the recent research use bank reserves as a proxy for market liquidity. Bank reserves are the sum of reserve requirements and settlement balances including excess reserves. In economies where reserve requirements are marginal, bank reserves directly reflect the demand for settlement balances and excess reserves. In the Indian case, although reserve requirements continue to be significant, data on required reserves is not published. Hence, the study uses total reserves rather than excess reserves. Besides, in view of frequent cash reserve ratio (CRR) changes, there is a need to adjust bank reserves for changes in reserve requirements (see Sengupta *et al.* (2000).

9. Repo rates for the period November 29, 1997 to June 5, 2000 are fixed rate repos. These rates are the cut-off rates based on the auctions made by the Reserve Bank. The fixed rate repo system was replaced by the introduction of the Liquidity Adjustment Facility (LAF) with effect from June 5, 2000 that operates with auction based repo (absorption) and reverse repo (injection) system. Whenever the repo (absorption) is non-existent, the rate has been calculated by taking the average of the previous day repo (absorption) rate and current reverse repo (absorption) rate.

assets. These spreads exist due to differences in liquidity, risk and maturity that can also be influenced by factors such as taxes and portfolio regulations. Cyclical changes in any of these factors can arise from monetary policy shifts leading to changes in financial spreads. The most commonly used financial spread is the yield spread whose role in predicting future changes in interest rates is documented in several articles including Campbell and Shiller (1991), Froot (1989), and Sarantis and Lin (1999).

The slope of the yield curve – the difference between the long-term interest rate and the short-term interest rate, measures the yield spread. According to the expectations hypothesis of the term structure, this yield differential provides an indication of the expected future inflation rate (Mishkin, 1989). It also provides a signal about growth in future output. For instance, tight monetary policy and high interest rates can imply a declining yield curve and thus a slowdown in future output growth.

Thus, variables included in the models are: yield spread (10 years minus 3-months Treasury Bill rate); inflation (calculated from wholesale price index using week-to-week changes and year-on-year changes); liquidity in the system; credit (food and non-food credit)[10]; bank rate/repo rate (indicator of monetary policy); foreign interest rates (Libor 3 months and 6 months); and forward premium (3 months and 6 months). The last two variables reflect the integration between domestic and global markets (Bhoi and Dhal, 1998).

The specific variables included in the various models are given below:

Model A

Call Money Rate: inflation (week-to-week); Bank Rate; yield spread; liquidity, foreign interest rate (3-months Libor), forward premium (3-months).

Model B

Treasury Bill Rate (15-91 days): inflation (year-on-year), Bank Rate; yield spread, liquidity, foreign interest rate (3-months Libor), forward premium (3-months).

10. Data on food and non-food credit are available on a fortnightly basis. The weekly data are generated taking the average of the previous year and succeeding year figures.

Model C

Government Security 1 year: inflation (year-on-year), bank rate; yield spread, liquidity, foreign interest rate (6-months Libor), forward premium (6-months).

Model D

Government Security 5 years: inflation (year-on-year), Bank Rate; yield spread, credit, foreign interest rate (6-months Libor), forward premium (6-months).

Model E

Government Security 10 years: inflation (year-on-year), bank rate; yield spread, credit, foreign interest rate (6-months Libor), forward premium (6-months).

In the present context, it is worth noting that the week-to-week inflation rate ($week_{i+1}$ relative to $week_i$) produces better forecasts for the call money rate than year-on-year inflation ($week_{i+52}$ relative to $week_i$) while for all other interest rates year-on-year inflation produces superior forecasts. This may be because the call money rate is more responsive to week-to-week changes.

The co-integration results indicate existence of co-integration in the above five equations[11]. A caveat here is that the co-integrating equations are estimated over a short span (five and a half years) and therefore cannot capture the long-run properties of the model. The purpose of estimating the equations is to establish the existence of a co-integrating relationship and thus justify estimating the VAR in levels. Nevertheless, we estimate the error correction model and examine the predictive ability of the variables using Granger causality tests. These results are reported in Table 2.2 and show that all the variables significantly Granger cause the various interest rates, thus justifying their inclusion in the model.

In addition to the level VAR and VECM models, several Bayesian vector autoregressive models are also estimated. We begin with the prior recommended by Doan (1992) – w=0.2, d=1, k=0.5). Four more priors are used to select the optimal prior – i.e., the combination

11. Details of co-integration tests are available in Dua *et al.* (2003).

of hyperparameters that yields the most accurate forecasts. Tighter priors compared to Doan (1992) for k=0.5 are: w=0.1, d=1; w=0.1, d=2; and w=0.2, d=2. A looser prior relative to Doan (1992) is obtained by increasing the interaction parameter, k, e.g., k=0.7, w=0.2, d=1.

The 'optimised' BVAR model for k=0.5, i.e., one that has the lowest overall U statistic is tabulated along with the other models while the remaining BVAR models are tabulated under 'alternative' models. Tables 2.3A-2.3E show the performance of alternative forecasting models while Figures 2.3A-2.3E show the out-of-sample forecast performance of the "best" univariate and multivariate models for 1, 4 and 12-week ahead forecast horizons.

Main Findings

Call Money Rate (Table 2.3A; Figures 2.3.1A, 2.3.2A, 2.3.3A)

- ARMA-GARCH model yields more accurate forecasts than the best-fit ARIMA model.
- ARMA-GARCH model outperforms all alternative (univariate and multivariate) models for very short-term forecasts (up to 9-weeks ahead). The model U statistic is < 1 for almost all forecast horizons, which indicates that the model strongly outperforms the random walk.
- Level VAR (LVAR) model provides more accurate forecasts relative to the naïve and other univariate models for more than 9 weeks forecast horizon.
- LVAR model generally provides more accurate forecasts than the Vector Error Correction Model (VECM).
- VECM yields the most inaccurate forecasts.
- BVAR models perform better than LVAR for longer-term forecasts, over 20 weeks ahead.
- Of the BVAR models, the model with a loose prior (w=.2, d=1 with k fixed at 0.5) outperforms the alternatives. Allowing k to increase (thus increasing the interaction) improves forecast accuracy. This model is superior to the random walk model for over 8-week-ahead forecasts as reflected in the Theil U statistic.

- The univariate models and VECM generally exhibit an increase in RMSE, i.e., a decrease in forecast accuracy with an increase in the forecast horizon. On the other hand, the level VAR model almost consistently shows decrease in RMSE while the BVAR models show some improvement in accuracy at the very long end.

Thus, for the Call Money Rate, an ARMA-GARCH model is best suited for very short-term forecasting while a BVAR model with a loose prior can be used for longer-term forecasting.

Treasury Bill Rate – 15-91 days (Table 2.3B; Figures 2.3.1B, 2.3.2B, 2.3.3B)

- ARMA model produces marginally more accurate forecasts compared to the ARMA-ARCH model. However, since the U statistic is greater than or close to 1 for all forecast horizons, the forecast performance is not superior to that of a random walk.
- For all univariate models (including the random walk) there is deterioration in accuracy with an increase in the forecast horizon.
- The LVAR model outperforms the VECM model consistently.
- The LVAR model also beats the BVAR models in terms of forecast accuracy.
- Performance of all BVAR models is reasonable and generally improves on loosening the prior. In the extreme case, with a very loose prior, the BVAR model converges to LVAR.

Therefore, for the 15-91 day Treasury Bill Rate, the LVAR models produce the most accurate short- and long-term forecasts.

Government Securities – 1-year (Table 2.3C; Figures 2.3.1C, 2.3.2C, 2.3.3C).

- ARMA model is generally more accurate than ARMA-GARCH.
- LVAR model almost consistently outperforms VECM forecasts.
- Performance of BVAR forecasts is satisfactory for short- and long-term forecasts and is almost consistently better than that of LVAR.
- Of the BVAR models, the model with w= 0.2, d=1 and k=0.5 performs best.

- All models are inaccurate for forecasts 16 through 22 weeks ahead. This can be attributed to the fluctuations in the interest rate from March to May 2002 (from 5.37 per cent to 7.22 per cent).

Thus, for 1-year Government Securities, BVAR models out-perform the alternatives at the short and long end.

Government Securities – 5-year (Table 2.3D; Figures 2.3.1D, 2.3.2D, 2.3.3D)

- ARMA model is generally more accurate than ARMA-GARCH. Accuracy of both models improves relative to the random walk for forecast horizons over 24 weeks.
- All models are inaccurate for forecasts 17 through 23 weeks ahead, which can be attributed to fluctuations in the interest rate from 6.43 to 7.29 per cent.
- LVAR and BVAR models produce inaccurate forecasts, generally worse than those from a random walk.
- VECM yields the most accurate forecasts and is almost consistently better than the random walk.
- ARMA-ARCH model is more accurate than LVAR and the BVAR models.

For 5-year Government Securities, the BVAR models do not perform well. Overall, VECM outperforms all the alternative models. VECM also generally outperforms the alternatives at the short and long forecast horizons.

Government Securities – 10-year (Table 2.3E; Figures 2.3.1E, 2.3.2E, 2.3.3E)

- Introducing ARCH effects in the ARMA model does not improve forecast accuracy.
- LVAR produces the most accurate short-term and long-term forecasts, better than all other models.
- VECM is generally out-performed by LVAR and BVAR models.
- Performance of all BVAR models is reasonable and generally improves on loosening the prior. In the extreme case, with a very loose prior, the BVAR model converges to LVAR, which in this case is the preferred model.

- All models consistently out-perform the random walk.
- The accuracy of all the univariate models deteriorates with the increase in the forecast horizons.
- LVAR and BVAR models generally show improvement in accuracy with the increase in the forecast horizons.

Therefore, for 10-year Government Securities, forecasting performance of all the models is satisfactory. The model that produces the most accurate forecasts is LVAR, or, in other words, a BVAR with a very loose prior. LVAR model produces the most accurate short- and long-term forecasts.

Thus, generally, BVAR models perform well and are able to beat the naïve forecast most of the time.

In the multivariate analysis above, the Bank Rate is used to capture the effect of monetary policy. Other variables included are: inflation, liquidity, credit, spread, libor 3-and 6-months, forward premium 3- and 6-months. In the above models, we also examine, if the repo rate can be used in place of the Bank Rate, i.e., if the repo rate is a better predictor of interest rates compared to the Bank Rate. It was found that the out-of-sample forecast accuracy (reflected in a decrease in U) for both these rates as measured by the Theil statistic. The results[12] show that the improvement (if any) in accuracy from using the repo rate is marginal at best. The maximum improvement occurs in the TB 15-91 and that too by less than 10 per cent. The Bank Rate can therefore be used as a satisfactory indicator of monetary policy.

5. Conclusions

This study discusses different models to forecast both short- and long-term interest rates. Future movements in interest rates are critical to the financial decisions of businesses and households. Forecasting the behaviour of interest rates thus helps to reduce the risk associated with large fluctuations in the interest rates. Forecasting any economic variable can be a difficult task since the forecasts will depend on the model used to generate them. Hence it is important to study the properties of forecasts generated from different models and select the "best" on the basis of an objective criterion.

---

12. Details of results are available in Dua *et al.* (2003).

This study also highlights the differences between modelling short- and long-term interest rates. This is reflected in the choice of variables in the multivariate models.

The conclusions for each interest rate are as follows:

- *For the Call Money Rate, an ARMA-GARCH model is best suited for very short-term forecasting while a BVAR model with a loose prior can be used for longer-term forecasting.*
- *For the 15-91 day Treasury Bill Rate, the LVAR models produce the most accurate short- and long-term forecasts.*
- *For 1-year Government Securities, BVAR models out-perform the alternatives at the short and long end.*
- *For 5-year Government Securities, the BVAR models do not perform well. Overall, VECM outperforms all the alternative models. VECM also generally outperforms the alternatives at the short and long forecast horizons.*
- *For 10-year Government Securities, forecasting performance of all the models is satisfactory. The model that produces the most accurate forecasts is LVAR, or, in other words, a BVAR with a very loose prior. LVAR model produces the most accurate short- and long-term forecasts.*

The selected models conform to expectations. Standard ARIMA models are based on a constant residual variance. Since financial time series are known to exhibit volatility clustering, this effect is taken into account by estimating ARCH/GARCH models. It is found that although the ARCH/GARCH effects are significant, the ARCH model produces more accurate out-of-sample forecasts relative to the corresponding ARIMA model only in the case of call money rate. This result is not surprising since the out-of sample period over which the alternative models are evaluated is relatively stable with no marked swing in the interest rates.

It is also found that the multivariate models generally produce more accurate forecasts over longer forecast horizons. This is because interactions and dependencies between variables become stronger for longer horizons. In other words, for short forecast horizons, predictions that depend solely on the past history of a variable may yield satisfactory results.

In the class of multivariate models, the Bayesian model generally outperforms its contenders. Unlike the VAR models, the Bayesian models are not adversely affected by degree of freedom constraints and overparameteistion. In two cases, i.e., for TB 15-91 and GSec 10, the level VAR performs best suggesting that a loose prior is more appropriate for these models. Notice that with a loose prior, the Bayesian model approaches the VAR model with limited restrictions on the coefficients.

The VECM model outperforms the others only in the case of the GSec 5-years rate. Although inclusion of an error correction term in a VAR is generally expected to improve forecasting performance if the variables are indeed co-integrated, this contention did not find support in this study. This may be because co-integration is a long run phenomenon and the span of the estimation period in this study is not sufficiently large to permit a rigorous analysis of the long-run relationships. Thus, it is not surprising that the VAR models generally outperform the corresponding VECM forecasts.

Thus, to sum up, the forecasting performance of BVAR models for interest rates is satisfactory. The BVAR models generally produce more accurate forecasts compared to the alternatives discussed in the study and their superiority in performance is marked at longer forecast horizons. The variables included in the BVAR models are: inflation, Bank Rate, liquidity, credit, spread, libor 3-and 6-months, forward premium 3- and 6-months. These variables are selected from a large set of potential series including the repo rate, cash reserve ratio, foreign exchange reserves, exchange rate, stock prices, advance (centre and state government advance by RBI), turnover (total turnover of all maturities), 3- and 6-months US Treasury Bill rate (secondary market), reserve money and its growth rates.

A closing remark may be made on one caveat on the research method used in the Study. BVAR forecasts have one important limitation. The search for an optimal prior requires an objective function (i.e., the Theil U-statistic) that is optimised over the out-of-sample forecasts. The chosen prior, therefore, may not be optimal beyond the period for which it was selected. This shortcoming is not limited to BVAR models; it is a problem for all models selected on the basis of out-of-sample forecasts. In other words, the selected specification may not produce the 'best' forecasts outside the sample for which the selection was made.

Table 2.2

Granger Causality Tests

Null Hypothesis	*Number of Lags*	χ^2 *(calculated)*	*Conclusion*
MODEL A : $i_{(Call)}$ = f (π_1†, Bank Rate, Spread, Liquidity, i^*_1, fp_1)			
$i_{(Call)}$ is not granger caused by Bank Rate	3	70.99 (.00)	Reject null hypothesis*
$i_{(Call)}$ is not granger caused by Spread	3	52.42 (.00)	Reject null hypothesis*
$i_{(Call)}$ is not granger caused by Liquidity	3	43.66 (.00)	Reject null hypothesis*
$i_{(Call)}$ is not granger caused by i^*_1	3	44.11 (.00)	Reject null hypothesis*
$i_{(Call)}$ is not granger caused by fp_1	3	61.51 (.00)	Reject null hypothesis*
MODEL B : $i_{(TB\ 15\text{-}91)}$ = f (π_2, Bank Rate, Spread, Liquidity, i^*_1, fp_1)			
$i_{(TB\ 15\text{-}91)}$ is not granger caused by π_2	2	54.94 (.00)	Reject null hypothesis*
$i_{(TB\ 15\text{-}91)}$ is not granger caused by Bank Rate	2	114.29 (.00)	Reject null hypothesis*
$i_{(TB\ 15\text{-}91)}$ is not granger caused by Spread	2	45.75 (.00)	Reject null hypothesis*
$i_{(TB\ 15\text{-}91)}$ is not granger caused by Liquidity	2	50.50 (.00)	Reject null hypothesis*
$i_{(TB\ 15\text{-}91)}$ is not granger caused by i^*_1	2	45.23 (.00)	Reject null hypothesis*
$i_{(TB\ 15\text{-}91)}$ is not granger caused by fp_1	2	115.37 (.00)	Reject null hypothesis*
MODEL C : $i_{(GSec\ 1)}$ = f (π_2, Bank Rate, Spread, Liquidity, i^*_2, fp_2)			
$i_{(GSEC\ 1)}$ is not granger caused by π_2	3	43.36 (.00)	Reject null hypothesis*
$i_{(GSEC\ 1)}$ is not granger caused by Bank Rate	3	140.92 (.00)	Reject null hypothesis*
$i_{(GSEC\ 1)}$ is not granger caused by Spread	3	39.47 (.00)	Reject null hypothesis*
$i_{(GSEC\ 1)}$ is not granger caused by Liquidity	3	34.28 (.00)	Reject null hypothesis*
$i_{(GSEC\ 1)}$ is not granger caused by i^*_2	3	27.75 (.00)	Reject null hypothesis*
$i_{(GSEC\ 1)}$ is not granger caused by fp_2	3	104.18 (.00)	Reject null hypothesis*

Contd. ...

Contd. ...

Null Hypothesis	*Number of Lags*	χ^2 *(calculated)*	*Conclusion*
MODEL D : $i_{(GSec\ 5)}$ = f (π_2, Bank Rate, Spread, Credit, i^*_2, fp_2)			
$i_{(GSEC\ 5)}$ is not granger caused by π_2	3	08.22 (.08)	Reject null hypothesis**
$i_{(GSEC\ 5)}$ is not granger caused by Bank Rate	3	87.95 (.00)	Reject null hypothesis*
$i_{(GSEC\ 5)}$ is not granger caused by Spread	3	19.99 (.00)	Reject null hypothesis*
$i_{(GSEC\ 5)}$ is not granger caused by Credit	3	08.77 (.07)	Reject null hypothesis**
$i_{(GSEC\ 5)}$ is not granger caused by i^*_2	3	11.52 (.02)	Reject null hypothesis*
$i_{(GSEC\ 5)}$ is not granger caused by fp_2	3	37.74 (.00)	Reject null hypothesis*
MODEL E : $i_{(GSec\ 10)}$ = f (π_2, Bank Rate, Spread, Credit, i^*_2, fp_2)			
$i_{(GSEC\ 10)}$ is not granger caused by π_2	3	10.31 (.04)	Reject null hypothesis*
$i_{(GSEC\ 10)}$ is not granger caused by Bank Rate	3	61.04 (.00)	Reject null hypothesis*
$i_{(GSEC\ 10)}$ is not granger caused by Spread	3	15.26 (.00)	Reject null hypothesis*
$i_{(GSEC\ 10)}$ is not granger caused by Credit	3	10.25 (.00)	Reject null hypothesis*
$i_{(GSEC\ 10)}$ is not granger caused by i^*_2	3	05.98 (.20)	Reject null hypothesis***
$i_{(GSEC\ 10)}$ is not granger caused by fp_2	3	26.31 (.00)	Reject null hypothesis*

Note: p-value in parenthesis. *, ** and *** denote significance at 5%, 10% and 20% levels, respectively. p_1 and p_2 denote week-to-week and year-on-year inflation respectively; i^*_1 and i^*_2 denote LIBOR-3 months and LIBOR-6 months respectively; and fp_1 and fp_2 denote 3 and 6 months forward premium respectively.

† Week-to-week Inflation has been used as an exogenous variable.

Table 2.3A

Accuracy of Out-of-Sample Forecasts: Call Money Rate (January – September 2002)

		ARMA (2,2)		ARMA (2,2) –GARCH (1,1)		LVAR (LAG 4)		VECM (LAG 4)		Optimal BVAR Models (w=.2, d=1, k=.5)		Alternative BVAR Models			
												(w=.1, d=2,k=.5)	(w=.1, d=1,k=.5)	(w=.2, d=2,k=.5)	(w=.2, d=1,k=.7)
Week-ahead	*N**	*U*	*4 Weeks Average U*	*U*	*4 Weeks Average U*	*U*	*4 Weeks Average U*	*U*	*4 Weeks Average U*	*U*	*4 Weeks Average U*	*4 Weeks Average U*	*4 Weeks Average U*	*4 Weeks Average U*	*4 Weeks Average U*
4	36	1.275	1.230	0.967	0.978	1.384	2.177	2.132	2.416	1.094	1.239	1.253	1.079	1.354	1.366
8	32	1.264	1.235	0.958	0.948	1.117	1.194	2.132	2.060	1.058	1.025	1.236	1.058	1.189	1.018
12	28	1.170	1.186	0.876	0.898	0.785	0.860	1.827	1.880	0.814	0.882	1.058	0.938	1.021	0.862
16	24	1.125	1.153	0.811	0.844	0.653	0.721	1.840	1.854	0.776	0.797	0.930	0.855	0.916	0.770
20	20	1.299	1.178	0.795	0.780	0.600	0.574	1.751	1.762	0.731	0.738	0.880	0.814	0.869	0.709
24	16	1.464	1.436	0.783	0.783	0.462	0.500	1.723	1.723	0.342	0.458	0.648	0.567	0.621	0.436
28	12	1.522	1.482	0.815	0.799	0.477	0.469	1.812	1.710	0.221	0.257	0.378	0.317	0.353	0.255
32	8	1.623	1.587	0.817	0.817	0.421	0.448	1.750	1.807	0.208	0.211	0.380	0.294	0.365	0.188
36	4	1.675	1.666	0.848	0.833	0.233	0.340	1.894	1.781	0.313	0.288	0.620	0.466	0.547	0.254
Average U			**1.350**		**0.853**		**0.809**		**1.888**		**0.655**	**0.821**	**0.710**	**0.804**	**0.651**

* N is the number of observations.

Variables: Inflation (week-to-week), Bank Rate, Spread, Liquidity, Libor-3months and fp-3months.

Table 2.3B

Accuracy of Out-of-Sample Forecasts: TB 15-91 days (January – September 2002)

		ARMA (3,0)		*ARMA (3,0) –ARCH (1)*		*LVAR (LAG 4)*		*VECM (LAG 4)*		*Optimal BVAR Models (w=.2, d=1, k=.5)*		*Alternative BVAR Models*			
												(w=.1, d=2,k=.5)	*(w=.1, d=1,k=.5)*	*(w=.2, d=2,k=.5)*	*(w=.2, d=1,k=.7)*
Week-ahead	*N**	*U*	*4 Weeks Average U*	*U*	*4 Weeks Average U*	*U*	*4 Weeks Average U*	*U*	*4 Weeks Average U*	*U*	*4 Weeks Average U*	*4 Weeks Average U*	*4 Weeks Average U*	*4 Weeks Average U*	*4 Weeks Average U*
4	36	1.024	1.026	1.090	1.086	0.871	1.264	1.474	1.624	1.163	1.311	1.177	1.189	1.518	1.260
8	32	0.984	0.981	1.085	1.062	0.840	0.838	1.585	1.505	0.968	1.004	1.182	1.115	1.241	0.925
12	28	0.985	0.982	1.137	1.113	0.696	0.742	1.578	1.578	0.834	0.881	1.097	1.008	1.083	0.824
16	24	0.928	0.950	1.131	1.127	0.666	0.643	1.718	1.582	0.844	0.801	1.008	0.926	1.002	0.750
20	20	0.999	0.942	1.362	1.240	0.769	0.763	2.254	2.088	1.185	1.075	1.352	1.242	1.363	1.011
24	16	1.050	1.052	1.356	1.392	0.605	0.693	1.392	1.723	0.817	0.964	1.255	1.146	1.298	0.904
28	12	1.025	1.028	1.297	1.304	0.527	0.537	1.120	1.135	0.631	0.674	0.832	0.773	0.899	0.639
32	8	1.024	1.026	1.305	1.303	0.511	0.534	0.811	0.944	0.583	0.615	0.723	0.678	0.800	0.593
36	4	0.973	1.002	1.257	1.287	0.517	0.511	0.703	0.713	0.431	0.472	0.503	0.488	0.591	0.464
Average U			**0.999**		**1.213**		**0.725**		**1.432**		**0.866**	**1.014**	**0.952**	**1.088**	**0.819**

* N is the number of observations.

Variables: Inflation (year-on-year), Bank Rate, Spread, Liquidity, Libor-3months and fp-3months.

Table 2.3C

Accuracy of Out-of-Sample Forecasts: 1-year Government Securities (January – September 2002)

Week-ahead	N*	ARMA (1,0)		ARMA (1,0) –GARCH (1,1)		LVAR (LAG 4)		VECM (LAG 4)		Optimal BVAR Models (w=.2, d=1, k=.5)		Alternative BVAR Models			
												(w=.1, d=2,k=.5)	(w=.1, d=1,k=.5)	(w=.2, d=2,k=.5)	(w=.2, d=1,k=.7)
		U	4 Weeks Average U	U	4 Weeks Average U	U	4 Weeks Average U	U	4 Weeks Average U	U	4 Weeks Average U	4 Weeks Average U	4 Weeks Average U	4 Weeks Average U	4 Weeks Average U
4	36	0.977	0.985	0.982	0.989	0.826	0.936	0.954	1.017	0.775	0.780	0.813	0.802	0.859	0.766
8	32	0.971	0.974	0.984	0.984	0.659	0.727	0.772	0.828	0.633	0.680	0.741	0.701	0.734	0.680
12	28	0.966	0.968	0.989	0.987	0.632	0.634	0.779	0.755	0.596	0.601	0.644	0.601	0.615	0.604
16	24	0.999	0.979	1.041	1.012	0.719	0.677	1.047	0.926	0.652	0.617	0.646	0.587	0.603	0.620
20	20	1.159	1.080	1.237	1.141	1.020	0.898	1.632	1.410	1.010	0.874	0.966	0.845	0.889	0.869
24	16	1.009	1.102	1.146	1.222	0.800	0.921	1.495	1.687	0.717	0.885	1.294	1.007	1.141	0.868
28	12	0.442	0.628	0.466	0.693	0.475	0.535	1.131	1.169	0.370	0.423	0.914	0.654	0.796	0.410
32	8	0.471	0.447	0.458	0.444	0.297	0.374	0.591	0.725	0.314	0.348	0.766	0.572	0.698	0.349
36	4	0.568	0.547	0.577	0.550	0.459	0.457	0.408	0.387	0.340	0.328	0.565	0.464	0.539	0.346
Average U			**0.857**		**0.891**		**0.684**		**0.989**		**0.615**	**0.817**	**0.693**	**0.764**	**0.612**

* N is the number of observations.

Variables: Inflation (year-on-year), Bank Rate, Spread, Liquidity, Libor-6months and fp-6months.

Table 2.3D

Accuracy of Out-of-Sample Forecasts: 5-year Government Securities (January – September 2002)

Week-ahead	N*	ARMA (2,0)		ARMA (2,0) -ARCH (2)		LVAR (LAG 4)		VECM (LAG 4)		Optimal BVAR Models (w=.2, d=1, k=.5)		Alternative BVAR Models			
												(w=.1, d=1,k=.5)	(w=.2, d=2,k=.5)	(w=.2, d=1,k=.5)	(w=.1, d=2,k=.7)
		U	4 Weeks Average U	U	4 Weeks Average U	U	4 Weeks Average U	U	4 Weeks Average U	U	4 Weeks Average U	4 Weeks Average U	4 Weeks Average U	4 Weeks Average U	4 Weeks Average U
4	36	0.955	0.974	0.939	0.946	1.288	1.317	0.918	0.950	0.904	0.901	0.954	0.910	1.010	0.901
8	32	0.929	0.938	0.938	0.939	1.390	1.308	0.759	0.806	0.965	0.928	1.016	0.957	1.106	0.940
12	28	0.917	0.921	0.938	0.936	1.494	1.447	0.614	0.663	0.993	0.984	1.103	1.028	1.226	1.006
16	24	0.952	0.933	1.017	0.978	2.014	1.763	0.569	0.573	1.342	1.167	1.320	1.216	1.476	1.193
20	20	1.529	1.175	1.798	1.339	5.514	3.540	0.983	0.744	3.877	2.442	2.730	2.518	3.027	2.491
24	16	0.717	1.166	0.971	1.468	3.982	5.198	0.696	0.910	2.897	3.776	4.214	3.862	4.670	3.845
28	12	0.351	0.404	0.424	0.530	1.821	2.412	0.406	0.467	1.344	1.769	1.994	1.800	2.224	1.800
32	8	0.302	0.319	0.319	0.359	1.441	1.573	0.355	0.369	1.108	1.163	1.315	1.178	1.466	1.180
36	4	0.384	0.327	0.358	0.293	0.970	1.135	0.318	0.298	0.834	0.965	1.066	0.971	1.165	0.976
Average U			**0.795**		**0.865**		**2.188**		**0.642**		**1.566**	**1.746**	**1.604**	**1.930**	**1.592**

* N is the number of observations.

Variables: Inflation (year-on-year), Bank Rate, Spread, Credit, Libor-6months and fp-6months.

Table 2.3E

Accuracy of Out-of-Sample Forecasts: 10-year Government Securities (January – September 2002)

		ARMA (1,0)		ARMA (1,0) –ARCH (1)		LVAR (LAG 4)		VECM (LAG 4)		Optimal BVAR Models (w=.2, d=2, k=.5)		Alternative BVAR Models			
												(w=.1, d=2,k=.5)	(w=.1, d=1,k=.5)	(w=.2, d=1,k=.5)	(w=.2, d=2,k=.7)
Week-ahead	*N**	*U*	*4 Weeks Average U*	*U*	*4 Weeks Average U*	*U*	*4 Weeks Average U*	*U*	*4 Weeks Average U*	*U*	*4 Weeks Average U*	*4 Weeks Average U*	*4 Weeks Average U*	*4 Weeks Average U*	*4 Weeks Average U*
4	36	0.942	0.958	0.940	0.947	0.725	0.729	0.797	0.776	0.777	0.803	0.824	0.815	0.789	0.796
8	32	0.891	0.919	0.895	0.923	0.600	0.626	0.691	0.708	0.691	0.692	0.704	0.696	0.698	0.687
12	28	0.837	0.860	0.855	0.876	0.486	0.532	0.619	0.650	0.535	0.588	0.594	0.591	0.615	0.587
16	24	0.761	0.787	0.785	0.813	0.445	0.474	0.601	0.626	0.435	0.486	0.486	0.506	0.560	0.496
20	20	0.636	0.662	0.659	0.689	0.478	0.499	0.703	0.701	0.530	0.517	0.494	0.562	0.667	0.547
24	16	0.661	0.625	0.701	0.659	0.267	0.346	0.615	0.668	0.293	0.407	0.398	0.426	0.499	0.423
28	12	0.638	0.642	0.687	0.686	0.173	0.196	0.544	0.566	0.213	0.242	0.260	0.230	0.235	0.229
32	8	0.613	0.624	0.675	0.681	0.112	0.128	0.433	0.471	0.130	0.150	0.174	0.136	0.134	0.131
36	4	0.589	0.600	0.665	0.672	0.056	0.043	0.346	0.363	0.038	0.056	0.071	0.059	0.098	0.054
Average U			**0.742**		**0.772**		**0.397**		**0.614**		**0.438**	**0.445**	**0.447**	**0.477**	**0.439**

* N is the number of observations.

Variables: Inflation (year-on-year), Bank Rate, Spread, Credit, Libor-6months and fp-6months.

CALL MONEY RATE

"Best" Univariate vs. "Best" Multivariate Model

Figure 2.3.1A

1-week-ahead Forecasts

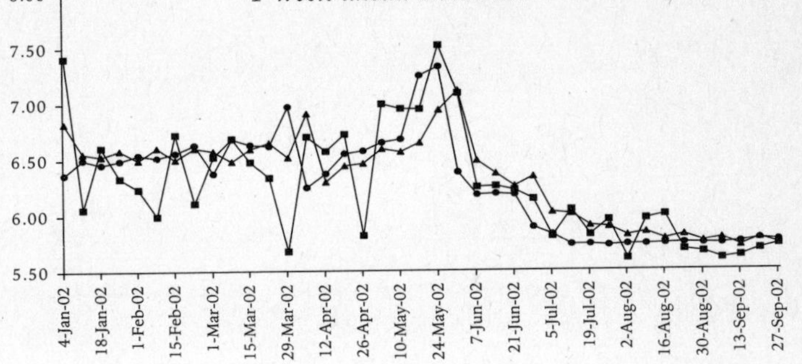

Figure 2.3.2A

4-week-ahead Forecasts

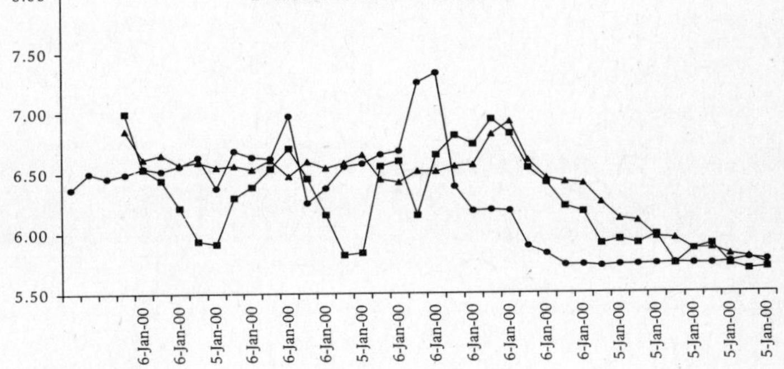

Figure 2.3.3A

12-week-ahead Forecasts

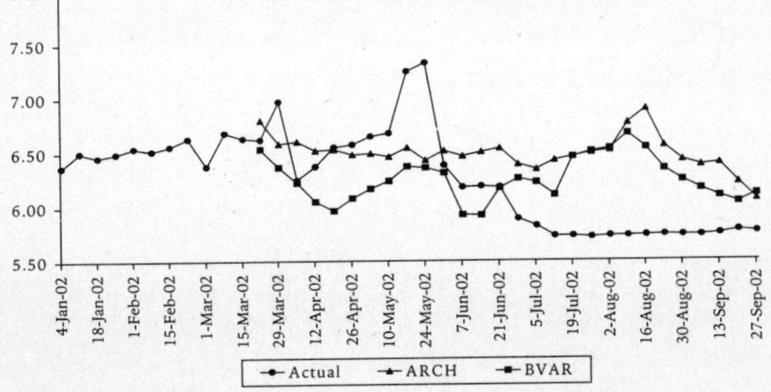

TB 15-91 DAYS

"Best" Univariate vs. "Best" Multivariate Model

Figure 2.3.1B

1-week-ahead Forecasts

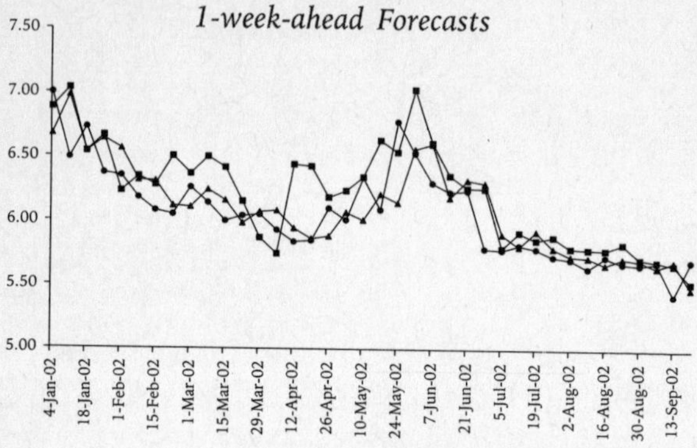

Figure 2.3.2B

4-week-ahead Forecasts

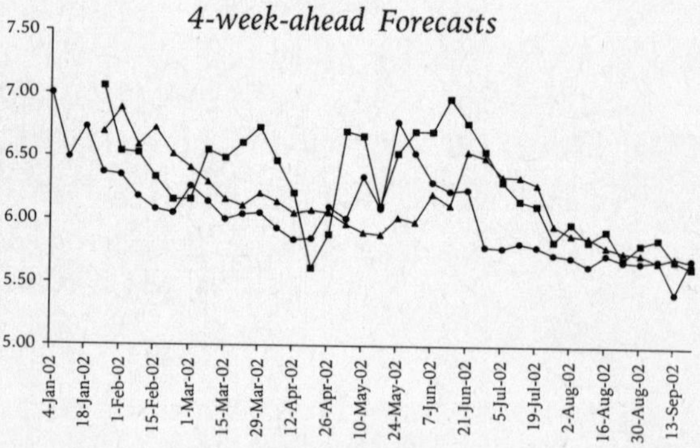

Figure 2.3.3B

12-week-ahead Forecasts

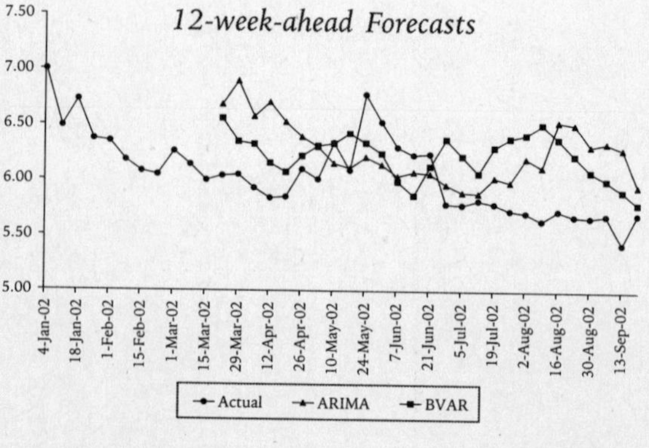

GSEC 1

"Best" Univariate vs. "Best" Multivariate Model

Figure 2.3.1C

1-week-ahead Forecasts

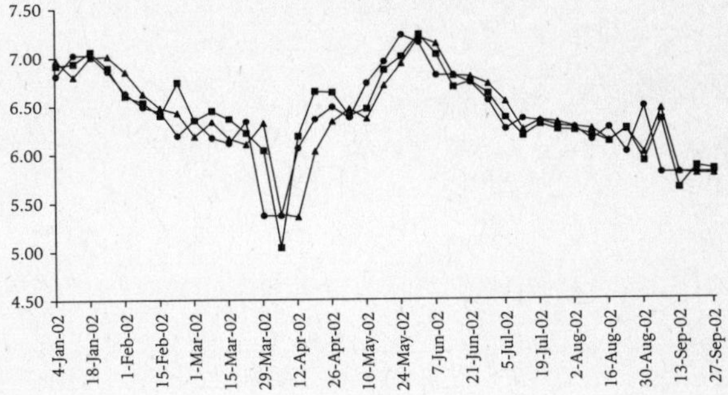

Figure 2.3.2C

4-week-ahead Forecasts

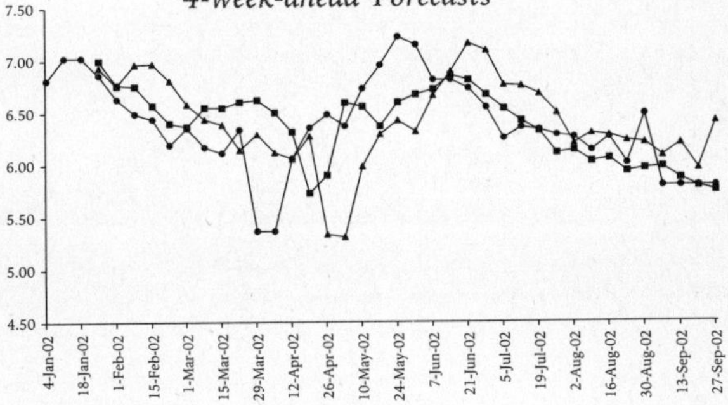

Figure 2.3.3C

12-week-ahead Forecasts

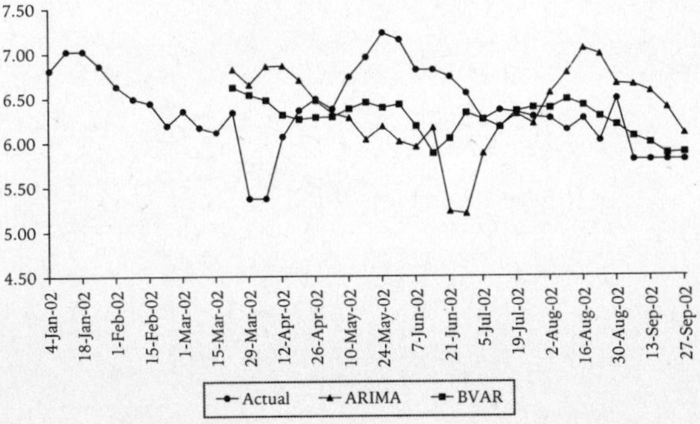

GSEC 5

"Best" Univariate vs. "Best" Multivariate Model

Figure 2.3.1D

1-week-ahead Forecasts

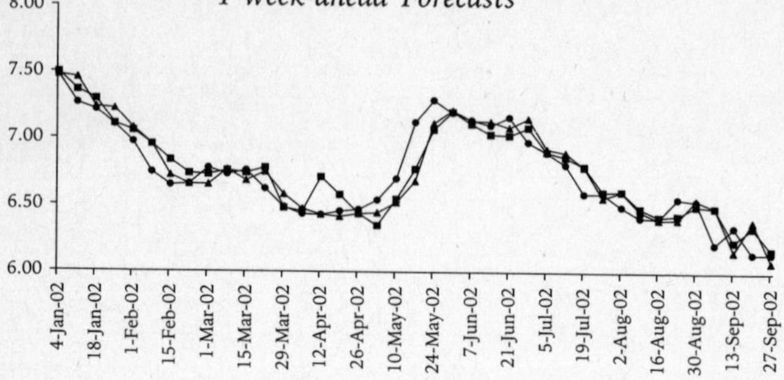

Figure 2.3.2D

4-week-ahead Forecasts

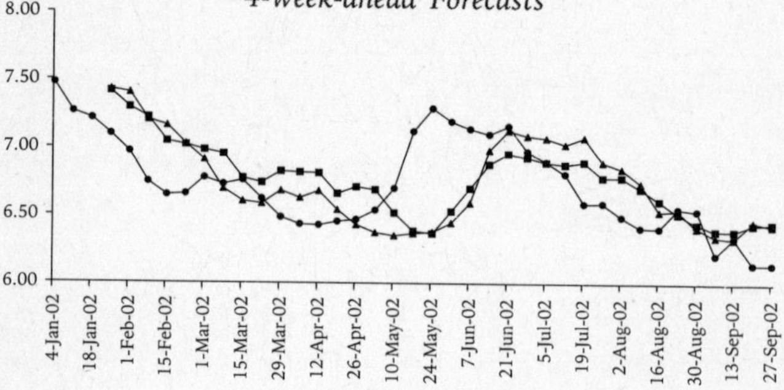

Figure 2.3.3D

12-week-ahead Forecasts

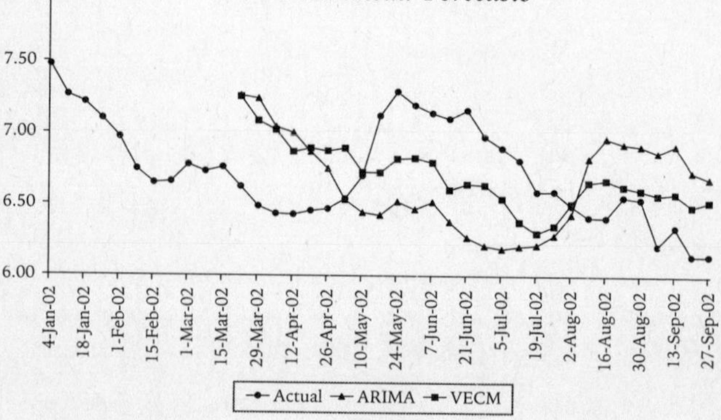

GSEC 10

"Best" Univariate vs. "Best" Multivariate Model

Figure 2.3.1E

1-week-ahead Forecasts

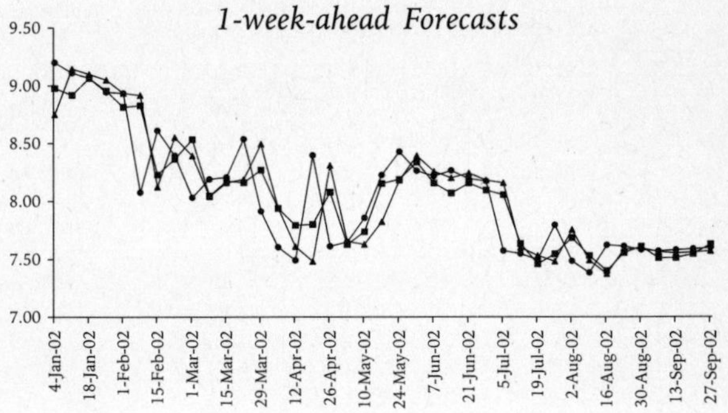

Figure 2.3.2E

4-week-ahead Forecasts

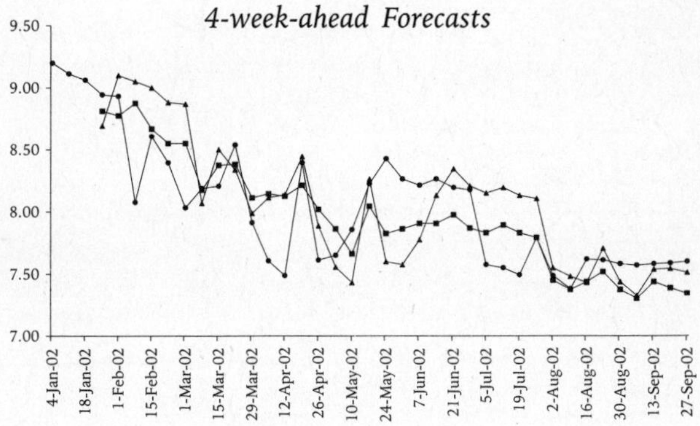

Figure 2.3.3E

12-week-ahead Forecasts

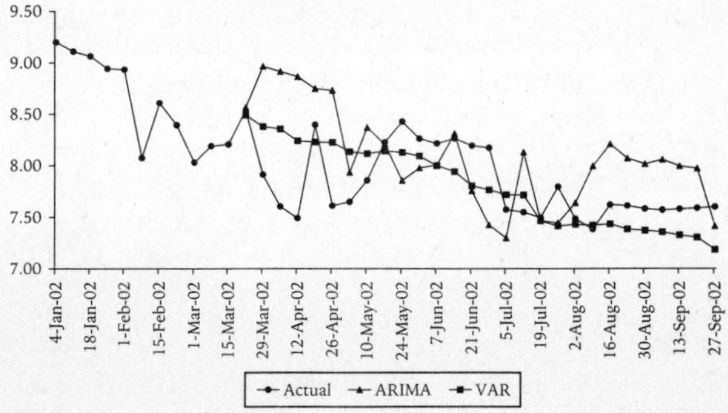

ANNEXURE

Data Definitions and Sources

Both the univariate and multivariate forecasting models have been carried out using a common sample from April 1997 to September 2002. The data definitions and sources of the variables are set out in the Table below.

Variable	*Definition*	*Source*
CALL	Weekly weighted average call money rates as compiled by the Reserve Bank. The call money rate upto 1997-98 is the weighted arithmetic average of the rate at which money was accepted and reported by select scheduled commercial banks at Mumbai, the weights being proportional to the amounts accepted during the period by respective banks. Data for the period 1998-99 till April 2001 relate to those reported by scheduled commercial banks, primary dealers and select financial institutions. Data since May 2001 include those of commercial banks, primary dealers, financial institutions, insurance companies and mutual funds.	Handbook of Statistics on the Indian Economy and RBI Bulletin
TB 15-91	Government of India Treasury Bills of residual maturity of 15-91 days based on the secondary market outright transactions in Government Securities (face value) as reported in Subsidiary Government Ledger (SGL) accounts at RBI, Mumbai.	Handbook of Statistics on the Indian Economy and RBI Bulletin
GSEC1	Government of India dated Securities of residual maturity of 1-year based on the secondary market outright transactions in Government securities (face value) as reported in Subsidiary Government Ledger (SGL) accounts at RBI, Mumbai.	Handbook of Statistics on the Indian Economy and RBI Bulletin
GSEC5	Government of India dated Securities of residual maturity of 5-years based on the secondary market outright transactions in Government Securities (face value) as reported in Subsidiary Government Ledger (SGL) accounts at RBI, Mumbai.	Handbook of Statistics on the Indian Economy and RBI Bulletin
GSEC10	Government of India dated Securities of residual maturity of 10-years and above based on the secondary market outright transactions in Government Securities (face value) as reported in Subsidiary Government Ledger (SGL) accounts at RBI, Mumbai.	Handbook of Statistics on the Indian Economy and RBI Bulletin
LIBOR 3-months	3-month LIBOR on USD deposits	Moneyline TeleRate
LIBOR 6-months	6-month LIBOR on USD deposits	Moneyline TeleRate
Bank Rate	Bank Rate	Handbook of Statistics on the Indian Economy
REPO	Repo Rate	See Note (1)

Contd. ...

Contd. ...

Variable	*Definition*	*Source*
fp 3-months	3-month forward premium	Handbook of Statistics on the Indian Economy and Weekly Statistical Supplement
fp 6-months	6-month forward premium	Handbook of Statistics on the Indian Economy and Weekly Statistical Supplement
LIQUIDITY	Liquidity indicator variable	See Note (2)
CREDIT	Total credit (Food and Non-food). Data on food and non-food credit are available on a fortnightly basis. The weekly data are generated taking the average of the previous year and succeeding year figures.	Weekly Statistical Supplement
INFLATION	Both week-to-week and year-on-year inflation rate have been used.	Weekly Statistical Supplement
SPREAD	10-Year Government Security rate *minus* 91-days Treasury Bills rate.	See Note (3)

Note:

(1) Repo Rate

Repo rates for the period November 29, 1997 to June 5, 2000 are fixed rate repos. These rates are the cut-off rates based on the auctions made by the Reserve Bank. The fixed rate repo system was replaced by the introduction of the Liquidity Adjustment Facility (LAF) with effect from June 5, 2000 that operates with auction based repo (absorption) and reverse repo (injection) system. Whenever the repo (absorption) is non-existent, the rate has been calculated by taking the average of the previous day repo (absorption) rate and current reverse repo (injection) rate.

(2) Estimation of the LIQUIDITY Variable

The LIQUIDITY variable, as an indicator of market liquidity is estimated from bank reserves. Most of the recent research use bank reserves as a proxy for market liquidity. Bank reserves are the sum of reserve requirements and settlement balances including excess reserves. In economies where reserve requirements are marginal, bank reserves directly reflect the demand for settlement balances and excess reserves. In the Indian case, although reserve requirements continue to be significant, data on required reserves is not published. Hence, the study uses total reserves rather than excess reserves. Besides, in view of frequent cash reserve ratio (CRR) changes, there is a need to adjust bank reserves for changes in reserve requirements (see Sengupta *et al.* (2000)).

(3) Yield Spread

The yield spread is defined as the difference between the Government of India dated Securities on residual maturity of 10-years and above and the 91-days treasury bills rate. It may be mentioned that the empirical models reported in this study use the Government of India Treasury Bills on residual maturity of 15-91 days based on the secondary market outright transactions in Government Securities (face value). Since data on exact 91-days are not available for the secondary market instruments, the 91-days Treasury Bills rate (primary market) has been used for calculating the yield spread.

References

Ang, A. and Bekaert (1998). "Regime Switches in Interest Rates," *NBER Working Paper*, No. 6508.

Artis, Michael J. and W. Zhang (1990). "BVAR Forecasts for the G7", *International Journal of Forecasting*, 6, 349-62

Barkoulas, J.T. and C.F. Baum (1997). "Fractional Differencing Modeling and Forecasting of Eurocurrency Deposit Rates", *Journal of Financial Research*, 20, 355-72.

Bhoi, B.K. and S.C. Dhal (1998). "Integration of Financial Markets in India: An Empirical Evaluation", *RBI Occasional Papers*, Vol.19, No.4, December.

Bidarkota, P.V. (1998). "The Comparative Performance of Univariate and Multivariate Models: An Application to Real Interest Rate Forecasting," *International Journal of Forecasting*, 14, 457-468.

Blejer, M.I. and J.G. Diaz (1986). "Domestic and External Factors in the Determination of the Real Interest Rate: The Case of Uruguay", *Economic Develpoment and Cultural Change*, 589-606.

Bollerslev, T. (1986). "Generalized Autoregressive Conditional Heteroscedasticity," *Journal of Econometrics*, 31, 307-27.

Campbell, J. Y. and P. Perron (1991). "Pitfalls and Opportunities: What Macroeconomists Should Know About Unit Root", *Technical Working Paper 100, NBER Working Paper Series*, April.

Campbell, J.Y. and R.J. Shiller (1991). "Yield Spreads and Interest Rate Movements: A Bird's Eye View", *Review of Economic Studies*, 58, 495-514.

Chiang, T.C. and D.R. Kahl (1991). "Forecasting the Treasury Bill Rate: A Time Varying Coefficient Approach", *Journal of Financial Research*, XIV, 327-336.

Cole, S.C. and W. Reichenstein (1994). "Forecasting Interest Rates with Euro Dollar Futures Rates", *Journal of Futures Markets*, 14, 37-50.

Cooley, T.F. and S.F. LeRoy (1985). "Atheoretical Macroeconometrics: A Critique," *Journal of Monetary Economics*, 16, 283-308.

Craine, R. and A. Havenner (1988). "Forecast Comparisons of Four Models of U.S. Interest Rates", *Journal of Forecasting*, 7, 21-29.

Deaves, R. (1996), "Forecasting Canadian Short-Term Interest Rates," *Canadian Journal of Economics*, 29, 615-634.

Dickey, David and Wayne A. Fuller (1979). "Distribution of the Estimates for Autoregressive Time Series with a Unit Root", *Journal of American Statistical Association*, 74, 427-31.

————. (1981). "Likelihood Ratio Statistics for Autoregressive Time Series Models: Tests and Implication", *Econometrica*, 49, 1057-72.

Doan, T. A. (1992). *RATS User's Manual*, III, Estima.

Doan, T. A., Litterman, R.B., and Sims (1984). "Forecasting and Conditional Projection Using Realistic Prior Distributions", *Econometric Reviews*, 3, 1-100.

Doldado, J., T. Jenkinson, and S. Sosvilla-Rivero (1990). "Co-integration and Unit Roots", *Journal of Economic Surveys*, 4, 249-73.

Dua, P. (1988). "Multiperiod Forecasts of Interest Rates", *Journal of Business and Economic Statistics*, 6, 381-384.

Dua, P. and S.M. Miller (1996). "Forecasting Connecticut Home Sales in a BVAR Framework Using Coincident and Leading Indexes", *Journal of Real Estate Finance and Economics*, 13, 219-235.

Dua, P., S.M. Miller and D.J. Smyth (1999). "Using Leading Indicators to Forecast U.S.Home Sales in a Bayesian Vector Autoregressive Framework", *Journal of Real Estate Finance and Economics*, 18, 191-205.

Dua, P. and B.L. Pandit (2002). "Interest Rate Determination in India: Domestic and External Factors", *Journal of Policy Modeling*, 24, 853-875.

Dua, P., N. Raje and S. Sahoo (2003). "Interest Rate Modelling and Forecasting in India", *Development Research Group Study No. 24*, Reserve Bank of India, Mumbai.

Dua, P. and S.C. Ray (1995). "A BVAR Model for the Connecticut Economy", *Journal of Forecasting,* 14, 217-227.

Dua, P. and Smyth, D.J. (1995). "Forecasting U.S. Home Sales Using BVAR Models and Survey Data on Households' Buying Attitudes for Homes", *Journal of Forecasting,* 14, 167-180.

Edwards, S. and M. S. Khan (1985). "Interest Rate Determination in Developing Countries: A Conceptual Framework", *IMF Staff Papers,* 32, 377-403.

Engle, R.F. (1982). "Autoregressive Conditional Heteroscedasticity with Estimates of the Variance of United Kingdom Inflation", *Econometrica,* 50, 987-1007.

Engle, R.E. and C.W.J. Granger (1987). "Co-integration and Error Correction: Representation, Estimation and Testing", *Econometrica,* 55, 251-76.

Fauvel, Y., A. Paquet, and C. Zimmermann,(1999). "A Survey on Interest Rate Forecasting", Center for Research on Economic Fluctuations and Employment, *Working Paper No. 87.*

Froot, K.A. (1989). "New Hope for the Expectations Hypothesis of the Term Structure of Interest Rates", *Journal of Finance,* 44, 283-305.

Gochoco, M.S. (1991). "Financial Liberalisation and Interest Rate Determination: The Case of Phillipines 1981-1985", *Journal of Macroeconomics,* Spring 1991,13(2), 335-350.

Gosnell, T. F. (1997). "Accuracy of International Interest Rate Forecasts", *Financial Review, 32,* 431-448.

Granger, C. W. J. (1986). "Developments in the Study of Co-integrated Economic Variables", *Oxford Bulletin of Economics and Statistics,* 48, 213-228.

Granger, C. W. J. (1988). "Some Recent Developments in the Concept of Causality", *Journal of Econometrics,* 39, 199-212.

Granger, C.W.J. and P. Newbold (1974). "Spurious Regressions in Econometrics", *Journal of Econometrics,* 2, 111-20.

Gray, S. (1996). "Modelling the Conditional Distribution of Interest Rates as a Regime Switching Process", *Journal of Financial Economics,* 42, 27-62.

Hafer, R.W., S.E. Hein, and S.S. MacDonald (1992). "Market and Survey Forecasts of the Three-Month Treasury-Bill Rate", *Journal of Business,* 65, 123-138.

Hakkio, C.S. and Rush, M. (1991). "Co-integration: How Short is the Long-Run?" *Journal of International Money and Finance,* 10, 571-581.

Holden, K. and J.L. Thompson (1996). "Forecasting Interest Rates from Financial Futures Markets", *Applied Financial Economics,* 6, 449-461.

Holden, K. and Broomhead, A. (1990). "An Examination of Vector Autoregressive Forecasts for the U.K. Economy", *International Journal of Forecasting,* 6, 11-23.

Iyer, S. and R.L. Andrews (1999). "Forecasting with Latent Structure Time Series Models: An Application to Nominal Interest Rates", *Journal of Forecasting,* 18, 395-409.

Johansen, S. and Katerina Juselius, (1990). "Maximum Likelihood Estimation and Inference on Cointegration with Application to the Demand for Money", *Oxford Bulletin of Economics and Statistics,* 52, 169-209.

————. (1992). "Testing Structural Hypothesis in a Multivariate Cointegartion Analysis of PPP and the UIP for UK", *Journal of Econometrics,* 53, 211-44.

Jondeau, E. and F. S—dillot (1999). "Forecasting French and German Long-Term Rates Using a Rational Expectations Model", *Weltwirtschaftliches Archiv,* 135, 413-436.

Jorion, P. and Frederic Mishkin (1991). "A Multicountry Comparison of Term-Structure Forecasts at Long Horizons", *Journal of Financial Economics,* 29, 59-80.

Kolb, R.A. and H.O. Stekler (1996). "How Well Do Analysts Forecast Interest Rates?, *Journal of Forecasting,* 15, 385-94.

Kwiatkowski, Denis, Peter C.B. Phillips, Peter Schmidt, and Yongcheol Shin (1992). "Testing the Null Hypothesis of Stationarity against the Alternative of a Unit Root." *Journal of Econometrics,* 54, 159-178.

———. (1981). "A Bayesian Procedure for Forecasting with Vector Autoregressions," *Federal Reserve Bank of Minneapolis, Working Paper.*

———. (1986). "Forecasting with Bayesian Vector Autoregressions – Five Years Experience," *Journal of Business and Economic Statistics*, 4, 25-38.

Mishkin, F.S. (1989). "The Information in the Longer Maturity Term Structure about Future Inflation," *NBER Working Paper No. 3126.*

Park, T.H. and L.N. Switzer (1997). "Forecasting Interest Rates and Yield Spreads: The Informational Content of Implied Futures Yields and Best-Fitting Forward Rate Models," *Journal of Forecasting*, 16, 209-24.

Perron, P. (1989). "Testing for a Random Walk: A Simulation Experiment of Power when the Sampling Interval is Varied," in B. Raj, ed., *Advances in Econometrics and Modeling*, Kluwer Academic Publisher.

Pesando, J.E. (1981). "On Forecasting Interest Rates: An Efficient Markets Perspective," *Journal of Monetary Economics 8, 305-318.*

Phillips, P. and P. Perron (1988). "Testing for a Unit Root in Time Series Regression", *Biometrica*, 75 335-46.

Prell, M.J. (1973). "How Well Do the Experts Forecast Interest Rates?" *Federal Reserve Bank of Kansas City Monthly Review*, September- October, 3-13.

Reddy, Y.V. (1999). "Monetary Policy in India: Objectives, Instruments, Operating Procedures and Dilemmas", Speech Given at the *Fourth Securities Industry Summit*, Organised by Invest India Private Ltd., Mumbai, May 26, 1999.

Roley, V.V. (1982). "Forecasting Interest Rates with a Structural Model" *Journal of Portfolio Management* 8, pp. 53-63.

Sarantis, N. and S.X. Lin (1999). "The Role of Financial Spreads in Macroeconomic Forecasting: Evidence for the UK," *Manchester School*, 67, 89-110.

Sen Gupta, Indranil, I. Bhattacharyya, Satyananda Sahoo and Siddhartha Sanyal (2000). "Anatomy of Liquidity Management", *RBI Occasional Papers*, 21(2 & 3), 291-321.

Shiller, R.J. and P. Perron (1985). "Testing the Random Walk Hypothesis: Power versus Frequency of Observation", *Economics Letters*, 18, 381-86.

Sims, C.A. (1980). "Macroeconomics and Reality", *Econometrica*, 48, 1-48.

Sims, C.A., J. Stock and M.W. Watson (1990). "Inference in Linear Time Series Models with Some Unit Roots", *Econometrica*, 58, 113-144.

Sola, M. and J. Driffill (1994). "Testing the Term Structure of Interest Rates Using a Stationary Vector Autoregression with Regime Switching", *Journal of Economic Dynamics and Control*, 18, 601-628.

Spencer, D.E. (1993). "Developing a Bayesian Vector Autoregression Forecasting Model," International Journal of Forecasting, 9, 407-421.

Theil, Henri (1966). *Applied Economic Forecasting*, Amsterdam, North Holland.

———. (1971). *Principles of Econometrics*, John Wiley and Sons, New York, and North-Holland Publishing Company, Amsterdam.

Throop, A.W. (1981). "Interest Rate Forecasts and Market Efficiency", *Federal Reserve Bank of San Francisco Working Paper*, 29-43.

Todd, R.M. (1984). "Improving Economic Forecasting with Bayesian Vector Autoregression", Quarterly Review, Federal Reserve Bank of Minneapolis, Fall, 18-29.

Zellner, A. (1979). "Statistical Analysis of Econometric Models", *Journal of the American Statistical Association*, 74, 628-643.

Zellner, A. and Palm, F. (1974). "Time Series Analysis and Simultaneous Equation Econometric Models", *Journal of Econometrics*, 2, 17-54.

3

Macroeconomic Effects of Changes in Selected Monetary and Fiscal Variables: A Simulation Analysis for India

A. SOUMYA
K.N. MURTY

1. Introduction

A macroeconometric model can be stated as a system of simultaneous equations, which relates the variables, and seeks to explain the behaviour of the economy at aggregate level, based on the received theories of macroeconomics. Macroeconometric modelling in general pursues two objectives: forecasting and policy analysis. The latter objective is the focus of this study. Fiscal and monetary policies are the foremost policies that are virtually analysed in macroeconometric models from their inception.

This paper attempts to utilise the tool of an aggregative, structural, macroeconometric model to analyse the macroeconomic effects of changes in selected monetary and fiscal variables for India. Before we give the details of the selected model, its estimation etc., it would be useful to briefly look at the literature on this topic pertaining to India.

2. Literature Review

A detailed review of macro models built for Indian economy is beyond the scope of this paper[1]. Since this study proposes to deal with the monetary sector, it would be worthwhile to look into how the monetary sector was modelled in the Indian context[2]. This will be useful for identifying the research issues pertinent to this study.

---

1. A comprehensive review of macroeconometric models and policy modelling for India can be found in Krishnamurty (2001), Bhattacharya *et al.* (2002) and Pandit and Krishnamurty (2004).
2. A good review of monetary sector models was provided by Jadhav (1990).

There was no mention about treatment of the monetary sector in the earlier models. After 1970s, modelling monetary sector and its links with fiscal and external sectors became a challenging task in India. Modelling money and monetary policy for the determination of real output and price level has increased considerably in India. These issues were highlighted in models built by Rangarajan and Arif (1990), as well as Rangarajan and Mohanty (1997). In these models, stock of money varies endogenously through feedback from reserve money, which changes to accommodate fiscal deficit and changes in foreign exchange reserves.

The price level is determined by money supply and production. The output supply is determined as a function of real money balances and investment with lags. In this formulation, it is argued that reserve bank credit to finance public sector investment leads to monetary expansion and investment, which together may lead to higher output with a lag. Some models attempt to link the real, monetary and fiscal sectors. Models by Rangarajan and Arif (1990) and Pandit and Krishnamurty (1984) exhibit this form of linking. Public capital expenditure adds to real capital stock which in turn affects the level of real output.

The analysis of effect of public investment on private investment indicates crowding-in, in the sense that the infrastructure facilities created by public investment provide incentives for the private sector to invest (Krishnamurty, 1985). More recent assessment suggests the weakening of this phenomenon in the last decade possibly due to resource constraint and the negative price effect of public sector investment financed by fiscal deficit (Krishnamurty, 2001).

Modelling the external sector was not a major concern in the earlier models, because of restrictions on trade. But in the recent years, several models emerged with detailed emphasis on the external sector and it's interlinks with the monetary and fiscal sectors. Krishnamurty and Pandit (1996) modelled the merchandise trade flows in supply-demand framework. Import supply function is specified to be infinitely inelastic at fixed import price and the level of domestic economic activity. In modelling exports, demand is specified to depend on the world GDP and relative price, while supply depends on relative price and level of domestic output.

Macroeconomic impact of fiscal deficit on balance of payments in India is an emerging issue in recent years since the inception of stabilisation programme. These issues were modelled by Bhattacharya *et al.* (1994) and Rangarajan and Mohanty (1997). It is postulated that fiscal deficit increases the absorption in the economy relative to output and the output effect of deficit follows with a lag.

There has been a shift from the net domestic assets to the net foreign assets on the resources side of money base. This is because of the recent policy of financial liberalisation and the ensuing changes in the monetary policy, i.e. relying more on market based indirect measures than the direct monetary controls. These issues have been addressed by modelling the money supply process in India during the 1990s (Rath, 2001). Professor Nachane, in a recent paper, discussed the impact of liberalisation on monetary policy and the link between monetary base and money supply for the post-reform period (Nachane, 2001).

3. Methodology

This paper attempts to utilise a recently built macroeconometric model for India by the first author, as part of her M.Phil. dissertation. A few improvements in that model to address the theme of this paper have also been made. The basic model in the cited study (as well as this paper) is monetarist in focus and extends the work of Rangarajan and Arif (1990) to include the external sector along with a few other modifications. The model emphasises the inter-relationships between money, output, prices and balance of payments.

The model strives for a balance between the two polarised approaches of the classicals and the Keynesians. While classicals contend that changes in money supply, ultimately results in changes in the price level, the Keynesians on the other hand postulate that the changes in money supply eventually leads to changes in output, under conditions of less than full employment. Viewing reality lying somewhere in between these two extremes, one can postulate that changes in money supply affect both the output and the price level. Thus, the model tries to capture the effects of changes in money supply resulting in both output and price level.

The model mainly focuses on the determination of money supply and its links with fiscal operations and on the impact of money stock on output. It is postulated that real money balances or credit along with the real capital stock affects output. An increase in real credit results in monetary expansion, which in turn has an effect on output, and price level. A rise in output through increase in credit dampens the rise in price level caused by monetary expansion.

Further, RBI credit to finance the resource gap, which is defined as government total expenditure less government total receipts, causes money supply to increase endogenously with the rise in reserve money. This monetary expansion again affects the price level and output to a lesser extent, and the cycle continues.

In addition, external sector is also modelled by including supply and demand for exports, demand for imports and the BOP identity. Assuming equilibrium in the exports market, the export supply function is specified as a price equation for unit value of exports. It also incorporates real income and relative price factors of India and the rest of the world. The export demand depends on relative export prices and world income excluding that of India, thereby capturing the influence of world economic activity on India's exports. The import demand function is based on the domestic income level, relative import prices and the (foreign exchange) reserves capacity to pay for imports. The model structure can be summarised as shown below:

4. Model

1. YR = f ((M3/WPI), KGR)
2. GCER = f (YR, GCER $_{(-1)}$)
3. GRR = f (YR*WPI)
4. GBBS = f (ADEP, SLR)
5. ADEP = f (M3)
6. WPI[3] = f (M3, YR, WPI $_{(-1)}$)
7. NID = f (WPI)
8. KPGR = f (GKER)
9. KPCGR = f (KPGR, YR $_{(-1)}$)

3. Interest rate was also included as an exogenous variable in the money demand function, but it was found to be statistically insignificant and hence omitted.

10. GCE = GCER*WPI
11. GKE = GKER*WPI
12. GTE = GCE+GKE
13. GMB = ΔGBBS + GBNB
14. GCR = GMB+GNMB+GEB
15. RM = RBCG+RBCC+RBCS+RBFA+GCL-RNML
16. M3 = M_t * RM
17. Y = YR*NID
18. KGR = KPGR+KPCGR+KPUGR
19. UVEXP = f (WPI/EXR, WP, WIR, YR, $EXPR_{(-1)}$,)
20. EXPR = f (UVEXP/WP, WIR, $EXPR_{(-1)}$)
21. IMPR = f ((UVIMP*EXR)/WPI, YR, RBFA/(UVIMP*EXR))
22. RBFA = $RBFA_{(-1)}$+EXR (UVEXP*EXPR - UVIMP*IMPR) +FDI+NIF

Endogenous Variables

1. YR : Real national income (NNP at FC)
2. Y : Nominal national income (NNP at FC)
3. GCE : Current account expenditure of the government
4. GKE : Capital expenditure of the Government
5. GTE : Total expenditure of the Government
6. GCER : Real current account expenditure of the Government
7. GRR : Revenue receipts of the Government
8. GCR : Capital receipts of the Government
9. GBBS : Borrowings of the Government from banks
10. GMB : Market borrowings of the Government
11. ADEP : Aggregate Deposits with Banks
12. RBFA : Net foreign exchange assets of RBI
13. RM : Reserve money (M1)
14. M3 : Broad money
15. NID : Price deflator for national income

16. WPI : Wholesale price index
17. KGR : Gross Real Capital Stock: Aggregate
18. KPGR : Gross Real Capital Stock: Public sector
19. KPCGR : Gross Real Capital Stock: Private corporate sector
20. EXPR : Real exports
21. UVEXP : Unit value of exports
22. IMPR : Real imports

Exogenous Variables

1. GKER : Real capital expenditure of the Government
2. GEB : Government external borrowings
3. RBCG : RBI credit to the Government
4. GBNB : Government borrowings form the non-baking financial institutions
5. RG : Resource gap
6. RBCC : RBI credit to the commercial and co-operative banks, and NABARD
7. RBCS : RBI credit to the commercial sector
8. SLR : Statutory liquidity ratio
9. GCL : Government current liabilities to the public
10. RNML : RBI's net non-monitory liabilities
11. KPUGR : Gross Real Capital Stock: Unorganised private sector
12. EXR : Exchange rate
13. IMPR : Real Imports
14. UVIMP : Unit value of imports
15. FDI : Foreign direct investment
16. NIF : Net inflows
17. WIR : World income excluding India
18. WP : World wholesale price index excluding India
19. DUMMY : Dummy variable for economic reforms
20. M_t : Money multiplier
21. GNMB : Non-market borrowings of the Government

As stated above, the model pays attention on the link between money supply and fiscal operations. The distinguishing feature of the model is to include the lagged real money balances (M3/WPI) or credit as a factor of production along with the lagged real capital stock (KGR) in the production function. The rationale for introducing the firm's real balances as an input in its production function is that holding real balances allows the firm to produce greater output with given amounts of labour and capital. If the firm did not hold any real balances, it would have greater difficulty in paying its employees and suppliers or selling it's output i.e. transaction cost of coordinating production activities would be higher. To avoid handling payments and receipts in money, the firm would have to divert part of its labour and capital to somehow arrange for payments and receipts directly in commodities, with such diversion reducing the amounts of labour and capital allocated to the production of output and thereby reducing the firm's output. Therefore, in an economy requiring the exchange of goods against money, real balances function as an input in the firm's production function, with higher real balances leading to higher output, Thus marginal productivity of real balances is positive.

The government operations are modelled by a set of seven equations. Total expenditure of the government (GTE) is taken as the sum of current expenditure (GCE) and capital expenditure (GKE). While the latter is taken as exogenous or policy determined, the current expenditure of the government in real terms (GCER) is determined according to a partial adjustment process related to the real income. Nominal revenue receipts of the government (GRR) are related to nominal income.

The nominal capital receipts of the government (GCR) consist of government market borrowings (GMB), non-market borrowings (GNMB) and external borrowings of the government (GEB). Market borrowings of the government is the sum of changes in government domestic borrowings from banks (ΔGBBS) that are reflected by the banks net-investment in government securities, and borrowings from financial institutions, other than banks (GBNB). Non-market borrowings comprises of small savings, provident funds, special borrowings from RBI against compulsory deposits and other capital receipts. Government borrowings from banks are a function of aggregate deposits with banks (ADEP), which in turn is related to money supply.

The resource gap is financed through credit from RBI (ΔRBCG), over and above other borrowings. The link between fiscal and monetary sectors is established by making RBI credit to government (RBCG) as a component of reserve money (RM), which in turn is related to money supply (M3) through money multiplier (M_t). The other components of reserve money are, RBI credit to commercial sector (RBCS) and commercial banks, co-operative banks (RBCC), net foreign exchange assets of the RBI (RBFA) and government currency liabilities (GCL) less net non-monetary liabilities of the RBI (RNML). Demand for money is expressed in terms of a price equation where price level (WPI) is related to money supply, real income and lagged prices. The national income deflator (NID) is related to WPI.

Real capital stock (KGR) is decomposed into gross real capital stock in public sector (KPGR), private corporate sector (KPCGR) and unorganised private corporate sector. KPGR is explained in terms of real capital expenditure of the government KPCGR depends on gross real capital stock on public sector and lagged real income.

Coming to the external sector, export supply equation is expressed in terms of unit value of exports (UVEXP), lagged exports, real income, WPI, world price (WP) and real income of rest of the world (WIR). Export demand (EXPR) is explained in real terms, as a function of relative prices, income of rest of the world and lagged exports. The import demand equation is specified as a function of unit value of imports (UVIMP) relative to WPI, real income and desired level of foreign exchange reserves given unit value of imports. The balance of payments (or change in reserves) is equal to the sum of net trade balance and net capital inflows where net capital inflows are decomposed into foreign direct investment and rest of capital inflows. A schematic view of the full model is shown in Chart-3.1.

5. Empirical Results

The model has 12 equations and 10 identities. Annual data on all the variables was collected for the period 1972-73 to 2001-02. However, the data for the period 1972-73 to 1998-99 was used only for model estimation and the observations from 1999-00 to 2001-02 were used for *ex-post* or post-sample validation of the model.

Since stationarity of variables is an important issue in econometric estimations, the data was tested for stationarity using the unit root tests[4]. Most of the variables were found to be non-stationary in levels but stationary in rate of change form. Hence, the required 12 equations are estimated in **rate of change**[5] form, using 3SLS method of estimation[6]. Thus, the estimates therefore, possess desirable properties like unbiasedness, consistency and efficiency, at least asymptotically.

While estimating the model, a TREND variable is included in most of the equations to capture the autonomous time related changes in the growth rates of the observed series of endogenous variables. A DUMMY variable to separate the pre- and post-liberalisation (1991-92 onwards) periods in the data is also included in the model. Interaction of this DUMMY variable with some of the explanatory variables is also considered.

The 12 estimated equations using 3SLS method are given in Appendix-3A.I. The selection of the final forms of these equations is based on usual statistical criteria like correct signs of coefficients, significant t-values and high goodness of fit. Since the estimated equations are in the growth-rate form, the regression coefficients can be treated as partial elasticities of the dependent variable with respect to independent variables. The elasticities are computed for the short- and long-run as well as pre- and post-reform periods. The partial elasticities of all the dependent variables w.r.t. selected independent variables are given in the Table 3.1. The implications of a few of these partial responses are discussed below.

---

4. Despite non-stationarity of variables, in simultaneous equation systems, the 2SLS but not the OLS estimators, are shown to produce consistent estimates (see for e.g. Hisio 1997). The authors are grateful to Professor V.N. Pandit for bringing this literature to their notice.

5. Estimating equations in stationary variables, here rate of change form, may result in loosing 'long-term' effects. It is recommended to use co-integration and error correction mechanism in the event of non-stationarity. But, this approach will be quite difficult for a large system of simultaneous equations present in a macro econometric model. Of late, vector error correction methods seem to be available in computer packages. Future work will consider this option.

6. EViews package has been used for the model estimation.

Chart 3.1

Schematic Diagram of the Model

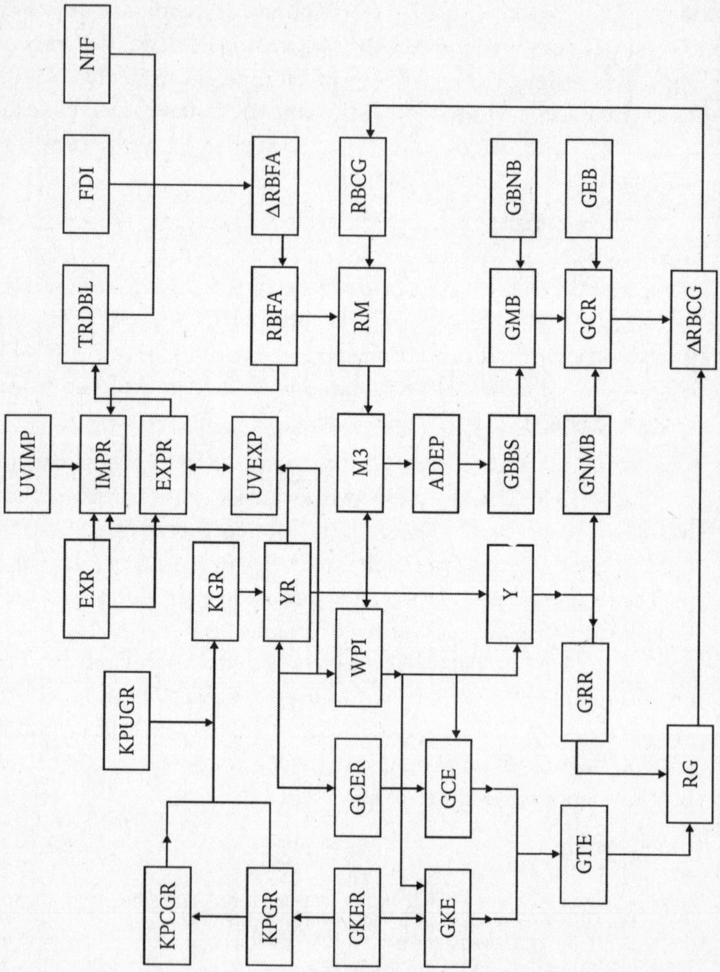

Table 3.1

Estimated Partial Elasticities of the Dependent Variables w.r.t. Selected Independent Variables

Dependent Variable	*Independent Variables*					
YR	**(M3/WPI)** 0.13				**KGR** 0.14	
WPI	**M3**				**YR**	
	Pre-Reform		*Post-Reform*			
	0.46 SR	1.11 LR	0.28 SR	0.60 LR	-1.16 SR	-2.82 LR
KPGR	**GKER**					
	Pre-reform		*Post-reform*			
	0.57		0.38			
KPCGR	**KPGR** 0.15				**YR_{-1}** 1.73	
GCER	**YR**					
	1.31 SR		1.50 LR			
GRR	**(YR*WPI)**					
	Pre-reform		*Post-reform*			
	0.70		0.58			
GBBS	**ADEP** 0.94				**SLR** 0.28	
ADEP	**M3** 1.15					
UVEXP	**WP** 0.37		**WIR** 0.22		**YR** 0.99	
EXPR	**(UVEXP/WP)**				**WIR**	
	-1.10 SR	-1.14 LR			0.41 SR	0.42 LR
IMPR	**(UVIMP*EXR/WPI)**				**YR**	
	-0.73 SR	-0.91 LR			1.53 SR	1.90 LR

SR: Short-run; LR: Long-run

Here, in the first regression, which is a production function, the regression coefficients are output elasticities with respect to factor inputs. From the table, it can be seen that due to a 10 per cent increase in each of these two factor inputs, ceteris paribus, the real aggregate output in the economy would increase by 1.3-1.4 per cent.

These elasticities are numerically small, implying low output response to changes in real credit or capital stock.

Like wise, from the estimated price equation, for every 10 per cent rise in money stock, general price level rises by 4.6 per cent during pre-reform period and 2.8 per cent in post-reform period. The long-run responses are even larger. A 10 per cent rise in real output, decreases the price level by 11.6 per cent in the short-run and 28.2 per cent in the long run. Coming to investment variables, a 10 per cent rise in government capital expenditure leads to 5.7 per cent and 3.8 per cent increase in capital stock during pre-reform period and in the post-reform period respectively. A 10 per cent rise in public sector capital stock increases private sector capital stock by 1.5 per cent as a crowding-in effect.

The government borrowings from banks seems to be affected by aggregate deposits with the banks equi-proportionally, while a 10 per cent increase in SLR will increase government borrowings from banks only by 2.8 per cent. Increase in money supply also will have almost an equi-proportional increase in aggregate deposits with banks. Government revenue receipts, ceteris paribus, will increase with rise in nominal income in the economy. But, the rate of increase in government revenue receipts seems to slow down marginally from 0.7 per cent during the pre-reform period to 0.6 per cent in the post-reform period.

Performance of the Model

To assess the empirical adequacy of the full model in describing the historical data, the predicted sample period values (levels) of the 12 endogenous variables are generated successively using the definition of 'rate of change' and the estimated rate of change values of each endogenous variable along with an appropriate initial value at the beginning of the series. The observed value in 1973-74 is taken as the initial value for each variable. Thus, the full model has 34 (=12+12+10) relationships in total for the purpose of simulation. EViews package was employed to solve the 34 relations together iteratively for each year using commonly required options, namely deterministic simulation and dynamic solving options for the entire sample period, 1972-73 to 2001-02. The simulated values, also called the 'base simulation', for the period 1972-73 to 1998-99 are sample period (*ex-post*) estimates. The 'base simulation' values are tuned for adjustment in levels by modifying only the initial 1973-74 values wherever necessary. The assessment of the full model is done by (a) comparing the time series plots of actual and base simulation values and (b) computing the summary measures MAPE, RMPE and Theil's inequality coefficient, separately for the sample and post-sample periods. Based on all these three criteria, the base simulation could trace the historical data quite well. Due to limitation of space, these details are omitted here.

6. Policy Simulations

The simulation methodology can also be conveniently used to analyse the impacts of counter factual scenarios about certain policy variables, among the exogenous variables. Hypothetical sustained changes in each policy instrument are incorporated for a specified sample period and the full model is solved for each year, during that sample period. The time path of each endogenous variable of such a policy simulation is compared and contrasted with the base simulation (not the actual series) as a reference path. Such comparison only can facilitate quantification of the impacts of policy change on the endogenous variables, without confounding the effects of the inaccuracies of estimated model.

The monetary policy variables chosen here for this purpose are RBI credit to commercial sector (RBCS), the statutory liquidity ratio (SLR) and the foreign direct investment in India (FDI). Counterfactual simulations are undertaken to illustrate the usefulness of the model for analysing the changes in monetary policy relating to these variables in a simultaneous equations framework.

For comparing the macroeconomic effects of changes in fiscal and monetary policies, another variant of the model is constructed. For this purpose, the base simulation is re-calibrated by making money supply (M3) exogenous in the model. Two additional policy simulations relating to changes in GKER and M3 were undertaken. The simulation results for a few important variables are plotted in Graphs.

The allocative and dynamic macroeconomic effects due to the above policy changes are also quantified as percentage changes, known as multipliers, with reference to base simulation values at four points of time, namely same year of exogenous change (immediate or instantaneous or impact), after one year (short-term), after five years (medium term) and after ten years (long-term).

It may be mentioned that these percentage responses are contemporaneous in nature (policy simulation *vs.* base simulation) and should not be treated as usual percentage rate of change over time. For this reason, these responses are likely to be different from the direct responses (both partial and net) implied by the estimated rate of change equations using 3SLS. The period 1991-2001 is used for all these policy simulations. The scenario results are presented in Tables 3.2-3.3.

(a) Sustained 30 per cent Increase in RBI Credit to Commercial Sector (RBCS)

RBI credit to commercial sector is an important monetary policy instrument to affect macro economy through changes in money supply. We consider a hypothetical or counterfactual simulation to visualise such a policy change. A sustained 30 per cent increase in RBCS from 1991-92 onwards is simulated. We shall discuss the impacts and dynamic responses of the policy change on all the endogenous variables.

Due to a 30 per cent increase in RBCS, as expected, the first change will occur in reserve money (RM), and thereby money supply. Reserve money and money supply have increased by 2.3 per cent as an immediate response. As a result, price level increased by 0.4 per cent. Since real money balances is a factor of production with positive and significant coefficient (0.13), real output rises marginally (0.2%). Sizeable increases occur in most of the monetary and fiscal variables, government market borrowings being the largest beneficiary (19.9%). Capital receipts of the government also rises (3.5%). Due to rise in real income, unit value of exports rise (0.3%), thereby reducing export demand (0.4%). Conversely, since unit value of imports being exogenous, rise in real income has led to rise in real imports (0.7%), thereby worsening the balance of payments (5.0%).

In the second and subsequent years, when the policy change is sustained, there will be **system-wide effects**, strengthening of some and weakening of other responses, with an overall slide down in the economy- fall in real output (0.2%), gross capital stock (0.1%), private corporate sector capital stock (0.1%), money supply (2.1%), government market borrowings (4.4%), government capital receipts (3.0%) and bank deposits (2.5%) by the year 2001-02. However,

Table 3.2

Impacts and Dynamic Multipliers (per cent) of Hypothetical Changes in Selected Exogenous Variables

Endogenous Variable	*Simulation-1*				*Simulation-2*				*Simulation-3*			
	1991-92	*1992-93*	*1996-97*	*2001-02*	*1991-92*	*1992-93*	*1996-97*	*2001-02*	*1991-92*	*1992-93*	*1996-97*	*2001-02*
YR	0.2	0.1	-0.1	-0.2	-0.0	-0.0	-0.2	-0.2	0.0	0.0	0.0	0.0
Y	0.6	0.4	-0.3	-0.7	-0.0	-0.1	-0.7	-1.4	0.0	0.0	0.0	0.0
NID	0.3	0.3	-0.2	-0.6	-0.0	-0.0	-0.5	-1.1	0.0	0.0	0.0	0.0
WPI	0.4	0.5	-0.3	-0.8	-0.0	-0.1	-0.7	-1.6	0.0	0.0	0.0	0.0
KGR	0.0	0.1	-0.1	-0.1	0.0	0.0	-0.1	-0.1	0.0	0.0	0.0	0.0
KPGR	0.0	0.0	0.0	0.0	0.0	0.0	0.0	0.0	0.0	0.0	0.0	0.0
KPCGR	0.0	0.4	-0.1	-0.1	0.0	-0.0	-0.2	-0.3	0.0	0.0	0.0	0.0
M3	2.3	0.9	-1.1	-2.1	-0.1	-0.2	-2.1	-3.2	0.0	0.0	0.0	0.0
RM	2.3	0.9	-1.1	-2.1	-0.1	-0.2	-2.1	-3.2	0.0	0.0	0.0	0.0
GCER	0.3	0.1	-0.2	-0.2	-0.0	-0.0	-0.3	-0.3	0.0	0.0	0.0	0.0
GRR	0.4	0.3	-0.2	-0.5	-0.0	-0.0	-0.5	-1.0	0.0	0.0	0.0	0.0
GBBS	2.4	1.0	-1.2	-2.2	-0.1	-0.2	-2.2	-3.4	6.7	6.7	6.7	6.7
ADEP	2.6	1.1	-1.3	-2.5	-0.1	-0.3	-2.4	-3.7	0.0	0.0	0.0	0.0
EXPR	-0.4	-0.2	0.1	0.3	0.0	0.0	0.3	0.5	0.0	0.0	0.0	0.0
IMPR	0.7	0.7	0.4	-0.2	-0.0	-0.1	-0.8	-1.6	0.0	0.0	0.0	0.0
UVEXP	0.3	0.1	-0.2	-0.4	-0.0	-0.0	-0.3	-0.5	0.0	0.0	0.0	0.0
Δ(RBFA)	-5.0	-5.4	-2.7	1.7	-0.5	-1.8	-5.9	-5.3	0.0	0.0	0.0	0.0
GCE	0.8	0.6	-0.5	-1.0	-0.0	-0.1	-1.0	-1.9	0.0	0.0	0.0	0.0
GKE	0.4	0.5	-0.3	-0.8	-0.0	-0.1	-0.7	-1.6	0.0	0.0	0.0	0.0
GTE	0.7	0.6	-0.4	-1.0	-0.0	-0.1	-0.9	-1.9	0.0	0.0	0.0	0.0
GCR	3.5	-1.5	-1.4	-3.0	-0.1	-0.3	-2.5	-2.0	9.7	2.8	3.3	0.0
GMB	19.9	-3.4	-2.3	-4.4	-0.5	-0.8	-4.1	-3.0	55.8	6.5	5.3	0.0

Note: Simulation-1: 30 per cent sustained increase in RBCS
Simulation-2: 30 per cent sustained decrease in FDI
Simulation-3: 30 per cent sustained increase in SLR

Table 3.3

Impacts and Dynamic Multipliers (per cent) of Hypothetical Changes in Selected Exogenous Variables

Endogenous Variable	*Simulation-4*				*Simulation-5*			
	1991-92	*1992-93*	*1996-97*	*2001-02*	*1991-92*	*1992-93*	*1996-97*	*2001-02*
YR	0.5	0.4	0.3	0.3	0.5	0.5	0.7	0.5
Y	0.7	0.9	1.2	1.3	0.1	-0.1	-0.6	-0.6
NID	0.3	0.5	0.9	1.0	-0.4	-0.7	-1.2	-1.2
WPI	0.4	0.7	1.2	1.5	-0.5	-0.9	-1.7	-1.6
KGR	0.0	0.2	0.2	0.2	4.0	3.8	3.8	2.9
KPGR	0.0	0.0	0.0	0.0	9.9	9.9	9.9	9.9
KPCGR	0.0	0.7	0.5	0.4	1.1	1.9	2.1	2.0
GCER	0.6	0.6	0.5	0.4	0.6	0.7	1.0	0.8
GRR	0.5	0.7	0.9	1.0	-0.0	-0.2	-0.6	-0.6
GBBS	3.3	3.3	3.3	3.3	0.0	0.0	0.0	0.0
ADEP	3.5	3.5	3.5	3.5	0.0	0.0	0.0	0.0
EXPR	-0.7	-0.6	-0.6	-0.7	-0.5	-0.4	-0.4	-0.3
IMPR	0.9	1.2	1.5	1.6	0.2	0.1	-0.3	-0.4
UVEXP	0.6	0.5	0.5	0.5	0.4	0.3	0.3	0.2
D(RBFA)	-9.8	-13.6	-6.5	-48.3	-3.0	-1.8	1.0	10.7
GCE	1.0	1.3	1.7	1.9	0.1	-0.2	-0.8	-0.8
GKE	0.4	0.7	1.2	1.5	29.3	28.8	27.8	27.9
GTE	0.8	1.1	1.6	1.8	8.5	7.4	5.2	3.8
GCR	6.0	1.2	1.5	1.4	0.0	0.0	0.0	0.0
GMB	25.2	3.2	2.5	1.7	0.0	0.0	0.0	0.0
RBCG	0.6	1.5	10.4	12.7	0.2	0.3	-0.3	-2.1

Note: Simulation-4: 3 per cent sustained increase in M3
Simulation-5: 30 per cent sustained increase in GKER

consumers may be benefited due to fall in general price level (0.8%). Balance of payments also seems to improve due to subsequent rise in real exports (0.3%) and fall in real imports (0.2%). Thus, sustained increase in RBI credit to commercial sector seems to result only in immediate to short-run benefits to the economy. The long-run effects are likely to be unfavourable. Some of these important scenario effects are shown in Figures 3.1-3.3.

Figure 3.1

Impact of 30 per cent Increase in RBCS on Money Supply

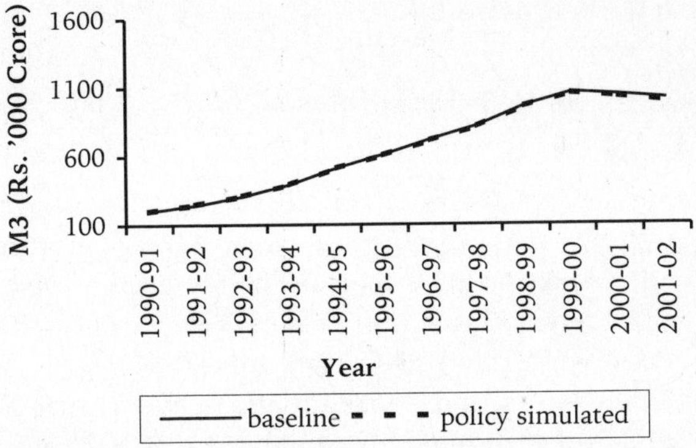

Figure 3.2

Impact of 30 per cent Increase in RBCS on Wholesale Price Index

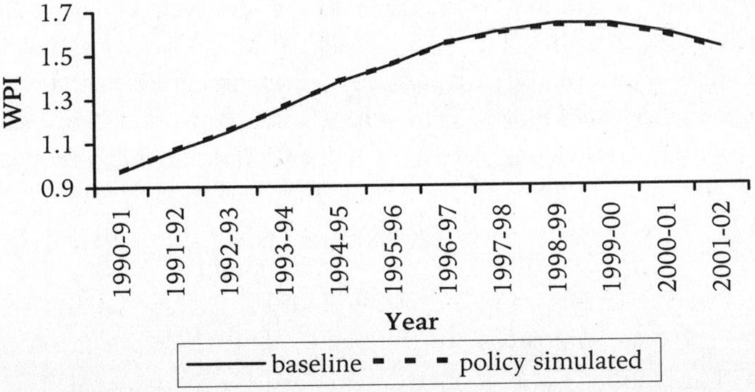

Figure 3.3

Impact of 30 per cent Increase in RBCS on Balance of Payment

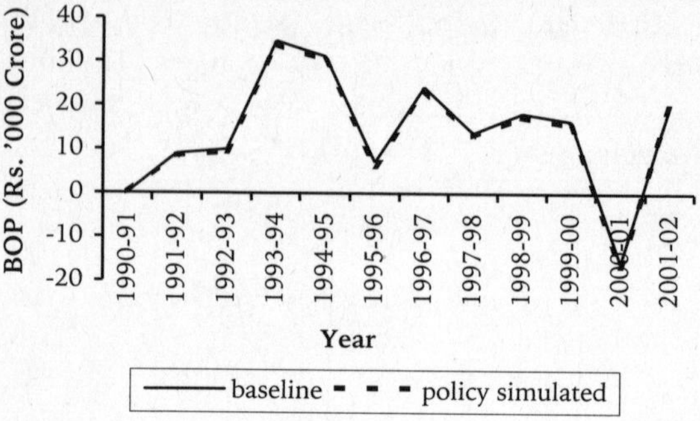

(b) *Sustained 30 per cent Decrease in Foreign Direct Investment (FDI)*

Foreign direct investment is a very crucial policy variable in the model. Changes in this variable can cause several macroeconomic impulses that are extremely important in the current discussion of globalisation and economic reforms. Fears are often expressed about the possible sudden withdrawal of foreign direct investment by foreign institutional investors and consequential adverse effects on the economy. Keeping this in mind, we simulated a 30 per cent sustained decrease in nominal foreign direct investment from 1991-92 onwards. The immediate and dynamic effects of such a scenario are quantified in comparison to the base simulation and are presented in Table 3.2. The FDI variable appears directly as a pure explanatory variable in the foreign exchange reserves (RBFA) identity. Therefore, the effects of reduction in FDI will start with this identity and they will percolate to all other relationships in the model in the same year, due to simultaneity. However, the magnitude of changes in 1991-92 for many of the endogenous variables seems numerically very small (less than or equal to 0.1%). Hence we see only the direction of changes, but not magnitudes in the table. Decline in FDI will directly reduce foreign exchange reserves, which will reduce base money (RM), money supply (M3) and real imports (IMPR). Reduction in nominal money supply will trigger a series of second round changes. These include decline in real output, aggregate deposits with the banks, and wholesale price index.

All the above second round effects will lead to more wide spread changes in the third and subsequent rounds in the same year of exogenous FDI reduction. The net year-end changes are noticeable (more than 0.1%) only in the case of two variables, namely balance of payments (-0.5%), and government market borrowings (-0.5%). These two changes are the result of a series of systemic effects, which are the hallmark of a simultaneous equations model. It may be mentioned that the direction of all other effects are in accordance with the postulated model.

In the second year, 1992-93, a few more endogenous variables will have sizeable changes. Due to sustained reduction in foreign direct investment, the reserves deplete further (-1.8%) thereby causing considerable reduction (-0.2%) in base money (RM) and money supply (M3). As a consequential change, the country's economic activity (YR) will slow down marginally, necessitating cuts in government borrowings from banks (GBBS) and aggregate deposits with banks (ADEP). The overall price level will decline in comparison to the base simulation. Due to reduction in FDI (and hence reserves), imports may be discouraged marginally.

The medium (1996-97) and long-term (2001-02) effects are stronger and exhibit continuation of above-mentioned trends. Interestingly, most of the endogenous variables are affected due to decline in foreign direct investment, signifying its importance to the Indian economy. Specifically, these macroeconomic changes include, marginal decline in output (-0.2%), price level (-1.6%); and money supply (-3.2%) by the year 2001-02. The real capital stock in private corporate sector (-0.3%) and hence in the economy is expected to decline marginally (-0.1%). The real imports will fall (-1.6%) and real exports demand will pickup (0.5%), but net balance of payments will decline (-5.3%).

Most of the fiscal and monetary variables also seem to suffer due to sustained reduction in foreign direct investment. Thus, there is justification for the fears expressed regarding adverse macroeconomic consequences on the Indian economy, particularly in the event of substantial (and sustained) reduction in foreign direct investment.

(c) Sustained 30 per cent Increase in Statutory Liquidity Ratio (SLR)

A sustained 30 per cent increase in SLR doesn't seem to affect any of the variables except government borrowings from banks (GBBS), government capital receipts (GCR) and government market borrowings (GMB). In the first year, GMB increased very rapidly (55.8%) than the other two variables. Government capital receipts have gone-up by 9.7

per cent in 1991-92, but the response seems to die down eventually. GBBS rose by 6.7 per cent through out, in conformity with its regression coefficient for SLR (0.28). The localisation of the effects due to changes in this crucial monetary policy variable can be attributed to the absence of link between government capital receipts (GCR) and monetised deficit (ΔRBCG). Originally, this link existed in the model, but it could not be retained due to problems of non-convergence of simulation routine. This limitation in the model needs further probing. Some of these important scenario effects are shown in Figures 3.4-3.6.

Figure 3.4

Impact of 30 per cent Increase in SLR on Government Borrowings

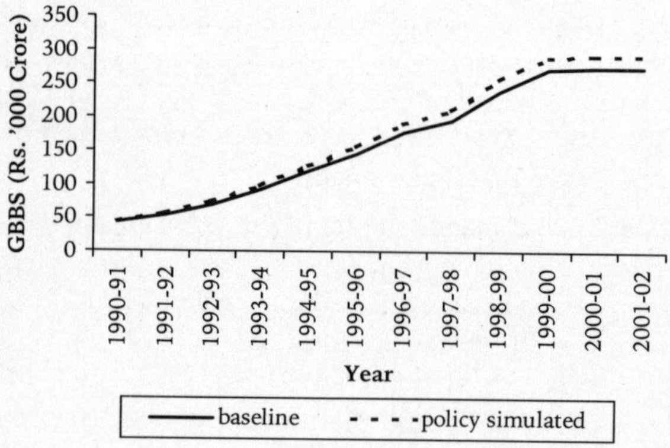

Figure 3.5

Impact of 30 per cent Increase in SLR on Government Capital Receipts

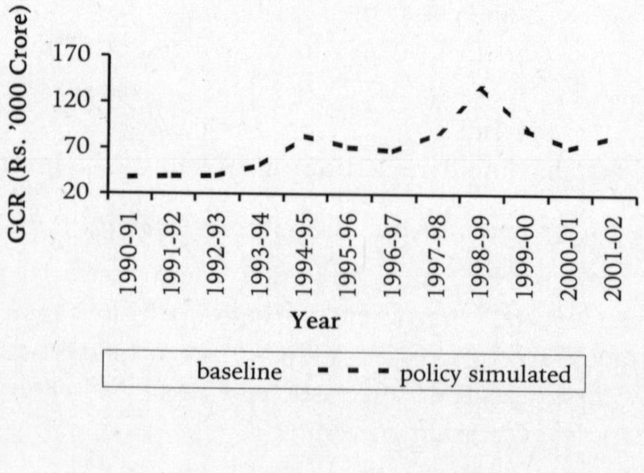

Figure 3.6

Impact of 30 per cent Increase in SLR on Government Market Borrowings

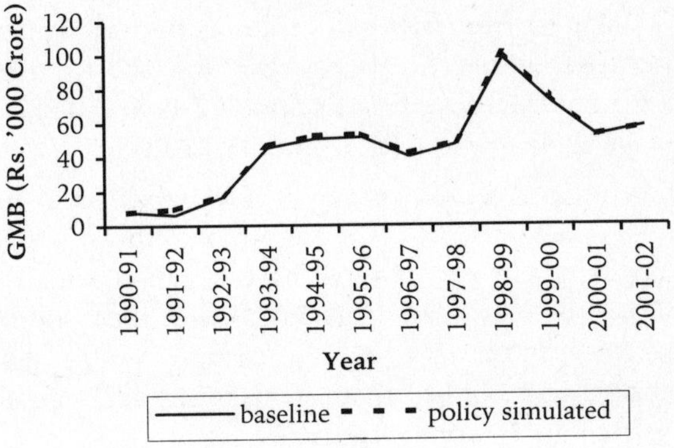

(d) *Sustained Increase in Money Supply versus Government Capital Expenditure*

Often the policymaker has to compare two or more policy options and opt for one among them for implementation. Two such competing policy options in our model framework are increase in money supply and increase in government real capital expenditure. To implement the first policy option, the existing model needs modification in which the money supply becomes a pure exogenous variable.

This requires dropping the reserve money and money supply identities, but bring in a new identity relating to Reserve Bank Credit to Central Government (RBCG). Changes in RBCG are usually termed as monetised deficit, which used to play a very important role in the Indian economy prior to the start of economic reforms process. Since the equations being estimated are unaffected by the above changes, all the 12 estimated growth rate equations using 3SLS remain intact. Only some identities get changed and after incorporating these changes in the model, the base simulation is re-calibrated. The modified base simulation will be used as reference path to compare the above mentioned two policy options.

Unlike in the earlier simulations, we try to bring in a common feature or 'standardisation' for comparison, namely equal percentage deviation in real output (0.5%) from base simulation in the year 1991-92, between the two policy scenarios. This is achieved by trial and error method of changing M3 and GKER variables. The M3 and GKER variables needed respectively 3 per cent and 30 per cent changes in 1991-92 to achieve a 0.5 per cent deviation in real output in 1991-92 alone. The same percentage changes in M3 and GKER are sustained till 2001-02. We believe that this facilitates better comparison than equal percentage change in policy variables. We first discuss the impacts of a 3 per cent sustained increase in money supply on all the remaining endogenous variables including RBCG.

As we mentioned earlier, money supply (which is assumed to be equal to money demand) is one of the most crucial variable in the model. Changes in this variable will have instantaneous system wide effects. This can be seen from Table 3.3. Few of them are represented in Figures 3.7-3.9. In the first round of changes, a 3 per cent increase in money supply in 1991-92 will raise aggregate real output in 1991-92 itself, since real money balances (or credit) is a factor of production with current time suffix. Aggregate deposits with the banks will rise due to increased liquidity. Wholesale price index will rise to clear the product market. These changes will lead to further changes in the second and subsequent rounds. Significant among these are increase in government borrowings from market (25.2%) and banks (3.3%). As a result, capital receipts of the government will increase (6.0%). Due to rise in domestic price level, unit value of exports will rise (0.6%), leading to fall in export competitiveness and hence real export demand (-0.7%). But, real imports will rise by 0.8% due to fall in relative prices and rise in real income. The net effect is a fall in balance of payments (-9.8%). The capital stock, both private and public, is unaffected in 1991-92 due to the exogenous rise in money supply. The fiscal variables are increased marginally.

In contrast, the following responses are noticed in 1991-92 due to a 30 per cent increase in government real capital expenditure in 1991-92. Due to this policy change, as expected, the largest endogenous change is in government nominal capital expenditure (29.3%) and government nominal total expenditure (8.5%). The real capital stock in the public sector (9.9%) as well as the economy as a whole will rise (4.0%). There are only minor changes in the other endogenous variables including a 0.5 per cent decline in the price level. Thus, the main difference between the two policy options seems to be changes in general price level, public sector capital stock and expenditure. Increase in money supply is inflationary, while increase in government capital expenditure is asset creating as well non-inflationary. Both leads to an identical rise in real output (0.5%) in 1991-92. These trends will continue into the future for both the scenarios. It is interesting to notice that there will be a switch over from government market borrowings to RBI credit as 3 per cent increase in money supply is sustained. In the case of 30 per cent sustained increase in government capital expenditure, there will be a decline in RBI credit to government. The balance of payments will also improve (10.7%). Some of these important scenario effects are shown in Figures 3.7-3.12.

Figure 3.7

Impact of 30 per cent Increase in M3 on Real Output

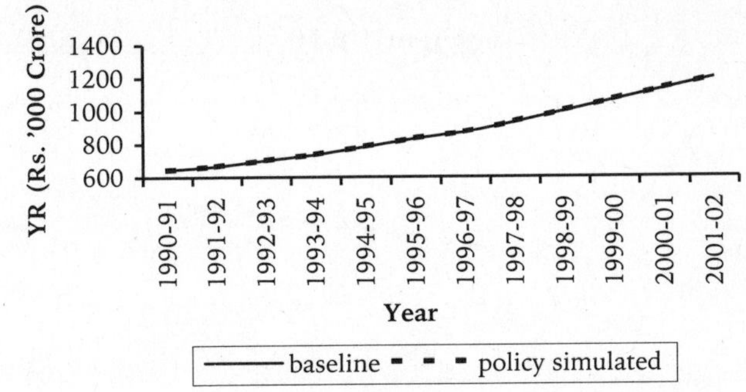

Figure 3.8

Impact of 30 per cent Increase in M3 on Aggregate Deposits with Banks

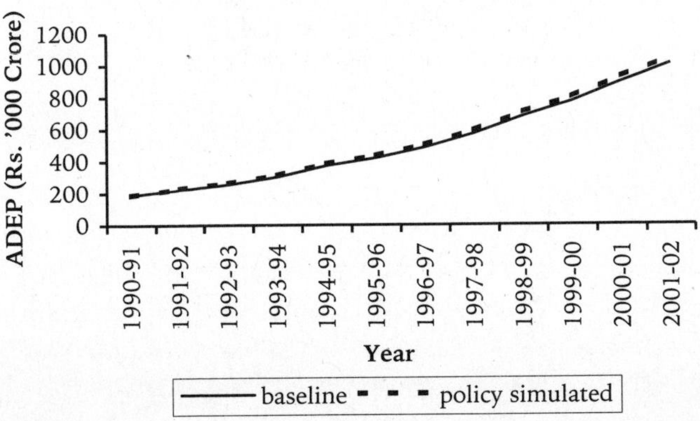

Figure 3.9

Impact of 30 per cent Increase in M3 on Balance of Payments

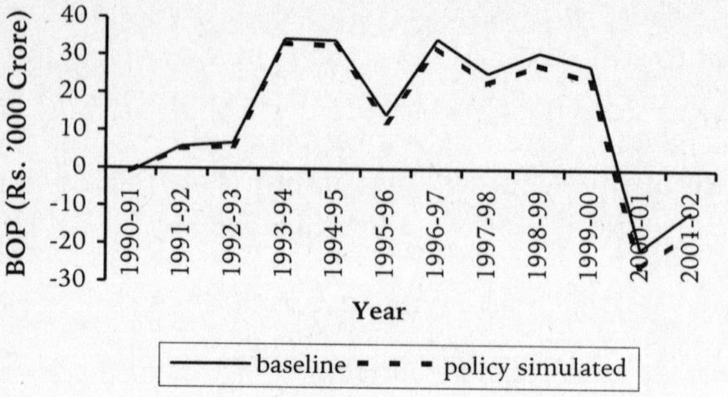

Figure 3.10

Impact of 30 per cent Increase in GKER on Wholesale Price Index

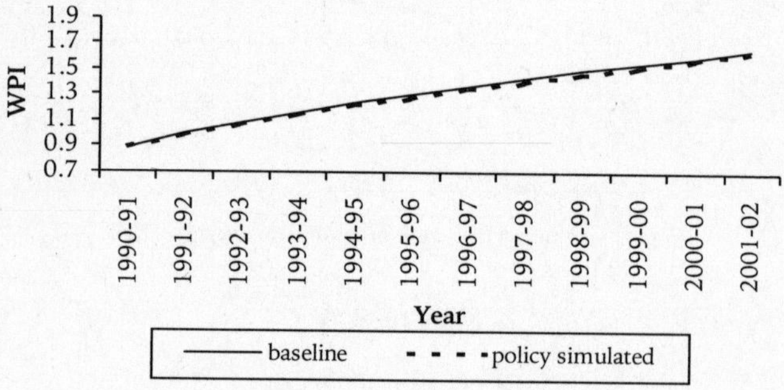

Figure 3.11

Impact of 30 per cent Increase in GKER on Capital Stock in Public Sector

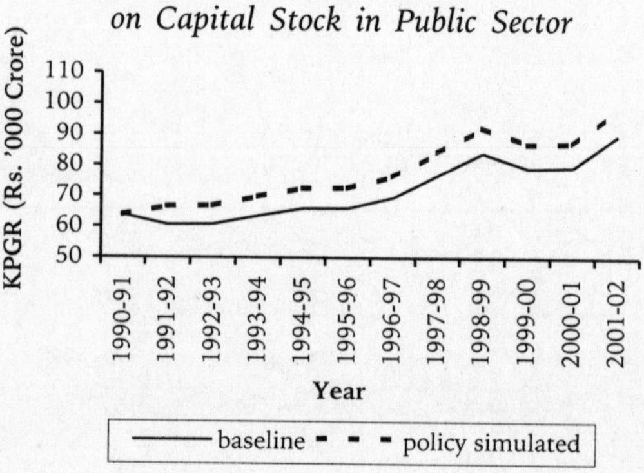

Figure 3.12

Impact of 30 per cent Increase in GKER on Capital Stock: Aggregate

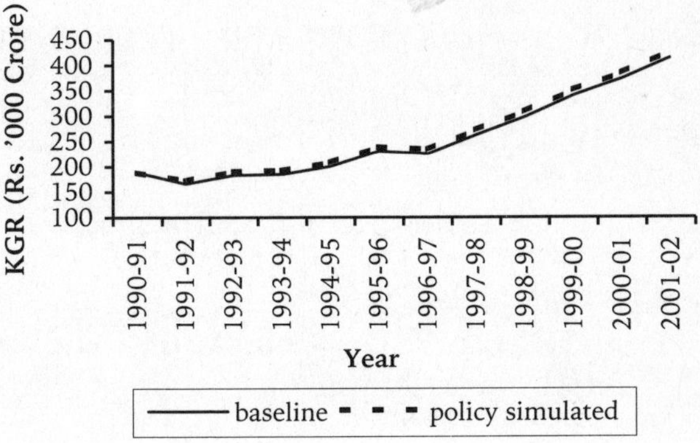

Thus, **to conclude**, this study has analysed the likely macroeconomic effects of changes in selected monetary and fiscal variables for India. The quantified effects include the allocative and dynamic responses of chosen policy change on important macroeconomic variables such as real output, investment in public and private sectors, money supply, general price level, real exports, imports and balance of payments in the Indian economy. The sign and magnitude of the effects differ between the two types of policy variables and they vary over time-immediate to long run.

Specifically, the effects of increase in monetary variable like RBI credit to commercial sector seem to be beneficial to the economy **only** in the immediate to short run. However, there can be sustained benefits to the consumer in terms of lower price level due to such a policy change. Sustained withdrawal of foreign direct investment will adversely affect the Indian economy in many ways. Between the two policy options of increase in real government expenditure and nominal money supply, as can be expected, the former will be more beneficial than the latter.

Appendix 3A.I

Estimated Equations Using 3SLS Method (t-values in parenthesis)

1) $$GrYR = \underset{(1.98)}{0.0191^{**}} + \underset{(2.03)}{0.1270^{**}}\ Gr\ (M3/WPI) + \underset{(2.53)}{0.1393^{*}}\ GrKGR + \underset{(1.56)}{0.0008^{***}}\ TREND - \underset{(-2.59)}{0.4158^{*}}\ AR\ (1)$$

$R^2 = 0.26$, $DW = 2.20$

2) $$GrGCER = \underset{(4.89)}{1.3133^{*}}\ GrYR - \underset{(-0.11)}{0.0001}\ TREND + \underset{(1.35)}{0.1217^{***}}\ GrGCER_{(-1)}$$

$R^2 = 0.14$, $DW = 1.90$

3) $$GrGRR = \underset{(5.97)}{0.7000^{*}}\ YR*WPI - \underset{(-0.60)}{0.1188}\ (DUMMY*Gr\ (YR*WPI)) + \underset{(1.83)}{0.0028^{**}}\ TREND$$

$R^2 = -0.30$, $DW = 1.74$

4) $$GrGBBS = \underset{(8.32)}{0.9372^{*}}\ GrADEP + \underset{(1.23)}{0.2769}\ GrSLR + \underset{(1.49)}{0.0021^{***}}\ TREND - \underset{(-2.53)}{0.3275^{*}}\ AR\ (1)$$

$R^2 = 0.30$, $DW = 2.49$

5) $$GrADEP = \underset{(32.99)}{1.150^{*}}\ GrM3 - \underset{(-2.97)}{0.0012^{*}}\ TREND$$

$R^2 = 0.52$, $DW = 2.56$

6) $$GrWPI = \underset{(5.18)}{0.4574^{*}}\ GrM3 - \underset{(-5.22)}{1.1586^{*}}\ GrYR - \underset{(-1.83)}{0.1771^{**}}\ (DUMMY*GrM3) + \underset{(1.21)}{0.0016}\ TREND + \underset{(6.57)}{0.5896^{*}}\ GrWPI_{(-1)}$$

$R^2 = 0.24$, $DW = 2.12$

7) $$Gr\ NID = \underset{(17.74)}{0.7322^{*}}\ GrWPI + \underset{(5.49)}{0.0016^{*}}\ TREND$$

$R^2 = 0.79$, $DW = 2.06$

8) $$GrKPGR = \underset{(4.01)}{0.5671^{*}}\ GrGKER - \underset{(-0.66)}{0.1820}\ (DUMMY*GrGKER) + \underset{(1.09)}{0.0013}\ TREND$$

$R^2 = 0.29$, $DW = 2.58$

9) $$GrKPCGR = \underset{(0.29)}{0.0281} + \underset{(0.35)}{0.1514}\ GrKPGR + \underset{(1.09)}{1.7279}\ GrYR_{(-1)}$$

$R^2 = 0.004$, $DW = 2.29$

10) $GrUVEXP = 0.2231\ Gr\ (WPI/EXR) + 0.3662^{***}\ GrWP + 0.2222^{**}\ GrWIR$
(0.82) (1.34) (2.13)

$+ 0.9923^{**}\ GrYR - 0.0050^{*}\ TREND + 0.1399\ GrEXPR_{(-1)}$
(2.22) (-3.25) (1.15)

$R^2 = 0.39$, DW = 2.11

11) $GrEXPR = -1.1024^{*}\ Gr\ (UVEXP/WP) + 0.4090^{*}\ GrWIR + 0.0330\ GrEXPR_{(-1)}$
(-7.33) (5.04) (0.31)

$R^2 = 0.49$, DW = 1.86

12) $GrIMPR = -\ 0.7325^{*}\ Gr\ ((UVIMP*EXR)/WPI) + 1.5321^{*}\ GrYR$
(-9.78) (3.82)

$+0.0040\ Gr(RBFA/(UVIMP*EXR)) + 0.00004\ TREND + 0.1942^{**}\ GrIMPR_{(-1)}$
(0.14) (0.03) (2.39)

$R^2 = 0.72$, DW = 2.19

*: Significant at 1% level, **: Significant at 5% level, ***: Significant at 10% level.

References

Bhattacharya, B.B, and Sabyasachi Kar (2002). *A Survey of Macro Econometric Models with Special Reference to India*, Discussion Paper, Institute of Economic Growth.

Bhattacharya, B.B., Agarwal, A. and Kar, S. (2000). *A Macroeconometric Model for Planning, Forecasting and Policy Analysis in India,* Development Planning Centre, Institute of Economic Growth, University Enclave, Delhi.

Hisio, C. (1997). "Statistical Properties of the Two Stage Least Squares Estimator Under Cointegration", *Review of Economic Studies,* Vol. 64, pp. 385-98.

Jadhav, Narendra (1990). "Monetary Modelling of the Indian Economy: A Survey", *Reserve Bank of India, Occasional Paper*, Vol. 11 (2), June.

Krishnamurty, K. (1984). "Inflation and Growth: A Model for India", *Indian Economic Review*, Vol. XIX (1), Jan-June; reprinted in K. Krishnamurty and V. Pandit. *Macroeconometric Modelling of the Indian Economy*, Hindustan Publishing Co., 1985.

Krishnamurty, K. (2001). "Macroeconometric Models for India; Past, Present and Prospects", *Economic and Political Weekly*, October 19-25.

Krishnamurty, K., Pandit, V.N. (1996). "Exchange Rate, Tariffs and Trade Flows: Alternative Policy Scenarios for India", *Indian Economic Review* (Jan-June 1996) (Mimeo Version 1995), reprinted in *Journal of Asian Economics*, Fall, 1997.

Nachane, D.M. (2001). *Financial Liberalisation and Monetary Policy: The Indian Evidence*, EUI Working Papers, European University Institute.

Pandit, V.N., Krishnamurty, K. (2004). *Economic Policy Modelling for India*, Oxford University Press.

Rangarajan, C. (1997). "Monetary Policy: Objectives and Targets", *Perspectives on Indian Economy* by Rangarajan, C., 1997.

Rangarajan, C. and Arif, R.R. (1990). "Money, Output and Prices: A Macroeconometric Model", *Economic and Political Weekly*, Vol.25, No.16.

Rangarajan, C. and Mohanty, M.S. (1997). "Fiscal Deficit, External Balance and Monetary Growth – A Study of Indian Economy", *Reserve Bank of India, Occasional Papers*, December 1997.

Rath, D.P. (2001). *Endogeneity Issues in the Money Supply Process of India*, Ph.D. Dissertation, Indira Gandhi Institute of Development Research, Mumbai.

This paper is based on the M.Phil dissertation of the first author submitted to the University of Hyderabad. An earlier version of this paper was presented in the Sixth Annual Conference of 'Money and Finance in the Indian Economy', at IGIDR, Mumbai. The authors would like to thank the discussant and the participants of the conference for their helpful comments. We would also like to thank Ms. Pallavi Bora for her careful reading of the manuscript and editorial suggestions. The usual disclaimer applies regarding the remaining errors, if any.

4

Money Demand in the Indian Economy: A Time Varying Parameter Approach

PAMI DUA
SRIVIDYA SUBRAMANIAM

1. Introduction

The objective of this paper is to estimate and test the stability of the money demand function in India following the economic liberalisation programme of 1991.

The relationship between the demand for money balances and its determinants is a critical component in the formulation of monetary policy. The stability of the function has important policy implications because the success of monetary targeting based policy crucially hinges on a stable money demand function. A stable demand for money implies a stable money multiplier and therefore stability makes it easier to predict the effect of a given money supply on the aggregate money income.

Instability in the money demand function can be a result of various factors like financial innovation such as introduction of new instruments, the changing institutional structure of the financial sector and the increasing economic integration of the global economies. These factors can reduce the transactions costs of converting money into other financial assets and thus allow money holders to keep smaller balances. These factors may also alter the responsiveness of money demand to changes in its determinants, thus rendering the policies based on money growth targets ineffective.

India presents an important case study for analysing the implications of financial market activities on money demand. The New Economic Policy (NEP) of structural adjustments and stabilisation programme was given a big thrust in India in June 1991. These reforms have encompassed the financial sector *viz.* banks, stock markets, government securities market, external sector and institutional development. In fact, the phase of gradual and progressive deregulation of interest rates, which began in 1985, received a big push in 1991 and is still continuing. Most of the interest rates in the economy were deregulated and a beginning was made towards market rates on government securities. Auction of 91-day Treasury bill commenced from January 1993 and a new money market instrument *viz.* commercial paper was introduced in 1990. In continuation with the liberalisation measures some more policy measures were taken in 1996-97, which included reduction of CRR, rationalisation of CRR on external deposits, deregulation of interest rates on domestic term deposits, greater autonomy to banks on matters of credit appraisal and fixation of PLR etc.

Reforms have also been made in the stock market and the external sector. Since 1991, the capital market in India has been influenced by wide-ranging reforms leading to changes in the number of issues, market capitalisation and trading volumes. Another important change in the capital market, which has wide ranging effects for money demand is the easy access allowed to the international capital market through euro-equity shares. Another important change is the entry of foreign capital in the Indian stock market through foreign institutional investors and joint ventures. The liberalisation measures have boosted stock market activities as the capital raised from new issue market, average turnover, activities of mutual fund, market capitalisation, foreign institutional investment all increased considerably.

Reforms in the external sector include introduction of the flexible exchange rate system. The Indian rupee was made partially convertible in 1992-1993.

The above measures, which have penetrated the different sectors of the economy, could have influenced the determinants of money demand and hence affected its stability. In this context we test the stability of the money demand function in India.

A vast amount of literature already exists on the estimation of the money demand function in the Indian economy. These studies differ in terms of explanatory variables used (income, interest rate, stock prices, exchange rate), time period of study, econometric methodology (OLS, co-integration) and frequency of data (annual, monthly). In some studies along with the role of real income, rate of inflation, or some other measure of the opportunity cost of holding money were the major concerns in formulating the money demand function. Moosa (1992) used co-integration technique and found a stable relation between demand for narrow money and income and interest rate. Employing OLS, Mathiyazhagan and Prusty (1998) find that the demand for money is a stable function of income and other variables. Attempt to include stock prices (Paul (1992), Barari (1996), (Apte (1997)) and exchange rate in the money demand function has been quite recent (Nag and Upadhyay (1993), Das and Mandal (2000)). In addition to estimating the money demand function, stability of the function has also been tested, using either OLS or co-integration technique. Stability tests have been conducted by Das and Mandal (2000) and Nag and Upadhyay (1993), within the co-integration framework.

In this paper, we model the demand for money as a function of income, interest rate, stock prices and exchange rate. This paper differs from earlier studies, as it adopts an alternative methodology *viz.* the Time-Varying Parameters Approach to estimate and test the stability of the money demand function. This is a flexible method, which allows for the adjustment process of the parameters in response to these measures.

The paper is organised as follows. Section 2 discusses the theoretical model used in this paper for estimating the money demand function. In Section 3, we present the econometric methodology i.e. the time varying parameter approach. In Section 4 we discuss the recent trends in interest rates due to financial sector reforms of 1991. Empirical results are given in Section 5. The paper concludes with Section 6.

2. Specification of the Model

The approach to money demand analysis used in this paper is based on the shopping time model of Mc Callum (1989), which is a simple stylised general equilibrium model. This employs intertemporal optimisation choices by individual economic agents whose transactions are facilitated by their holdings of money.

In this model the medium of exchange role of money is used to acquire consumption goods. For this, the household must expend time and energy in shopping. Money is introduced into the utility function by assuming that money balances they save on shopping time and hence are leisure enhancing. So the leisure function is of the form

$$l_t = \phi\ (C_t, M_t / P_t) \qquad ...(1)$$

The function ϕ (.) defines transactions technology-saved shopping time in the model, where ϕ_1 <0-higher consumption implies more shopping time and hence less leisure time and ϕ_2 >0-higher real money balances (M_t / P_t) help reduce shopping time and thereby free up more time for leisure.

Agents maximise an intertemporal utility function defined over leisure and consumption goods, which is separable across time:

$$\sum_{i=0}^{\infty} \beta^i U(C_{t+i}, l_{t+i}) \qquad ...(2)$$

where U_1, U_2 >0 and β is a discount rate satisfying $\beta \equiv 1/(1+\rho)$ where ρ is the consumer's subjective rate of time preference. Assume that labour is supplied inelastically, so that agents allocate their time between only shopping and leisure each period. Agents receive real income, y_t each period, with this amount unaffected by the household's choices. The household does however have significant choices to make with regard to its borrowing or lending of wealth. B_t is the nominal quantity of loans made (bonds purchased by the household in t+1. The household budget constraint can be written as

$$P_t\, y + M_{t-1} + (1 + R_{t-1})\, B_{t-1} = P_t\, C_t + M_t + B_t \qquad ...(3)$$

where the LHS defines income and the RHS expenditure; P_t is the price of the consumption bundle.

The consumer's problem then is to maximise (2) subject to (1) and (3) by choice of M_t, C_t and B_t. To carry out the maximisation problem formulate a Lagrange expression L_t

$$L_t = U\,[C_t, \phi\ (C_t, M_t/P_t)] + \beta\, U\,[C_{t+1}, \phi\ (C_{t+1}, M_{t+1}/P_{t+1}) + \text{——} + \lambda_t \{(1+ R_{t-1})\, B_{t-1} - [(P_t\,(C_t - y) + (M_t - M_{t-1})] - (1 + R_t)^{-1} [P_{t+1}\,(C_{t+1} - y) + (M_{t+1} - M_t)] \text{——}]\}$$

The first order conditions are:

$$\frac{\partial L_t}{\partial C_t} = U_1\,[C_t, \phi\,(C_t, M_t/P_t)] + U_2\,[C_t, \phi\,(C_t, M_t/P_t)]\, \phi\,(C_t, M_t/P_t)] - \lambda_t P_t = 0 \qquad ....(4)$$

$$\frac{\partial L_t}{\partial M_t} = \frac{U_2[C_t, \phi(C_t, M_t/P_t)]\ \phi_2(C_t, M_t/P_t)]}{P_t} - \lambda_t + \lambda_t\{1+R_t)^{-1}\} = 0 \quad ...(5)$$

Using (4) and (5) gives us the following Euler equation,

$$U_2\ [C_t, \phi\ (C_t, M_t/P_t)]\ \phi_2\ (C_t, M_t/P_t)] = [1-(1+R_t)^{-1}]\ \{U_1\ [C_t, \phi\ (C_t, M_t/P_t)] + U_2\ [Ct, \phi\ (C_t, M_t/P_t)]\ \phi\ (C_t, M_t/P_t)] \quad ...(6)$$

Inspection of the above reveals that this necessary condition for household optimality involves only three variables C_t, M_t/P_t and R_t and assuming that it can be uniquely solved for (M_t / P_t), equation (6) can be rewritten as

$$M_t/P_t = L(C_t, R_t) \quad ...(7)$$

Thus the model yields a portfolio balance relationship between real money balances demanded, a variable measuring the volume of transactions conducted (C_t) and the nominal interest rate (Mc Callum (1987)). This can be interpreted as a money demand function. It can be shown that for reasonable specification of the utility and shopping time functions L (.,.) will be increasing in its first argument and decreasing in the second. (Mc Callum (1987)).

A logarithmic or a semi-logarithmic money demand model would be obtained depending upon the specification of the utility and transactions technology function. However, it is the semi-logarithmic money demand specification, which is often used to represent the basic money demand relation, which is more a matter of convenience (McCallum (1989)). This can be written as follows:

$$m_t = \beta_0 + \beta_1\ y_t + \beta_2\ r_t + \varepsilon_t \quad ...(8)$$

Where m_t = real money balances

y_t = real income

r_t = interest rate, lower case letters denote logs

The behavioural assumptions require that $\beta_1 > 0$ and $\beta_2 < 0$.

This standard money demand relationship does not directly include stock prices in the list of potential explanatory variables. However the above model can be extended to include stock prices as an additional explanatory variable (Friedman (1988)). This is because stock prices can influence money demand directly through two channels consisting of a positive wealth effect and a negative substitution effect.

The wealth effect of stock prices consists of the following components:

- An increase in stock prices implies an increase in nominal non-human wealth. This would lead to an increase in demand for money balances. This is one component of the so-called wealth effect.
- Increase in stock prices leads to an increase in the expected return from risky assets. Unless this is accompanied by a decrease in investor's risk aversion it would induce them to increase their holdings of safer assets such as money to restore the overall risk of their portfolios. This is the second component of the wealth effect of stock prices on money demand.
- The third component of the wealth effect is due to the increased volume of trading on the stock market, which is an accompaniment of increase in stock prices. This should result in incremental transactions demand for money balances.

The wealth effect causes a positive relationship between stock prices and money holdings.

On the other hand, an increase in the expected returns on stocks increases the opportunity costs of holding money. This induces a shift away from money. This is the 'substitution effect', which causes a negative relationship between stock prices and money holdings.

To investigate the effect of stock prices on money demand, we include deflated stock price in the list of explanatory variables to get the following closed economy money demand model (CEM)

$$(M_t/P_t) = \beta_0 + \beta_1(Y_t/P_t) + \beta_2 r_t + \beta_3 S_t + \varepsilon_t \qquad ...(9)$$

where S_t = deflated share price index

If $\beta_3 > 0$, Wealth effect dominates the Substitution effect.

$\beta_3 < 0$, Substitution effect dominates the Wealth effect.

The above model is applicable in a closed economy, where agents consider money as part of the portfolio consisting of only domestic -financial and real - assets. However in the light of the growing integration of world economies, the importance of the exchange rate as an international determinant of money demand cannot be dismissed. The exchange rate is included as an open economy or international determinant of money demand. This is to capture the substitution between domestic and foreign assets. When the exchange rate depreciates for a net debtor country the home currency value of wealth falls and this reduces the demand for money. The open economy money demand model (OEM) can be written as follows:

$$(m_t) = \beta_0 + \beta_1 (y_t) + \beta_2 r_t + \beta_3 s_t + \beta_4 e_t + \varepsilon_t \qquad ...(10)$$

where e is the exchange rate and $\beta_4 > 0$.

The above model includes the effect of both domestic and external factors in determining the demand for money.

Based on the above theoretical framework, we now estimate the open economy money demand model. The econometric methodology used for this purpose is explained in the next section.

3. Econometric Methodology

We use the time varying parameter approach to estimate and test the stability of the money demand function in India. In this approach, we first formulate the money demand equation as a Kalman filter state space model and then use a recursive algorithm to maximise the log-likelihood function. We proceed as follows.

The first step in any time series analysis is to test the stationarity of the series. If the variables are found to be non-stationary then classical regression techniques cannot be used. This is because the classical regression model requires that the dependent and independent variables in a regression be stationary in order to avoid the problem of 'spurious regression' (Granger and Newbold (1974)). However, in contrast to linear regression techniques, Kalman filters and smoothers are designed to work with non-stationary data because the filters and smoothers produce distribution of the so-called state variables that are conditional on the previous realisation of the states. For that reason, non-stationarity in itself presents no problem and ergodicity can be satisfied implying that the distributions of the coefficient have a meaningful interpretation.[1] The next step is to estimate the time varying parameters model.

1. See (Bomhoff (1991)).

3.1 Time Varying Parameters Approach

The random walk time varying parameters model is

$$y_t = x_t'\beta_t + \varepsilon_t \qquad t = 1,2,\text{———}T \qquad ...(1)$$

where ε_t ~NID $(0, \sigma^2)$ and vector β_t is generated by the process

$$\beta_t = \beta_{t-1} + \eta_t, \ \eta_t \sim (0, \sigma^2 Q) \qquad ...(2)$$

The first equation is known as the observation (or measurement) equation and the second is known as the state (or transition) equation. The state equation describes the dynamics of β_t. Since β_t is non-stationary, it is able to evolve in such a way that the model can accommodate fundamental changes in structure. The state variable is assumed to follow a random walk since we believe that shocks to the random coefficients persist indefinitely. The k*k positive semidefinite matrix Q determines the extent to which β_t can vary. If Q=0, the model collapses to a regression model like

$$y_t = x_t'\beta_t + \varepsilon_t$$

since $\beta_t = \beta_{t-1}$.

On the other hand if Q is PD all k parameters will be varying. So $\sigma^2 Q$ is a measure of variability of the parameter β_t.

Suppose we consider a particular state variable

$$\beta_{it} = \beta_{1t-1} + \eta_{it}, \ \eta_{it} \sim (0, v_i^2)$$

If we want to test $v_i=0$, this will involve non-standard statistics and thus the associated standard errors will be meaningless (Harvey, pg. 286). In addition if $v_i=0$, then the associated parameter is constant and standard t-test can be used to evaluate if the β_i is statistically different from zero. If $v_i \neq 0$, then the associated coefficient varies overtime and it is possible to evaluate its significance in each time period. A graph can report the time profile of the coefficient and the 95 per cent confidence interval.

The model is estimated by applying the Kalman filter to the sample period. The Kalman filter is a tool to estimate the state vector in an optimal way and to update the estimate when new observations become available. This requires maximising the likelihood function using an optimisation algorithm. The Kalman filter is to time series models in state space form as least squares computations are to a regression model. The covariance matrix of the observation and state equation are restricted to be diagonal.

After the model has been estimated one can derive the smoothed state series. The aim of smoothing is to take account of information made available after time t. The smoothed series is the best estimate of the state series using the full sample T as it is in terms of mean squared error. The smoothed estimator is based on more information than the filtered estimator and will have a mean square error, which in general is smaller than that of the filtered estimator.

We can now write the money demand model of Section 2 in the state space framework.

3.2 *Money Demand Model in State Space Framework*

The specification of the model follows Stracca (2000). We convert the open economy money demand model to the state-space formulation as follows:

$$m_t = \beta_{0t} + \beta_{1t} y_t - \beta_{2t}(r_t) + \beta_{3t} s_t + \beta_{4t} e_t + \varepsilon_t \quad \ldots(1)$$

$$\beta_{0t} = \beta_{0t-1} + \omega_{0t} \quad \ldots(2)$$

$$\beta_{1t} = \beta_{1t-1} + \omega_{1t} \quad \ldots(3)$$

$$\beta_{2t} = \beta_{2t-1} + \omega_{2t} \quad \ldots(4)$$

$$\beta_{3t} = \beta_{3t-1} + \omega_{3t} \quad \ldots(5)$$

$$\beta_{4t} = \beta_{4t-1} + \omega_{4t} \quad \ldots(6)$$

Equation (1) is the observation equation. It states that the level of the real money balances equals the sum of a shift parameter, the product of the income elasticity of and the income measure y_t, (-)ve of the production of interest rate elasticity and the interest rate plus the product of the stock price elasticity and stock prices, plus the product of the exchange rate elasticity and the exchange rate and an error term ε_t This observation equation is identical to an ordinary regression equation. The Kalman filter methodology adds equations (2), (3), (4), (5) and (6), the so-called state update equation. The state vector is composed of all regression coefficients. Together the transition equations and the measurement equation represent a state space model.

The reforms introduced in the monetary sector may have affected the parameters of the money demand function *viz.* income elasticity, interest rate elasticity, etc. and hence make the demand function unstable. To capture and test the effect of these measures on money demand all state variables are assumed to follow a random walk. If we model each regression coefficient as a random walk, the state variables can change, as new information becomes available (Engle and Watson (1985)).

The above set of equations can be written as follows:

$$m_t = X_t' \beta_t + \varepsilon_t$$

$$\text{where } X_t = \begin{bmatrix} 1 \\ y_t \\ r_t \\ s_t \\ e_t \end{bmatrix} \text{ and } \beta_t = \begin{bmatrix} \beta_{0t} \\ \beta_{1t} \\ \beta_{2t} \\ \beta_{3t} \\ \beta_{4t} \end{bmatrix}$$

$$\beta_t = \beta_{t-1} + \omega_t$$

β_t is driven by a multivariate random walk. We complete the model by assuming that v_t and w_t are independent white noise processes,

$$v_t \sim N(0, \sigma_v^2) \text{ and } \omega_t \sim N(0, \sigma_w^2)$$

$$\text{where } \sigma_w^2 = \begin{bmatrix} \sigma_{w0}^2 \text{--------} 0 \\ \text{-----------} \\ \text{-----------} \\ \text{-----------} \\ \text{---------} \sigma_{w4}^2 \end{bmatrix}$$

is a diagonal matrix. The initial state β_0 is assumed to be normally distributed and independent of v_t and w_t.

Assuming that a sample $\mathbf{y} = (y_1, \ldots\ldots\ldots y_T)$ is available, the log-likelihood function of the model is

$$\log l(\sigma_v^2, \Sigma_w^2, \overline{\beta_0}, \Sigma_0 \mid y) = -\frac{T}{2}\log(2\Pi) - \frac{1}{2}\sum_{t=1}^{T}\log\left|\Sigma_y(t \mid t-1)\right|$$
$$-\frac{1}{2}\sum_{t=1}^{T}(y_t - y_{t|t-1})^2 / \Sigma_y(t \mid t-1)$$

where $\Sigma_y(t \mid t-1)$ is a scalar(1*1) matrix as y is a univariate variable. The log likelihood function may be evaluated with the

Kalman filter recursions for given parameters $\sigma_v^2, \Sigma_w, \bar{\beta}_0, \Sigma_0$ the maximisation problem may be solved with an iterative algorithm. Once estimates of the parameters σ_v^2, Σ_w are available, estimates $\beta_{t/T}$ of the coefficients of the money demand function may be obtained with the smoothing recursions. Σ_w is a measure of the variability of the parameters.

4. Exploratory Analysis of the Data

Before estimating the money demand function, we undertake an exploratory analysis of the explanatory variables - interest rates, stock prices and the exchange rate - over the sample period to identify distinct phases in their movements and aberrations if any. This information is important for our analysis since it will help us in judging whether the variation (if any), in any particular parameter estimate is due to its own volatility or a result of the reform measures.

Data Sources: In this study we have used both the narrow and broad measures of money supply. Three alternative definitions of the interest rate *viz.* call money rate (CMR), Treasury bill rate (Tbill) and commercial paper rate (CPR) are used. Output is proxied by IIP. For share prices BSE Sensex has been used. The real values of the variables are calculated by deflating their nominal values by the wholesale price index. Data has been collected from various issues of the monthly bulletin of statistics, RBI, various issues of report on currency and finance and RBI handbook of statistics.

4.1 Movements in Interest Rates

The movement of the call rate shows a distinct jump around mid-1989, due to the removal of the ceiling w.e.f. May 1989. After this period the call rate has fluctuated widely and its volatility has increased over the years (Chart 4.1c). The extent of variation in the call rate overtime can also be gauged from its standard deviation which increased from 1.7 in 1980:04-1989:02 to 6.08 in 1989:04-2003:09. The measures introduced in 1996-97 led to excess liquidity, and the call money market remained remarkably easy during this period.

The Treasury Bill rate was an administered as well as the lowest rate of interest till 1993. An auction system for trading of the 91-day

Treasury Bills was introduced with effect from 1 Jan 1993, after which the Treasury Bill rate became market determined. However, the policy induced cut in CRR and inflow of capital led to a significant downward drift in the cut-off yield of 91-day Treasury Bills during 1996-97 (Chart 4.1e)

A new money market instrument, Commercial Paper was introduced in Jan. 1990. Interest rates on Commercial Paper are market determined. It increased between 1993-94 to 1995-96 (Chart 4.1d). Easy liquidity conditions due to factors mentioned earlier gave a fillip to the issue of Commercial Paper during 1996-97 and the interest rates on Commercial Paper have also moved down since April 1996. summary statistics of interest rates is given in Table A–4.9.

4.2 Movements in Stock Prices and Exchange Rates

The fluctuation in share prices are more after 1990 than in the period before it. There is a steep increase in mid-1991 after, which there are greater fluctuations. (Chart 4.1a). This may be due to the reform measures. The plot of the exchange rate shows a declining trend till 1990, a steep drop in 1991 and a slow increase thereafter (Chart 4.1b).

5. Empirical Results

On the basis of the above exploratory analysis, our estimation procedure is as follows.

- We estimate and test the stability of the money demand function in India, over different sample periods and with different sets of explanatory variables. Three alternative measures for interest rates *viz.* call money rate, treasury bill rate and commercial paper rate have been used. Data on call money rate is available for a longer time period, so we estimate the money demand equation first with call money rate over 1980:04-2003:09. We then break this period into two non-overlapping sub-samples *viz.* 1980:04-1989:02 and 1989:04-2003:09[2]. Data on the deregulated T-bill rate and commercial paper rate are available only from 1993 onwards; hence the estimation period with these begins in

2. We take 1989:04 as the cut-off point for the two sub-periods, since from this period the ceiling on Call Money Rate was removed.

1993:04. The money demand models are also estimated and tested for stability in the sub-period from 1996:09-2003:09.

- The open economy version of the money demand model (OEM) is used for our analysis. We have also estimated the closed economy version of the model (CEM) and the difference if any in results has been reported. We have used both the narrow and broad measures of money supply.

Model Estimates with Call Money Rate

We begin with the longer sample period of 1980:04-2003:09. The money demand model is estimated with broad measure of money supply (M3). The Kalman filter maximum likelihood estimates of the variances of the state variables are given in Table A–4.4.[3] Figure 4.1 shows a time plot of the point value of β as well as a band of two standard error of the residuals. We find that the state variable of the call money rate fluctuates since its variance is different from zero (Figure 4.1). The variability increases after 1990. This may be due to removal of ceiling in 1989. A steep decline is also witnessed around 1996, which can be due to the excess liquidity in the system due to monetary policy measures. Sensex emerges as an important determinant of money demand. There is presence of the wealth effect as shown by the positive coefficient. The signs of all coefficients confirm with theory. However call money rate is insignificant (Table A–4.1). We also find high correlation between stock prices and exchange rate (-0.90). If we drop exchange rates, we find that there is instability only in the state variable of the interest rate as shown by the estimates of the variance in Table A–4.4.

Estimating the model over 1980:04-1989:02, we find that the variance estimates of the state series of all variables are quite small, nearly equal to zero, implying stability in the parameter estimates. (Table A–4.2, Figure 4.2).

In the sub-sample 1989:04-2003:09 the results are different from that obtained for the first sub-sample. Both call money rate and exchange rate become insignificant (Table A–4.3). This could be due to high multicollinearity between exchange rates and interest rate. There is instability in state variable of call money (Figure 4.3). Dropping exchange rates and estimating the model again we find that

3. Estimates of the state variables with the t-statistics are given in the Appendix.

the instability in call money rate remains; stock prices too display variation as seen from the variance, although other variables are time invariant.

Therefore we find that state variable of call money rate is stable during the period 1980:04-1989:02. However, for the period 1989:04-2003:09, it displays instability. This can be attributed to the volatility of the call rate itself since it became market determined in May, 1989.

Model Estimates with Treasury Bill Rate as the Opportunity Cost Variable

We next conduct the analysis using the deregulated treasury bill rate, as the proxy for the opportunity cost variable. There is presence of wealth effect. of stock prices on money demand. The insignificance of the exchange rate may be due to high collinearity with Treasury bill rate. The treasury bill rate has the correct sign, but is insignificant (Table A–4.5). However, all state variables are found to be stable over the sample period considered (Figure 4.4). Estimating the closed economy version of the model does not change the result of stability of parameters (Table A–4.6).

We find that despite deregulation treasury bill rate did not emerge as a significant determinant of broad money in the post-1993 period. However it does become a significant determinant of money demand in the post-1996 period[4]. Neither the interest rate elasticity nor the coefficient of any other determinant displays any time variation in both periods. Hence the money demand model estimated using treasury bill rate could be said to be stable.

Model Estimates with Commercial Paper Rate

We next estimate the money demand model with commercial paper rate as the relevant opportunity cost variable. The income elasticity has the correct sign and is significant. The positive sign of the share price coefficient indicates the presence of a wealth effect (Table A–4.7). This coefficient displays stability over the time period considered (Table A–4.8). The commercial paper rate does not have the correct sign although the coefficient displays stability over the time period considered. The wrong sign of the commercial paper rate

4. This result is obtained only for the closed economy version of the model.

could be due to the high spike observed in the series from March 1996-May 1996. When the sample is taken from 1996:09-2003:09, we find that the commercial paper rate has the correct sign and is significant in determining broad money balances. Also there is no instability.[5] Thus the money demand function is stable.

The results obtained in this section regarding the stability of the state variable of the alternative interest rates can be summarised as follows.[6]

Table 4.1

State Variable of the Interest Rates – Summary Results on Stability

Interest Rate	*Model*	*1980:04-2003:09*	*1980:04-1989:02*	*1989:04-2003:09*	*1993:04-2003:09*	*1996:09-2003:09*
CMR	OEM	No	Yes	No	No	No
	CEM	No	Yes	No	No	No
Tbill	OEM	—	—	—	Yes	Yes
	CEM	—	—	—	No	Yes
CPR	OEM	—	—	—	Yes	Yes
	CEM	—	—	—	Yes	Yes

Note: No-Unstable, Yes-Stable, OEM-Open Economy Model, CEM-Closed Economy Model

The money demand models were estimated with the narrow measure of money supply over all the sample periods as above[7]. It was found that exchange significantly influence narrow money. However this function too displays stability over 1993:04-2003:09.

6. Summary and Conclusion

In this paper we estimated the money demand function for India and tested its stability in the light of the liberaralisation measures using the time varying parameters approach. We found that the demand for broad money is determined by income, interest rate and stock prices. Income and the exchange rates emerge as significant determinants of the demand for narrow money balances.

---

5. We obtain this result for the closed economy version of the model.
6. The state variables of the other explanatory variables are found to be stable across all models. Hence they have not been mentioned in the table.
7. Detailed results have not been reported due to space constraints.

We conducted the stability tests using three alternative definitions of the opportunity cost variable *viz.* call money rate, treasury bill rate and commercial paper rate over different sample periods. Using the call money rate, the results of the time varying parameters methodology show that the money demand function in India is stable. This result confirms the results that we obtained using the Hansen (1992) stability test within a co-integration framework[8]. The stability result also is in line with that obtained by Das and Mandal (2000), Subramanian and Pradhan (1997) and Nag and Upadhyay (1993) using the co-integration framework. The volatility observed in the state series of call money rate is due to its own variation and not a result of liberalisation measures. The stability tests conducted with treasury bill rate and commercial paper rate confirmed the stability result.

On the basis of the above econometric exercise we can conclude that the financial liberalisation measures of 1991 and of subsequent periods do not have any effect on the stability of the demand for money in India. This means that broad money could be a useful long run target.

8. Co-integration results have not been reported due to space constraints. For more details see Srividya, K (2003).

APPENDIX A

Chart 4.1

Graphs of Stock Prices, Exchange Rate, Call Money Rate and Treasury Bill Rate

(a) Sensex 1980:04-2003:09

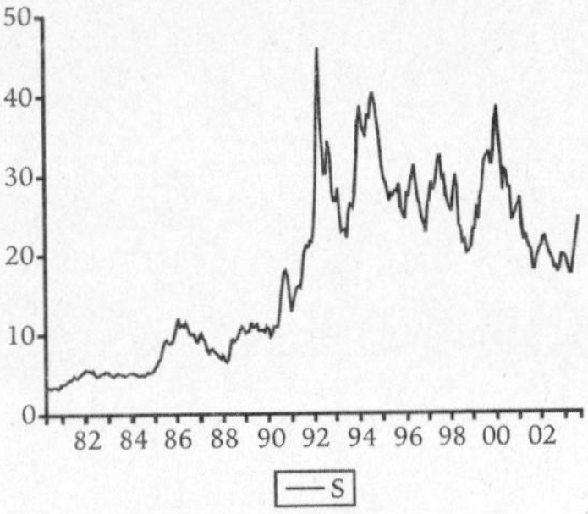

(b) REER 1980:04-2003:09

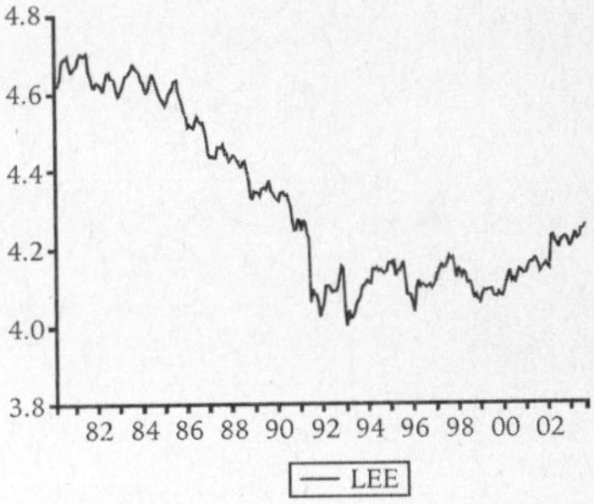

(c) CMR 1980:04-2003:09

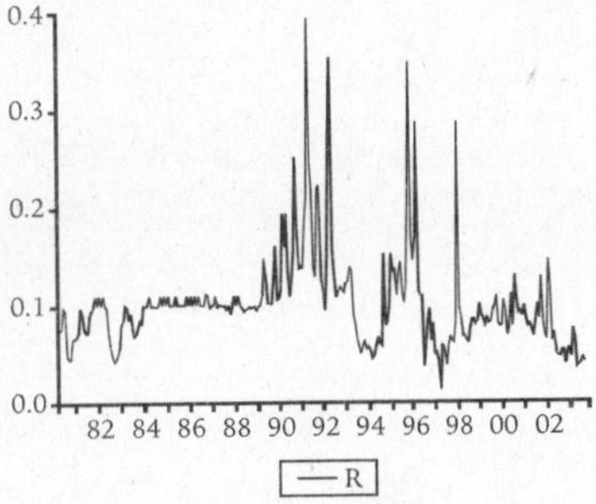

(d) CP 1993:04-2003:09

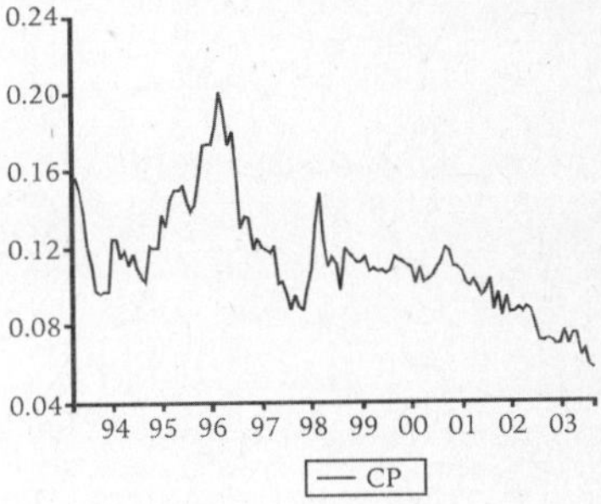

(e) TB 1993:04-2003:09

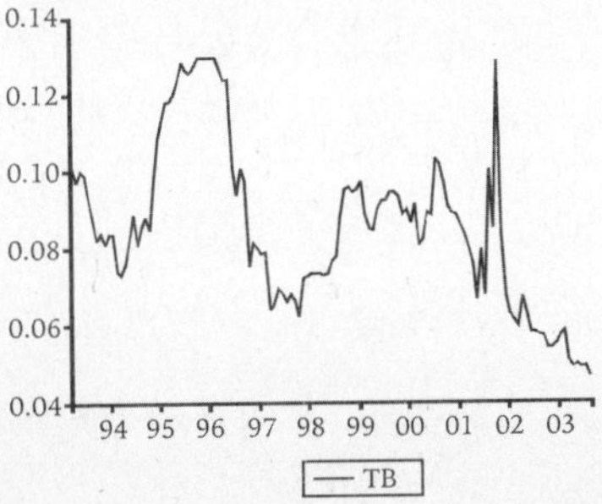

Figure 4.1

Plot of the Smoothed State Series of OEM with Call Money Rate, 1980:04-2003:09

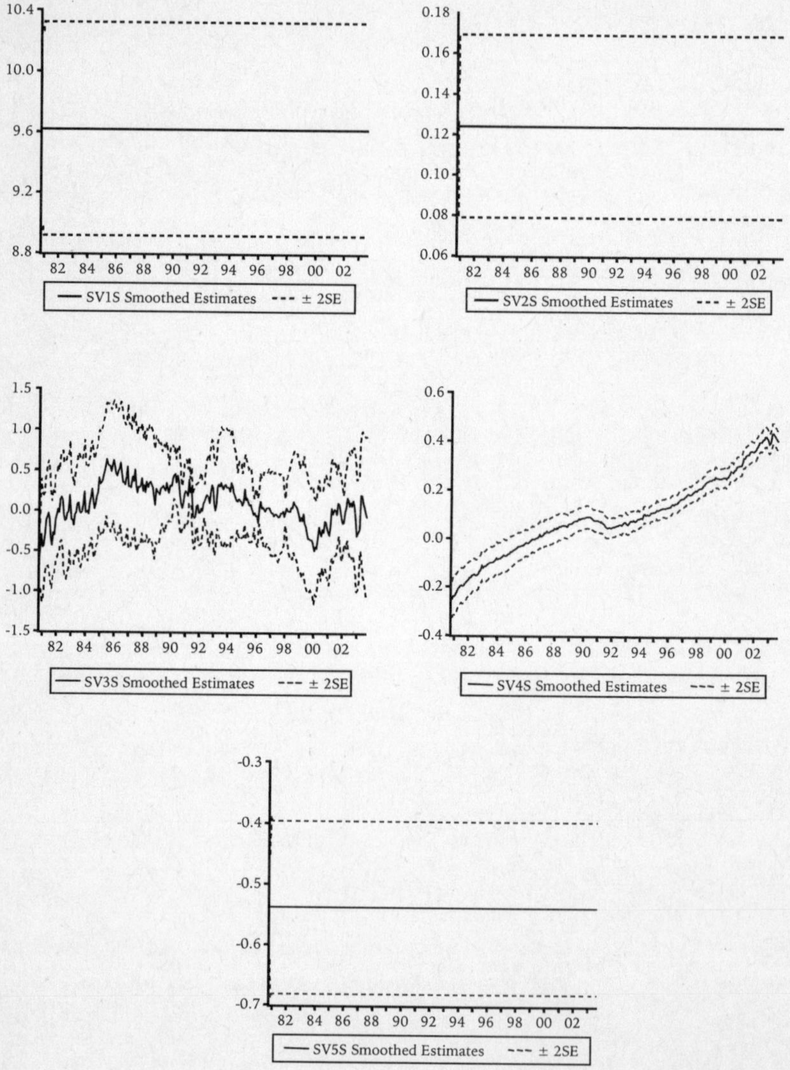

Figure 4.2

Plot of Smoothed State Series of OEM with Call Money, 1980:04-1989:2

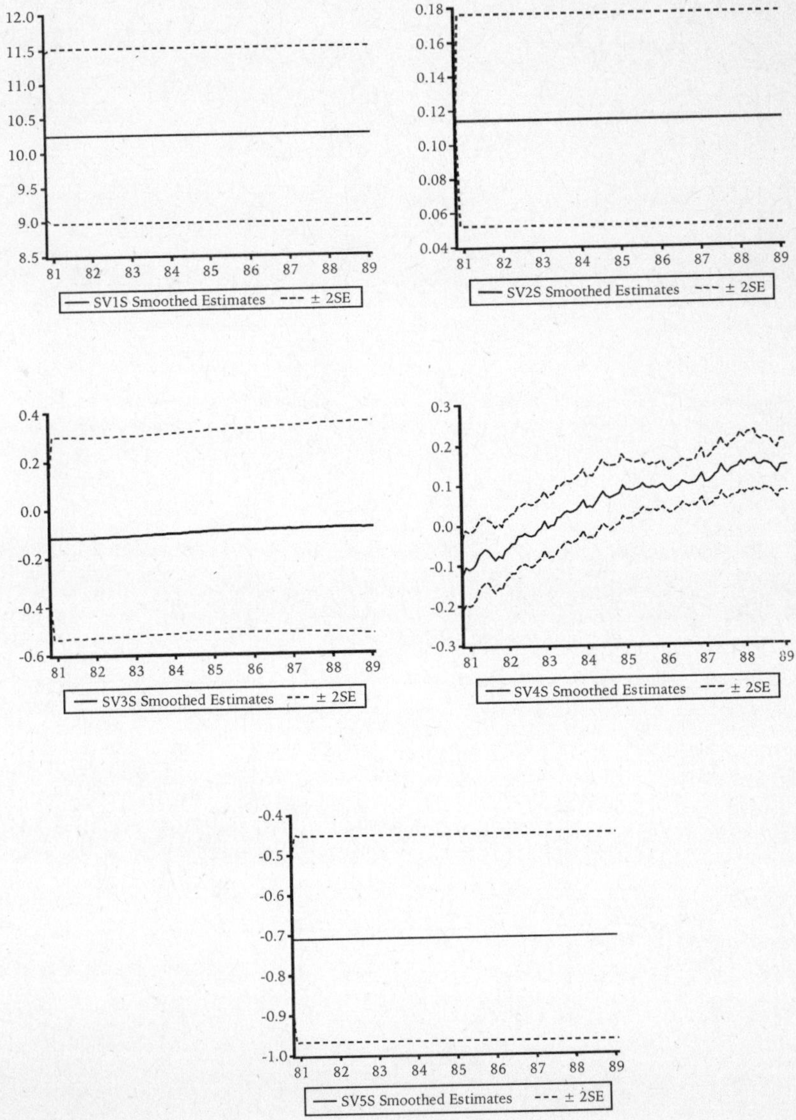

Figure 4.3

Plot of Smoothed State Series of OEM with Call Money Rate, 1989:04-2003:09

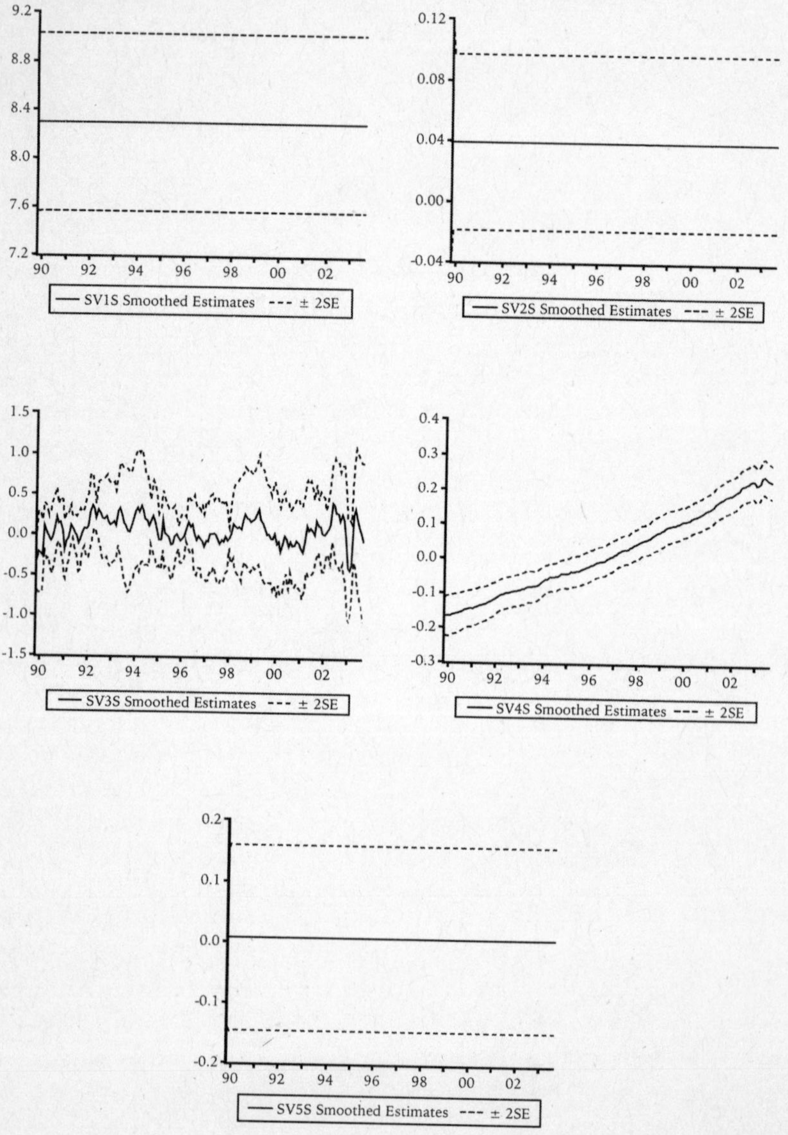

Figure 4.4

Plot of the State Series of OEM with Treasury Bill Rate, 1993:04-2003:09

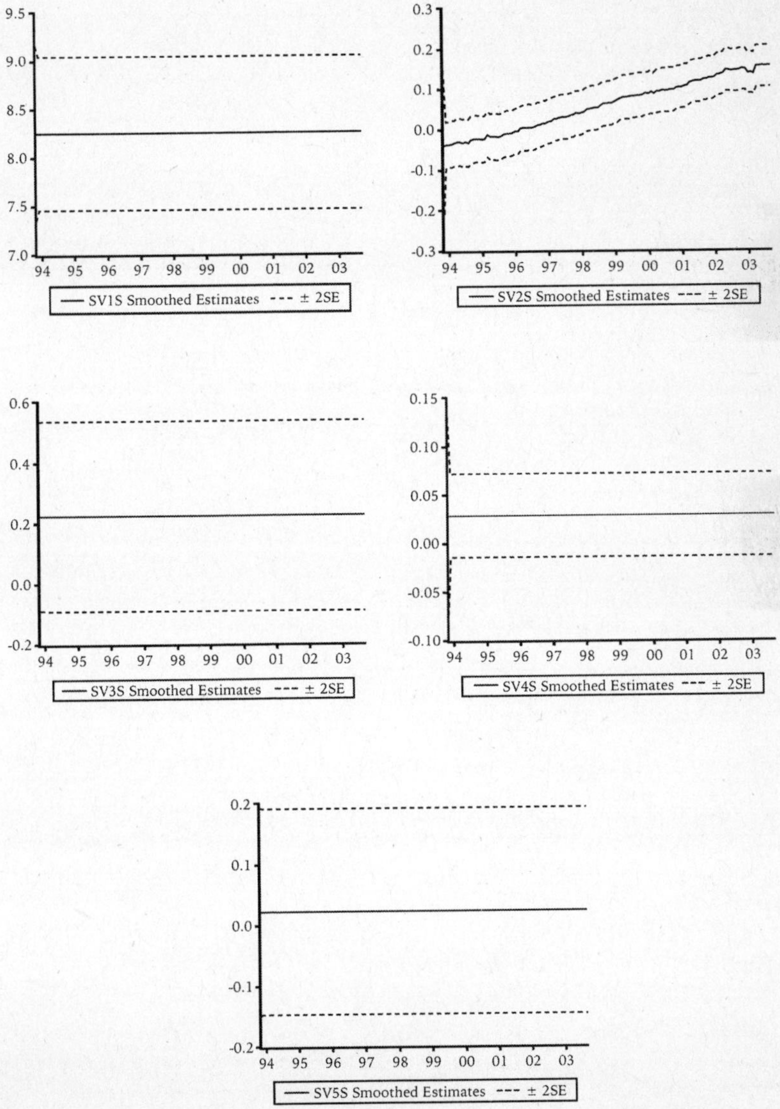

APPENDIX B

Table A–4.1

Estimates of Money Demand Model (CMR) for 1980:04-2003:09

Parameter	CEM			OEM		
	Est.	t-stat	σ^2	Est.	t-stat	σ^2
β_0	7.09	61.85	4E-13	—		
β_1	0.13	5.47	1.83E-9	0.30	8.59	1.27E-12
β_2	–0.17	–0.33	0.021	–0.50	–0.10	0.0103
β_3	0.45	20.76	6.85E-05	0.56	16.32	0.00026
β_4	—	—	—	1.35	37.64	1.39E-32

Table A–4.2

Estimates of Money Demand Model (CMR) for 1980:04-1989:02

Parameter	CEM			OEM		
	Est.	t-stat	σ^2	Est.	t-stat	σ^2
β_0	6.8	45.05	4.92E-12	10.24	16.11	1.42E-09
β_1	0.13	3.96	6.65E-10	0.114	3.68	4.03E-32
β_2	0.25	1.13	6.49E-17	-0.082	-0.37	0.000113
β_3	0.23	6.8	0.000130	0.144	4.29	9.85E-05
β_4				-0.710	-5.53	1.81E-24

Table A–4.3

Estimates of Money Demand Model (CMR) for 1989:04-2003:09

	CEM			OEM		
	Est.	t-stat	σ^2	Est.	t-stat	σ^2
β_0						
β_1	1.38	43.05	7.16E-23	0.30	8.59	1.27E-12
β_2	–0.78	–0/97	0.000261	–0.05	–0.10	0.0130
β_3	0.64	11.49	0.038418	0.56	16.32	0.00026
β_4	—	—	—	1.35	37.64	1.39E-32

Table A–4.4

Estimates of Variances of State Variables of the Money Demand Models with CMR

	1980:04-2003:09		*1980:04-1989:02*		*1989:04-2003:09*	
	OEM	*CEM*	*OEM*	*CEM*	*OEM*	*CEM*
β_0	7.53E-12	4E-13	2.42E-10	4.92E-12	1.57E-12	
β_1	1.70E-125	1.83E-9	4.03E-32	6.65E-10	3.32E-12	7.16E-23
β_2	0.025355	0.021	1.27E-06	6.49E-17	0.035975	0.038418
β_3	4.09E-05	6.85E-05	3.32E-05	0.000130	1.83E-05	0.000261
β_4	1.24E-12	—	1.81E-24		6.94E-89	

Table A–4.5

Estimates of Money Demand Model for 1993:04-2003:09 with Tbill

Parameter	*CEM*			*OEM*		
	Est.	*t-stat*	σ^2	*Est.*	*t-stat*	σ^2
β_0	8.36	54.46	1.41E-11	8.27	19.49	9.46E-11
β_1	0.153	5.78	1.71E-05	0.153	5.57	1.17E-05
β_2	-0.0284	-0.16	1.24E-64	-0.028	0.1617	3.33E-10
β_3	0.028	1.32	9.79E-11	0.029	1.30	2.90E-34
β_4				0.0193	0.214	1.52E-11

Table A–4.6

Estimates of Variances of the State Variable of Money Demand Model for Tbill

	1993:04-2003:09		*1996:09-2003:09*	
	OEM	*CEM*	*OEM*	*CEM*
β_0	9.46E-11	1.41E-11	2.14E-10	2.58E-09
β_1	1.17E-05	1.71E-05	1.52E-10	1.01E-05
β_2	3.33E-10	1.24E-64	1.30E-09	7.52E-21
β_3	2.90E-34	9.79E-11	1.52E-10	2.42E-10
β_4	1.52E-11		2.04E-11	

Table A–4.7

Estimates of Money Demand Model for 1993:04-2003:09 with CPR

Parameter	*CEM*			*OEM*		
	Est.	*t-stat*	σ^2	*Est.*	*t-stat*	σ^2
β_0	8.35	54.09	5.65E-09	8.25	20.73	3E-11
β_1	0.153	5.7	1.08E-05	0.35	5.94	1.04E-05
β_2	0.23	1.42	1.55E-05	0.22	1.42	4.27E-43
β_3	0.029	1.33	2.03E-07	0.028	1.33	1.89E-12
β_4				0.022	0.26	7.31E-15

Table A–4.8

Estimates of Variances of the State Variable of Money Demand Model for CPR

	OEM	*CEM*	*OEM*	*CEM*
b_0	3E-11	5.65E-09	1.12E-11	4.91E-11
b_1	1.04E-05	1.08E-05	1.12E-05	1.21E-15
b_2	4.27E-43	1.55E-05	2.74E-19	9.3E-11
b_3	1.89E-12	2.03E-07	9.30E-25	3.20E-05
b_4	7.31E-15		4.39E-21	

Table A–4.9

Summary Statistics of Interest Rates

Sample Period	*CMR*				*91-day TB*				*CP*			
	Mean	*Max*	*Min*	*Sd*	*Mean*	*Max*	*Min*	*Sd*	*Mean*	*Max*	*Min*	*Sd*
1980:04-2003:09	10.06	39.42 5/91	4.2 9/82	6.08								
1980:04-1989:02	9.1	11.10 10/96	4.27 9/82	1.7								
1989:04-2003:09	10.6	39.4 5/91	1.2 4/97	6.08								
1993:04-2003:09	8.6	34.8 11/95	1.2 4/97	4.7	7.7	12.96 11/95-4/96	4.6 9/03	2.14	11.25	20.15 3/96	5.6 9/03	1.8
1993:04-1996:08	10.74	34.8 11/95	3.5 7/96	6.4	10.36	12.96 11/95-4/96	7.3 4/94	1.9	13.7	20.15 3/96	9.6 93/1 0	2.8
1996:09-2003:09	7.6	28.7 1/98	1.2 4/97	3.2	8.5	12.86 11/1	4.6 9/3	1.6	10.03	14.86 3/98	5.6 9/03	2.8

References

Apte, Prakash G (1997). "Money, Stock Prices & Industrial Activity: Long Run Relationships and Causality", *Indian Economic Review*, Vol 32, No. 2, Pg 179-198.

Barari, Mahua (1996). "The effect of financial market activities on money demand: A case study of India", *Indian Economic Journal*, Vol 1, pg 47-63

Bomhoff, Eduard J. (1991). "Stability of Velocity in the Major Industrial Countries", *IMF Staff Papers*, Vol 38, No.3, September, pg.626-42

Chadha, Jagjit S., Haldane, Andrew G and Janssen, Norbert G.J. (1998). "Shoe Leather Costs Reconsidered", *The Economic Journal*, 108, pg. 363-382

Das, Samarjit and Mandal, Kumarjit (2000). "Modelling Money Demand in India: Testing Weak, Strong and Super Exogeneity", *Indian Economic Review*, Vol 35, No. 1, pg. 1-19

Friedman, Milton (1988). "Money and the Stock Market", *Journal of Political Economy*, Vol 96, No. 2, pg. 221-243

Hall, Stephen G (1993). "Modeling Structural Change Using the Kalman Filter", *Economics of Planning*, 26, 1,pg. 1-13

Harvey, Andrew (1989). *Forecasting, Structural Time Series Models and the Kalman Filter*, Chapter 4, Cambridge University Press

Joshi, Himanshu and Saggar, Mridul (1995). "The Demand for Money in India: Stability Revisited", *RBI Occasional Papers*, Vol 16, No. 2, pg. 79-97

McCallum Bennett T and Goodfriend Marvin S (1987). "Money: Theoretical Analysis of the Demand for Money", *NBER Working Paper*, No. 2157, February.

Moosa, Imad A. (1992). "The Demand for Money in India: A Cointegration Approach", *Indian Economic Journal*, Vol 41, No 1, pg. 101-115

Mathiyazhagan, K. and Prusty, Sadananda (1998). "Demand for Money Under Economic Reforms in India: A Further Empirical Evidence", *Artha Vijnana*, Vol XL, No.3, pg. 292-309

Nag and Upadhyay (1993). "Estimating Money Demand Function: A Cointegration Approach", *RBI Occasional Papers*, Vol 14, No.1, March, pg. 47-65

Pradhan, Basanta K and Subramanian A (1997). "On the Stability of the Demand for Money in India", *Indian Economic Journal*, July-Sep, Vol.45, 1, pg.106-117

Paul, Thomas M. (1992b). "Demand for Money, Inflationary Expectation and Stock Market", *Indian Economic Journal*, 40, pg. 36-62

Nag and Upadhyay (1993). "Estimating Money Demand Function: A Cointegration Approach", *RBI Occasional Papers*, Vol 14, No.1, March, pg. 47-65

Pradhan, Basanta K. and Subramanian A. (1997). "On the Stability of the Demand for Money in India", *Indian Economic Journal*, July-Sep, Vol.45, 1, pg.106-117

Srividya, K. (2003). *Modelling the Demand for Money in India*, M.Phil Thesis, Department of Economics, Delhi School of Economics, University of Delhi.

Stracca Livio (2001). "The Functional Form of The Demand For Euro Area M1", *European Central Bank Working Paper*, No.51, March

5

Search for Stable Money Demand Function for India: A Co-integration Approach

A.K. GIRI
B. KAMAIAH

1. Introduction

A stable demand function for money has long been perceived as a pre-requisite for the use of monetary aggregates in the conduct of monetary policy. Proper management of monetary policy and its effectiveness to influence the real economy call for a stable relationship between money demand and its determinants such as real GNP, prices and interest rate. A necessary condition for stable money multiplier is a stable money demand function. An unstable demand for money would make impossible or difficult to predict the effect on interest rate and hence, on aggregate expenditure of a given change in the money supply. Hence, the efficacy of targeting money supply essentially rests on the stability of money demand function.

One of the major concern of the monetary authorities is to have a fairly accurate idea about the monetary transmission mechanism to have a predictable influence of monetary targeting. The classicals and monetarists maintain that there exist a stable and predictable link between money and the ultimate goal variables - income and price level. This assertion has major implications. First, changes in money supply would produce predictable changes in real income and price level. Second, the monetary authority can bring about changes in prices and income by controlling money supply. Therefore, monetarists consider monetary aggragates (bank reserves, monetary base, money supply etc.) as the most important target of monetary policy. By controlling monetary aggregates, the central bank can achieve its policy objectives, namely, price stability economic growth and full employment. Friedmen and Schwartz (1963) has asserted that, "applicable changes in the rates of growth of money stock is a necessary and sufficient condition for applicable changes in the rates of growth of money income". The theoritical and policy conclusions stated above are based on a stable money demand function.

The transmission mechanisms of how money affects the economy is neither static nor uniform across countries and over the years. Since mid-1970s, sweeping changes have been taking place in the financial systems all over the world. It is but natural for the transmission mechanism to undergo changes possibly making the earlier channels less effective compared to the new ones. Moreover, the stability property of demand for money has been seriously questioned after the missing money episode of 1973.

There is a conceptual problem also with respect to measurement of liquidity after the changes have ocurred in the financial system. Firms and households have diversified their potfolios and hold a variety of assets to optimise their return. It has become increasingly difficult as to which assets should be included in the measure of liquidity. In the whole spectrum of financial assets, instruments with investment characteristics are genarally excluded from the measure of liquidity although they can be converted into liquid assets without much difficulty. The conversion cost, in fact, declined dramatically over time. It is this chracteristic of assets which generates instability in the system in a number of ways. One such instability discussed in the literature relates to the demand function. One is therefore, naturally encouraged to explore to what extent the financial innovations and deregulatory changes have been responsible for money demand instability. Such an attempt is made in the present paper by considering the Indian case.

It has been recognised that money demand models based on Goldfeld (1976) or one of its variants, suffer from spurious inference, since the least square techniques have been applied on relationships involving non-stationary variables. There is therefore, a need to re-estimate the money demand relation in India by employing co-integration techniques. Further, the long run equilibrium relationship that assumed to exist between real money balances and a given set of variables will be examined in the present paper.

Thus, the present paper focuses on the issue of stability of demand for money and the long run relationship underlying the money demand function, so that the transmission mechanism can be better understood in the light of phenomenal changes in the Indian financial sector. Accordingly, the remaining part of this paper is organised as follows: Section 2 gives an account of previous research on the topic. Section 3 carries out relevant discussion on regarding the methodology and estimation techniques and the empirical evidences are documented in Section 4. Finally, Section 5 presents the conclusions.

2.1 Survey of Empirical Studies on Stability of Money Demand Function

Evidence on demand for money at least prior to mid-1970s, suggested a stable relationship between money, output and prices in a large number of countries. Laidler (1977) asserted that the large body of research carried out over the post-War period showed a stable demand for money function. The situation thereafter has changed. Studies (Artis and Lewis, 1976; Goldfeld, 1976; Hacche, 1974) undertaken thereafter questioned the stability of demand for money relation.

Most of the studies undertaken during 1960s and early-1970s (for instance Meltzer (1963), Brunner and Meltzer (1963), Laidler (1966) and Goldfeld (1973) for the US and Laidler and Parkin (1970) for the UK) have found stable and well determined money demand functions. The precise form of equation and the type and period of data used varied across the studies; static long run equations were common for annual data, while studies using quarterly data generally estimated short-run equations which allowed for adjustment and expectational lags. The results, for the US in particular, were broadly invariant to the precise data period involved and the particular definition of money, interest rate and scale variables used. Consequently, nobody seriously questioned that the demand for money was stable. At this juncture, it is pertinent to quote Laidler (1971) who claimed that, "the evidence for Britain certainly points to the existence of a stable demand for money function in that economy. For the United States the evidence is overwhelming, and for Britain it is at the very least highly suggestive".

In contrast, studies undertaken since the mid-1970s, using quarterly data for both the UK and US, have often had difficulty in modelling the money market and have consequently questioned the existence of a stable demand for money relation. Indeed, this problem was not solely confined to the UK and US. The period since the mid-1970s has been marked by unusual economic conditions such as supply shocks, high and variable inflation, recession etc., in many countries. The period also coincided with substantial institutional changes brought by financial innovation and deregulation. As a result, what has been really thought of as "money" ceased to remain the same. The role of demand deposits as a close substitute to cash holding through prohibition of interest payment has since changed. Commercial banks in fact have been offering compensation to demand deposits by way of repurchases of securities at higher prices, cash management services at rates tied to market interest rate etc.. The concentration account, zero balance account allow firms to manage their deposit balances more carefully (Simpson and Porter, 1980). Among the regulatory changes, authorisation to commercial banks to open interest bearing checkable deposits and growth of negotiable order of withdrawals (NOW) in the US have blurred the distinction between interest bearing and non-interest bearing deposits. Non-inclusion of these innovations might have contributed to instability of the money demand functions.

Thus, with the deepening and widening of the financial systems across the countries tended to provide a very severe test to the stability of demand for money relationships. During this period, a number of shortcoming in the conventional money demand functions have been exposed. Repeated break down of the existing models in the face of newly emerged data has compelled the researchers to improve the demand for money function, in terms of more sophisticated examination of dynamics, functional forms and expectations.

Empirical studies of money demand function generally adopted a partial adjustment model which typically treats the real money demand as a dependent variable, with real GNP and interest rate as well as lagged dependent variable, as an explanatory variable. The representative of these studies is the study by Goldfeld (1973). At least prior to the mid-1970s, the relationship suggested a stable relationship underlying the money demand function. In the mid-1970s, however, this model began to lose its adequacy in explaining developments in money demand as major divergence emerged between the forecasted and the actual values (Goldfeld, 1976). This phenomenon persisted despite effort to rectify the situation such as adding new explanatory variables to the conventional functions. This situation led many monetarists to suggest that financial innovation and deregulation resulted in the shift in money demand function (the "missing money" phenomenon).

The episode of missing money phenomenon led to two strands of research on money demand studies. First, a number of researchers have modified the existing specifications to capture the effects of innovation and financial deregulation since 1970s. Research on this line had been carried out by including extra variables such as interst rate rachets (Goldfeld, 1976), yield on certificate of deposits (Hacche, 1974), Bank debits (Goldfeld, 1976, Hamburger, 1977), time trend (Liberman, 1977), Brokerage fees proxies (Porter and Offenbacher, 1982) in the money demand functions. Second, the experience during the mid-1970s led others to re-evaluate the conventional money demand specifications. Artis and Lewis (1976), Carr and Darby (1981) presented empirical models emphasising the problem of endogeneity of money supply. And the research on this line led to modelling "buffer stock" approach to demand for money. In addition, Gordon (1984), Granger and Newbold (1974) and Laidler (1980), raised some important isues concerning the econometric properties of estimated money demand equations. Granger and Newbold asserted that non-stationarity in the log-level or log-difference of the economic variables produced spurious regression results, throwing most of the research result into serious doubt and prompting the researchers to revisit the money demand function. The concept of co-integration, proposed by Engle-Granger (1987) is an attempt to salvage the regression techniques from the problem of non-stationarity. Since then, co-integration and error correction framework has become a standard tool to determine long run equilibrium relationship underlying money demand function. Since then studies (Dickey, *et al.* (1991), Hall *et al.* (1990), Miller (1990;1991), Hendry, (1995), Hendry *et al.* (1992)), have investigated the presence of long run equlilibrum and stability of money demand function using this technique.

Searching for the stability property of money demand relation has undergone an evolution since the "missing money" episode. The researchers across countries have revisited the money demand function to incorporate the instruments of innovation and deregulation to arrive at a stable money demand relation for the purpose of effective monetary targeting. The financial innovation and deregulation is not limited to a particular country. Economies have experienced this changes over different period of time. In India too, the above changes have taken place in the recent past, which brought about a new element in the money and securities markets. In the light of this, money demand would have to be studied afresh with an eye on the possible shift in the function. Further, the framework for empirical testing has also undergone a radical change, as most of the recent studies in the literature have used co-integration framework to test the stability property of money demand. Hence, it is essential to use the co-integration framework in the present conext to test the stability propety of the function.

2.2 Empirical Evidence on Stability of Demand for Money in India

A vast amount of literature exists on the stability of demand for money function in India. Controversy regarding the estimation of the money demand function centred around the appropriate measure of money (i.e., M1 or M2 or M3), the choice of appropriate scale and opportunity cost variables, for monetary targeting. Much of the existing research has been done to ascertain the stability property of money demand function since 1970s.

In India, there have been several attempts over the years to estimate the stability of money demand function considering either narrow or broad definition of money. The search for stability centres around the choice of appropriate measure of money and the suitable determinants of the money demand function. Most of the studies support the hypothesis of stable demand function for money with a few exception (Bhoi, 1992, Gupta, 1979, Ram and Biswas, 1983). The studies that found the evidence of instability have suggested that structural breaks or instability of the money demand has occured due to (i) inappropriate methdology used and (ii) misspecification (inadequate to capture the changes in financial innovation and deregulation). Dissatisfied with the conventional methods, the studies during 1990s, started using Engle-Granger (Moosa, 1991,

Bhattacharya, 1995) and Johansen-Juselius (Joshi and Sagar, 1995, Nag and Upadhyay, 1993) methods and confirmed that long run equilibrium relation existed either for both the aggregates (Joshi and Sagar, 1995, Nag and Upadhyaya 1993) or that narrow money aggregate was more stable compared to that of broad definition of money (Bhattacharya, 1995 and Moosa, 1991).

Though there have been regular attempts to resolve various issues associated with the money demand relation, still the issue of stability of money demand function is far from settled in the Indian case. The issue needs further empirical attention in an environment of phenomenal change of financial innovation, deregulation and institutional changes during recent past. Further, the framework for empirical testing for stability of money demand function has undergone radical changes. Hence, it is essential to use co-integration approach to test the money demand function in the present context of the phenomenal changes. Specifically, the focus of the present chapter is to find out an appropriate monetary aggregate for effective monetary targeting for India.

3. Methodology: An Overview

3.1 Testing Unit Root and Co-integration

Before estimating the co-integartion models, it is essential to examine the time series properties of the variables in level or in first differences. If the equation is estimated with data that are non-stationary, the application of OLS method would not yield a consistent parameter estimator. That is, the t-statistics of the estimated coefficients are unreliable since the underlying time series would have theoretically infinite variance (Hendry, 1986, Granger, 1986). Moreover, in estimating the co-integration, it is necessary that the variables should be non-stationary. Hence, the following, Dickey-Fuller (DF), Augmanted Dickey-Fuller (ADF), Phillips-Perron (PP) and KPSS unit root tests are performed to know whether the process governing the concerned variables is stationary or not.

3.1.1 Dickey-Fuller (DF) and Augmented Dickey-Fuller (ADF)

It is necessary to start with a unit root test to check whether a given series say Xt is stationary or not. The Dickey-Fuller and

Augmented Dickey-Fuller unit root tests are popular in the literature. The tests require estimation of the follwing equation:

$$\Delta X_t = \mu + \alpha X_{t-1} + \sum_{i=1}^{k} \gamma_i \, \Delta X_{t-1} + \varepsilon_t \qquad ...(1)$$

where k is the value which ensure ε_t be a white noise series, Δ is the difference operator, α and γi are parameters. The above procedure is known as the ADF test. The DF test follows a special case of ADF test when summation part of the equation (1) is zero, that is when k = 0. The test statistics of DF and ADF are tested under the null hypothesis of non-stationarity against the alternative of stationarity.

3.1.2 Phillips-Perron

Phillips and Perron (1988) have suggested an alternative unit root test. The advantage of this test is that it is neutral to the selection of lag-length in the ADF equation. Further, the error term over there could be serially correlated and heteroscedastic. This test also tested with the null hypothesis of non-stationarity and alternative of stationarity for which the procedure requires that the test statistics are to be negative and statistically significant in comparision to the tabulated value.

3.1.3 KPSS Unit Root Test

An alternative explanation for the common failure to reject a unit root is simply that the standard unit root due to Kwiatkowski, D, Phillips, P C B, Schmidt, P and Shin, Y (1992) tests are not very powerful against the relavant alternatives. Hence it has been suggested (Dejong and Whiteman (1991), Diebold and Rudebusch (1991)) that it would be useful to perform test of null hypothesis of stationary as well as of unit root. KPSS unit root test provides a test of null hypothesis of stationarity against an alternative of unit root, to test whether the series is diferenced stationary.

3.2 Co-integration

Co-integration theory was developed by Granger and his associates to examine whether long run equilibrium exist between the variables (Granger, 1986, Engle and Granger, 1987).

Consider initially a pair of series X_t and Y_t, each of which is said to be integrated of order one, denoted by I(1) and having no drift or trend in mean. It is generally true that any linear combination of these variables will also be integrated of order one. However, it is possible that there exist a linear combination say Z_t, such that it is I(0) or stationary, it is said that X_t and Y_t are co-integrated.

However, when X_t is the vector of N components time series, each without trend in mean and each I(d), d>0. Then X_t will be said to be co-integrated CI (d,b) if there exist a vector such that $Zt = \alpha' X_t$ is I (d-b), b>0.

The case considered earlier has N = 2 and d = b = 1. Moving to a general values for N, d, b, adds a large number of possible inter-relationships and models. In particular, α will not be unique, as there will be several equilibrium relationship linking N>2 variables. If there are r vectors α, each of which produces Z's integrated of order less than d, then r is called the "order of integration" and is easily seen that r<N-1.

3.2.1 Tests of Co-integration

(i) Engle Granger Two Step Procedure

Suppose that by using the unit root tests described above, we have detected that variables are non-stationary at levels or having random walk, but at first differences they are stationary. It is then quite easy to test whether the combination of the variables are co-integrated. To ascertain this, Engle Granger (1987) propose a two step pocedure, where the first step is running the OLS regression of the combination of variables and extracting the residuals from the regression. And the second step is testing or ascertaining the statianarity of these residuals. To test the stationarity of the residuals, the usual unit root tests are followed.

(ii) Johansen-Juselius (JJ) Pocedure

Tests of co-integration such as Engle Granger two step procedure allows for the estimation and testing of unique co-integrating vector, even though there could be as many as the number of variables involved less one. As well since this single equation method estimates the co-integrating vector with the data on the levels only, it has been criticised for ignoring potentially valuable information contained in

Table 5.1(a)

Description of Variables
(Monthly Data : 1981:04 to 2003:03)

Variables	*Definitions*
ASRM1	Real Narrow Money
ASRM3	Real Broad Money
ASIP	Index of Industrial Production
ASCALL	Call Money Rate at Bombay, average of week.
ASREER	Real Effective Exchange Rate
ASBSE	BSE Index
ASRBI	RBI Share Index

Note: All the variables are seasonally adjusted using an additive deseasonalisation procedure.

Table 5.1(b)

Money Demand Specifications

Sl. No.	*Dependent Variable*	*Independent Variables*
1	LASRM1	LASIP, LASCALL, LASREER
2	LASRM1	LASIP, LASCALL, LASREER, LASRBI
3	LASRM1	LASIP, LASCALL, LASREER, LASBSE
4	LASRM1	LASIP, LASCALL, LASRBI
5	LASRM1	LASIP, LASCALL, LASBSE
6	LASRM3	LASIP, LASCALL, LASREER
7	LASRM3	LASIP, LASCALL, LASREER, LASRBI
8	LASRM3	LASIP, LASCALL, LASREER, LASBSE
9	LASRM3	LASIP, LASCALL, LASRBI
10	LASRM3	LASIP, LASCALL, LASBSE

the short run fluctuation of the variables. Moreover, the Engle-Granger test procedure relies on the OLS residuals for the estimation of the test statistics. Johansen (1988) outlined a method which was later expanded by Johansen and Juselius (1990), which allowed for the testing of more than one co-integrating vector in the data and for the calcualtion of maximum likelihood of these vectors. This procedure yields two test statistics of the number of statistically significant co-integrating vectors. One is - λmax, which compares the null hypothesis $H_0(r)$ with an alternative $H_1(r+1)$ where r is the co-integrating vector. The second test is the trace test which examines the same null of $H_0(r)$ *versus* a general alternative, $H_1(p)$ where p is the number of variables. In this framework, it is desirable to obtain atleast one co-integrating vector, r = 1 to establish the model. If one gets r = 2, then one could in principle assume that the system is stable in more than one dimension.

4. Empirical Results

4.1 Unit Root Evidence

The unit root tests are employed to test the presence of stochastic trend of deseasonalised monthly macroeconomic variables that are used in formulating the alternative money demand specifications over the total sample from 1981:04 to 2003:03 and two sub-samples: 1985:04 to 1991:06 and 1991:07 to 2003:03. The variables considered are m1, m3, call money rate, index of industrial production, RBI and BSE share index and real effective exchange rate. The data are monthly deseasonalised and in logs. For the test of unit root, the present study used Dickey-Fuller (DF), Augmented Dickey Fuller (ADF), Phillips-Perron (PP and KPSS unit root tests both with trend and without trend for three sample periods. The results are presented in Tables from 5.2 to 5.7.

Table 5.2 presents the unit root tests statistics for DF, ADF and PP tests for the sample period 1981:04 to 2003:03. Looking at the results in the upper tier of the Table 5.2 for DF test without trend, the hypothesis of unit root in the level data is not rejected at the 1 per cent critical level across all the series, save one (LASCALL - call money rate). But DF test with trend indicates that some variables (call money rate, m1) are trend stationary. Here, in the present study the order of ADF test (value of lag-length, (k)) is selected by following FPE criterion. The test results confirm that for all (save LASCAL) the series both with and without trend, the statistics are not statistically significant to reject the null hypothesis of non-stationarity. The test statistics for tests shows that all the series are non-stationary at levels barring call money rate and REER. Further, the same test confirm that call money rate, m1, m3, REER, index of industrial production and BSE share index are trend stationary.

Table 5.2

Unit Root Test for Deseasonalised Monthly Series: 1981:04 to 2003:03

	Without Trend			With Trend		
	DF	ADF	PP	DF	ADF	PP
LASBSE	–1.5740	–0.0226(2)	–2.0992	–1.0670	–1.3293(2)	–3.8974
LASRBI	–1.4499	–0.4097(8)	–1.7788	–1.2704	–1.4953(8)	–3.6154
LASIP	–0.7127	–1.5103(13)	–0.9168	–1.7303	–3.8856(13)	–6.4471
LASREER	–1.8601	–0.4977(4)	–3.6733	–0.9119	–1.1254(4)	–4.7041
LASRMI	–0.5711	0.7896(13)	–0.1526	–3.2934	–3.0789(13)	–4.0017
LASRM3	–0.1009	–0.4206(13)	–0.1183	–1.6414	–1.8858(13)	–8.0175
LASCALL	–2.8751	–3.0456(6)	–3.9471	–3.0016	–3.1288(6)	–4.3151
ΔLASBSE	–10.2152	–10.2633(2)	–14.6528	–10.3171	–10.4054(2)	–14.6579
ΔLASRBI	–5.1479	–5.2365(7)	–10.6601	–5.3204	–5.3959(6)	–10.6883
ΔLASIP	–5.1951	–5.2245(13)	–22.3843	–5.2335	–5,2469(13)	–22.4163
ΔLASREER	–9.0552	–9.1440(3)	–12.5755	–9.2276	–9.3267(3)	–12.5738
ΔLASRMI	–3.9489	–4.0775(13)	–16.7459	–3.9634	–4.0892(13)	–6.7454
ΔLASRM3	–3.2293	–3.7559(13)	–32.1708	–4.8422	–13.948(13)	–32.3684
ΔLASCALL	–9.1787	–9.2581(05)	–15.2956	–8.5157	–12.6023(5)	–15.2864

Table 5.3

Unit Root Tests for Deseasonalised Monthly Series: 1985:04 to 1991:06

	Without Trend			With Trend		
	DF	ADF	PP	DF	ADF	PP
LASBSE	–1.3631	–0.3288(10)	–1.1446	–4.2276	–2.7630(10)	–3.8777
LASRBI	–0.7177	–0.4251(02)	–0.5887	–2.8319	–2.4648(02)	–2.6135
LASIP	–0.9218	–0.1848(10)	–0.4751	–6.3719	–1.5945(10)	–6.4471
LASREER	–0.7310	–0.8081(01)	–0.7549	2.8839	–3.0286(01)	–3.1456
LASRMI	–0.6361	–0.5535(02)	–0.6048	–3.7038	–3.1475(01)	–3.8471
LASRM3	–1.4031	–1.6757(07)	–1.2088	–8.3383	–1.6967(07)	–8.7419
LASCALL	–4.3322	–2.1469(04)	–3.9471	–4.6219	–2.3192(04)	–4.3151
ΔLASBSE	–13.6057	–9.2609(03)	–15.2860	–13.2616	–13.2616(03)	–14.6579
ΔLASRBI	–10.7727	–5.6442(04)	–10.8154	–10.6995	–5.6157(04)	–10.6883
ΔLASIP	–19.9790	–9.4716(01)	–22.3686	–19.9268	–12.4430(01)	–22.4163
ΔLASREER	–12.5584	–8.1468(01)	–12.6273	–12.4689	–8.1187(01)	–12.5738
ΔLASRMI	–16.0609	–8.9324(01)	–16.6808	–15.9792	–11.9009(01)	–16.7454
ΔLASRM3	–22.7879	–9.9774(03)	–32.4901	–22.5009	–11.0141(03)	–32.3684
ΔLASCALL	–14.0511	–9.3474(01)	–15.2624	–13.9370	–11.3039(01)	–15.2864

Table 5.4

Unit Root Tests for Deseasonalised Monthly Series: 1991:07 to 2003:03

	Without Trend			With Trend		
	DF	*ADF*	*PP*	*DF*	*ADF*	*PP*
LASBSE	–2.9862	–2.5139(02)	–1.1446	–3.2843	–2.0304(02)	–20.4934
LASRBI	–2.9848	–2.6565(03)	–2.5887	–2.9250	–2.8452(03)	–20.4328
LASIP	–0.1865	–1.2693(10)	–1.9693	–1.9774	–3.2339(10)	–6.4471
LASREER	–1.5611	–1.2626(04)	–0.7549	–2.5742	–2.8039(04)	–19.4916
LASRMI	–0.8282	–1.3415(02)	–0.4962	–2.1754	–3.7836(02)	–3.8471
LASRM3	–0.7903	–0.4866(08)	–0.1070	–2.1851	–2.0646(08)	–8.6584
LASCALL	–2.6904	–2.1765(04)	–3.9471	–3.0544	–2.8988(04)	–5.0917
ΔLASBSE	–7.7204	–7.7142(02)	–144.043	–7.8513	–7.9308(02)	–144.612
ΔLASRBI	–6.9286	–6.8357(02)	–105.999	–6.9761	–6.9757(02)	–106.531
ΔLASIP	–9.5671	–9.3958(10)	–174.663	–9.5307	–9.3534(10)	–174.257
ΔLASREER	–7.0341	–7.1495(03)	–103.239	–7.0209	–7.1592(03)	–102.686
ΔLASRMI	–5.7079	–5.6689(10)	–54.2360	–5.7093	–5.6213(10)	–53.9398
ΔLASRM3	–5.2075	–5.2801(01)	–91.6028	–5.6078	–5.5307(01)	–90.875
ΔLASCALL	–8.2615	–8.3674(03)	–154.577	–8.2431	–8.3751(03)	–154.111

Note: In Table 5.2 – 5.4, DF: Dickey-Fuller, ADF: Augmented Dickey-Fuller, PP: Philips-Perron. The values inside parentheses corresponding to ADF statistics (column 3 and 6) indicate appropriate lag length is the difference operator.

Table 5.5

KPSS Unit Root Test Statistics for Deseasonalised Series: 1981:04 to 2003:03

	With Trend				Without Trend			
	K=1	*K=2*	*K=3*	*K=4*	*K=1*	*K=2*	*K=3*	*K=4*
LASBSE	0.2456	0.2045	0.2005	0.1982	1.3840	0.9743	0.8214	0.7124
LASRBI	0.1543	0.1340	0.1243	0.1198	1.3404	0.9282	0.7445	0.6201
LASIP	0.4242	0.4043	0.3898	0.3092	2.3035	1.6125	1.2598	1.0698
LASREER	0.1841	0.0821	0.0710	0.0612	0.5474	0.5123	0.5014	0.4921
LASRMI	0.4521	0.4212	0.4121	0.4012	2.1432	1.9843	1.8124	1.7124
LASRM3	0.1743	0.0714	0.0453	0.0400	2.5121	1.9812	1.5298	1.4293
LASCALL	0.4053	0.3913	0.3012	0.2912	0.9424	0.9045	0.8243	0.7143
ΔLASBSE	0.0612	0.0601	0.0578	0.0514	0.1617	0.1423	0.1434	0.1512
ΔLASRBI	0.0843	0.0742	0.0612	0.0543	0.2134	0.2042	0.1843	0.1841
ΔLASIP	0.0243	0.0212	0.0159	0.0141	0.0786	0.0843	0.0914	0.1189
ΔLASREER	0.0461	0.0379	0.0281	0.0198	0.0943	0.0912	0.0878	0.0743
ΔLASRMI	0.0472	0.0418	0.0398	0.0312	0.0743	0.0842	0.0881	0.0892
ΔLASRM3	0.0201	0.0215	0.0324	0.0414	0.0214	0.0242	0.0342	0.0412
ΔLASCALL	0.0395	0.0381	0.0441	0.0651	0.1469	0.1743	0.2120	0.2681

Table 5.6

KPSS Unit Root Test Statistics for Deseasonalised Series: 1985:04 to 1991:06

	With Trend				Without Trend			
	K=1	K=2	K=3	K=4	K=1	K=2	K=3	K=4
LASBSE	0.1788	0.1406	0.1242	0.1122	5.4284	3.7338	2.8765	2.3471
LASRBI	0.4043	0.2957	0.2424	0.2075	5.4196	3.6869	2.8138	2.2823
LASIP	0.2016	0.1637	0.1454	0.1355	6.1247	4.1297	3.1261	2.5238
LASREER	0.8197	0.5675	0.4409	0.3648	5.9342	4.0068	3.0391	2.5468
LASRMI	0.1699	0.1272	0.1043	0.0915	6.1907	4.1710	3.1581	2.5493
LASRM3	0.4331	0.3931	0.3595	0.3327	6.1641	4.1664	3.1589	2.5520
LASCALL	0.2254	0.1876	0.1729	0.1643	3.4431	2.5607	2.1048	1.8030
ΔLASBSE	0.0205	0.0219	0.0323	0.0581	0.0205	0.0219	0.0323	0.0582
ΔLASRBI	0.0184	0.0198	0.0288	0.0503	0.0444	0.0476	0.0685	0.1170
ΔLASIP	0.0168	0.0206	0.0251	0.0290	0.8187	0.0229	0.0279	0.0322
ΔLASREER	0.0817	0.0754	0.0729	0.0747	0.3101	0.2854	0.2755	0.2808
ΔLASRMI	0.0241	0.0311	0.0306	0.0343	0.0629	0.0809	0.0794	0.0886
ΔLASRM3	0.0087	0.0129	0.0170	0.0216	0.0244	0.0363	0.0476	0.0603
ΔLASCALL	0.0138	0.0163	0.0228	0.0341	0.0198	0.0234	0.0326	0.0486

Table 5.7

KPSS Unit Root Test Statistics for Deseasonalised Series: 1991:07 to 2003:03

	With Trend				Without Trend			
	K=1	K=2	K=3	K=4	K=1	K=2	K=3	K=4
LASBSE	0.5423	0.4782	0.4123	0.3745	7.4253	6.2514	4.4279	2.2221
LASRBI	0.8423	0.7843	0.7241	0.6242	7.5253	5.2423	3.2312	3.0913
LASIP	0.6576	0.6242	0.6041	0.5312	7.8242	5.8243	4.4221	3.2123
LASREER	0.4523	0.4224	0.4013	0.3817	8.0123	6.4312	6.1213	5.4123
LASRMI	0.8541	0.8242	0.8014	0.7542	7.0214	6.7813	5.4312	4.9812
LASRM3	0.9214	0.9040	0.8145	0.7525	7.4123	6.2430	5.4032	4.7812
LASCALL	0.4728	0.4123	0.3878	0.3232	2.5613	1.2312	1.0714	1.0023
ΔLASBSE	0.0143	0.0267	0.0298	0.0345	0.0215	0.0244	0.0231	0.0315
ΔLASRBI	0.0452	0.0487	0.0543	0.0624	0.0482	0.0512	0.0698	0.0621
ΔLASIP	0.0352	0.0389	0.0456	0.0678	0.0178	0.0192	0.0241	0.0278
ΔLASREER	0.0452	0.0512	0.0579	0.0672	0.0342	0.0313	0.0331	0.0314
ΔLASRMI	0.0262	0.0314	0.0394	0.0412	0.0312	0.0372	0.0412	0.0452
ΔLASRM3	0.0098	0.0156	0.0176	0.0216	0.0261	0.0364	0.0398	0.0412
ΔLASCALL	0.0182	0.0215	0.0279	0.0315	0.0198	0.0220	0.0298	0.0310

Note: In Table 5.5 to 5.7, K refers to lag-length. The critical values for the test at 5 per cent level of significance with trend and without trend are 0.146 and 0.463 respectively.

The lower tier of the Table presents the unit root test statistics for all the variables at their first differences. From the results it is found that the DF, ADF and PP, test statistics are statistically significant for almost all the series. Hence, the evidence across the tests indicates that the given macroeconomic variables are difference stationary (i.e., (I(1))).

4.1.1 KPSS Unit Root Test Evidence

It is important to note that the unit root tests empolyed above have the presence of unit root as the null hypothesis and the way in which these tests are carried out ensure that the null hypothesis is accepted unless there is strong evidence against it. Hence, the standard unit root tests discussed above, are not powerful against the relevant alternatives. So, Dejong *et al.* and Whiteman (1991) and Diebold and Rudebush (1991) after finding that these tests are weak, suggested that in trying to decide by classical methods whether a given economic data are stationary or integrated, it shoud be useful to perform test of the null hypothesis of stationarity as well as test of the null hypothesis of unit root.

The present test known as KPSS unit root test provides the test statistics under the null hypothesis of stationarity against the alternative of a unit root, to test that the series is differnced stationary. Following the methodology provided by Kwiatkowski, D, Phillips, P C B, Schmidd, P and Shin, Y (1992), the test statistics are calculated for all the macroeconomic variables at levels and at first differencs with trend and without trend. Table 5.5 presents the test statistics calculated by following KPSS methodology for the sample period 1981:04 to 2003:03. It is to be noted that the 5 per cent critical values of the test with trend and without trend are 0.146 and 0.463 respectively. A rejection of null hypothesis (at 5 per cent level) requires statistically significant test statistics more than 0.146 for with trend and 0.463 for with out trend. The upper tier of the Table presents the test statistics with and without trend for k = 1 to k = 4. The results shows that all the test statistics are significant enough to reject the null hypothesis of stationary both with and without trend. Hence, all the variables are non-stationary at levels. The lower tier of the Table shows the test statistics for all the series at their first differences. It is checked that all the calculated values are below the critical tabulated values for both with and without trend. In otherwords, none of the statistics are significant enough to reject the null hypothesis of stationary. Hence, it is concluded that the series are differenced stationary i.e., integrated of order one (I(1)).

Hence, the overall evidence from the unit root tests suggests that all the variables examined here for total sample period: 1981:04 to 2003:03, are first differenced stationary i.e., integrated of order one (I(1)). Hence, the search for co-integration among the variables is initiated, as the necessary condition (all the variables are being integrated of the same order, I(1) in this case) is satisfied.

4.1.2 Unit Root Results From Sub-Sample Data

The tests of unit roots have also been carried out for two sub-samples: 1985:04 to 1991:06 and from 1991:07 to 2003:03. Table 5.3 contains the unit root test statistics for DF, ADF and PP test for the sub-sample 1985:04 to 1991:06. The upper tier of the Table presents the test statistics for all the variables with and without trend at their levels and the lower tier presents the statistics for the variables at their first differences. Looking at the upper tier results it is confirmed that the null hypothesis of unit root is not rejected at 5 per cent significance level and without trend for all the variables except call money rate. Wheras, DF and PP test with trend indicate that variables call money rate, m1, m3, index of industrial production and BSE index are level stationary. However, the ADF test results indicate that for all the series, with and without trend, the statistics are not significant enough to reject the null hypothesis of non-stationary. Therefore, according to ADF test, all the series are non-stationary at their levels. The test results in the lower of the Table show that for all the unit root tests-DF, ADF and PP, the test statistics rejects the null hypothesis of non-stationary. And hence, the evidence across tests for all the macro economic variables confirm the presence of unit root - the variables are differenced stationary (i.e., I(1)).

Table 5.6 presents the test statistics for KPSS unit root test of all the variables both with and without trend for the sub-sample period 1985:04 to 1991:06 The calculated statistics at levels shows that with k = 1, all the variables with trend are statistically significant to reject the hypothesis of stationarity. However, at k = 2 and with trend, the variables BSE index and m1 and at k = 3, the variable index of industrial production, failed to reject the null hypothesis. However, the results confirmed that for all the series without trend, the statistics are significant enough to reject the null hypothesis of stationarity. Again, the test statistics for the variables at their first differences confirm that all the series, with and without trend and for all levels of k, are stationary. Hence, the test confirms that the given variables are differenced stationary for the given sample period.

Table 5.4 presents the unit root test statistics for the second sub-sample period, 1991:07 to 2003:03. Here also, the upper tier of the Table contains the test statistics of all the unit root tests (DF, ADF and PP) for the macroeconomic variables at their levels and the lower tier contains the test statistics for the variables at their first differences. Here also, DF and PP tests suggest that all the variables are non-stationary without trend save, the call money rate. Whereas, variables like call money rate, m1, m3, index of industrial production are found to be trend stationary. However, the ADF test results confirm that all the variables are non-stationary at levels both with and without trend. The result from the lower tier of the Table confirm that all the variables both with and without trend are stationary. The null hypothesis is rejected across tests to confirm that the given variables are differenced stationary (i.e.I(1)).

The KPSS unit root test results for the sub-sample from 1991:07 to 2003:3 are presented in Table 5.7. Looking at the results in the upper tier of the Table for without trend, the hypothesis of unit root for the level data is accepted at 5 per cent critical level across all the series, save one (real effective exchange rate). But the test statistics indicate that with k = 2, variables like BSE and RBI share index and at k = 1, the real effective exchange rate and m3, fails to reject the null hypothesis. However, it is observed that the test statistics for all the variables in their first differences and with and without trend are below the critical levels. Hence, the null hypothesis of stationarity is accepted for all the variables at their first differences. So, the evidences suggest that the given variables are difference stationary (i.e., I(1)).

Hence, the overall evidences from all the unit root tests for all three samples indicate that all the variables examined are first difference stationary i.e., integrated of order one (I(1)). Hence, the search for co-integration among the variables is initiated here.

4.2 Co-integration Tests

Co-integration tests are employed to check the long run equilibrium relationship among the observed time series variables. The essence of the co-integration analysis is that if the variables are individually integrated of the same order, say I(1), but a linear combination of the variables exists such that it is I(0), then it may be stated that there exists stable long run equilibrium relation among them, though each tends to drift away from the others over time.

In this study we examine the evidence of co-integraton on the demand for money functions using both Engle-Granger two step procedure proposed by Engle and Granger (1987) and Johansen-Juselius technique proposed by Johansen (1988) and Johansen and Juselius (1990).

4.2.1 Testing for Co-integration: The Engle-Granger Two-Step Procedure

In this section we present the result of co-integration test using the Engle-Granger two-step method. In computing these results, the first step is to estimate a co-integration regression (in the present case, money demand specifications whch are listed in Table 5.1 and extract residuals from the regressions. In the second step, the stationarity of the residuals derived from the regressions are examined. The DF, ADF and PP tests are carried out to test the null hypothesis of non-stationarity of the residuals obtained from the co-integration regressions. The tests for co-integration have been carried out for three samples: 1981:04 to 2003:03, 1985:04 to 1991:06 and 1991:07 to 2003:03.

Table 5.8 presents the co-integration test results computed using the residuals derived from the alternative money demand specifications for the total sample period, *viz*., 1981:04 to 2003:3. The statistics are computed by using the methodology of DF, ADF and PP tests. It is clear from the results that the DF and PP tests are able to reject the non-stationarity of residuals both with and without trend. However, the ADF test fails to reject non-stationarity of error at 5 per cent level of significance for both m1 and m3 regression using index of

Table 5.8

Co-integration Test: The Engle-Granger Two-Step Procedure for Deseasonalised Monthly Series for the Period: 1981:04 to 2003:03

Specifications	*Without Trend*			*With Trend*		
	DF	*ADF*	*PP*	*DF*	*ADF*	*PP*
1	-6.7076	-4.4363(13)	-7.4232	-6.8567	-4.4056(13)	-7.1813
2	-11.2206	-4.9607(13)	-11.3452	-11.3245	-4.9567(13)	-11.3456
3	-10.8194	-3.1641(13)	-10.3456	-11.9456	-3.0645(13)	-10.275
4	-8.4158	-4.1590(13)	-7.7845	-8.5437	-4.2728(13)	-7.3334
5	-10.7310	-4.0593(13)	-9.6947	-10.8657	-4.1234(13)	-8.8577
6	-10.1334	-4.7543(03)	-10.1334	-10.2345	-4.8026(03)	-10.102
7	-9.8299	-2.2982(03)	-9.4546	-9.9456	-2.2345(03)	-9.6788
8	-9.6351	-2.3432(03)	-9.9394	-9.6845	-2.3145(03)	-9.4562
9	-7.7246	-5.6969(03)	-7.8456	-7.8768	-4.9876(03)	-7.4354
10	-7.5960	-2.4404(03)	-7.5657	-7.9867	-2.2799(03)	-7.1971

* Specifications (1) to (10) are the same as listed in Table 5.1(b).

industrial production, call money rate and BSE index (specifications 5 and 10) as explanatory variables. Again, the test fails to reject the non-stationarity of error at 1 per cent level of significance for m1 specification using index of industrial production, call money rate, real effective exchange rate and BSE index (specification 3) and m3 specification using industrial production, call money rate, real effective exchange rate and either RBI or BSE share index (specification 7 and 8) as the explanatory variable for both with and without trend.

So, the co-integration test (Engle-Granger two-step procedure) for the total sample data suggests that each of the monetary aggregates (both m1 and m3) has a long run trend relationship with the appropriate determinants examined.

Table 5.9 contains the co-intgration test statistics obtained from the OLS regression of ten alternative money demand specifications for the first sub-sample, *viz.*, 1985:04 to 1991:06. The test statistics computed for DF and PP tests with and without trend suggest that the errors of all the specifications are stationary at levels confirming the presence of long run equilibrium relationship. However, the ADF test fails to reject the null hypothesis of non-stationarity of errors at 5 per cent level of significance for m1 regression using index of

Table 5.9

Co-integration Test: The Engle-Granger Two-Step Procedure for Deseasonalised Monthly Series for the Period: 1985:04 to 1991:06

Specifications	*Without Trend*			*With Trend*		
	DF	*ADF*	*PP*	*DF*	*ADF*	*PP*
1	-6.6941	-3.5528(01)	-7.1440	-6.6746	-3.5339(01)	-7.1713
2	-6.3837	-2.9039(10)	-6.6331	-6.3587	-2.9893(10)	-6.6524
3	-6.6198	-3.7016(01)	-7.0189	-6.6041	-3.6763(01)	-7.0475
4	-7.0974	-4.8340(01)	-7.2414	-7.1944	-4.8728(01)	-7.3895
5	-7.5018	-4.7450(01)	-7.6947	-7.6260	-4.8154(01)	-7.8577
6	-9.7951	-4.8152(03)	-10.122	-9.7301	-4.8006(03)	-10.143
7	-9.7413	-4.8809(03)	-10.142	-9.6744	-4.8502(03)	-10.128
8	-9.7538	-5.7838(02)	-10.095	-9.6899	-5.7535(02)	-10.102
9	-7.6623	-4.6996(01)	-7.8314	-7.6742	-4.7074(01)	-7.9014
10	-7.9671	-4.2766(02)	-8.1221	-7.9862	-4.2799(02)	-8.1971

* Specifications (1) to (10) are the same as listed in Table 5.1(b).

industrial production, call money rate and real effective exchange rate (specification (1)) and the same set of variable with either RBI or BSE share price index (specification 2 and 3) as explanatory variables. The test again fails to reject the hypothesis of no co-integration for m3 specification using index of industrial production, call money rate and BSE index (specification (10)) as the explanatory variable for both with and without trend.

The co-integration test results for the second sub-sample period, i.e., 1991:07 to 2003:03 are presented in the Table 5.10. The test statistics computed for DF, ADF and PP tests on the residuals derived from the alternative specifications presents an intersting inference on the long run equilibrium relationships. By looking at the results it is confirmed that the statistics for DF and PP tests for all the specifications are significant enough to reject the null hypothesis of non-stationarity of errors for both with and without trend. However, the ADF test statictics fail to reject the null for all the above specifications. Again, the results for all the m3 money specifications shows that the DF, ADF, PP test statistics fails to reject the null hypothesis of non-stationarity (no co-integration) even at 5 per cent

Table 5.10

Co-integration Test: The Engle-Granger Two-Step Procedure for Deseasonalised Monthly Series for the Period: 1991:07 to 2003:03

Specifications	*Without Trend*			*With Trend*		
	DF	*ADF*	*PP*	*DF*	*ADF*	*PP*
1	-8.5666	-4.7627(10)	-8.5636	-8.6846	-4.5339(10)	-8.2674
2	-8.5717	-3.9843(10)	-8.5342	-8.3687	-3.9893(10)	-8.4356
3	-8.4890	-4.2549(10)	-8.0234	-8.2341	-4.1763(10)	-8.0034
4	-8.3833	-4.0464(10)	-8.2345	-8.1945	-4.2345(10)	-7.8657
5	-8.3074	-4.4217(10)	-7.9876	-7.9870	-4.2348(10)	-7.5678
6	-4.0763	-3.0102(02)	-4.0045	-4.0034	-3.0023(03)	-4.3456
7	-4.2435	-3.1339(02)	-3.9856	-4.1234	-3.2342(03)	-3.2435
8	-4.2323	-3.2226(02)	-3.5678	-4.1254	-3.1234(03)	-3.3456
9	-4.3378	-3.1589(02)	-4.0123	-4.2342	-3.0023(03)	-3.9867
10	-4.0822	-2.9546(02)	-3.7656	-3.9876	-2.6789(03)	-3.4567

Note: In Table 5.8 – 5.10, DF: Dickey-Fuller, ADF: Augmented Dickey-Fuller, PP: Philips-Perron. The values inside parentheses corresponding to ADF statistics (column 3 and 6) indicate appropriate lag length. is the difference operator.

* Specifications (1) to (10) are the same as listed in Table 5.1(b).

level of significance for with and without trend. Hence, it is confirmed that m3 money demand functions do not have long run co-integration relationship for the sample period.

The co-integration test (Engle-Granger two-step procedure) suggests that each of the monetary aggregates (m1 and m3 in our case) has a long run co-integration relationship with the appropriate determinanats for the total sample period from early 1981 to end of 1995. This result suggest that there exist an equilibrium long run relationship for both m1 and m3 money demand functions. However, the results for the sub-sample period of 1990s show that the long run trend relationship does exist for m1 money demand functions in contrast to the m3 counterparts. So, the findings suggest that whereas either of the monetary aggregates can be used as the guide for monetary targetting in 1980s, only m1 suits well to be the appropriate aggregate for monetary targetting during the 1990s and early 2000.

4.2.2 Testing for Co-integration: The Johansen and Juselius (JJ) Procedure

Tests of co-integration such as Engle-Granger two-step procedure (Engle and Granger, 1987) allowed for the estimation and testing of unique co-integrating vector, even though there could be as many co-integrating vectors as the number of variables involved less one. As well, since this single equation method estimates the co-integrating vector with the data in levels only, it has been criticised for ignoring potentially valuable information contained in the short-run fluctuations of the variables. Moreover, the Engle-Granger test procedures relies on the OLS residuals for the estimation of test statistics. In the past few years, there has been a movement towards estimating co-integrating relationships in a system of equation framework to make better use of all the information available in the long run and short run fluctuation of each variable. Johansen (1988) outlined a method, which was later expanded by Johansen and Juselius (1990), that allowed for the testing of more than one co-integrating vector in the data and for the calculation of maximum-likelihood estimates of these vectors. Again, the procedure also allows direct hypothesis tests on the co-efficients in the co-integrating vectors.

The present study makes use of the Johansen and Juselius (1990) technique on deseasonalised monthly data for the total sample - 1981:04 to 2003:03 and of its two sub-samples - 1985:04 to 1991:06 and 1991:07 to 2003:03. The lag-lengths for the VARs were selected according to the Akaike Information Criterion for each specification.

Table 5.11 reports the results of co-integration tests using the Johansen and Juselius technique for the total sample period (1981:04 to 2003:03) on selected alternative specifications. This study relies upon only the trace statistics to determine the number of co-integrating vectors. The results of the trace statistic rejects the null hypothesis of r = 0 for all specifications, both of m1 and m3. Hence, it may be concluded that a long run equilibrium relationship exist among money (both narrow and broad), output, interest rate, real effective exchange rate and share price index for Indian economy. However, it is found that the first three specifications for m1 (specification (1), (2) and (3)) the statistics imply the existence of three co-integrating vectors and specifications (4) and (5) signify the presence of two co-integrating vectors. As against this, m3

Table 5.11

Co-integration Test: The Johansen-Juselius Procedure for Deseasonalised Monthly Series for the Period: 1981:04 to 2003:03

Specifications	*Co-integrating Vector*	*Trace Statistics*	*Specifications*	*Co-integrating Vector*	*Trace Statistics*
1	r = 0	71.4102	6	r = 0	47.1759
(Lag = 03)	r ≤ 1	36.8349	(Lag = 03)	r ≤ 1	20.4784
	r ≤ 2	30.3477		r ≤ 2	6.6749
	r ≤ 3	2.4777		r ≤ 3	0.4901
2	r = 0	107.3894	7	r = 0	74.0432
(Lag = 03)	r ≤ 1	56.0144	(Lag = 03)	r ≤ 1	39.2496
	r ≤ 2	29.6981		r ≤ 2	20.4331
	r ≤ 3	8.3232		r ≤ 3	7.9894
	r ≤ 4	0.0894		r ≤ 4	0.4710
3	r = 0	94.2301	8	r = 0	64.3660
(Lag = 03)	r ≤ 1	54.7969	(Lag = 03)	r ≤ 1	36.4561
	r ≤ 2	29.7948		r ≤ 2	17.6538
	r ≤ 3	10.1070		r ≤ 3	7.6143
	r ≤ 4	0.0094		r ≤ 4	0.1289
4	r = 0	72.1473	9	r = 0	48.9647
(Lag = 03)	r ≤ 1	35.1663	(Lag = 03)	r ≤ 1	21.4487
	r ≤ 2	9.1000		r ≤ 2	8.9606
	r ≤ 3	0.8880		r ≤ 3	1.0001
5	r = 0	68.1380	10	r = 0	41.8047
(Lag = 03)	r ≤ 1	32.9440	(Lag = 03)	r ≤ 1	17.6039
	r ≤ 2	10.0387		r ≤ 2	7.7643
	r ≤ 3	0.8547		r ≤ 3	0.1797

* Specifications (1) to (10) are the same as listed in Table 5.1(b).

specifications imply the existence of two co-integrating vectors for specification (7) and (8), one for specification (6), (9) and (10). So, the above results suggest that though there exist a long run equilibrium relationship underlying the money demand functions, a more stable relationship is detected for m1 aggregates than that of m3 aggregates.

Table 5.12 presents the results of the Johansen-Juselius co-integration test for the sub-sample period: 1985:04 to 1991:06. The test results reject the null hypothesis of zero co-integrating vectors for

Table 5.12

Co-integration Test: The Johansen-Juselius Procedure for Deseasonalised Monthly Series for the Period: 1985:04 to 1991:06

Specifications	*Co-integrating Vector*	*Trace Statistics*	*Specifications*	*Co-integrating Vector*	*Trace Statistics*
1	r = 0	175.6721	6	r = 0	121.6417
(Lag = 28)	r ≤ 1	28.2458	(Lag = 28)	r ≤ 1	43.7206
	r ≤ 2	10.9612		r ≤ 2	14.9526
	r ≤ 3	3.2832		r ≤ 3	1.0600
2	r = 0	135.7963	7	r = 0	110.1012
(Lag = 23)	r ≤ 1	66.9014	(Lag = 23)	r ≤ 1	49.2883
	r ≤ 2	39.0860		r ≤ 2	17.1523
	r ≤ 3	13.0159		r ≤ 3	4.3069
	r ≤ 4	1.3751		r ≤ 4	0.0297
3	r = 0	109.6959	8	r = 0	82.8886
(Lag = 23)	r ≤ 1	59.4242	(Lag = 23)	r ≤ 1	53.1897
	r ≤ 2	33.4986		r ≤ 2	27.7762
	r ≤ 3	15.0618		r ≤ 3	10.8382
	r ≤ 4	5.5962		r ≤ 4	0.0197
4	r = 0	104.3607	9	r = 0	101.1002
(Lag = 23)	r ≤ 1	47.7809	(Lag = 23)	r ≤ 1	54.1252
	r ≤ 2	11.2238		r ≤ 2	21.7875
	r ≤ 3	0.6300		r ≤ 3	1.1945
5	r = 0	116.4276	10	r = 0	106.0949
(Lag = 23)	r ≤ 1	47.5197	(Lag = 23)	r ≤ 1	48.9177
	r ≤ 2	8.3125		r ≤ 2	15.4164
	r ≤ 3	0.3599		r ≤ 3	4.6542

* Specifications (1) to (10) are the same as listed in Table 5.1(b).

all the money demand specifications. However, the test suggests the existence of three co-integrating vectors for two m1 specifications (specifications (2) and (3)), two significant vectors for specifications (4) and (5) and one for specification (1). Whereas, the test find only two significant co-integrating vectors for four specifications (specifications (7), (8), (9) and (10)) and one significant vector for specification (6). The above results suggest that a long run equilibrium relationship exists underlying the money demand relationships for the chosen sample period and few specifications with m1 money as dependent variable and selected explanatory variables are more stable compared with the m3 counterpart.

The results for the second sub-sample period i.e., 1991:07 to 2003:03 are presented in Table 5.13. While searching for significant co-integrating vectors, the results support the existence of long run

Table 5.13

Co-integration Test: The Johansen-Juselius Procedure for Deseasonalised Monthly Series for the Period: 1991:07 to 2003:03

Specifications	*Co-integrating Vector*	*Trace Statistics*	*Specifications*	*Co-integrating Vector*	*Trace Statistics*
1	r = 0	80.8327	6	r = 0	41.4331
(Lag = 10)	r ≤ 1	29.7698	(Lag = 09)	r ≤ 1	23.0345
	r ≤ 2	7.1608		r ≤ 2	7.5836
	r ≤ 3	0.1772		r ≤ 3	1.5836
2	r = 0	98.2142	7	r = 0	89.6556
(Lag = 10)	r ≤ 1	47.8139	(Lag = 10)	r ≤ 1	48.2705
	r ≤ 2	22.5702		r ≤ 2	20.7830
	r ≤ 3	4.6298		r ≤ 3	3.9848
	r ≤ 4	0.4084		r ≤ 4	1.3226
3	r = 0	99.1221	8	r = 0	98.6196
(Lag = 10)	r ≤ 1	47.7228	(Lag = 10)	r ≤ 1	52.2696
	r ≤ 2	22.5534		r ≤ 2	23.2071
	r ≤ 3	4.5470		r ≤ 3	4.9696
	r ≤ 4	0.7251		r ≤ 4	0.9986
4	r = 0	96.2349	9	r = 0	69.6963
(Lag = 10)	r ≤ 1	25.6715	(Lag = 10)	r ≤ 1	26.1085
	r ≤ 2	5.7234		r ≤ 2	13.1107
	r ≤ 3	0.3832		r ≤ 3	3.8704
5	r = 0	69.8767	10	r = 0	71.9805
(Lag = 10)	r ≤ 1	22.9144	(Lag = 10)	r ≤ 1	28.6816
	r ≤ 2	4.0397		r ≤ 2	9.5698
	r ≤ 3	0.0097		r ≤ 3	2.6515

* Specifications (1) to (10) are the same as listed in Table 5.1(b).

equilibrium relationship for alternative money demand functions for the selected sample period as well. The results show that the null hypothesis of zero co-integating vector could be rejected for specifications all of the m1 specification and of m3 specifications save specification (6). Whereas, specifications (2) and (3) for m1 specifcations and (7) and (8) of m3 specfications are having more than or equal to two significant co-integrating vectors. So, the result suggests that for the second sub-period, which covers the 1990s, both the monetary aggregates are having stable long run equilibrium relationship.

5. Concluding Remarks

In the present paper, an attempt has been made to re-examine the issue of stability of demand for money in India. The search for long run equilibrium money demand relationship is attemted here with the help of multivariate co-integration tests. Before going for co-integration tests, unit root tests are employed to check the presence of stochastic trends in the data. The present study has used Dickey-Fuller, Augmented Dickey-Fuller, Phillips-Perron, and KPSS unit root tests for the purpose. These unit root tests confirmed that the macroeconomic variables examined here were found to be differenced stationary. Hence, the initiation is taken for the analysis co-integration with the help of both Engle-Granger two-step and Johansen-Juselius test. The findings from Engle-Granger test reveal that an equilibrium long run relationship does exists for either of the monetary aggregates (m1 or m3). However, for the sub-period of 1990s and early 2000, long run trend relationship exist only for m1 function in contrast to that of m3. So the results suggest that either of the monetary aggregate act as a guide for monetary targeting during 1980s, but only m1 serves as the suitable monetary aggregate during 1990s and early 2000. The test results from the use of Johansen-Juselius co-integration procedure confirms that there exist a stable long run equilibrium relationship among money, output, interest rate, stock prices and exchange rate. Moreover, the procedure suggests that a more stable long run equilibrium relationship does exist for m1 function compared to those of m3 functions.

The stability of the money demand function is being questioned in an environment of deregulation, globalisation and rapid defusion of financial innovation during the 1980s. In view of this, the quantum of money channel seem to have lost some of their significance, suggesting the monetary authorities to shift out from the quantitative targeting to targeting the rate variables (i.e., interest rate, exchange rate). However, the findings of the existence of long run equilibrium relationship underlaying money demand relation suggests that monetary authorities can have faith on the effectiveness of monetary transmission mechanism. But during the 1990s and in the future, narrow monetary aggregate will be an appropriate target variable for monetary targeting in India.

References

Artis, M.J. and Lewis, M.K. (1976). "The Demand for Money in the UK", *Manchester School of Economics*, Vol. 44. pp. 147-181.

Bhattacharya, R. (1995). "Co-integration Relationship in the Demand for Money in India", *Indian Economic Journal*, Vol. 43, pp. 69-75.

Bhoi, B.K. (1992). "Issues of Instability in Money Demand Analysis: A Perspective", *RBI Staff Papers*, No. 9.

Brunner, K. and Metlzer, A.H. (1963). "Predicting Velocity: Implications for Theory and Policy", *Journal of Finance*, Vol. 18, pp. 319-354.

Carr, J. and Darby, M. (1981). "The Role of Money Supply Shocks in the Short Run Demand for Money", *Journal of Monetary Economics*, Vol 8, pp.183-199.

Dickey, D.A., Dennis, W.J. and Daniel, L.T. (1991). "A Primer on Co-integration with an Application to Money and Income", *Fedral Reserve Bank of St. Louis*, (March/April), pp. 48-78.

Engle, R.F. and Granger, C.W.J. (1987). "Co-integration and Error Correction: Representation, Estimation and Testing", *Econometrica*, Vol. 55, pp. 251-276.

Friedman, M. (1977). "Finanacial Flow Variables and the Short Run Determination of the Long Term Interest Rate", *Journal of Political Economy*, Vol. 85, pp. 661-689.

Friedman, M. and Schwartz, A.J. (1963). "Money and Business Cycles", *Review of Economic and Statistics*, Vol. 45 (Suplementary), pp. 32-78.

Goldfeld, S.M. (1973). "The Demand for Money Revisited", *Brooking Papers on Economic Activity*, Vol 3, pp.577-646.

Goldfeld, S.M. (1976). "The Case of Missing Money", *Brooking Papers on Economic Activity*, Vol 3, pp.683-739.

Gordon, R.J. (1984). "The Short-run Demand for Money: A Reconsideration", *Journal of Money Credit and Banking*, Vol 16, pp.403-434.

Granger, C.W.J and Newbold, P. (1974). "Spurious Regression in Econometrics", *Journal of Econometrics*, Vol 2.

Gupta, S.B. (1979). "*Monetary Planning for India*", Oxford University Press: Delhi.

Hall, S.G., Henry, S.G.B. and Wilcox, J.B. (1990). "The long run Determination of the UK Monetary Aggragates",*Bank of England, Discussion Papers* , No. 41, London.

Hamburger, M.J. (1977). "Behavour of the Money Stock: Is there a Puzzle?", *Journal of Monetary Economics*, Vol. 3, pp. 265-288.

Hendry, S. (1995). "Long-Run Demand for M1, *Bank of Canada Working Papers*, 95-11.

Hendry, D.F. and Ericsson, N.R. (1991). "Modelling the Demand for Narow Money in the United Kingdom and the United States", *Europian Economic Review*, Vol. 35, pp. 833-886.

Johansen, S. (1988). "Statistical Analysis of Co-integrating Vectors", *Journal of Economic Dyanamic and Control*, Vol. 12, pp. 231-254.

Johansen, S. and Juselius, K. (1990). "Maximum Likelihood Estimation and Inference on Co-integration with Application to Demand for Money", *Oxford Bulletin of Economics and Statistics*, Vol. 52, pp. 169-210.

Joshi, H. and Saggar, M. (1995). "The Demand for Money in India: Stability Revisited", *RBI Occassional Papers*, Vol. 16, pp. 79-97.

Judd, J.P. and Scadding J.L. (1982). "The Search for a Stable Money Demand Function: A Survey of the Post-1973 Literature", *Journal of Economic Literature*, Vol. 20, pp. 993-1023.

Kamaiah, B. (1985). "Functional Misspecification and Stability of Macro Money Demand Function in India", *Prajnan*, Vol. 14, pp. 181-198.

Kwiatkowski, D., Phillips, P.C.B., Schmidt, P. and Shin, Y. (1992). "Testing the Null Hypothesis of Stationary Against the Alternative of a Unit Root", *Journal of Econometrics*, Vol. 54, pp. 159-178.

Laidler, D.E.W. (1966). "Some Evidence on the Demand for Money", *Journal of Political Economy*, Vol. 74, pp. 55-68.

Laidler, D. (1971). "The Influance of Money on Economic Activity: A Survey of Some Current Problems, in *G Clayton, J C Gilbort and R Sedgwick (ed), Monetary Theory and Policy in the 1970s*, Oxford: Oxford University Press.

Laidler, D. (1977). "The Demand for Money: Theories and Evidence", (2nd edn), New York: Dun-Donnely.

Laidler, D. (1980). "The Demand for Money in the United States: Yet Again", in Brunner K and Meltzer, A (ed), The State of Macro Economics, Carnegie

Rochester Conference Series on Public Policy, Vol. 12, Amsterdam: North Holland.

Mahajan, Y.L. (1979). "Stability of the Demand for Money in India", *Indian Economic Journal*, Vol. 27, pp. 95-109.

Miller, S.M. (1990). "Money Demand Instability : Has it Ended?, *Economic Letters*, Vol.30, pp. 345-349.

Miller, S.M. (1991). "Monetary Dynamics: An Application of Co-integration and Error Correction Modelling", *Journal of Money, Credit and Banking*, Vol. 23. pp. 139-154.

Moosa, I. (1992). "The Demand for Money in India: A Co-integration Approach", *Indian Journal of Economics*, Vol. 40, pp. 101-115.

Nag, A.K. and Upadhyay, G. (1993). "Estimation of Money Demand Function: A Co-integration Approach", *RBI Occassional Papers*, Vol. 14, pp. 47-66.

Phillips, P.C.B and Perron, P. (1988). "Testing for Unit Root in Time Series Regression", *Biometrica*, Vol. 75, pp. 335-346.

Ram, R. and Biswas, B. (1983). "Stability of Demand for Money in India: Some Further Evidence", *Indian Economic Journal*, Vol. 31, pp. 77-88.

Rangarajan, C. (1989). "Issues in Monetary Management", *Indian Economic Journal*, Vol. 36, pp. 1-13.

6

Optimising Growth and Inflation: Some Empirical Results Relating to the Indian Economy Using Control Theory

BALWANT SINGH
SUSHILA AUGUSTINE

Introduction

The derivation of macroeconomic stabilisation policies in a control theoretic framework is an important area of theoretical and empirical economic research. This is because such a stance presents an ideal blend of skillfully interweaving the essential theoretical ingredients of the contemporary macroeconomic paradigms with specific structural features of the country under reference. This technique enables the policymaker to build up alternative policy evidences and thus this approach proves far superior to alternative approaches based on intuitive or judgmental criteria. With this backdrop, this paper attempts to develop a small macro model incorporating some of the recent features of the Indian economy. The model tries to represent the structure of the Indian economy in the post-reform period so that its results are more relevant for policy design purposes. The paper as such is divided into four Sections. In Section 1, we present discussion on the specification and empirical results of the individual equations of the model. Section 2 is devoted to evaluate collective performance of the model. Results of some control theoretic experiments are discussed in Section 3. Summary and broad conclusion of the study are given in Section 4 and references are given at the end.

This paper is dedicated to the memories of (late) Prof. M.J. Manohar Rao, architect of the applications of control methods in India.

1 EQUATIONS OF THE MODEL

1.1 Basics and Modeling Strategy

The basic premises of the model are that monetary sector changes are the reflections of the changes in fiscal and external sectors. Fiscal sector changes itself occur due to the developments in real sector and price level. Changes in external sector, in the exports and imports of goods, occur due to developments in the domestic and to a certain extent in the world economy. Changes in the real sector and price level, takes place due to a combination of factors, including monetary and fiscal impacts. Thus, the model captures inter-linkages of the economy in a simultaneous framework. With such a macro-economic system as background, Reserve Bank of India maintains desired liquidity in the economy, in line with the set objectives of inflation control and to meet credit needs of the economy, by making adjustments in credit supply (through adjustments in cash reserve ratio) and the Bank rate. From the fiscal side, model includes government development expenditure as one of the policy variable.

The model is a very aggregated representation of the Indian economy. There are five blocks of equations relating to output and investment; government revenue and expenditure; money; prices and external trade. The model has a single production function for the whole economy, implicitly assuming similar production functions for the different sectors of the Indian economy. The assumption of homogenous production function with respect to different sectors of the Indian economy (agriculture, industry and services sector) may not be very realistic. Agriculture is essentially supply driven whereas non-agriculture has now become considerably sensitive to aggregate demand as well (Sastry and Singh, *et al.*, 2003). Similarly, the model does not have separate investment functions for agriculture and non-agriculture sectors (as in Pani's model of 1984) and thus investment functions, as assumed in this model may not capture inter-sectoral sensitivity of investment, especially of the public sector investment on the macro variables. Relaxing theses assumptions is an area for future work.

The model covers two distinct phases of the Indian economy– highly regulated and deregulated and, therefore, some of coefficients, especially those, which have gained prominence in the post-reform period, are unlikely to turn statistically significant. However, considering their importance in the emerging Indian economy, they have been retained in the model. The model consists of 17 equations, of which 10 are stochastic and 7 are identities. The parameters are estimated using annual time series data for the fiscal years from 1985-86 to 2001-02.

Modeling strategy involves an application of a more rigorous approach rather estimating equation either in levels or in a growth rate form. At the first stage, a long-run relationship is estimated. While estimating a long run relationship, in some equations, coefficients of some of the variables were restricted (to 1) to obtain theoretically appropriate results. The appropriateness of the long-run relationship is judged on the basis of the signs of the regression coefficients and whether the residual series of the long-run relationship is stationary or not, evaluated using Dicky-Fuller (DF) test. The final relationship is estimated in an ECM framework, including both long run and short-run information. Like-wise long run relationship, in some ECM equations as well, coefficient of the residual terms, which was less than minus 1, was restricted to minus 1. These problems prominently occurred in those variables which were substantially affected by the reform process and whose modeling otherwise are also inherently difficult, as in case of the private investment. The choice of variables of the equations, long run as well short-run, is made on the basis of theoretical and statistical criteria. Needless to say, several alternative specifications were tried (not reported for lack of space) to arrive at the best fit of the equations. In many cases dummy variables have been incorporated to neutralise the effects of outliers and irregular changes. Dummy variables are also used to cover two different policy regimes, wherever felt essential. The list of endogenous and exogenous variables used in the model is given in Annexure 6A.1.

1.2 Real Sector

1.2.1 Output

The long run relationship of real output could be specified as a conventional production function in which output is determined by fixed capital (K), labour (L) and total factor productivity. However, in respect of a country like India, the lack of quality data on employment, especially relating to the unorganised sector, means that including labour in the production function may not be realistic. Perhaps, in view of such considerations, earlier modeling exercises in India (Rangarajan and Arif (1990), Bhattachraya, Barman and Nag (1994)) and others) have not included labour in the production functions specified in their studies. Therefore, real output is postulated as a function of capital stock alone. However, a dummy variable representing the pre-reform period is considered to take account of the impact of the policy regime on the production function. In the short-run, however, output in India could be affected by variety of demand- and supply-oriented factors.

One of the most important factors is rainfall. Rainfall affects the overall growth prospects, primarily through its impact on agricultural sector which in turn affects industry as a supply factor in agro-based industries, and through demand (Sastry, Singh, *et al.* 2003). Another factor, which continues to affect the performance of the Indian economy, is the availability of bank credit, essential for working capital needs. Earlier, Rangarajan and Arif (1990) used real (broad) money balances as one of the variable in their output function. We used real bank credit rather than real money balances in the output equation. Bank credit appears to be more appropriate for many reasons. In the Indian set-up, there is a vast unorganised sector, which relies on bank credit to meet its working capital and investment needs as this sectors lack its own resources. Another explanation is that bank credit could be considered as a proxy for the potential utilisation as well. An increase in the (growth rate of real) bank credit (especially if caused because of demand factors) generally reflects higher use of the existing resources (capital stock, etc.). Given this, real output is postulated to be a function of changes in capital stock, lagged by one year ($\Delta \log Kr_{-1}$), changes in (real) bank credit to the commercial sector (Δlog (Bccs/Wpi)) and rainfall (Rif[1])and one lagged residual series of the long-run equation.[2]

1. There was a doubt whether excessive rainfall would adversely affect output performance and so whether there is a need to include quadratic form of the rainfall index as one of the explanatory variable, which should bear negative sign. However, data did not support this hypothesis.
2. Other factors, which also could be considered, are the export performance and government expenditure affecting through the external and domestic demand, respectively (Bhattacharya, Barman and Nag (1994)).

Long-run equation:

$$Log\ Yr = 2.2712 + 0.76609\ Log\ Kr + 0.04358\ Der$$
$$t\quad (8.35)\quad (42.20)\qquad\qquad (2.82)$$

ECM equation:

$$\Delta LogYR = 0.0140 + 0.2936 \Delta LogKr_{-1} + 0.1696\ \Delta Log\ (Bccs/Wpi)$$
$$t\quad (0.42)\quad (0.72)\qquad\qquad (2.99)$$
$$+ 0.07793\ Rif - 0.6612\ Resyr(-1)$$
$$(2.58)\qquad (4.11)$$

$R^{2(adj.)} = 0.78$ DW=2.17 SEE=0.00892

The above equation was also estimated using a credit demand function discussed in the monetary sector as an instrument because of the endogeneity of bank credit. That is, by replacing actual values of bank credit by their estimates, as obtained through a credit demand function.

ECM equation using instrument variable for ΔLog (Bccs/Wpi):

$$\Delta LogYr = 0.0088 + 0.2942 \Delta LogKr_{-1} + 0.2705\ \Delta Log\ (Bccs/Wpi)\hat{}$$
$$t\quad (0.31)\quad (0.85)\qquad\qquad (3.99)$$
$$+ 0.0599\ Rif - 0.6280\ Resyr_{(-1)}$$
$$(2.26)\qquad (4.50)$$

$R^{2(adj.)} = 0.84$ *DW=2.28 SEE=0.0076*

1.2.2 Investment Equations

Investment data in India are available for the household, corporate and public sectors. For the purpose of this study, data for corporate and household sectors is clubbed together and is treated as capital formation in the private sector, also occasionally referred to as investment in the private sector. Initially, regression equations in nominal terms for capital formation in the private (Ipn) and public sectors (Ign) are estimated separately and then are added-up and converted into real terms (Ir) by using deflator for the capital formation deflator (Idf).

1.2.2.1 Capital Formation in the Private Sector

Long-run nominal capital formation in the private sector (Ipn) could be postulated as a function of (nominal) output (Yn) and certain other factors, e.g. foreign resources. Since the data for the other factors, especially foreign resources in India is not readily available, they have been proxied by a time trend. Private investment is thus estimated as function of (nominal) output and a time trend. The regression coefficient of Yn turned out to be greater than one, which is theoretically impossible[3]. Therefore, the equation was re-estimated by restricting the coefficient of Yn to one. This is still unattractive from a theoretical point of view because it implies that investment output ratio (IPN/YN) grows over time. Though this is impossible in the long run, however, it might be possible in the medium-term.

$$\text{Log Ipn} = -2.19762 + 1.0 \text{ Log Yn} + 0.0156 \text{ Time}$$

In the short-run, capital formation in the private sector is likely to be affected by growth in nominal income, the cost of capital, proxied by prime lending rate adjusted for expected inflation ($Plr\text{-}P^e$). To test the competing hypotheses of 'crowding-in' or 'crowding-out' of private sector investment by the public sector investment, growth in capital formation in the public sector (ΔLog Ign), is also included,[4] as an additional variable (Blejer and Khan, 1984). The estimated coefficient on the ECM was less than minus one and, therefore, equation was re-estimated restricting its (error term) coefficient to one, which is still inappropriate.

ECM equation:

$$\Delta\text{Log Ipn} = 0.031 - 1.491\ (Plr\text{-}P^e) + 1.603\ \Delta\text{Log Yn}(-1) + 0.202$$
$$t \quad (0.21) \quad (1.47) \qquad (1.82) \qquad (0.61)$$
$$\Delta\text{Log Ign}(-1) - 1.00\ \text{Resipn}_{(-1)}$$

$$R^{2(adj)} = 0.68 \quad DW = 2.63 \quad SEE = 0.0811$$

1.2.2.2 Capital Formation in the Public Sector

Long-run capital formation in public sector is modelled as a function of government development expenditure (Gde), where development expenditure used is that of the Central Government.[5]

$$\text{Log Ign} = -0.1311 + 1.00 \text{ Log Gde}$$
$$t \quad (0.32) \quad (27.88)$$

3. Long-run coefficient of Yn greater than one will imply that in the long-run entire Yn is used for investment and thus there will be no consumption.
4. The empirical result indicated that the public sector investment has the maximum 'crowding-in' effect on the private sector investment with one year lag.
5. States expenditures are not included. We assume their exclusion will not alter the results.

ECM equation:

$$\Delta \text{Log Ign} = 0.0679 + 0.3311\ \Delta\ \text{Log Gde} - 0.6168\text{Resign}_{(-1)}$$
$$t \quad (3.16) \quad (1.90) \quad (3.23)$$

$R^{2(adj)} = 0.40$ DW $=2.01$ SEE$=0.0521$

1.3 Fiscal Sector

The fiscal sector of the model involves equations for non-development expenditure and revenue receipts of the Central Government. Non-development expenditure was also initially estimated as a function of nominal output. However, the empirical results were considered inappropriate, as the residual series obtained from the long-run equation was not stationary. Accordingly, the equation was modified and re-estimated as a function of real output (Yr) and wholesale price index (Wpi)[6].

$$\text{Log Nde} = -16.2881 + 1.8544\ \text{Log Yr} + 0.4957\ \text{Log Wpi}$$
$$t \quad (7.29) \quad (8.56) \quad (3.12)$$

ECM Equation:

$$\Delta\ \text{Log Nde} = 0.0597 + 0.7923\ \Delta\ \text{LogYr} + 0.5058\ \Delta\ \text{Log Wpi}$$
$$t \quad (1.58) \quad (1.96) \quad (1.67)$$
$$+\ 0.021\ \text{Der} - 0.8151\ \text{Resnde}_{(-1)}$$
$$(1.35) \quad (3.96)$$

$R^{2(adj.)} = 0.53$ DW$=2.47$ SEE$=0.0267$

Revenue receipts is modeled as a function of nominal output.

$$\text{Log Rr} = -1.3205 + 0.9304\ \text{Log Yn} + 0.0543\ \text{Der}$$
$$t \quad (3.72) \quad (36.52) \quad (1.42)$$

ECM equation

$$\Delta\ \text{Log Rr} = 0.0489 + 0.5627\ \Delta\text{Log Yn} - 1.00\ \text{Resrr}_{(-1)}$$
$$t \quad (0.96) \quad (1.50) \quad -$$

$R^{2(adj.)} = 0.57$ DW$=2.21$ SEE$= 0.040$

Finally, the gap between total expenditure (non-development expenditure plus development expenditure) and revenue receipts, represented as gross fiscal deficit, is financed either by market

6. The similar specification was attempted for revenue receipts as well which was considered inappropriate as the coefficient of the residual series of the long-run relationship in the ECM equation turned out to be much greater than one.

borrowings, including borrowings from the commercial banks and other market borrowings, or borrowings from the Reserve Bank of India. For the purpose of this model, borrowings of the Central Government from commercial banks and RBI are clubbed together, represented as ΔBcg.

1.4 Monetary Sector

Monetary sector is modeled at the aggregate level (M_3). By identity, M_3,

$$M_3 = Bcg + Bccs + Nfea + Om_3$$

Of these, Bcg and Nfea have been endogenised and Bccs and 'Om_3' are treated as exogenous variables.

1.4.1 Bank Credit to the Government

Bank credit to the government (Bcg) equals the fiscal gap between revenue receipts, other receipts and total expenditure by identity.

$$\Delta Bcg = Nde + Gde - Rr - Otrc$$

1.4.2 Bank Credit to the Commercial Sector and Prime Lending Rate

Bank credit to the commercial sector (Bccs) has been as a kept as an exogenous variable. The credit demand function is estimated for its use in the output as an instrument. This equation is also used while conducting a policy simulation experiment of assessing the impact of changes in the Bank rate on the other macro variables. Banks credit to the commercial sector could be assumed to be exogenous (policy variable) since the RBI can influence the supply of bank credit to the commercial sector (Bccs) by adjusting the cash reserve ratio (CRR) while keeping the reserve money unchanged.[7] In this framework, changes in Bccs would influence prime lending rate, which in turn is likely to influence investment, especially in the private sector. Real bank credit to the commercial sector, (i.e. Bccs/Wpi) is estimated as a function of real output (Yr), the real prime lending rate ($Plr\text{-}P^e$) and a dummy variable for pre-reform period.

7. Reduction in CRR causes a rise in the money multiplier and thus the same reserve money causes more monetary expansion.

Long-run equation:

$$\text{LogBccs/Wpi} = -4.2277 + 1.2277\text{Log Yr} - 0.6189\ (\text{Pl-P}^{e}) + 0.1211\text{Der}$$
$$t \quad (5.14)\ (20.53) \qquad (1.27) \qquad (3.10)$$

ECM equation:

$$\Delta\ \text{LogBccs/Wpi} = 0.0372 + 0.4844\ \Delta\ \text{Log Yr} - 0.7281\text{Resbccs}_{(-1)}$$
$$t \quad (1.39) \quad (1.04) \qquad (2.98)$$

$R^{2(adj.)} = 0.49$ DW= 1.11 SEE=0.0305

The lending rate (Plr), in the long run, is estimated as a function of the Bank rate (and a dummy variable for the pre-reform period).

$$\text{Plr} = 0.0470 + 1.00\ \text{Br} + 0.0175\ \text{Der}$$
$$t \quad (2.53) \quad (5.62) \quad (2.52)$$

Plr in the short-run is estimated as a function of changes in Br and changes in the bank credit to the commercial sector, representing liquidity conditions in the market.

ECM equation:

$$\Delta\text{Plr} = 0.0066 + 0.8340\ \Delta\text{Br} - 0.0577\ \Delta\text{Log Bccs} - 0.7964\ \text{Resplr}_{(-1)}$$
$$t \quad (0.49) \quad (1.86) \quad (0.62) \qquad (2.40)$$

$R^{2(adj)} = 0.18$ DW=1.90 SEE=0.0126

Although the equation seems appropriate in itself, its impact on the collective performance of the model was not satisfactory especially when the model was solved in a dynamic mode. In view of these limitations of this ECM equation, for policy simulation purposes, a long-run relationship has been considered.

1.5 External Sector

In this model, we estimated empirical relationships for exports of goods (Expg) and imports of goods (Impg) whereas net invisible receipts (Ninvr) and capital account (Cap) are treated exogenously. Finally, the net effect of these changes in the external sector components are linked with the monetary sector through an identity:

$$\Delta\ Nfea = Expg + Ninvr - Impg + Cap + Eom$$

Eom is the balancing factor between changes in Nfea on the monetary side and changes in the reserves on the balance of payments side.

1.5.1 Exports of Goods

In India external trade is generally invoiced in foreign currency denominations and then converted into rupees. Thus, changes in exchange rate leads to rupee value of exports and imports with no change in fundamental factor. In order to eliminate this problem, these two variables are estimated by measuring them in US $ terms (as in Rao and Singh (1995)). Because India's share of trade in the world trade is relatively small, the long run relationship for exports of goods from India is postulated as a function of its real output. The reforms to this sector, especially the opening of the Indian economy, have also significantly affected the external trade. A number of proxy variables were considered as potential indicator of 'openness' for the export equation. The variables tried were the ratio of net foreign exchange assets to broad money (Nfea/M_3) and a time trend. However, these measures of 'openness' were found to be empirically inappropriate. Another possible variable is the reduction in the restrictions on imports. Since information on effective custom duty is readily available from 1993, it was used as a proxy variable representing 'openness' in the external sector in India. Thus, the long-run relationship for exports was estimated as a function of real output and a dummy variable for the pre-reform period and a variable indicating effective custom duty (Impord). In the short-run, exports of goods is considered to be affected by the changes in the real output of industrial countries (dlgdpic) and changes in the real exchange rate (Leavgr=Log (Wpi*(Eavg/Wpi)). A large part of exports, especially diamond related items, is re-exported. To capture such an effect, (changes in) imports in the previous year, is included as an additional variable.

Long-run equation:

$$\text{Log Expg/ Eavg} = \underset{(-4.60)}{-10.9303} \underset{(9.09)}{+1.4166} \text{ Log Yr} \underset{(1.72)}{-0.1515} \text{ Log imord} \underset{(1.12)}{-0.0766} \text{ Der}$$

t (-4.60) (9.09) (1.72) (1.12)

ECM equation:

$$\Delta\text{LogExpg/Eavg} = -0.0154 + 2.4496\Delta\text{LogGdpic} + 0.4649\Delta(\text{LogImpg/Eavg})_{-1}$$

t (0.21) (1.07) (2.32)

$$+\ 0.3414\ \Delta\text{Log Eavgr}_{(-1)}\ -0.5632\text{Resexpg}_{(-1)}$$

(0.92) (2.20)

$R^{2(adj.)}=0.32$ DW=1.45 SEE=0.0722

1.5.2 Imports of Goods

Imports of goods, measured in USA \$, are postulated as a function of real output in the long run. To take into account of the shift in policy, a pre-reform dummy variable is included. The reduction in custom duty (Imord), is also included in the relationship for the same reasons as discussed above.

Long-run equation:

$$\text{Log Impg/Eavg} = \underset{(3.28)}{-8.3926} + \underset{(7.72)}{1.2892}\ \text{Log Yr} + \underset{(1.96)}{0.1432}\ \text{Der} - \underset{(3.04)}{0.2861}\ \text{Log Imord}$$

t values in parentheses.

Imports of goods in the short-run are modeled as a function of changes in real output and changes in the real exchange rate.

ECM equation:

$$\Delta\text{Log Impg/Eavg} = -\underset{(1.54)}{0.0827} + \underset{(3.68)}{3.0243}\ \Delta\text{Log Yr} - \underset{(1.32)}{0.3874}\ \Delta\text{Log Eavgr} - \underset{(2.88)}{0.8084}\ \text{Resimpg}_{(-1)}$$

t values in parentheses.

$R^{2(adj.)} = 0.76$ DW=1.97 SEE=0.0630

1.6 Prices

1.6.1 Investment and GDP Deflators

The GDP deflator is obtained as a function of Wpi and unit value index of imports (Mp).

$$\text{Log Ydf} = -\underset{(3.20)}{0.5159} + \underset{(20.20)}{0.9951}\ \text{Log Wpi} + \underset{(1.62)}{0.0929}\text{Log Mp} + \underset{(1.66)}{0.03597}\ \text{Der}$$

t values in parentheses.

ECM Equation:

$$\Delta\text{Log Ydf} = \underset{(2.27)}{0.0207} + \underset{(6.05)}{0.7202}\ \Delta\text{Log Wpi} + \underset{(1.42)}{0.0566}\ \Delta\text{Log Mp} - \underset{(2.06)}{0.4260}\ \text{Resydf}_{(-1)}$$

t values in parentheses.

$R^{2(adj.)}=0.73$ DW=1.49 SEE=0.0125

The above equation suggests that in the short-run a 1 per cent rise in the price level raises the income deflator by 0.72 per cent. In long run, however, this impact works out to be around 1 per cent.

Similarly, investment deflator is modelled as a function of Wpi and the unit value index of imports.

Long-run relationship

$$\text{Log Idf} = -0.0705 + 0.7453 \text{ Log Wpi} + 0.2134 \text{ Log Mp}$$
$$t \quad (-1.01) \quad (16.43) \quad (4.86)$$

ECM equation:

$$\Delta \text{ Log Idf} = 0.0022 + 0.7616\ \Delta \text{ Log Wpi} + 0.2033\ \Delta \text{ Log Mp}$$
$$t \quad (0.21) \quad (5.98) \quad (4.09)$$
$$- 1.00 \text{ Residf}_{(-1)}$$
$$(3.71)$$

$R^{2(adj.)} = 0.77$ DW=1.30 SEE=0.0130

A 1 per cent rise in the price level, increase the income deflator by 0.76 per cent in the short-run and by a similar magnitude in the long-run.

1.6.2 Price Level

In the long run, inflation in India is assumed to be a monetary phenomenon and the long-run link between money and price is assumed to be in the quantity theory framework. Though, some studies suggest that the link between narrow money and prices is stronger (Bhattacharya, Barman and Nag, 1994), we use broad money (M_3) since in India monetary policy is primarily concerned with it. The definition of narrow money also varies across time.[8] Thus, the long run relationship for WPI is postulated as a function of broad money (M_3) and real output (Yr). Two dummy variables, for the years 1999-2000 and 2001-20002, when inflation in India was moderate despite strong monetary expansion, and another for the period from 1985-86 to 1989-90, have also been included in the equation. The Long run impact of the money on the prices is assumed to be unity.

$$\text{Log Wpi} = 11.4565 + 1.00 \text{ Log } M_3 - 1.4602 \text{ Log Yr} - 0.0525 \text{ Der}$$
$$t \quad (1.54) \quad - \quad (24.36) \quad (1.64)$$
$$-0.0559 \text{ dwp20}$$
$$(1.62)$$

8. For analytical purposes of monetary management in India, reference may be made to Vasudevan (1991).

The elasticity of money demand at 1.46 is very close to 1.50 used by the RBI while following monetary targeting approach till very recent period. In the short-run, however, wholesale prices in India are likely to be affected by changes in the prices of food articles, energy prices as well money and output. Accordingly, short-run changes in WPI are postulated as a function of both demand and supply factors. Changes in food articles and energy prices are included as supply shock variables whereas changes in broad money represent the demand side factor.

$$\Delta LogWpi = 0.0272 + 0.2764\,\Delta Log\,M_3 - 0.2677\Delta Log\,Yr + 0.1836\Delta LogWpifa$$

$$t \quad (0.58) \quad (1.16) \qquad (1.05) \qquad (1.63)$$

$$+0.0463dwpi20 + 0.0828\,Log\,Wpie \; -0.4554\,Reswpi_{(-1)}$$

$$(2.64) \qquad (0.95) \qquad (2.94)$$

$$R^{2(adj.)} = 0.64 \quad DW=1.43 \quad SEE=0.0167$$

1.7 Discussion

Real output turned out to be a satisfactory function of the capital sock in the long run. In the short-run, however, bank credit and rainfall have major influence on the output performance. Private investment is determined as a function of (nominal) output and to a certain extent by real prime lending rate also. Impact of public sector investment on the private investment turned out to be positive but comparatively low. Incidentally, public sector investment turned to be an exact function of the government development expenditure. Revenue receipts can be successfully modeled as a function of nominal output, implying identical impact of real output and prices, whereas in case of non-development expenditure, real output and prices show differential effect. Prime lending rate responds to the Bank rate satisfactorily in the long run whereas in the short-run their relationship is weak. Export equation turned out to be poor as compared to import equation. In both the equations, factor affecting them indicated desired impact. But statistically, many were insignificant in the export equation. GDP and investment deflators turned out to be satisfactory function of price level and unit value index of imports. A long run relationship for prices could be determined in the quantity theory framework, though the use of two dummy variables became essential to satisfy stationarity properties of the residuals of the (long-run) relationship. In the short-run, impact of food articles turned out to be stronger as compared to energy prices, both in terms of 'size' and 't' values of the coefficients.

2. COLLECTIVE PERFORMANCE OF THE MODE

Before conducting policy simulations or making use of the model for policy design purposes or obtaining forecasts, it is essential to evaluate the collective performance of the model. In other words, though the estimates of the individual equations of the model may be satisfactory, it is necessary to test their collective performance and goodness of fit as a whole by obtaining a simultaneous solution. The technique of simulation has been used for this purpose. In simulation, an iterative procedure is used to solve the simultaneous equation system for the set of endogenous variables. Both static and dynamic simulation solutions are obtained. In static simulation, the actual lagged values of the endogenous variables are used in obtaining the solution whereas in dynamic simulation only the initial values of the data are used. Simulated values are used for the subsequent periods. Thus, in static simulation the results represent a step-ahead solution, without any inter-period linkages through the values of endogenous variables generated by the model in the previous periods. In the dynamic simulation, estimates of the various endogenous variables are linked over the period and, therefore, the solution reflects a dynamic time-path of the endogenous variables. Both simulations were conducted for a period of 17 years, from 1985-86 to 2001-02. The simulation has been conducted at levels, by suitable transformation of the growth rates.

In assessing the goodness of fit of the model, two measures of collective performance have been considered: (i) mean absolute percentage error (MAPE) and (ii) root mean square percentage error (RMSPE). MAPE and RMSPE of the important endogenous variables are given in Table 6.1.

These results are reasonably encouraging. Though the model is small but the structure of the Indian economy changed markedly over the same period, the errors are not too large. They are relatively big for investment and trade data, partly because of the issues discussed earlier and partly because that these variables seem to be inherently difficult to model. The result suggests that the model could be used for control theoretic exercises, discussed in the Section.

Table 6.1

Mean Absolute Percentage Error and Root Mean Square Percentage Error of the Important Endogenous Variables-Static and Dynamic Simulation Smpl: 1985-86- 2001-02

(Per cent)

Variable	*Static Simulation-MAPE*	*Static Simulation-RMSPE*	*Dynamic Simulation-MAPE*	*Dynamic Simulation-RMSPE*
Yr	0.82	1.04	1.29	1.53
Wpi	1.17	1.40	2.46	2.96
Kr	0.37	0.46	1.04	1.18
Ir	4.71	5.91	4.82	5.71
Ipn	4.64	6.46	6.92	8.53
Ign	7.87	9.71	6.40	7.66
Nde	2.48	3.58	2.76	3.72
Rr	3.43	3.97	3.79	4.46
M_3	1.30	1.70	1.72	1.96
Expg	6.40	7.94	6.94	9.00
Impg	3.64	4.91	4.78	5.69
Idf	4.72	1.93	2.54	2.96
Ydf	2.50	1.20	1.90	2.33

3. SETTING UP THE OPTIMAL CONTROL EXPERIMENTS

The application of control theory for deriving policy options in fact involves minimising the objective function:

$$J = 1/2\sum_{t=1}^{T}\left[\left(X_t - X_t^*\right)Q\left(X_t - X_t^*\right) + \left(U_t - U_t^*\right)R\left(U_t - U_t^*\right)\right]$$

Such that

$$X_t = A\,X_{t-1} + B\,U_t + C\,Z_t + D$$

Where X_t^* and U_t^* indicates the desired values of the state (Xt) and control (Ut) variables, respectively. Zt represent exogenous variables. A, B and C are regression coefficient of the lagged state variables, control variables and exogenous variables, respectively. D represents intercept terms. Q and R are the penalty matrices for the state and control variables, respectively. The application of control theory involves either using dynamic programming or the discrete maximum principle and obtaining a feedback equation, known as Ricatti equation in control literature, as given below:

$U_t = g_t + G_t X_{t-1}$

Where g_t and G_t embody the desired values of both the state and control variables, estimated coefficients and the exogenous variables. Thus once U_1 is obtained using given values of X_0, the optimal values of the state variables in time period 1, i.e, X_1 are obtained which in turn yield U_2. Thus the entire sequence of U_t and X_t can be computed recursively. In case the model is non-linear in nature, it involves two approaches. As per the first approach, non-linear model could be linearised appropriately and make use of the control methods. Alternative approach is to treat the problem of minimising a policy objective function subject to a non-linear programming problem.

3.2 The Cost Functional

One should remember that we are penalising for per cent deviations from the nominal in each case and because the variables are scaled differently, their assigned weights will have different scales.

Since all variables are not of equal size, in order to have equal relative weights, the actual weights have to be compensated for the size of the variables. The actual weight of any two variables could be calculated from the formula:

$$(X_1 - \overline{X}_1)^2 * W_1 = (X_2 - \overline{X}_2)^2 * W_2$$

Since the size of each variable varies through time, actual weights to be assigned to each variable can be approximated by using their mean values. For instance, if variable X_2 has an average magnitude of 100 and variable X_1 has a magnitude of 10, an equal 10 per cent deviation from their desired paths will imply, according to the above formulae:

$(10)^2 * W_1 = (1.0)^2 * W_2$

Normalising and setting $W_1 = 1.00$ yields:

$W_2 = [(10)^2 / (1)^2] = 100$

Therefore, in order to have equal relative emphasis, the weight of X_2 , i.e., W_2 has to be hundred times larger. Following the above procedure, the relative weights for the state and control variables have been worked out and are reported below in Tables 6.2 and 6.3 respectively. Desired trajectories of the state variables (*viz.* Yr and Wpi) are given in Table 6.4.

Table 6.2

Equal Relative Weights for the State Variables

(Q Matrix)

Sr. No	*Variable*	*Mean*	*(Mean)²*	*Relative Weight*
1.	Wpi	147.16	21656	798852401
2.	Yr	1169233	1.37E+12	12.65
3.	Kr	4155591	1.73E+13	1
4.	Ir	294698	8.68E+10	199.2
5.	Gcfr	305868	9.36E+10	184.91
6.	Gcfn	432578	1.87E+11	92.45
7.	Ipn	306820	9.41E10	183.77
8.	Ign	125757.8	1.58E+10	1093.90
9.	Idf	140.7	19802.7	8.7E+08
10.	Nde	173794	3.02E+10	572.7
11.	RR	171781	2.95E+10	586.2
12.	Ydf	152.6	23299	7.43E+08
13.	Yn	1751199	3.07E+12	5.64
14.	M3	1147938	1.32E+12	13.12
15.	Dbcg	59562	3.55E+09	4876
16.	Bcg	451415	2.04E+11	84.89
17.	Nfea	217269	4.72E+10	366
18.	Dnfea	41847	1.75E+09	9878.9
19.	Impg	235195	5.53E+10	312.7
20.	Expg	166567	2.77E+10	623.5
21.	Plr	0.124	0.0153	1.13E+15

Table 6.3

Equal Relative Weights for the Control Variables

(R Matrix)

Sr. No	*Variable*	*Mean*	*(Mean)²*	*Relative Weight*
1.	Eavg	43.18	1865	180157902
2.	Gde	135230	1.83E+10	18
3.	Br	0.08	0.0064	5.25E+13
4.	Obccs	579290	3.36E+11	1.0

Table 6.4

Trajectories of the Target Variables

Year	*Wpi*	*Yr*
1997-98	132.8 (4.3)	1016594 (4.7)
1998-99	138.8 (4.5)	1062166 (7.0)
1999-00	145.0 (4.5)	1152264 (7.0)
2000-01	151.5 (4.5)	1212084 (7.0)
2001-02	158.4 (4.5)	1291582 (7.0)

Note: Figures in brackets represent their growth rates.

3.3 The Results

In all the following experiments, numerical solutions are obtained using specific cost functional form, which are suitably modified in accordance with the results of the previous experiments, so as to iteratively extract an optimal set of weights from dynamic responses of the model.

When actually carrying out the experiments and interpreting the results, it is important to realise the fact that the cost functional accumulates penalties only over the finite planning horizon. As a result many a time we notice anomaly that has generally manifested itself in the form of peculiar behaviour pattern in the optimal paths of certain control variables towards the planning period. The practical solution to this problem has been to extend the planning horizon beyond the period of actual interest by as many time periods as the maximum control delay.

Another problem, which we encountered while solving this model, is that the optimal values of the state and control variables fluctuated widely over the planning horizon. We understand that such results are the manifestation of the structure of the model estimated in the error-correction form, which inherently assumes the economic system to be moving from equilibrium to dis-equilibrium and again back to equilibrium. In view of these results, discussion on the optimal values is based on the average values of the state and control variables for the three years, omitting first and the last year of the planning horizon.

3.3.1 Base Run

In this run base level solution is obtained keeping all the target variables at their actual levels. Similarly penalty matrices for both the state and control variables (Q and R matrices) have been retained keeping equal weights to all variables. In a way the solution so obtained is the identical to the 'shadow pricing' of the state and control variables. The difference between the actual and optimal values of the state variables could be considered as the level of dis-equilibrium between them.

Table 6.5

Actual Versus Optimal Values of the State and Control Variables

(Per cent)

Sr. No	*Variable*	*Actual*	*Optimal*
1.	Inflation	5.3	5.0
2.	Growth	5.5	5.9
3.	Money supply	15.6	14.5
4.	Bank credit	14.9	12.9

Empirical results of the above Table reflects that during the period of 1998-99 to 2000-01 the performance of the Indian economy, in terms of inflation, growth, money supply expansion and bank credit was largely in consonance with the economic structure. Based on these results, optimal growth works out a little above at around 6 per cent, as against actual growth of 5.5 per cent. Incidentally optimal values of monetary aggregates, in terms of money supply and bank credit were placed about 1 percentage point and 2 percentages point lower than actually observed reflecting that monetary policy during these years has been comparatively more flexible and accommodative in nature in order to accelerate the growth performance.

3.3.2 Optimising Growth Rate

In this experiment we have attempted to stabalise the economy at a higher growth level by way of enhancing public sector investment.

Empirical results suggests that in order to raise the average growth rate from 5.5 per cent as observed during the period under consideration public sector investment should be accelerated by about 12 per cent more. This policy however leads to price rise by about 0.6 percentage point. Optimal values of the state and control variables are as given in Table 6.6.

Table 6.6

Optimal Values of the State and Control Variables

(Per cent)

Sr. No	*Variable*	*Optimal*
1.	Inflation	5.9
2.	Growth	6.3
3.	Money supply	16.7
4.	Bank credit to commercial sector	15.0

Note: Optimal values in money growth and bank credit works out to be 16.7 per cent and 15.0 per cent, respectively.

3.3.3 Optimising Inflation Rate

In this experiment attempt has been made to work out the policy options to reduce the inflation rate, say at 4.5 per cent. For this experiment reduction in monetary aggregates has been effected through the reduction in bank credit to the government, which in turn necessitates fall in government capital expenditure. Empirical results of the policy option are as given in Table 6.7.

Table 6.7

Optimal Values of the State and Control Variables

(Per cent)

Sr. No	*Variable*	*Optimal*
1.	Inflation	4.6
2.	Growth	5.8
3.	Money supply	14.2
4.	Bank credit to commercial sector	14.5

Empirical results suggest that for maintaining inflation rate at around 4.6 per cent, given prices of the food articles and energy prices intact, desired monetary expansion works out to be around 14.2 per cent. Similarly, desired level of the bank credit rise work out to be around 14.5 per cent and likely growth could be around 5.8 per cent, respectively.

3.3.4 Optimising Growth and Inflation Rate

In this experiment an attempt is made to work out the policy options to maintain lower inflation, at around 4.5 per cent, and higher growth at around 7 per cent. In this experiment, policy options are based on monetary and fiscal variables. However, appropriately policy variables like interest rate, etc. also could be attempted. Initial experiments revealed the infeasibility of keeping low inflation and attaining high growth within the existing structure. One of the limitations which reflected that though higher growth is feasible by way of augmenting higher level of government development expenditure but the same policy options also resulted in a higher level of money supply, causing an unfeasible solution for the lower price level. The only feasible policy option appears to raise the government development expenditure, as high as about 1.5 per cent of the existing level and neutralise its monetary expansion effect either by reducing non-development expenditure or way of raising resources by expanding the tax base and also improving the tax collection mechanism. As regards monetary sector, the feasible growth rate work out to be about 13 per cent in money supply and about 16.5 in bank credit to the commercial sector.

Table 6.8

Optimal Values of Target and Control Variables

Sr. No	*Variable*	*Optimal*
1.	Inflation	4.4
2.	Growth	6.8
3.	Money supply	13.1
4.	Bank credit	16.7

3.3.5 Policy Implications of the Above Control Experiments

These results appear to have policy implications both from the methodology of control theory as well as political economy point of view.

1. In this paper the model is estimated in an ECM framework. This implicitly assumes that economy moves from dis-equilibrium to equilibrium and then again to dis-equilibrium. In this framework, the control policy experiments may have dual objectives. First objective could be to restore the equilibrium of the target variables, say growth and inflation around their mean levels, as reflected from the existing economic system. Alternatively, the objective could be to raise the equilibrium itself of the economy, from low growth and high inflation. Empirical results of this paper revealed that trajectories of the control variables were not very smooth, rather revealed a fluctuating behaviour. The analysis in this paper, therefore, is based on average values (of the state and control variables).
2. Another important policy implications appears to be that policy design should be comparatively flexible in nature, especially when the policy objectives are to maintain the equilibrium rather than to attain a certain equilibrium level.
3. Another implication of this study, specifically to the Indian economy, appears to be that the issue of gross fiscal deficit needs to be resolved by raising more revenue resources rather than curtailing expenditure, especially development expenditure. Thus, in order to raise the level of equilibrium of the economy to a higher growth trajectory, say 7 per cent, revenue receipts should be raised substantially, say by 50 per cent above the existing level. Though these findings appears to be un-plausible but an international comparison of tax performance suggests inevitability of such policy measures. As per IMF, total tax to gross domestic product (GDP) ratio of the industrial countries was placed at 31.60 (in 1985) in relation to tax to GDP ratio of the low-income-countries at 14.60 per cent (Linn and Wetzel, IMF, 1990). This reflects

that in case similar to the industrial countries, if in India also revenue resources are enhanced by widening the tax base i.e. by bringing all sectors of the economy under the purview of taxation, there would be an increase in the capital formation, which in turn should lead to raise the trajectory of growth to a higher level without inducing any inflationary pressure in the economy.

4. SUMMARY AND BROAD CONCLUSIONS

In this paper a model relating to the Indian economy is estimated in the error correction framework, thus encompassing long-run and short-run dynamics into it. Thereafter model is simulated in a dynamic mode and its collective performance turned out to be satisfactory. Based on the model so evaluated certain control theoretic experiments have been conducted with a view to obtain policy options in order to stabilise the economy (a) at a high growth trajectory of 7 per cent and no constraint on prices; (b) low inflation at 4.5 per cent and no constraint on growth, and finally (c) high growth and low inflation.

Our empirical results suggest that high growth of about 6.86 per cent is feasible within the existing economic structure accompanied with a relatively higher (as compared to the existing level) of around 5.5 per cent. Desired level of broad money supply expansion works out to be around 15 per cent and desired level of bank credit to the commercial sector works out to be around 14 per cent. As regards lower level inflation, at around 4.6 per cent, the growth rate also turns out to be lower at around 5.8 per cent accompanied with monetary expansion and bank credit increase at around 14 per cent both. Further, empirical results indicated that over a longer horizon it may not be feasible to maintain higher growth and low inflation unless public sector investment is stepped up substantially and resources for the higher level of private investment are generated either downsizing non-development expenditure or by of augmenting revenue receipts by way of covering all the sectors of the economy for tax purposes rather than raising tax rate.

Annexure 6A.1

List of Endogenous Variables

Sr. No.	*Variable*	*Description*	*Unit*
1.	Yr	Gross domestic product at factor cost	Amount in Rs. at 1993-94 prices
2.	Yn	Gross domestic product at factor cost	Amount in Rs. at current prices
3.	Kr	Capital stock (cumulated investment from 1970-71 onwards)	Amount in Rs. at 1993-94 prices
4.	Ir	Investment during the year	Amount in Rs. at 1993-94 prices
5.	In	Investment during the year	Amount in Rs. at current prices
6.	Ipn	Private investment during the year	Amount in Rs. at current prices
7.	Ign	Public sector investment during the year	Amount in Rs. at current prices
8.	Rr	Revenue receipts of the Central government	Amount in Rs. at current prices
9.	Nde	Non-development expenditure of the Central government	Amount in Rs. at current prices
10.	Bcg	Banks' credit to the government	Amount in Rs. at current prices
11.	M_3	Broad money	Amount in Rs. at current prices
12.	Wpi	Whole sale price index	Index, 1993-94=100
13.	Ydf	Deflator for nominal income	Index, 1993-94=100
14.	Idf	Deflator for nominal investment	Index, 1993-94=100
15.	Impg	Imports of goods	Amount in Rs. at current prices.
16.	Expg	Exports of goods	Amount in Rs. at current prices
17.	Nfea	Net foreign exchange assets of the banking sector	Amount in Rs. at current prices
18.	Plr	Prime lending rate (advance rate of the State Bank of India)	Rate

List of Exogenous Variables

Sr. No.	*Variable*	*Description*	*Unit*
1.	Br	Bank rate	Rate
2.	Pe	Expected inflation	Rate
3.	Gde	Government development expenditure	Amount in Rs. at current prices
4.	Rif	Rainfall index	Index
5.	Bccs	Banks' credit to the commercial sector	Amount in Rs. at current prices
6.	OM3	Other components of broad money supply (=M3—Bcg-Bccs-Nfea)	Amount in Rs. at current price
7.	Eavg	Exchange rate	Rs per US$
8.	Wpic	Price index for industrial countries	Index, 1997=100
9.	Gdpic	Output index for industrial countries	Index, 1997=100
10.	Cap	Capital account balances	Amount in Rs. at current prices
11.	Eom	Balancing factor between BoP and monetary identity	Amount in Rs. at current prices
12.	Imord	Effective custom duty rate	Rate
13.	Ninvr	Net invisible receipts	Amount in Rs. at current price
14.	Wpie	Wholesale price index for energy price	Index, 1993-94=100
15.	Wpifa	Wholesale price index for food articles	Index, 1993-94=100
16.	Mp	Unit value index of imports	Index,
17.	Otrc	Other receipts of the Central government	Amount in Rs. at current prices
18.	Der	Dummy for pre-reform period	'1' for the period 1985-86 to 1989-90 and '0' for rest of the period.
19.	Dwp20	Dummy for Wpi	'1' for 1999-00 and 20001-02 and '0' for rest of the period
20.	Time	Time trend	1,2,.......,17

References

Anjaneyulu. D.(1993). "Macro Economic Linkages in the Indian Economy: Inter-Links between Imports, Output, Exchange Rate and External Debt", *RBI Occasional Papers*, December 1993.

Aoki, M. (1976). *Optimal Control and Systems Theory in Dynamic Economic Analysis*, North-Holland, Amsterdam.

Barnanke, B.S. and M. Gertler (1995). "Inside the Black Box; the Credit Channel of the Monetary Policy Transmission", *Journal of Economic Perspective*, 9(4),Fall.

Bhattacharya, B.B, R.B. Barman and A.K. Nag (1994). "Stabilisation Policy Options— A Macro-econometric Analysis", *RBI, Development Research Group*, 8.

Blejer, M.I. and M.S. Khan (1984). *Government Policy and Private Investment in Developing Countries*, International Monetary Fund, Washington, D.C.

Chow, G.C. (1975). *Analysis and Control of Dynamic Economic Systems*, John Wiley & Sons , New York.

Engle, R.F. and C.W.J. Granger (1987). *Cointegration and Error Correction: Representation and Testing*, Econometrica, 55.

Engle, R.F. and C.W.J. Granger, (eds.) (1991). *Long Run Economic Relations: Readings in Cointegration*, Oxford University Press, Oxford.

Jadhav, Narendar and Balwant Singh (1990). "Fiscal – Monetary Dynamics in India – An Econometric Model", *Economic and Political Weekly*, January 29, 1990.

Kendrick, D. (1981). *Stochastic Control for Economic Models*, McGraw Hill, Inc., New York.

Linn, F. Johannes and Deborah L. Wetzel (eds) (1990). "Public Finance, Trade and Development: What Have We Learned?", in *Fiscal Policy in Open Developing Economies*, I.M.F., Washington, D.C.

Lucas Jr. R.E. (1976). "Econometric Policy Evaluation: A Critique", in Brunner, K. and Meltzer, A. (eds), The Phillips Curve and Labour Markets, *Supplement to the Journal of Monetary Economics*.

Mahadeva, L and P. Sinclair (2001). *The Transmission of Monetary Policy*, Mimeo, Centre for Central Banking Studies, Bank of England.

Palanivl, T. and Lawrence Klein (1999). "An Econometric Model for India with Special Reference to Monetary Sector", *The Developing Economies* (XXXVII).

Pani, P. K. (1984). "An Econometric Model of the Indian Economy with Special Reference to Output, Demand and Prices", *RBI Occasional Papers*, 1984.

Rangarajan, C. and R.R. Arif (1990). "Money, Output and Prices: A Macro-Econometric Model", *Economic and Political Weekly*, April 1990.

Rao, M.J. Manohar (1987). *Filtering and Control of Macroeconomic Systems*, North-Holland, Amsterdam.

Rao. M.J. Manohar and Balwant Singh (1995). "Analytical Foundations of Financial Programming and Growth Oriented Adjustment", *RBI, Development Research Group*, 10.

Reddy, Y.V. (1999). "Monetary Policy Operating Procedures in India", *BIS Policy Papers*, 5, March 1999.

Reserve Bank of India, *Report on Currency and Finance*, 2000-01 and 2001-02".

Sarma, Y.S.R. (1982). "Government Deficit, Money Supply and Inflation in India", *RBI Occasional Papers*.

Sarma, Y.S.R. (1991). "Money, Output and Prices", *RBI Occasional Papers*, December 1991.

Sastry, D.V.S., Balwant Singh and Indernil Bhattacharya (2001). "Money, Output and Prices: A Small Macro-model Relating to the Indian Economy", *Mimeo, Paper presented at a Seminar at the Department of Economics*, Mumbai University, Mumbai.

Sastry, D.V.S, Balwant Singh, Kaushik Bhattachryaand and N.K. Unnikrishnan(2003). "Sectoral Linkages and Growth Prospects: Some Reflections on the Indian Economy", *Economic and Political Weekly*, June, 2003.

Singh Balwant (2003). "A Forecasting and Policy Simulation Oriented Small Macro-Model for the Indian Economy", *Mimeo, Paper Prepared at the Centre for Central Bank Studies (CCBS), Bank of England,* London, from June 9 to August 29, 2003, as a follow-up of the research workshop on *Forecasting in Central Banks*.

Vasudevan, A. (1991). "Analytics of Monetary Management", *RBI Occasional Papers*, December 1991.

7

Comparing Measures of Core Inflation for India

AJIT R. JOSHI
RAJASHREE RAJPATHAK

Introduction

One of the major objectives of the central banks, all around the world, is maintaining price stability. The price stability does not, however, mean maintaining constant prices. The objective of price stability translates into maintaining low and stable inflation rate, which is considered to be conducive to economic growth and employment generation. In some countries, the central banks have additional policy objectives such as maintaining stable exchange rate, ensuring fast economic growth, etc. However, among these objectives price stability has an overriding role in most countries, sometimes in the explicit form as inflation targeting.

Therefore, measurement of inflation correctly has been a matter of debate. As the traditional measures of inflation have been found to be inadequate in capturing the underlying inflation process, new set of measures derived from the traditional price statistics, termed as core inflation have been in use. In the literature, several methods of computing the core inflation measures have been suggested. While each measure of core inflation has certain advantages, it is necessary that an acceptable measure satisfies certain criteria. The present study compares core inflation measures constructed using two popular methodologies, namely exclusion and trimmed means in the Indian context against a widely accepted set of evaluation criteria.

The next section surveys various measures of core inflation suggested in the literature. Section 2 provides details of the core inflation measures computed and compared in this study. Section 3 discusses the tests proposed for the core measures are discussed along with their rationale and applicability in the Indian context. Empirical results are discussed in Section 4 and the last section provides concluding observations.

SECTION 1: CORE INFLATION MEASURES IN LITERATURE

Definition of Core Inflation

Some countries, particularly developed ones, have adopted explicit inflation targeting framework for the monetary policy. While adopting inflation targeting, the question whether the headline inflation rate measured by the Consumer Price Index (CPI) is an appropriate measure to be targeted, or not, arises. The headline inflation rate, particularly the monthly rate measured as growth over the corresponding month of the previous year, is considered to be too volatile. Such headline measures may get affected due to one-off price changes. The transient shocks to the system also get mixed up with the underlying inflationary trend and therefore, such measure might provide confusing signals to the policymakers. There is also the so-called "base effect" where the unusual movements in the previous year also affect the measured inflation rate in the current year. Apart from the issues of "noise" in the price index data, there are also arguments, which suggest that the ability (or otherwise) of the central bank to control the prices of the commodities included in the price index basket should also be taken into account while constructing an appropriate measure of inflation.

The persistent components of inflation have been termed by many commentators as *Core Inflation or Underlying Trend Inflation*. In spite of wide spread use of the term "core inflation", there is no unanimity among the researchers about the definition of core inflation. Some definitions of core inflation found in the literature are as follows: (i) Bryan and Cecchetti (1993) have suggested that core inflation relates to the growth rate of the money supply; (ii) Blinder (1997) identifies core inflation with the 'durable' part of inflation; and (iii) Quah and Vahey (1995) define core inflation as '...that component of measured inflation that has no medium to long-run impact on real output'.

Conceptually, a distinction can be made between measures designed for policy assessment (i.e. to define inflation target) and those designed to help set policy to achieve a given objective (i.e. as leading indicators of the inflation target). If the core inflation measure is intended as a target variable, it is crucial that it is credible, transparent and not subject to revision, in order to facilitate policy assessment. The emphasis may be on finding a measure of underlying inflation which excludes transient fluctuations, and perhaps also price disturbances which are 'out of the control' of the monetary authorities. If, however, the core inflation measure were designed to help set policy then, we would be interested in a measure that provides good information about the future inflation. The focus is then on finding a good leading indicator of inflation, rather than on measuring true current inflation rate. However, the distinction is less obvious in practice, and empirical approaches to core inflation tend to strip out similar sorts of shocks, whether the measure is intended as a target or as a leading indicator.

In India, the inflation rate is measured in terms of Wholesale Price Index (WPI), in absence of a comprehensive and All India Consumer Price Index (CPI). Although Indian monetary policy has not adopted inflation-targeting approach, the issues relating to the appropriateness of using core inflation measures for monitoring the price developments are relevant in the Indian context also.

Methods of Computing Core Inflation

For computation of core inflation, various methodologies have been proposed in the literature. One class of these methodologies is statistical in nature while the other class makes the use of economic theory for estimating core inflation measures. What follows is a brief review of various methods proposed in the literature.

Exclusion Based Measures: Exclusion based measures of core inflation are based on the premise that prices of some commodities get unduly affected by supply shocks and seasonal factors and hence introduce noise in the headline inflation rate. The commodities, where the prices are controlled by some administrative authority are also typically considered for exclusion. In the construction of exclusion-based measures of core inflation, selected commodities are excluded from the price index basket and inflation rate of remaining basket is termed as "core inflation". These measures are considered to be suitable for inflation targeting frameworks, as they represent that component of inflation, on which the central banks have some control. The central banks are not in a position to control the factors responsible for price increase such as supply constraints or the price changes effected by some authorities. Therefore, for the purpose of targeting, a measure, which deviates from its desired path due to price changes of such commodities, is not considered to be appropriate. In many inflation targeting countries, the targets are set in terms of such exclusion based core measures, where the commodities such as food, energy, mortgage interest payments and government controlled prices (depending upon specific country situation) are excluded from the price index. Major limitation of using such core inflation measures is that the prices of excluded commodities may have useful information for predicting future inflation rates and to that extent there is information loss by using exclusion based measures of core inflation for policy purposes.

One of the earliest studies on core inflation in the Indian context was by Samanta (1999). He constructed four different measures by excluding different combinations of Primary Food Articles, Primary Non-food Articles, Food Products under Manufactured Products and commodities with administrative price control. He found that WPI obtained by excluding Primary Food Articles, Primary Non-food Articles and commodities with administrative price control performs the best among the four constructed measures.

Clarke (2001) has compared six different core measures in the context of New Zealand. Among these measures, three measures are based on exclusion of certain commodities. The measures considered by Clarke were CPI ex-food and energy, CPI ex-energy and CPI ex-8 components. The last one was worked out by excluding the 8 most volatile components of CPI. Each of these components were at least 3 times as volatile as CPI and were among the 9 components most frequently excluded while trimming. As expected, all these measures had lower volatility than the headline CPI, with CPI ex-8 components showing the least volatility. However, all these measures were found to be inferior to the trimmed mean, in terms of both volatility and ability to predict inflation, one and two years ahead.

Among the core measures based on exclusion, the CPI ex-energy appears to be superior to other exclusion based measures for New Zealand.

In the context of Canada, Hogan *et al.* (2001) have compared two measures of core inflation based on exclusion. CPIxFET, is a measure regularly published by Statistics Canada, excluding the food, energy and effects of indirect taxes. This measure is officially adopted as an operational target for policy by the Bank of Canada. Another exclusion based measure considered by Hogan *et al.* is CPIX, which excludes eight components, which are most volatile. The choice of these eight components is also based on their frequency of exclusion from the calculation of weighted average of truncated distribution (trimming). They conclude that the different measures of core inflation perform well on different dimensions. Therefore, they suggest that, selecting one measure as the most superior might not be sufficient. They note that the Bank of Canada regularly monitors four different measures of core inflation.

Measures Based on Trimming: The core inflation measures based on trimming of the commodities basket are also more or less similar to the exclusion-based measures. However, for constructing such measures, the commodities to be excluded from the basket are not chosen *a priori.* While computing trimmed mean, the commodities accounting for the largest and the smallest price changes are removed from the basket. The major difference between exclusion and trimming is that the commodities excluded at each time point may be different depending on whether they fall at the extreme ends of price change distribution.

Method of Computing Trimmed Mean

- Price changes for each commodity are computed for the given period
- They are arranged in ascending order of price change
- Cumulative weights of these commodities are computed
- The commodities representing the extreme 'n' per cent weight are excluded and inflation rate for the remaining basket is treated as "Core".

Measures of core inflation based on trimming were studied by Mohanty, Rath and Ramaiah (2000) in the Indian context. They found that 20 per cent trimmed mean performs better than the exclusion-based estimates. The exclusion-based measure considered by them excluded 17 most volatile commodities. This study was for a 16-year period from April 1983 to March 1999.

Clarke considered 16 per cent trimmed mean, by excluding 8 per cent smallest and 8 per cent largest price changes from the basket for New Zealand. Clarke found that the trimmed mean is the most suitable core measure in terms of both minimum volatility and more importantly, ability to predict inflation rate of headline CPI 2 year ahead.

Measures Based on Smoothing: One of the reasons for computing core inflation is to separate out the "noise" part from the "signal". This can also be done by making use of statistical techniques, which are used to separate out the underlying trend in a time series. One such method of computing core inflation is to apply Hodrick-Prescott (HP) filter to the inflation rate time series. This filter is expected to filter out seasonal, cyclical and random components from the time series. Although this technique appears to be useful *prima facie*, its application in the Indian context (Samanta and Bhattacharjee, 2000) suggests that this measure has not performed better as compared with other measures. This has been found to be unsuitable in terms of its predictive power also. One major problem with such measures is that addition of new data will affect the computed core values for the previous periods also.

Core Inflation Based on Whole Price Distribution: The core inflation measures calculated using *a priori* exclusion of commodities or trimming, effectively assign Zero weight to the excluded commodities. Prices of some of the commodities, which thus get excluded, may have the tendency to persist or to affect the prices of the remaining commodities in future. In order to make use of full information available in the price index, Blinder (1997) suggested that instead of assigning Zero weight to the commodities which are considered to be having transient price changes, the weighting pattern of the index basket could be recast based on certain criteria, which will give higher weight to the persistent components and reduce the weight of transient components. This measure is expected to have better predictive power as it uses the complete set of price data and it focuses on persistent inflation.

Model Based Core Inflation: The measures of core inflation discussed above are essentially statistical, and hence atheoretic in nature. Another set of measures of core inflation are based on economic theory. They make use of econometric and multivariate techniques and use non-price variables in calculating core inflation. As is the case with theory-based models, these measures are sensitive to the exact model specification and identification scheme. Moreover, the restrictions imposed in the process of model building are rarely uncontroversial. In view of these limitations, these measures of core inflation are discussed with much lesser intensity in the literature as compared with their statistical counterparts.

The motivation for the use of economic theory is usually based on the assumption that the changes in the stock of base money affects the prices of all commodities and this effect should be isolated in a measure of core inflation. It is also well recognised that there is a distinction between cost of living and the monetary inflation that is of concern to central banks. Quah and Vahey (1995) adopted this approach to construct their measure on the basis of assumption that long-run Phillips curve is vertical. It is assumed that output and inflation have stochastic trends, but are not co-integrated. Similar approaches have also been implemented by Fase and Folkertsma (1996), Claus (1997), Jacquinal (1998), Garter and Wehinger (1998). The Major problem with this approach is the presumption that Phillips curve is vertical in the long run. However, if this assumption is to be accepted, it invites the question that if inflation is neutral with respect to output in the long run, why the central banks would ever be concerned about price stability? Wynne (1999) notes that a more realistic assumption that the Phillips curve is upwardly sloping from left to right was proposed by Friedman (1997). However there are lots of difficulties in operationalising this notion in constructing a core measure. These implementations typically using econometric models are sensitive to validity of assumption about the data and therefore, are far from controversial.

SECTION 2: CORE MEASURES IN THE PRESENT STUDY

Database for the Study

The study covers the 20 year period from April 1983 to March 2003. The Wholesale Price Index (WPI) with base year 1981-82 was in operation till early 2000. When the new WPI series was released, the WPI data in respect of years since 1994-95 was released. Therefore, inflation rate data for period starting with April 1995 is based on the new series. Earlier data relates to the 1981-82 series. As the data relates only to the inflation rates, no need was felt to compute a combined series. While working out growth rate, index from the same series has been used. For computation of various measures of inflation, the WPI basket was considered at 80 sub-groups at two levels below the main groups, *viz.* (i) Primary Articles, (ii) Fuel, Power, Light and Lubricants and (iii) Manufactured Products. The reason for not considering the basket at further level of disaggregation was to ensure that there are no missing values in the data series. Another advantage of considering the series at somewhat aggregated level is that it enables better comparison of two different baskets. A few commodities from the 1981-82 basket, which could not be appropriately combined with any group, accounting for less than 8 per cent weight have been dropped from the basket for the purpose of comparability. The details of the components of WPI used in the current study are provided in the Annexure 7A.I. Core measures constructed and used in this study are described below.

Core Measures Based on Exclusion Principle

As noted earlier, typical measures of core inflation based on exclusion exclude some combinations of food and energy commodities. In Indian situation also, the logic of excluding the food and energy related commodities is applicable due to their supply related price movements. It may be seen from the following Figure 7.1 that the inflation rates for food and energy commodities have been far more volatile than the headline inflation rate. However between these two groups, the energy price rises tended to be systematically higher than the overall price rise, whereas, the same is not true about food prices. It is felt that exclusion of these volatile components might yield an underlying trend, which could be more permanent in nature. Therefore, we constructed three measures based on exclusion of (i) food articles alone, (ii) food and energy and (iii) energy alone.

Figure 7.1

Inflation Rate – Headline, Food and Energy

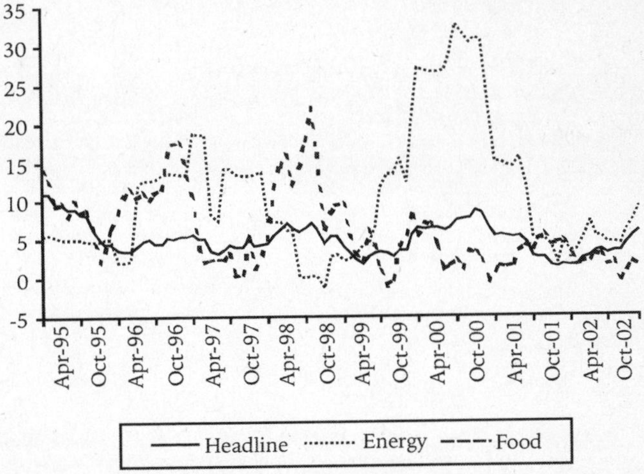

Samanta (1999) had also considered four different measures of core inflation, but he considered administrative controls on prices as important criteria for exclusion. With liberalisation of the economy, the price control mechanisms have been dismantled substantially. Therefore, while constructing our core measures, we have not emphasised on administered prices as a significant exclusion criteria. However, for the sake of comparability with the study of Samanta, we have constructed a measure, which closely corresponds with the core measure, which Samanta found to be the best among his set of four measures. This measure, however, suffers from the limitation that it excludes nearly 50 per cent of the weight from the WPI basket and thus could be considered to be inadequate in representing the price changes at the overall level.

Following some of the studies in other countries, we also tried to construct an exclusion-based measure by excluding those commodities, which are most volatile in terms of their coefficient of variation. The commodities to be excluded are chosen so that the total weight of the excluded commodities is comparable with that of food items or energy items, each having approximately 15 per cent in the WPI basket. Thus the fifth measure constructed by us excludes 12 most volatile commodities. List of the excluded commodities for this measure is given in Annexure 7A.2.

Table 7.1

Exclusion Based Measures

Name	*Description*	*Weight of Excluded Commodities*
Core-1 (x Food)	WPI obtained by excluding primary food articles (cereals, pulses, fruits and vegetables, milk, eggs, meat and fish, condiments and spices and other food articles)	15.40
Core-2 (x Food and Energy)	WPI excluding primary food articles, coal, mineral oils and electricity	29.63
Core-3 (x Energy)	WPI obtained by excluding the coal, mineral oils and electricity	14.23
Core-4 (xFEAdm)	WPI obtained by excluding primary food articles, primary non-food articles, energy, fertilisers, Iron and Steel	43.57
Core-5 (x 12)	WPI obtained by excluding the 12 commodities with most volatile prices (based on CV of the inflation rates).	14.15

Core Measures Based on Trimming

We constructed three measures of core inflation based on trimming with 10, 15 and 20 per cent of extreme price changes excluded from the basket. For computing the trimmed means, the WPI basket was divided into 80 components. The details of WPI components and corresponding basket weights are presented in Annexure 7A.1. Various evaluation criteria used for comparing these measures are discussed in the next section.

SECTION 3: EVALUATION OF VARIOUS MEASURES OF CORE INFLATION

The various measures of core inflation are compiled in order to provide relatively noise-free data to the policymakers. The concepts and the objectives of various measures suggest some basic criteria for evaluating the performance of these measures. The literature on core inflation has suggested several criteria to evaluate how well the core indicator tracks the underlying trend and how well it is able to predict future overall inflation. Irrespective of the utility of core inflation measure, certain desirable properties for such measures have been identified in the literature. These are as follows:

- Robustness – should be able to distinguish between persistent and transient movements
- Unbiased to the headline – in the long term, the average difference between core and headline inflation rate should be zero
- Timeliness – it should be available in a timely manner so as to be of use for policy purpose
- Credibility – it should be easy understandable and verifiable by outsiders.

In principle, each core inflation measure has advantages and disadvantages. Hence, whether one indicator is better than another depends on practical considerations such as objective, empirical performance and complexity. Moreover, as noted earlier, a distinction should be made between measures designed for policy assessment (i.e. to define inflation target) and those designed to help set policy to achieve a given objective (i.e. as leading indicators of the inflation target). In the later case, the core inflation measure should be monitored for its movements and not the exact value as in the former case. If a measure is being used as a leading indicator, it should be able to give a fair idea about the future path of the headline inflation. The evaluation of measures of core inflation should also be, therefore, done keeping a set of objectives in mind and as such tests suitable for such evaluation will also depend on the objectives.

The emphasis in the present study is to identify a core inflation measure with good forecasting ability and the ability of tracking the trend in the headline inflation. Therefore, from the various evaluation criteria suggested in the recent literature, the ones considered to be in line with this objective are briefly reviewed below.

Marques *et al.* (2000) have proposed certain necessary conditions to be satisfied by a core measure. They suggest that additional conditions may also be imposed in order to further rank various indicators. These conditions have been used by Mankikar *et al.* (2002) for evaluating various core measures for UK. These tests are:

1. Targeted and core inflation should be co-integrated with a unit coefficient,
2. Core inflation should be an 'attractor' of targeted inflation, and
3. Targeted inflation should not be an attractor of core inflation (i.e. core inflation should be strongly exogenous)

Mankikar *et al.* explain these conditions as follows. "The attraction of the tests is that they attempt to formalise the relationship between targeted and core inflation exploiting information contained in the differential between the two. The conditions essentially imply that the inflation in the long run should converge to core inflation but not *vice versa.*"

The utility and credibility of the core measure will essentially depend upon its being able to track the headline inflation in the long run and not diverging away from it. The co-integration between the two variables will ensure that they have a long run relationship. The deviation of headline inflation from the underlying trend will be essentially due to factors, which are short-term and transient in nature, and therefore, one would expect that as soon as these factors vanish, the headline inflation should move towards its long run trend. This feature can be evaluated by testing whether the core inflation is an 'attractor' of the headline inflation or not. On the other hand, the core inflation should not move towards the headline, when both deviate, because the assumption is that it is the headline inflation which is away from its long run path and should therefore return to it, rather than core following it on its detour from the long-run path. This justifies the third part of the test, of core inflation being 'not an attractor' but being exogenous. For testing the conditions 2 and 3 above, we have employed Granger's causality tests.

For evaluating the forecasting ability, we have followed Clarke (2001). The methodology used by Clarke is in line with the tests proposed by Marques. As we expect the core inflation to be an attractor of the headline inflation, the difference between these two measures at a given point in time should be able to predict the direction and quantum by which headline inflation will move at some time in future. Using this logic, we have used the regression below. Here it is assumed that the difference between these two measures will be able to forecast the headline inflation at some time in future. The forecast horizon will depend upon the transmission channels between various prices in the economy and could be different for each country. While testing this regression, we have tried to assess the measure, which will give us the best forecast, sufficiently ahead for the policy purposes.

Accordingly when current overall inflation is below core, overall inflation should rise. Thus, the predictive content in alternative measures of core inflation can be gauged from regressions of "the change in overall inflation from today to some point in the future" on "the current gap between core and overall inflation". More specifically, the ability of core inflation to predict future overall inflation is quantified by using monthly data to estimate the regression

$$\Pi_{t+h} - \Pi = \alpha + \beta\,(\Pi_t^{core} - \Pi_t) + \varepsilon_t$$

Where Π denotes overall WPI inflation and Π^{core} refers to one of the indicators of core inflation, both measured on a year-on-year basis. A policymaker may be interested in the inflation path in short-term as well as long-term, a core inflation, therefore, is assessed for it's ability to forecast the overall inflation in both short-term and long-term. A single measure of core inflation may not be suitable for both the purposes but different measures of core inflation may be useful for the purpose. In particular, we may find different measures appropriate for different forecast horizons. Therefore, we tested the measures for various values of the parameter h such as 6 and 12 months. Many other variables potentially useful for forecasting inflation could be added to the model. But this simple formulation captures the predictive content of core inflation indicators as they are often used. Empirical results based on these tests are discussed below.

SECTION 4: EMPIRICAL RESULTS

Unbiasedness and Volatility

The measures of core inflation chosen for assessment here are either exclusion-based or trimmed mean based. All these measures can be calculated in the real time. Further, availability of additional data does not change the history of the measures. Hence all the measures are verifiable at any time. Moreover the measures are robust to the sample size chosen. Most of these measures, however, consistently under-estimate the inflation rate. This is evident from the Tables 7.2 and 7.3. In the recent decade (1993-2003), only the WPI x Food seemed to have average closer to the headline inflation, as compared with much lower averages of xFood & Energy, x Energy, xFEAdm. On the other hand, x12 showed higher average than the headline inflation rate during this period. Among the trimmed means, none had average closer to headline inflation, and all were consistently under-estimating the headline inflation. Although this test is very important from the viewpoint of credibility of the inflation measure, if the difference is consistent, the same can be considered to be structural and adjustment could be made while interpreting the measures.

The exclusion-based measures, where a few commodities from the overall commodity basket are excluded, are simple to understand for a common man. The x12 measure computed by excluding the 12 most volatile commodities is a bit complex. Trimmed-mean based measures are further complicated to understand because of the calculation involved. Although simplicity is a desirable criterion for a core inflation measure, it should not be over-emphasised at the cost of utility of the measure for the policymakers. Hence, even if a measure is understandable by a limited group of academicians or critics and can be transparently computed, it should be acceptable. On this ground, we are considering all the measures are equal for further evaluation.

The inflation rates based on the core measures excluding "food and energy", "energy" and "food, energy and administered" are systematically lower than the headline inflation rate, with only a few exceptional time periods. This is mainly on account of exclusion of energy, which has shown higher inflation rates than headline inflation rates consistently over the last decade or so (see Figure 7.1). Therefore, only one core measure of the above, i.e. xFood, passes the test of being (more or less) unbiased with respect to the headline inflation. Inflation rates based on the exclusion based core measures are presented in the Figures 7.2 and 7.3 below.

In the following Table, summary statistics related to the five exclusion based measres of core inflation are presented. The measures of core inflation are expected to remove noise from the headline inflation and therefore should be less volatile than the headline inflation. However, except x12, all other exclusion based measures exhibited higher coefficient of variation than the headline inflation.

Table 7.2

Summary Statistics of Exclusion Based Measures

	Headline	*X Food*	*X Food & Energy*	*X Energy*	*X FEAdm*	*X 12*
1983-93						
Average	8.14	7.84	7.84	8.18	7.77	8.01
SD	2.93	2.58	2.75	3.03	2.68	2.90
CV	0.36	0.33	0.35	0.37	0.34	0.36
1993-2003						
Average	5.97	5.94	4.85	5.10	4.61	6.26
SD	2.72	3.04	3.57	3.26	3.19	2.33
CV	0.46	0.51	0.74	0.64	0.69	0.37

The trimmed means based core measures also tend to underestimate WPI over long run. The extent of underestimation is however lower than most of the exclusion based measures. Clarke (2001) had also observed this feature of trimmed mean based measures in the case of New Zealand. The systematic under-estimation of core inflation reflects the asymmetry in the distribution of price changes. On the volatility comparisons, trimmed means are no better than the headline inflation rates but do not show higher volatility than headline as exhibited by some of the exclusion based measures.

Figure 7.2

Core Measures – Exclusion Based

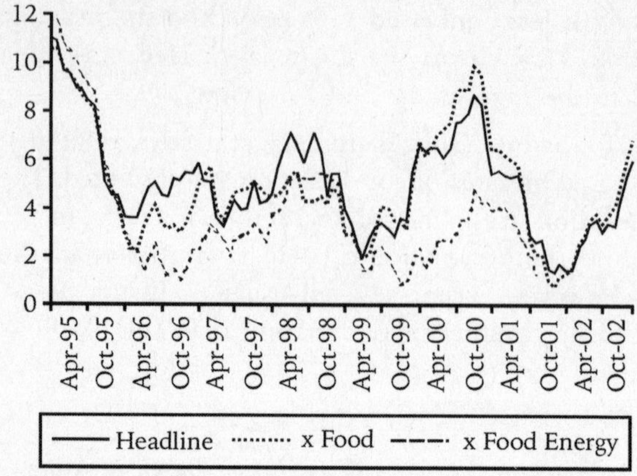

Figure 7.3

Core Measures – Exclusion Based

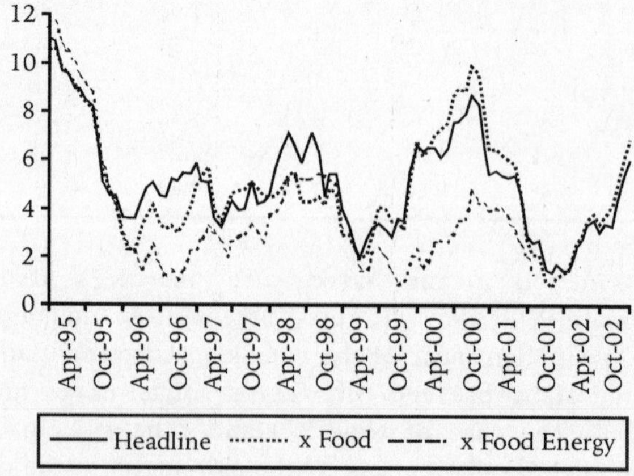

Co-integration with Headline Inflation

Before proceeding to apply the criteria suggested by Marques, the inflation measures were tested for unit root and it was found that all the core measures and the headline inflation rates are I(1). It can be seen from the Annexure 7A.3 that all the measures based on trimmed-mean are co-integrated with the headline inflation. Moreover the co-efficient is also close to one, suggesting that the long-term relationship between the core inflation measure and headline inflation is not diverging. Among the exclusion-based measures, xFood measure is co-integrated with the headline inflation, with a unit co-efficient while other exclusion-based measures do not satisfy this criterion.

Table 7.3

Summary Statistics of Trimmed Means

	Headline	*Trim 10*	*Trim 15*	*Trim 20*
1983-93				
Average	8.14	7.79	7.67	7.56
SD	2.93	2.69	2.66	2.64
CV	0.36	0.35	0.35	0.35
1993-2003				
Average	5.97	5.42	5.32	5.24
SD	2.72	2.57	2.54	2.52
CV	0.46	0.47	0.48	0.48

Figure 7.4

Core Measures – Trimmed Mean

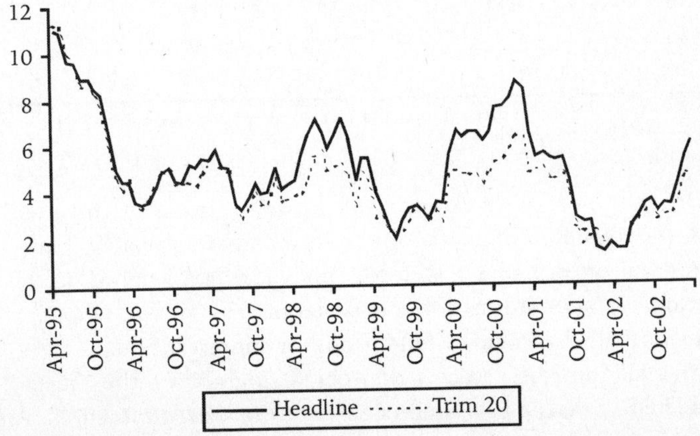

All the core measures under consideration except x12 are attractors of the headline inflation. Further among these only xfood, xfood 'n' energy and Trim 20 are strongly exogenous, not getting attracted by the headline inflation. As these measures are exogenous, they are also expected to be useful for forecasting the headline inflation.

Forecasting Ability

On the comparison of the ability to predict the 12-month ahead inflation rate, the trimmed-mean based measures perform better than the exclusion-based measures. The Trim 20 measure has the highest R^2 of the regression among the trimmed means (Annexure 7A.4), showing a potential of being a better predictor of the headline inflation rate. None of the exclusion based measures showed performance closer to trimmed means.

Table 7.4

Summary of Findings

Criteria	*Co-integrated*	$\pi_t^* \rightarrow \pi_t$	π_t^* *is Exogenous*	*Forecasting Ability 12m*
x Food	✓	✓	✓	×
x Food Energy	×	✓	✓	×
x Energy	×	✓	×	×
x FE Admin	×	✓	×	×
x 12	×	×	✓	×
Trim 10	✓	✓	×	✓
Trim 15	✓	✓	×	✓
Trim 20	✓	✓	✓	✓

Note: A tick indicates that the measure meets the requirement and cross indicates that the requirement is not met.

On the short-term forecasting horizon, none of the measures showed reasonably high R^2. This indicates that probably some more exploration on devising a suitable core measures leading indicator of inflation for short-term horizon is necessary. On the whole, all the exclusion-based measures fail in one or more criteria. Only x Food satisfies all the tests, except the forecasting ability, thus it could be considered to be the best among all exclusion-based measures. Among the trimmed-mean based measures, Trim 20 satisfies almost all the criteria under consideration. It emerges out to be the measure which can be used for the prediction and tracking of the future headline inflation rate. It is, however, not very much useful for short-term forecast of headline inflation rate.

SECTION 5: CONCLUDING OBSERVATIONS

The headline measure of inflation gets affected by not only the long-term inflationary trends, but also by the transient factors, which introduce noise in the time series. In order to separate out the noise from the underlying trends, different measures of core inflation have been proposed. The construction of core measures depends upon the purpose for which the measure is to be used. The literature on this topic as well as the results of the present study suggest that one measure of core inflation may not necessarily satisfy all the requirements of an ideal measure, but they might be suitable for the purpose for which they are constructed. Among the exclusion-based measures, xFood performs the best on the basis of unbaisedness, co-integration and other related criteria. It, however, exhibits almost as much volatility as the headline inflation rate. The 20 per cent trimmed mean satisfies most of the evaluation criteria, but its shortcoming is that it consistently under-estimates the headline inflation rate. On the whole, while the exclusion based measures are more appropriate for inflation targeting purposes, the measures based on trimming may be better for identifying the underlying trends and also in providing a robust forecast of future inflation rates.

Annexure 7A.1

WPI Components Used in Computations of Various Core Inflation Measures

Commodity Name	*Weight in WPI Basket*
Cereals	4.40629
Pulses	0.60320
Fruits & Vegetables	2.91655
Milk	4.36708
Eggs, Meat & Fish	2.20774
Condiments & Spices	0.66233
Other Food Articles	0.23927
Fibres	1.52331
Oil Seeds	2.66617
Other Non-Food Articles	1.94864
Metallic Minerals	0.29677
Other Minerals	0.18790
Coal Mining	1.75290
Liquified Petroleum Gas	1.83731
Petrol	0.88815
Kerosene	0.68928
Aviation Turbine Fuel	0.16953
High Speed Diesel Oil	2.02034
Light Diesel Oil	0.16015
Naptha	0.41885
Bitumin	0.14900
Furnace oil	0.49335
Lubricants	0.16367
Electricity	5.48369
Dairy Products	0.68696
Canning, Preserving & Processing of Fish	0.04651
Grain Mill Products	1.03343
Bakery Products	0.44148
Sugar, Khandsari & *Gur*	3.92876
Manufacture of Common Salts	0.02126
Cocoa Chocolate Sugar & Confectionery	0.08736
Edible Oils	2.75515
Oil Cakes	1.41578
Tea & Coffee Processing	0.96733
Other Food Products n.e.c	0.15380
Wine Industries	0.26892
Malt Liquor	0.04285
Soft Drinks & Carbonated Water	0.05274

Contd. ...

Contd. ...

Commodity Name	*Weight in WPI Basket*
Manufacture of *Bidi*, Cigarettes, Tobacco & *Zarda*	0.97461
Cotton Yarn	3.31243
Cotton Cloth - Mills	0.90306
Man Made Textiles	4.71892
Woolen Textiles	0.18959
Jute Hemp & Mesta Textiles	0.37551
Other Misc. Textiles	0.30041
Plywood Commercial Planks	0.05699
Timber Planks	0.11606
Paper & Pulp	1.22881
Manufacture of Board	0.23715
Printing & Publishing of Newspapers, Periodicals etc.	0.57807
Footwear Western type	1.01933
Tyre & Tubes	1.28627
Plastic Products	0.93687
Other Rubber & Plastic Products	0.16505
Basic Heavy Inorganic Chemical	1.44608
Basic Heavy Organic Chemical	0.45456
Fertilisers & Pesticides	4.16386
Paints Varnishes & Lacquers	0.49576
Dyestuffs & Indigo	0.17503
Drugs & Medicines	2.53187
Perfumes, Cosmetics, Toiletries etc	0.97768
Turpentine, Synthetic Resins, Plastic Materials etc.	0.74628
Matches Explosives & Other Chemicals n.e.c.	0.94010
Structural Clay Products	0.22952
Glass Earthenware Chinaware & their Products	0.23674
Cement	1.73105
Cement Slate & Graphite Products	0.31860
Iron & Steel	3.63656
Foundries for Casting Forging & Structurals	0.89559
Pipes Wires Drawing & Others	1.58887
Ferro Alloys	0.08510
Non-Ferrous Metals	1.46625
Metal Products	0.66949
Non-Electrical Machinery & Parts	3.37871
Electrical Industrial Machinery	1.81050
Wires & Cables	1.07625
Dry & Wet Batteries	0.27479
Electrical Apparatus & Appliances	1.82306
Locomotives Railway Wagon & Parts	0.31767
Motor Vehicles, Motorcycles, Scooters, Bicycles & Parts	3.97707

Note: The weight relates to that in basket for 1993-94 series.

Annexure 7A.2

Commodities Excluded on the Basis of Volatility for x12

1. Fibres
2. Other Food Articles
3. Wires & Cables
4. Basic Heavy Organic Chemical
5. Cotton Yarn
6. Other Minerals
7. Metallic Minerals
8. Sugar, *Khandsari* & *Gur*
9. Edible Oils
10. Timber Planks
11. Glass Earthenware Chinaware & their Products
12. Manufacture of Common Salts

Annexure 7A.3

Results of Co-integration and Causality Tests

Criteria	*π_t and π_t^* should be Co-integrated EG Test – A=DF, B=ADF, C=Coeff.*	*π_t^* Granger causes π_t Granger's Causality Test*	*π_t^* is Strongly Exogenous Granger's Causality Test*
xFood	A **-3.7495**	**F = 5.49**	**F = 1.02**
	B **-4.6485**	**p = .0047**	**p = .4287**
	C **0.95852**		
x Food and Energy	A **-3.2294**	**F = 8.35**	**F = 2.30**
	B **-3.7800**	**p = .0042**	**p = .1023**
	C *0.76879*		
x Energy	A *-2.6056*	**F = 7.42**	*F = 3.15*
	B *-3.2164*	**p = .0070**	*p = .0152*
	C *0.82048*		
x FEAdm	A **-3.1102**	**F = 12.53**	*F = 4.84*
	B **-3.7318**	**p = .0005**	*p = .0001*
	C *0.75294*		
x 12	A *-2.6544*	*F = 1.16*	**F = 2.53**
	B *-2.9561*	*p = .3113*	**p =.0817**
	C **1.0550**		

Contd. ...

Contd. ...

Criteria	*π_t and π_t^* should be Co-integrated EG Test – A=DF, B=ADF, C=Coeff.*	*π_t^* Granger causes π_t Granger's Causality Test*	*π_t^* is Strongly Exogenous Granger's Causality Test*
Trim 10	A **-3.7936**	**F = 5.18**	F = 3.06
	B **-4.0533**	**p=.0018**	*p=.0489*
	C **1.0318**		
Trim 15	A **-3.8411**	**F = 5.02**	*F = 2.87*
	B **-4.1321**	**p=.0022**	*p=.0240*
	C **1.0364**		
Trim 20	A **-3.7998**	**F = 4.62**	**F = 1.34**
	B **-4.2117**	**p=.0037**	**p=.2633**
	C **1.0401**		

Note: Bold face indicates that the desired condition is satisfied and italics indicate otherwise. All the tests have been done at 5 per cent level of significance.

Annexure 7A.4

Assessing Forecasting Ability of the Core Inflation Measures

Core Inflation Measures	*Regression R^2*	*Coefficient (s.e)*	*t-statistic*
	6 Months Ahead (h = 6)		
x Food	0.30	0.93 (0.72)	1.30
x Food & Energy	0.23	0.66 (0.61)	1.08
x Energy	0.12	-2.87 (3.84)	-0.75
x FEAdm	0.44	0.80 (0.45)	1.79
x 12	0.27	2.29 (1.86)	1.23
Trim 10	0.43	1.99 (1.15)	1.74
Trim 15	0.44	1.72 (0.97)	1.77
Trim 20	0.40	1.49 (0.90)	1.65
	1 Year Ahead (h =12)		
x Food	0.00	0.00 (0.55)	0.00
x Food & Energy	0.00	0.01 (0.49)	0.02
x Energy	0.13	-3.36 (2.70)	-1.25
x FEAdm	0.11	0.62 (0.56)	1.11
x 12	0.30	2.38 (1.14)	2.08
Trim 10	0.61	4.30 (1.09)	3.96
Trim 15	0.72	4.04 (0.79)	5.12
Trim 20	0.81	3.63 (0.56)	6.46

References

Blinder, A.S. (1997). "Commentary", *Review* Vol. 79 (3) on "Measuring Short-Run Inflation for Central Bankers" by Stephen G. Cecchetti, Federal Reserve Bank of St. Louis, May/ June.

Clark, Todd E. (2001). "Comparing Measures of Core Inflation", *Economic Review*, Vol. 86 (1), Federal Reserve Bank of Kansas City.

Cutler, Joanne (2001). "Core Inflation in the UK", *MPC Discussion Paper No. 3*, Bank of England.

Diebold, Francis X., and Lutz Kilian. (2001). "Measuring Predictability: Theory and Macroeconomic Applications," *Journal of Applied Econometrics*. Vol.16 (6).

Freeman, Donald G. (1998). "Do Core Inflation Measures Help Forecast Inflation?" *Economic Letters*, 58, pp. 143-147.

Hogan, S, M. Johnson and T. Lafleche (2001). "Core Inflation", *Bank of Canada Technical Report No. 89*.

Mankikar, Alan and Jo Paisley (2002). "What Do Measures of Core Inflation Really Tell Us?", *Bank of England Quarterly Bulletin*, Winter.

Marques, C.R., P. D. Neves, and L.M. Sarmento (2000). "Evaluating Core Inflation Indicators," *Bank of Portugal Working Paper* No. 3-00, April.

Mohanty, Deepak, D.P. Rath and M. Ramaiah (2000). "Measures of Core Inflation for India", *Economic and Political Weekly, January 29*.

Quah, D. and Vahey, S.P. (1995). "Measuring Core Inflation", *Economic Journal*, Vol. 105 (September), pp. 1,130–44.

Roger, Scott (1998). "Core Inflation: Concepts, Uses and Measurement", *Reserve Bank of New Zealand Discussion Paper G 98/9*.

Samanta, G.P. (1999). "Core Inflation in India: Measurement and Policy Perspectives", *Reserve Bank of India Occasional Papers*, Vol. 20(1), Summer.

Samanta, G.P. and M. Bhattacharjee (2000). "Are Seasonal Adjustment Methods and HP-Filter Useful for Estimating Core Inflation in India?", *International Journal of Development Banking*, Vol. 18(2).

Wynne, Mark A. (1999). "Core Inflation: A Review of Some Conceptual Issues", *Working Paper 99-0*, Federal Reserve Bank of Dallas.

Maddala, G.S. and In-Moo Kim (1998). *Unit Roots, Co-integration and Structural Change*, Cambridge University Press, UK.

Granger, C.W.J. (1988). "Some Recent Developments in a Concept of Causality", *Journal of Econometrics*, 39, pp. 199-211.

This paper was presented at the 40th Annual Conference of the Indian Econometric Society held at the Institute of Social and Economic Change, Bangalore during February 13 to 15, 2004. Authors are thankful to the participants for their useful comments. The views expressed in this paper are of the authors and not the institution to which they belong.

8

Endogenous Distribution, Politics and the Growth-Equity Tradeoff

SATYA P. DAS
CHETAN GHATE

1. Introduction

A burgeoning literature now analyses the impact of wealth and income distribution on economic growth.[1] Its general finding is that greater equality implies higher long-run growth. In one class of models, the exogenous initial distribution of wealth engenders a balance of power in which distributive conflict influences optimal policy choices in equilibrium (Bertola, 1993; Perotti, 1993; Alesina & Rodrik, 1994; Persson & Tabellini, 1994; Aghion & Howitt, 1998). In these models, a greater level of inequality leads to voted policies which reflect a higher demand for redistribution. In Alesina-Rodrik model for example, less inequality reduces the political demand for transfer by the median household, and, the transfer being funded by a tax on capital, it implies a lower tax on capital, higher after-tax return to capital, higher investment, resulting in a lower equilibrium growth rate.

An alternative class of models links wealth distribution to economic growth when capital markets are imperfect (Loury, 1981; Galor & Zeira, 1993; Banerjee & Newman, 1993; Benabou, 1995; Aghion & Bolton, 1997; Aghion & Howitt, 1998). In these models, redistributive policies that reduce investment inequality foster aggregate production by relaxing the credit constraints imposed by imperfect capital markets. This raises growth in the long-run.

Initial empirical evidence - by Alesina-Rodrik and Persson-Tabellini - was supportive of the finding that inequality harms growth. But more recent empirical works - notably by Li and Zou (1998), Forbes (2000),

1. See Benabou (1995) and Aghion *et al.* (1999) for an exhaustive survey of this literature.

Banerjee and Duflo (2003), and Lundberg and Squire (2003) - have found some evidence of the contrary: namely, more inequality may promote economic growth. For instance, in a structural regression accounting for the simultaneous endogeneity between growth and equality, Lundberg and Squire (2003, p. 336, Table 2) find that the point estimate on the Gini coefficient is positive (where growth is the dependent variable). Similarly, Banerjee and Duflo (2003) find that changes in inequality *in any direction* are associated with lower future growth rates. Indeed, these findings appear to resurrect the traditional tradeoff between growth and equity. However, to the best of our knowledge, there doesn't exist to date any model of endogenous growth with re-distributive politics that predicts, in a strong way, *a negative* causal relationship from an equity-enhancing policy to growth.

The purpose of this paper is to develop a model which implies such a negative link. Interestingly, to show this, one need not look for a framework that is drastically different in character from the existing models of distribution and growth. We use the well-known Alesina-Rodrik (A-R) model and generalise it in two important aspects. The end-product is capable of establishing a negative tradeoff between equity and growth.

In A-R, households live indefinitely. There is an initial distribution of labour and capital holdings across households. The production function is of the "AK" variety and a variant of Barro (1990). These assumptions imply no transitional dynamics. Hence the initial distribution (even though capital grows for each household) of the *ratio* of capital to labour holding remains unchanged over time, i.e., the "distribution of factor ownership is time-invariant" (A-R, page 473). In addition, the politically determined tax on capital fixes the net return to capital and the long-run growth rate.

Using this framework, our model first *endogeneises* wealth and income distribution. This is done by postulating that households have finite lifetimes and there is a bequest motive, i.e., it is a warm-glow model with one-sided altruism. For simplicity, households are assumed to live for a single period and their utility function has, as arguments, their own consumption and the amount they bequest, with positive and diminishing marginal utility from each argument (Picketty, 1997; Aghion and Bolton 1997). Interestingly, such a framework endogeneises wealth and income distribution. It is because limited lifetimes together with diminishing marginal utility from bequests (equal to savings) imply that households would not want to 'jump' to their steady-state capital holdings immediately. Thus, there are transitional dynamics, even though the production function is of the 'AK' variety.[2] This makes the evolution of wealth distribution endogenous - independent of the initial distribution.[3] This is our first generalisation.

Our second generalisation allows for both a non-political and political redistributive policy. To wit, in the A-R model as well as in Persson and Tabellini's, there is only one redistributive policy (a tax) which is politically determined - and hence, *endogenous*. However, the policy implication that emerges from these models - that a more equal distribution of wealth affects economic growth positively - must require the existence of an *exogenous* redistributive policy to achieve this. But there is no explicit exogenous re-distributive policy in either model. To make it logically complete so-to-speak, we introduce a transfer scheme *in addition* to a tax on capital or total income. We consider two cases: one in which the former is political (hence endogenous) while the latter is not, and, the *vice versa*.

Given this construct, our main finding makes appealing economic sense: *a non-political tax policy, which is more redistributive but contributes toward growth-enhancing productive inputs does promote long-run growth, whereas a non-political and equity-enhancing transfer policy reduces economic growth*. It is also shown that the position of the political equilibrium plays a role in the mechanism in which redistributive policies affect growth.

The paper proceeds as follows. Section 2 develops our basic finite-lifetime model. It assumes a single policy, tax on capital, which is

---

2. Indeed, our approach contrasts with Jones and Manuelli (1990) who append to a standard AK technology a production process that exhibits diminishing returns to capital. Such diminishing returns give rise to transitional dynamics. Put differently, 'convexity' in Jones and Manuelli (1990) arises from the production side. In our model, it arises from the preferences of finitely-lived households with one-sided altruism.

3. While there is some similarity between the notion of endogenous distribution here and in Matsuyama (2000), there is one major difference. In Matsuyama (2000), there is no source of heterogeneity across households other than initial wealth (similar to A-R actually). Hence, in the presence of transitional dynamics, complete equality as well as initial-period dependent inequality are both non-trivial possibilities in the steady state. In contrast, in our model, as we shall see, heterogeneity in the distribution of innate skill implies that perfect equality cannot occur in the long run. Moreover, at least locally, the steady-state distribution is independent the initial distribution of wealth.

political. This is same as the A-R model but the important difference is that there is transitional dynamics and the long-run wealth distribution is endogenous. Section 3 introduces a transfer scheme, along with tax on capital. One of these policies is non-political. None of our results are sensitive to the assumption that only capital or capital income is taxed. Section 4 analyses a general income tax *a la* Barro (1990). In this model also, a more redistributive tax policy improves long-run growth, but a more redistributive transfer scheme reduces it. Section 5 concludes.

2. The Basic Model

The population or the number of households in the economy is given. Each household has one unit of labour, inelastically supplied to the market. Households are differentiated on the basis of a basic skill level, L_h, whose distribution is continuous on a finite support in $\Re_+$. This distribution is primitive and constitutes the basic source of heterogeneity.[4] No further assumption such as skewness is necessary for the analysis of this section. For simplicity however, we assume that the distribution of L_h is skewed to the right, i.e., L_m, the median skill, is less than $\bar{L}$, the mean skill level. It permits us, as will be seen later, to use the capital holding of the median household relative to that of the mean household as a simple index of wealth inequality. Let $\int_{h\in H} L_h dh \equiv L$, where H is the total number of households and L is the total endowment of skill. For notational convenience, we normalise $H = 1$. Thus $L = \bar{L}$.

2.1 Production

A single good is produced. The production function follows Barro (1990) and A-R:

$$Q_t = A\bar{K}_t^{\alpha} G_t^{1-\alpha} \bar{L}^{1-\alpha}, \qquad \text{...(1)}$$

where Q_t is output at time t, $\bar{K}_t$ denotes the mean/aggregate capital, G_t is a public-infrastructure input and A > 0 is an index of technology[5]. Following the endogenous growth literature, we interpret

4. Alternatively, we can interpret L_h as just labour time supplied by household *h*, its distribution being based on how 'lazy' households are *vis-a-vis* one another.

5. By assuming a Cobb-Douglas specification, we maintain consistency with the literature. But, more generally, the results hold as long as the production function is linearly homogeneous in capital and labour and the infrastructure input plays the role of labour augmentation.

K as physical as well as human capital. Hence, α is the private return to physical and human capital. We require a regularity condition: $\alpha > 1/2$, which, as will be seen later, ensures that the net return to capital in equilibrium is positive.[6]

As in A-R, the input G_t is financed by a (specific) tax on capital income, which is equivalent to a wealth tax.[7] The government budget constraint is satisfied in all time periods, i.e., $G_t = \tau_t \overline{K}_t$. The competitive factor rewards are:

$$r_t = \psi(\tau_t) \equiv \alpha A \tau_t^{1-\alpha} \overline{L}^{1-\alpha}, w_t = \phi(\tau_t)\overline{K}_t \text{ where } \phi(.) \equiv (1-\alpha) A \tau_t^{1-\alpha} \overline{L}^{-\alpha}, \quad ...(2)$$

where r_t is the rent earned by capital and w_t denotes the wage rate. Note that an increase in τ enhances the marginal product of both factors. This constitutes the source of gain to household income and the economy's growth rate. As in A-R, without loss of generality, we let the rate of capital depreciation be zero.

2.2 *The Household's Problem*

Following Aghion and Bolton (1997), Picketty (1997), and Das (2000, 2001), every one lives for a single period. At the end of the period, a replica is born to each agent, and agents pass on a bequest to their children. Households derive utility from consumption, C_{ht}, and the amount of the good bequested (at time t) to time $t+1$, K_{ht+1}. Production occurs in the beginning of each period. Once production occurs, agents make consumption and bequest decisions. Hence, the bequest can be interpreted as inherited capital.

The utility function, $U: \Re_+^2 \rightarrow \Re_+$, satisfies the standard properties. For the sake of tractability, it is Cobb-Douglas: $U_{ht} = C_{ht}^{1-\beta} K_{ht+1}^{\beta}, 0 < \beta < 1$. The budget constraint facing an agent h is given by

$$C_{ht} + K_{ht+1} \leq \phi(\tau_t)\overline{K}_t L_h + [1 + \psi(\tau_t) - \tau_t] K_{ht}. \quad ...(3)$$

---

6. With a narrower interpretation of K as physical capital, it would be empirically implausible to assume $\alpha > 1/2$, but it is not so when capital is interpreted more broadly as we do here. Further, according to Barro and Sala-i-Martin (1995, page 38), even a value of α equal to 0.75 is quite reasonable.

7. We later show that our results are robust to G being funded by a proportional tax on capital earnings or on total income of a household.

We assume that the skill level of a household does not change over time or generations[8]. Each household is identified by a given L_h. There is no dynamic stochastic process governing the evolution of L_h.[9]

The tax rate is already known when households make their consumption and bequest decisions. Their optimisation exercise implies the following Euler equation for consumption: $C_{ht} = \frac{1-\beta}{\beta} K_{ht+1}$. It also leads to the following individual and aggregate accumulation equations:

$$K_{ht+1} = \beta\{\phi(\tau_t)L_h\overline{K}_t + [1+\psi(\tau_t)-\tau_t]K_{ht}\}, \qquad ...(4)$$

$$\overline{K}_{t+1} = \beta\{\phi(\tau_t)\overline{L} + [1+\psi(\tau_t)-\tau_t]\}\overline{K}_t. \qquad ...(5)$$

Substituting the Euler equation for consumption into the utility function yields

$$U_{ht} = \text{Constant}\cdot K_{ht+1}. \qquad ...(6)$$

Finally, substituting eq. (4) into eq. (6) yields the household's indirect utility function:

$$V_{ht} = Constant\cdot\{\phi(\tau_t)L_h\overline{K}_t + [1+\psi(\tau_t)-\tau_t]K_{ht}\}. \qquad ...(7)$$

It is sufficient to note that for any value of $\overline{K}_t$ and K_{ht}, the indirect utility is single peaked with respect to τ_t. This implies that the median household's optimal tax rate defines equilibrium under majority voting. However, before characterising the prefered tax rate of the median voter, we first prove that the median household is unique - which is an implication of our assumption that for any given h, L_h does not vary over time. The invariance of the median voter's identity over time ensures analytical tractability of our model.

2.3 Uniqueness of the Median Household

Define $n_{ht} \equiv K_{ht}/\overline{K}_t$. Dividing (4) by (5),

$$n_{ht+1} = n_{ht}\left[1+\frac{\phi(\cdot)(L_h/n_{ht}-\overline{L})}{\phi(\cdot)\overline{L}+1+\psi(\cdot)-\tau_t}\right]. \qquad ...(8)$$

8. In a very different context this is assumed, for instance, by Das (2000) and Ranjan (2001).

9. The benefit of this assumption is that it offers considerable analytical tractability. The cost is that it does not permit to say anything about social mobility. However, social mobility, although an important problem in its own right, is not our focus.

Let us start to track the economy from an initial period in which the tax rate is exogenous, not politically determined. Note then that the dynamic process (8) leads to a steady state where

$$n_h^* = \frac{L_h}{\bar{L}} \Rightarrow \phi(\tau)\bar{K}^* + [1+\psi(\tau^*) - \tau^*]\frac{K_h^*}{L_h} = \bar{K}^*\left[\phi(\tau^*) + \frac{1+\psi(\tau^*)-\tau^*}{\bar{L}}\right]. \quad ...(9)$$

The asterisks mark the steady-state values. The relation (9) implies that K_h^*/L_h is same for all h, i.e. the ranking of households in terms of capital held and disposable income is the same in terms of L_h. This 'alignment' of K_h^* with L_h in terms of ranking implies that the median household is identified by the ranking of L_h only, i.e. by $L_h = L_m$.

Now suppose that the tax rate 'becomes' political. The economy goes off the steady state. However, *irrespective* of what the tax rate is, (4) implies that the next period's capital stock holding of household *h* also has the same ranking as L_h. Further, this remains true for all successive time periods, off or on the steady state, as long as the households do not face asymmetric skill or preference shocks so as to change the initial ranking of households on the L_h scale. We assume away such shocks, which implies that the median household's identity is unchanged even though τ may change over time.

2.4 Analysis of Optimal Tax

How does the optimal tax rate compare across the households? Given (7), since the indirect utility of any particular household *h* is single-peaked with respect to τ_t, its optimal tax is given by the first order condition:[10]

$$\frac{\phi'(\tau_t)L_h}{n_{ht}} + \psi'(\tau_t) - 1 = 0. \quad ...(10)$$

From this equation, we can regard the marginal cost (MC) of a tax increase on disposable income as equal to 1, while the marginal benefit (MB) of a tax increase on disposable income (actually the MB/MC ratio) equal to $\phi'(\tau_t)L_h/n_{ht} + \psi'(\tau_t)$. These are illustrated in Figure 8.1. Consider two households: one is labour-rich and capital-poor and the other is labour-poor and capital-rich, i.e., the ratio L_h / n_{ht} is more for the former. Notice that the MB of a tax increase on disposable income is greater for the former. As a result, the

10. The second-order condition can be easily verified.

optimal tax for the former household is higher as shown $(\tau_1 > \tau_2)$. Intuitively, a labour-rich-capital-poor household cares less about net capital income than a labour-poor-capital-rich household. Hence, the optimal tax rate is higher for the former.

Figure 8.1

Optimal Tax for Households with Different Factor Holding Compositions

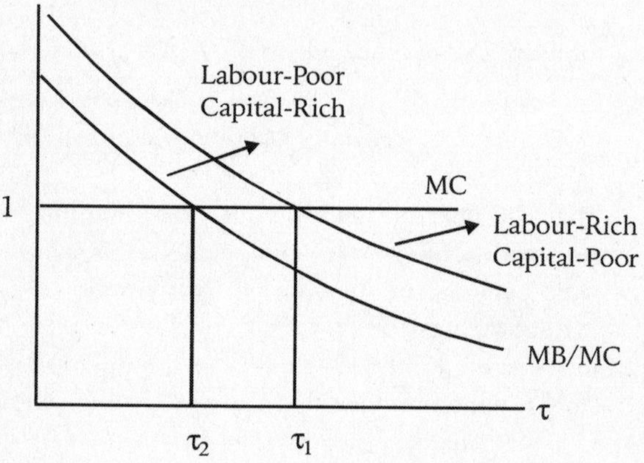

Using the definitions of $\phi(\cdot)$ and $\psi(\cdot)$ functions, the eq. (10) yields the following closed-form expression for the optimal tax rate of the hth household at time t, τ_{ht}:

$$\tau_{ht} = \left\{ A(1-\alpha)\bar{L}^{-1-\alpha}\left[\frac{(1-\alpha)L_h}{n_{ht}\bar{L}} + \alpha\right]\right\}^{\frac{1}{\alpha}}. \qquad ...(11)$$

Eq. (11) implies that the most preferred tax rate for a particular household depends on the ratio of two ratios, namely, $n_{ht}/(L_h/\bar{L})$. From now on, unless specified otherwise, let "relative" mean relative to the mean household. Thus, quite intuitively, τ_{ht} is negatively related to the ratio of its relative capital holding to its relative skill. Also, note that the optimal tax rate for any household is always positive. Moreover, this is bounded from below by the tax rate which will be chosen if a household's labour income were zero.[11]

11. This is equal to the tax rate which maximises the after-tax return to capital, $r_t - \tau_t$.

In particular, the equilibrium tax rate is equal to the optimal tax of the median household. This is given by substituting $h = m$ in (11):

$$\tau_{mt} = \left\{ A(1-\alpha)\bar{L}^{-1-\alpha} \left[\frac{(1-\alpha)L_m}{n_{mt}\bar{L}} + \alpha \right] \right\}^{\frac{1}{\alpha}}, \qquad ...(12)$$

where n_{mt} is the relative capital holding of the median household.

2.5 Steady State

The dynamics of the economy is fundamentally described by (8) with $h = m$ and eq. (12).

They contain two variables, n_{mt} and τ_{mt}.

Substituting $n_{mt+1} = n_{mt} = n_m^*$ in (8), it follows that, along the steady state,

$$n_m^* = \frac{L_m}{\bar{L}} \Leftrightarrow \frac{K_m^*}{L_m} = \frac{\bar{K}^*}{\bar{L}}. \qquad ...(13)$$

That is, the median household's composition of factor holdings is equal to that of the mean household. Indeed, (8) holds for all households, i.e.,

$$n_h^* = \frac{L_h}{\bar{L}} \Leftrightarrow \frac{K_h^*}{L_h} = \frac{\bar{K}^*}{\bar{L}} \; \forall h. \qquad ...(14)$$

In other words, compared to any given household, a more skilled household accumulates more capital in the long run and there is complete convergence of capital-labour ratio holdings across households in the steady state. This does *not* mean that there is (perfect) equality: although K_h^*/L_h is same for all households, for any two households say i and j such that $L_i \neq L_j$, we have $K_i^* \neq K_j^*$.

Interestingly, (14) implies that every household's preferred tax rate is the same, i.e., there is unanimity in the long run. Indeed, this is a general result, independent of Cobb-Douglas technology or that only capital is being taxed. A moment's reflection suggests that this is also natural: in the long run every one accumulates capital in proportion to his/her basic skill.

Graphically, note that in terms of the MB/MC and MC curves depicted in Figure 8.1, each household's MB/MC curve collapses to that of the mean household and its intersection with the MC=1 line gives τ in equation (15). This does not happen in the A-R model because factor ownership compositions are time-invariant.

In our model the unanimously agreed equilibrium tax rate is equal to[12]

$$\tau = \left[A(1-\alpha)\bar{L}^{1-\alpha} \right]^{\frac{1}{\alpha}}. \qquad ...(15)$$

We note a technical point here. Using (15), the net return to capital, $\kappa \equiv r - \tau$, is equal to $(2\alpha - 1)\tau/(1-\alpha)$, which may not positive for all $\alpha < 1$. This is where our regularity condition (R1), i.e. $\alpha > 1/2$, comes in; it assures that $\kappa > 0$.

Turning to the economy's growth rate, let us define it by $g_t \equiv K_t/K_{t-1}$. From (5),

$$g_{t+1} = \beta\left[\phi(\tau_t)\bar{L} + 1 + \psi(\tau_t) - \tau_t\right] = \beta(1 + A\bar{L}^{1-\alpha}\tau_t^{1-\alpha} - \tau_t). \qquad ...(16)$$

This shows a non-monotonic relationship between growth and the tax rate. On one hand, an increase in τ increases the marginal products of labour and capital and thus tends to increase disposable income. On the other hand, it lowers after-tax income. Hence, there is a trade-off. Moreover, similar to the A-R model, there is a unique growth-maximising tax rate equal to

$$t_g = \left[A(1-\alpha)\bar{L}^{1-\alpha} \right]^{\frac{1}{\alpha}}. \qquad ...(17)$$

However, unlike in A-R, this is *same* as the equilibrium tax rate in the steady state given by equation (15), i.e. *long-run growth is maximised at the political equilibrium*. It follows from the convergence of capital-labour ratio holdings across households. This, we believe, is a very interesting departure from the exogenous-distribution framework, and, a useful benchmark case where political equilibrium coincides with maximisation of growth. The benefit of identifying this economic environment is that the inefficiency resulting from politics in a more realistic economy can be seen insightfully in terms of a deviation from

12. In Galor and Moav (2002), there is also unanimity. However, our model contrasts from theirs in two respects. in their model unanimity occurs in a very different context: i.e., once the descendants of workers are sufficiently rich to invest in their human capital. Further, there is unanimity in both the short run and the long run. In our model, it holds in the long run only.

such an environment. In the next section, we will indeed analyse such deviations.

In terms of comparative statics, we note from (15) that $d\tau/dA > 0$. This is because a positive technology shock enhances the marginal product of both labour and capital and thus raises the marginal gain from a tax increase. Hence, everyone's preferred tax rate is higher. Next, differentiating (16) and using the expression of $d\tau/dA > 0$, we find $dg/dA > 0$. Thus a permanent positive technology shock increases both the equilibrium tax rate and the equilibrium growth rate. An important corollary of this is that the cross-country correlation between the tax rate and the growth rate may be positive when countries are ranked in terms of their levels of technology. This contrasts with an *intra-country* relationship between the tax and growth rates, which may be negative or positive depending on what the tax rate is.[13]

We have not talked about inequality yet. Our assumption that $L_m < \bar{L}$ implies that in the steady state, $n_m = K_m/\bar{K} < 1$. Hence, we can take n_m, the median-mean wealth ratio, as the indicator of inequality, and, a higher n_m implies a more *equal* distribution of wealth. Note also that, along the steady state, a household's disposable income and indirect utility are both proportional to a household's holding of capital. Hence, the magnitude of n_m would also indicate inequality in terms of income and utility. In other words, inequality in terms of wealth, income and utility are synonymous in our model.

Further, we observe directly from (13) that the long run wealth inequality is the same as the inequality in skill, i.e., more generally, the distribution of long-run wealth is the same as that of the skill. Within the purview of the model this is only natural.[14] Since the innate skill distribution is exogenous, unlike the tax rate or the growth rate, the level of inequality is not affected, for example, by a technology shock.[15]

13. It is easy to see that an increase in the preference parameter β does not affect the tax rate but leads to an increase in the growth rate.

14. If skill can be enhanced by education and there are capital market imperfections, then the distribution of long-run wealth or income inequality will not be equal to that of the innate skill distribution.

15. However, a uniform additive skill shock to all households would increase n_m and lower inequality.

More generally, we can define inequality in terms of coefficient of variation.[16] From (14) that the standard deviation of K_h equals $c_L \overline{K}_t$, where c_L is the coefficient of variation of L_h. Hence the coefficient of variation of wealth is equal to c_L, which is also invariant with respect to a technology or preference shock.

2.6 *Comparing with the A-R Model*

Figure 8.2 illustrates the comparison and reconciliation with the A-R model in a simple manner. The non-monotonic relationship between the growth rate and the tax rate - given by eq. (16) - is depicted in the top panel. We call it the 'growth-tax curve.' The tax rate that maximises the aggregate/average welfare is also the one that maximises the growth rate (This holds in the A-R model as well as in Barro (1990).)

The bottom panel graphs eq. (11): the optimal tax as a negative function of the ratio of relative capital holding to relative skill. In the A-R model the median voter's relative capital holding is *assumed* to be less than its relative skill. Hence, $\rho_m \equiv n_m/(L_m/L) < 1$. Accordingly, the economy operates effectively in the right-hand side of the growth-tax curve. Suppose that initially $\rho_m = \rho_m^0$. The tax rate is read off the horizontal axis and the economy's growth rate is g^0. Now, if ρ_m increases to ρ_m^1 i.e., the distribution becomes more equitable, we see that the tax rate falls and the economy's growth rate jumps up to g^1. In contrast, in our model, the distribution is endogenous. Every household's relative capital holding adjusts and converges in the steady state to its relative skill. That is, $\rho_h = 1$, for all *h*, including the median household. Thus political equilibrium implies the growth-maximising tax rate, τ_g. There is no conflict between politics and efficiency.

2.7 *Transitional Dynamics*

Suppose there are skill shocks to households (without changing their ranking in terms of L_h) such that initially the median voter's relative capital holding is not equal to its steady state value. How does the economy adjust over time? The transitional dynamics are governed by equations (8) and (12).

---

16. See Caselli and Ventura (1999) and Das (2000, 2001).

Figure 8.2

Comparison with the Alesina-Rodrik Model

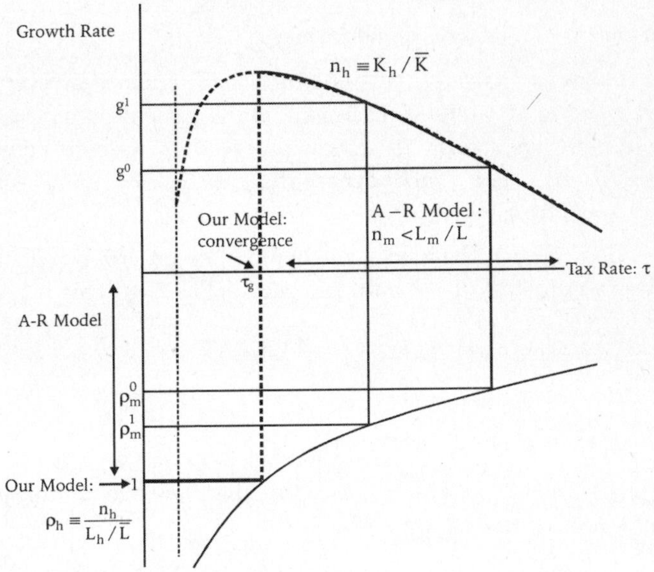

Totally differentiating equation (8) and evaluating the derivative by using the steady state condition $L_m/n_{mt} = \overline{L}$, , we get

$$0 < \left.\frac{dn_{mt+1}}{dn_{mt}}\right|_{n_{mt} \to L_m/\overline{L}} = \frac{1+\psi(\tau)-\tau}{\varphi(\tau)\overline{L}+1+\psi(\tau)-\tau} < 1. \qquad ...(18)$$

This implies that, locally the transition path of inequality is monotonic and stable. Starting from $n_{m0} \neq L_m/\overline{L}$, the economy converges monotonically to the long run level of inequality defined by the basic source of heterogeneity in L_h. Given the dynamics of n_{mt}, the dynamics of the tax rate are evident from (12). The optimal tax along the transition path decreases or increases over time as $n_{m0} \lesseqgtr L_m/\overline{L} \Leftrightarrow \rho_m \lesseqgtr 1$.

How does the growth rate change during transition? Interestingly, from Figure 8.2, we can readily infer that it increases over time - and tends to converge to the maximised growth rate - irrespective of whether $\rho_{m0} \lesseqgtr L_m/\overline{L}$ initially. Furthermore, since increase in ρ_{mt} means more equality, the contemporaneous correlation between growth and equality is negative and positive as $\rho_{m0} \lesseqgtr L_m/\bar{L}$ initially.

This completes the analysis of our basic model.

2.8 Proportional Tax on Capital Earnings

We now demonstrate that our bench-mark result that everyone's relative holding of capital to basic skill is the same does not hinge on our assumption of specific tax on capital earnings, which is equivalent to a wealth tax.[17] Let τ_t now denote the *proportion* of capital earnings that is taxed. Then $G = \tau_t r_t K_t$.

Working through the model, the optimal tax for any household h is governed a the first-order condition analogous to (10). This is given by

$$\frac{\breve{\phi}'(\tau_t)L_h}{n_{ht}} - \breve{\psi}(\tau_t) + (1-\tau_t)\breve{\psi}'(\tau_t) = 0 \quad \text{where}$$

$$\breve{\psi}(\tau_t) = \widetilde{\psi}(\tau_t)^{\frac{1}{\alpha}}, \breve{\phi}(\tau_t) = A^{\frac{1}{\alpha}}(1-\alpha)\alpha^{\frac{1-\alpha}{\alpha}}\tau_t^{\frac{1-\alpha+\alpha^2}{\alpha}}\bar{L}^{\frac{1-2\alpha}{\alpha}}.$$

Likewise, similar to eqs. (4) and (5), the individual and aggregate accumulation equations are:

$$K_{ht+1} = \beta\left\{\breve{\phi}(\tau_t)L_h\bar{K}_t + (1-\tau_t)\breve{\psi}(\tau_t)K_{ht}\right\}$$

$$\bar{K}_{t+1} = \beta\left\{\breve{\phi}(\tau_t)\bar{L} + (1-\tau_t)\breve{\psi}(\tau_t)\right\}\bar{K}_t. \qquad \text{...(19)}$$

Given (19), wealth distribution evolves according to

$$n_{ht+1} = n_{ht}\left[1 + \frac{\breve{\phi}(\cdot)(L_h/n_{ht} - \bar{L})}{\breve{\phi}(\cdot)\bar{L} + (1-\tau_t)\breve{\psi}(\cdot)}\right]. \qquad \text{...(20)}$$

Hence, along the steady state,

$$n_h^* = \frac{L_h}{\bar{L}} \Leftrightarrow \frac{K_h^*}{L_h} = \frac{\bar{K}^*}{\bar{L}}. \qquad \text{...(21)}$$

Every household's composition of factor holdings is the same. There is unanimity. Further, following the reasoning before, it is easy to see that convergence to the steady state is smooth and monotonic.

In sum, whether it is a tax on wealth or capital earning, the endogeneity of wealth distribution implies a configuration of the

17. Nor does it depend on the assumption of Cobb-Douglas technology.

long-run growth rate, tax rate, and the degree of inequality, which is quite different from the case where the distribution of wealth is exogenous.

However, this is only our bench-mark model with endogenous long-run distribution. As our second generalisation, we now introduce an additional distributive policy. Unanimity, we shall see, now breaks. Richer possibilities arise.

3. Political and Non-Political Policies

As discussed in the introduction, any policy inference from redistribution to growth must presume that the policy is independent or non-political. Accordingly, suppose that there is also a transfer policy, where θ denotes the fraction of tax revenues disbursed back uniformly across households. Thus, there are two policies: τ and θ. Both are redistributive as well as have implications towards the growth. However, θ is relatively more redistributive, whereas τ is primarily more targeted towards growth (as it finances the public input G). Assuming that one of the two policies is political and the other is not, we ask how an exogenous change in the policy that is non-political affects the other policy through the political process and thereby affects distribution and growth.

There are two possibilities: (a) τ is political as before, while θ is not and (b) τ is non-political and θ is political. For simplicity, let us revert back to the assumption (as in A-R) that τ represents specific tax on capital earnings.

3.1 τ *Political and* θ *Non-Political*

Let the policy which is political have time subscript, whereas the other doesn't. We have $G_t = (\tau_t - \theta)\overline{K}_t$, where $S_t \equiv \theta K_t$ is transferred back uniformly to all households. Denote $T_t \equiv \tau_t - \theta$, the net tax on capital. Normalising $A = 1$ for the sake of notational simplicity, the competitive rewards are then

$$w_t = \widetilde{\phi}(T_t)\overline{K}_t\,;\; r_t = \widetilde{\psi}(T_t) \text{ where}$$

$$\widetilde{\phi}(\cdot) = (1-\alpha)T_t^{1-\alpha}\overline{L}^{-\alpha}\,;\; \widetilde{\psi}(\cdot) = \alpha(T_t\overline{L})^{1-\alpha}. \qquad \text{...(22)}$$

Solving out the household problem exactly as before we obtain the following expressions of K_{ht+1}, K_{t+1} and the indirect utility:

$$K_{ht+1} = \beta\left\{\widetilde{\phi}(T_t)L_h K_t + \left[1+\widetilde{\psi}(T_t)-\tau_t\right]K_{ht} + \theta K_t\right\} \qquad ...(23)$$

$$\overline{K}_{t+1} = \beta\left\{\widetilde{\phi}(T_t)\overline{L} + 1 + \widetilde{\psi}(T_t) - T_t\right\}\overline{K}_t\ , \qquad ...(24)$$

$$V_{ht} = Constant \cdot \left\{\widetilde{\phi}(T_t)L_h \overline{K}_t + \left[1+\widetilde{\psi}(T_t)-\tau_t\right]K_{ht} + \theta K_t\right\}. \qquad ...(25)$$

Maximising indirect utility with respect to τ_t for a given $\overline{K}_t$ and K_{ht} gives the most preferred tax rate of household *h*. The first-order condition is $\widetilde{\phi}'(T_t)L_h\overline{K}_t + \left[\widetilde{\psi}'(T_t) - 1\right]K_{ht} = 0$, which effectively gives the optimal *net* tax on capital. This leads to an analog of (11):

$$T_{ht} = \left\{(1-\alpha)\overline{L}^{-1-\alpha}\left[\frac{(1-\alpha)L_h}{n_{ht}\overline{L}} + \alpha\right]\right\}^{\frac{1}{\alpha}}. \qquad ...(26)$$

Next, dividing (23) by (24) gives the dynamics for the household accumulation of relative capital holdings:[18]

$$n_{ht+1} = n_{ht}\left[1 + \frac{\widetilde{\phi}(T_t)\left(L_h / n_{ht} - \overline{L}\right) + \theta\left(1/n_{ht} - 1\right)}{\widetilde{\phi}(T_t)\,\overline{L} + 1 + \widetilde{\psi}(T_t) - T_t}\right]. \qquad ...(27)$$

Steady-state conditions are obtained by substituting $h = m$ in (26) and (27):

$$T_m^* = \left\{(1-\alpha)\overline{L}^{-1-\alpha}\left[\frac{(1-\alpha)L_m}{n_m^*\overline{L}} + \alpha\right]\right\}^{\frac{1}{\alpha}} \qquad ...(28)$$

$$(1-\alpha)\,(\overline{L}T_m^*)^{1-\alpha}\left(n_m^* - \frac{L_m}{\overline{L}}\right) = \theta(1-n_m^*). \qquad ..(29)$$

In view of our assumption that the median skill is less than the mean, i.e., $L_m < \overline{L}$, eq. (29) implies that $L_m/\overline{L} < n_m^* < 1$.[19] Hence factor compositions are not equalised and there is no unanimity. Furthermore, the median household holds a higher capital/skill ratio than the mean household. It is because the proportion of transfers received relative to pre-transfer income is higher for the median than the mean household. This does *not* however imply that the median

18. It is straight forward to verfity that the transitional dynamics are monotonic and stable.

19. Suppose $n_m^* \geq 1$. Then, from (29), $n_m^* \leq L_m/\overline{L}$. Thus $L_m < \overline{L}$ implies $n_m^* < 1$, which is a contradiction.

household is richer than the average. Although $K_m^*/L_m > \overline{K}^*/\overline{L}$, we have, as in the basic model, $K_m^* < \overline{K}^*$ and $L_m < \overline{L}$.[20]

From (26), the optimal τ for a household rises with the relative skill and falls with the relative capital holding and thus negatively related to the ratio of relative capital holding to relative skill. Since this ratio is higher for the median household than for the mean, τ_m is lower than the mean household's τ. This implies that, at given θ, the optimal net tax rate of the median household, equal to the equilibrium net tax rate, is less than that of the mean household. But the mean household net tax rate coincides the growth maximising net tax rate, say T_g.[21] Hence, $T_m^* < T_g$, i.e., the political equilibrium lies in the left-hand side of the growth-tax curve.

Figure 8.3

τ Political; θ Non-Political

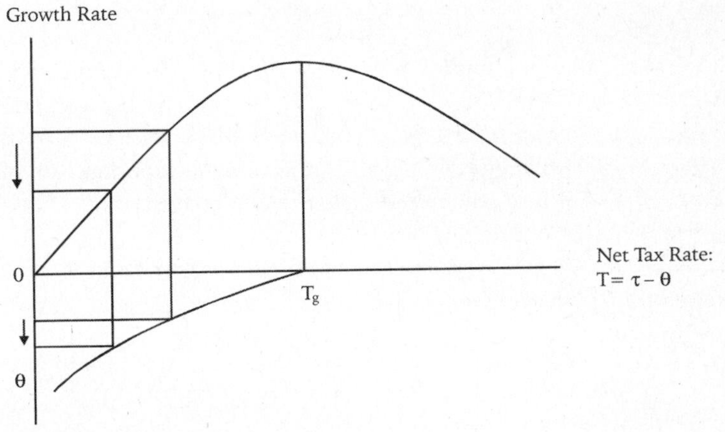

20. Also, in Appendix A8.1, we prove that, despite the median household holding more capital/labour ratio than does the average household, the capital-holding and the after-tax income ratios are equal between the two households.

21. By equating n_h to $L_h/\overline{L}$ in (26), $T_g = [(1-\alpha)\overline{L}^{1-\alpha}]^{1/\alpha}$.

In terms of comparative statics, the two steady-state conditions yield $dn_m^*/d\theta > 0$.[22] Intuitively, more transfers leads to less inequality. This, in turn, implies, in view of (28), $dT_m^*/d\theta < 0$: less inequality lessens the political demand for less net tax on capital.

The effect of an increase in θ on long-run growth is now straightforward. Since $T_m^* < T_g$ and $dT_m^*/d\theta < 0$, the growth rate falls. In other words, a transfer policy that reduces inequality *hurts* growth.

3.2 τ *Non-Political and* θ *Political*

This is the case where the tax rate is exogenous and the transfer policy is political. Using the expression of indirect utility, the most preferred "transfer rate" of household h is given by

$$\theta_{ht} = \tau - \left\{(1-\alpha)\bar{L}^{-1-\alpha}\left[\frac{(1-\alpha)L_h}{\bar{L}} + \alpha n_{ht}\right]\right\}^{\frac{1}{\alpha}} \qquad \text{...(30)}$$

$$\Leftrightarrow T_{ht} \equiv \tau - \theta_{ht} = \left\{(1-\alpha)\bar{L}^{-1-\alpha}\left[\frac{(1-\alpha)L_h}{\bar{L}} + \alpha n_{ht}\right]\right\}^{\frac{1}{\alpha}}. \qquad \text{...(31)}$$

It is obvious but important to note that the optimal transfer rate falls with a household's relative skill as well as relative capital holding. It is because the richer the household - either in terms of skill or capital - the larger is the marginal benefit of an increase in the net tax rate and hence *greater* is the marginal detrimental effect of a rise in θ - which tends to reduce the net tax rate - on its disposable income. This implies that a richer household will demand less θ and therefore a higher net tax.

---

22. Substituting (28) into (29), eliminating T_m^* and log-differentiating the resulting equation give $dn_m^* / d\theta = 1/(a\theta)$, where

$$a \equiv \frac{1}{1-n_m^*} + \frac{1}{n_m^* - L_m} - \frac{1-\alpha}{\alpha}\frac{(1-\alpha)L_m}{n^*[(1-\alpha)L_m + \alpha n_m^*]}.$$

Given our regularity condition $\alpha > 1/2$

$$a > \frac{1}{1-n_m^*} + \frac{1}{n_m^* - L_m} - \frac{(1-\alpha)L_m}{n^*[(1-\alpha)L_m + \alpha n_m^*]} > \frac{1}{1-n_m^*} + \frac{1}{n_m^* - L_m} - \frac{1}{n^*}$$

$$= \frac{1}{1-n_m^*} + \frac{L_m}{n_m^*(n_m^* - L_m)} > 0.$$

This implies $dn_m^* / d\theta > 0$.

There is a qualitative difference with the previous case: here the net tax rate increases with relative capital, whereas it decreased with relative capital in the previous case.

The equation governing the dynamics of n_{ht} is same as in the previous case, except that τ is now exogenous and θ is a variable. In the steady state however, this equation reduces exactly to (29).[23] Thus, as before, $L_m/\bar{L} < n_m^* < 1$.

The median household being skill-poor and capital-poor relative to the mean, in view of (31), T_m^* is less than the optimal net tax rate of the mean household. Accordingly $T_m^* < T_g$ and like in the previous case, the equilibrium lies on the left-hand arm of the growth-tax curve.

In the steady state we have

$$(1-\alpha)(\bar{L}T_m^*)^{1-\alpha}\left(n_m^* - \frac{L_m}{\bar{L}}\right) - T_m^*(1-n_m^*) = \tau(1-n_m^*) \qquad \dots(32)$$

$$T_m^* = \left\{(1-\alpha)\bar{L}^{-1-\alpha}\left[\frac{(1-\alpha)L_m}{\bar{L}} + \alpha n_m^*\right]\right\}^{\frac{1}{\alpha}}, \qquad \dots(33)$$

where the former is a restatement of (29) and the latter follows from eq. (31).

It is easy to compute that $dn_m^*/d\tau > 0$ and $dT_m^*/d\tau > 0$. Both implications are intuitive. The former implies less inequality and the latter implies higher growth, as τ increases. This is shown in Figure 8.4. Thus, a policy which is more redistributive but primarily a growth-enhancing increases long-run growth.

4. A General Income Tax

The same policy conclusions hold when the input G is, instead, funded by a general tax on income. However, the nature of the equilibrium may be quite different compared to when capital or capital income is taxed.

Let τ_{yt} denote a proportional tax on the sum of labour and income from capital, and let $S_t = \theta_{yt}Q_t$ be the amount transferred back uniformly to the households. Thus $G_t = (\tau_{yt} - \theta_{yt})Q_t \equiv T_{yt}Q_t$.[24] The

23. It is easy to derive that the local dynamics is locally stable and monotonic.

24. This can be viewed as a generalisation of Barro (1990). In Barro, $\theta_{yt} = 0$.

production function is the same, and, for notational simplicity, let $A = \bar{L} = 1$. There are again two cases: τ_y is not political, whereas θ_y is, and, the vice versa. We consider these in turn.

Figure 8.4

τ Non-Political; θ Political

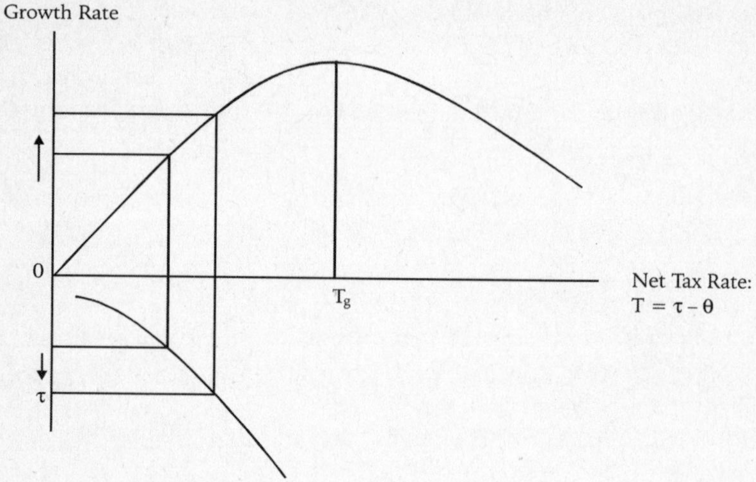

4.1 τ_y Non-Political and θ_y Political

This is quite similar to the previous case.

Given that the tax base is a household's total income, the factor rewards have the following expressions: $w_t = \hat{\varphi}\bar{K}_t$ *and* $r_t = \hat{\psi}$, where $\hat{\varphi} = (1-\alpha)T_{yt}^{1/\alpha}$ *and* $\hat{\psi} = \alpha T_{yt}^{1/\alpha}$. A household's budget constraint is given by $C_{ht} + K_{ht+1} \leq (1-\tau_y)(w_t L_h + r_t K_{ht}) + S_t$. However, the household optimisation leads to the same first-order condition. Together with the budget constraint, it gives rise to

$$K_{ht+1} = \beta\{(1-\tau_y)[\hat{\varphi}(T_{yt})L_h\bar{K}_t + [1+\hat{\psi}(T_{yt})]K_{ht}] + \theta_{yt}T_{yt}^{1/\alpha}\bar{K}_t\}, \quad ...(34)$$

$$V_{ht} = Constant \cdot \{(1-\tau_y)[\hat{\varphi}(T_{yt})L_h\bar{K}_t + [1+\hat{\psi}(T_{yt})]K_{ht}] + \theta_{yt}T_{yt}^{1/\alpha}\bar{K}_t\} \quad ...(35)$$

where we have utilised that $Q_t = w_t + r_t\bar{K}_t = (\hat{\varphi}+\hat{\psi})\bar{K}_t = T_{yt}^{1/\alpha}\bar{K}_t$, such that $S_t = \theta_y T_{yt}^{1/\alpha}\bar{K}_t$.

Maximising (35) with respect to θ_{yt} yields the net tax as a function of τ_y and n_{ht}:

$$T_{yht} \equiv \tau_y - \theta_{yt} = \frac{\tau_y + (1-\tau_y)[(1-\alpha)L_h + \alpha n_{ht}}{1+\alpha}. \qquad \ldots(36)$$

Analogous to the previous case, the rate of transfer falls and the net tax rate rises with both relative skill and relative capital holding.

Using (34) and aggregating it, the dynamics for the median household's accumulation of relative capital holdings is given by

$$n_{mt+1} = n_{mt}\left[1 - \frac{(1-\alpha)(1-\tau_y)(1-\frac{L_m}{n_{mt}}) + (\tau_y - T_{yt})(1-\frac{L_m}{n_{mt}})}{1-T_{yt}}\right] \qquad \ldots(37)$$

In the steady state then

$$T_y^* = \frac{\tau_y + (1-\tau_y)[(1-\alpha)L_m + \alpha n_m^*}{1+\alpha} \qquad \ldots(38)$$

$$(1-\alpha)(1-\tau_y)(n_m^* - L_m) = (\tau_y - T_y^*)(1-n_m^*) \qquad \ldots(39)$$

The last two equations are respectively obtained from (36) and (37). Eq. (39) implies $L_m < n_m^* < 1$. Differentiating these equations, we obtain $\partial T_y^*/\partial\tau_y$ *and* $\partial n_m^*/\partial\tau_y$ both positive.[25] The intuition is similar to the previous case.

Aggregating (34) gives a slightly different expression of growth as a function of the net tax, namely, $g^* = \beta(1-T_y)T_y^{1/\alpha}$. But the trade-off is analogous. There is a growth-maximising net tax rate, and, this is given by $T_{yg} = 1/(1+\alpha)$. We see from (38) that $T_y^* < T_{yg}$.[26] Thus the political equilibrium lies in the left-hand side of the growth-tax curve.

How does an increase in τ_y affect growth? Since $\partial T_y^*/\partial\tau_y > 0$, it follows that it increases long-run growth. This is shown in Figure 8.5. As in case of tax on capital, an increase in the tax rate on total income enhances both growth and equity.

---

25. Substituting (38) into (39) and eliminating T_y^* gives

$$\frac{(1-\alpha^2)(n_m^* - L_m)}{1-n_m^*} + (1-\alpha)L_m + \alpha n_m^* = \frac{\alpha\tau_y}{1-\tau_y}.$$

This yields $\partial n_m^*/\partial\tau_y > 0$. Using this, eq. (38) implies $\partial T_y^*/\partial\tau_y > 0$.

26. In (38) the coefficient of $1-\tau_y$ is less than one. Hence the numerator, which a weighted average of $\tau_y(<1)$ and $1-\tau_y$, is less than one. This implies $T_y^* < 1/(1+\alpha) = T_{yg}$.

Figure 8.5

τ_y Non-Political; θ_y Political

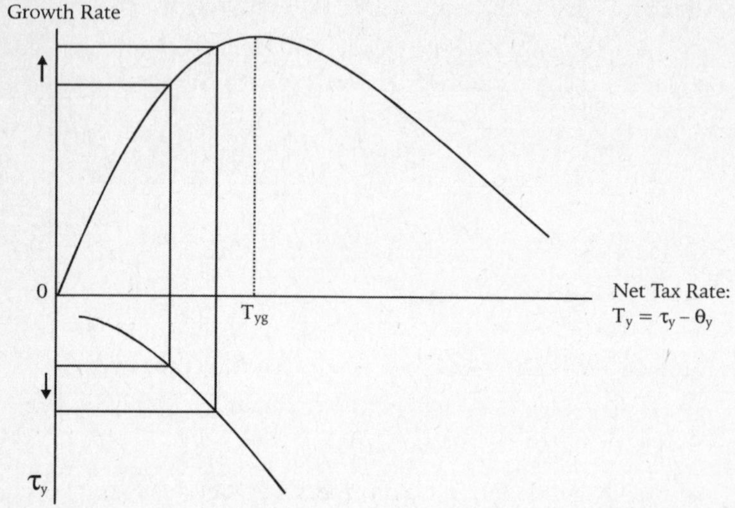

4.2 τ_y Political and θ_y Non-Political

It will be shown that an increase in θ_y, the rate of transfer, will reduce growth - which is similar to what was obtained in case of tax on capital only. But, interestingly, the mechanisms at work are quite different.

Proceeding as in earlier cases, the equilibrium tax rate is given by

$$\tau_{yht} = \theta_y + \frac{1}{1+\alpha} + \theta_y\left[\frac{1}{(1-\alpha)L_h + \alpha n_{ht}} - \frac{1}{1+\alpha}\right]. \qquad ...(40)$$

Note that, in contrast to the very first case where the political demand for the tax rate rises with the relative skill but falls with relative capital, here it falls with respect to both - because it is a tax on total income, not just on capital.

In the steady state and for the median household, eq. (40) gives the following expression of the net tax rate:

$$T_y^* = \frac{1}{1+\alpha} + \theta_y\left[\frac{1}{(1-\alpha)L_m + \alpha n_m^*} - \frac{1}{1+\alpha}\right]. \qquad ...(41)$$

The other steady state is condition (39) which can restated as:

$$\frac{1-n_m^*}{n_m^*-L_m}=\frac{(1-\alpha)(1-\theta_y-T_y^*)}{\theta_y}. \qquad ...(42)$$

Note that if $\theta_y=0$, then $n_m^*=L_m$. Unanimity holds. But given $\theta_y>0$ it does not, and the last equation gives $L_m<n_m^*<1$.

Notice from (41) that $T_y^*>1/(1+\alpha)=T_{yg}$, that is, unlike in the previous three cases, the political equilibrium lies in the right-hand side of the growth-tax curve. The median household is both skill- and capital-poor relative to the mean household, and, as derived earlier, the optimal income tax rate falls with relative skill and relative capital holding. Hence its preferred tax rate on income is *higher* than that of the mean household. At any given θ_y it translates to the equilibrium tax rate being higher than the growth-maximising tax rate.

Figure 8.6

τ_y Political; θ_y Non-Political

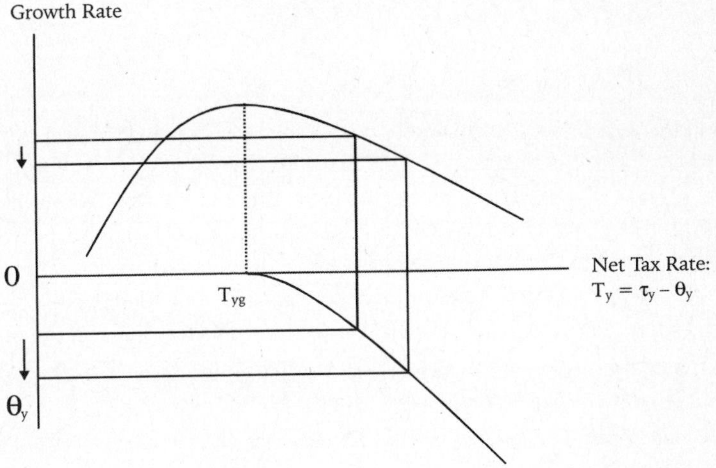

For comparative statics, it is easier to substitute (41) into (42), obtain

$$\frac{(1+\alpha)T_y^*-1}{1-T_y^*}=\frac{1-\alpha}{\alpha+L_m/(n_m^*-L_m)} \qquad ...(43)$$

and treat (41) and (43) as two equations having two variables, T_y^* and n_m^*. Totally differentiating these equations with respect to $\theta_y, dn_m^*/d\theta_y > 0;$ as expected, a higher rate of transfer brings more equity. What may not be so apparent is that $dT_y^*/d\theta_y > 0$. This means that an increase in transfer not only increases the politically determined tax rate, it does so by more than the increase in transfer - i.e. $\partial\tau_y^*/\partial\theta_y > 1$.

Intuitively, a rise in the net tax rate increases earning (both from labour and capital) *as well as* the transfer income (because transfers are funded from total income). Therefore, an increase in θ_y raises the marginal gain of a rise in the net tax on disposable income. This leads to a demand for a higher net tax rate.

The implications towards growth is now immediate. Since the economy operates on the right-hand side of the growth-tax curve and the net tax rate increases with θ_y, growth rate falls (Figure 8.6). In other words, quite interestingly, the position of the political equilibrium and the effect of an increase in the transfer rate on the net tax rate are both opposite of what they are in case of tax on capital income only. But in tandem, the two opposites together lead to the same policy implication.

5. Summary

This paper has formulated a model in which inequality and growth are jointly determined in a political equilibrium. There is a unique non-degenerate distribution of wealth and income in the steady state, independent of the initial distribution. In terms of the political equilibrium, our model follows the median-voter approach of Alesina-Rodrik and Persson-Tabellini. More specifically, the model is closer to the former. Our model also allows for a non-political policy instrument.

Endogeneity of distribution together with a non-political distributive policy offers novel insights. Table 8.1 summarises the results. When the growth-oriented redistributive policy is politically determined, a rise in the (non-political) transfer rate raises equality but reduces long-run growth. In this sense there is a *negative* tradeoff between growth and equity. This sharply contrasts the existing, central, (theoretical) result that more equality is growth-enhancing. But our result is consistent with recent empirical work by several authors such as Li and Zou (1998), Forbes (2000), Banerjee and Duflo

(2003), and Lundberg and Squire (2003) which argues that equality and growth may be negatively related. Politics determines the mechanism behind how redistributive policies affect growth.

Table 8.1

Summary of Results

Tax on Capital	*Equilibrium Net Tax Rate*	*Effect on Growth/Equity*
τ_t political, θ non-political; $\theta \uparrow$	$T^* < T_g$	Less growth/more Equity
τ non-political, θ_t political; $\tau \uparrow$	$T^* < T_g$	More growth/more Equity
General Income tax	*Equilibrium Net Tax Rate*	*Effect on Growth/Equity*
τ_{yt} political, θ_y non-political; $\theta_y \uparrow$	$T_y^* > T_{yg}$	Less growth/more Equity
τ_y non-political, θ_t political; $\tau_y \uparrow$	$T_y^* < T_{yg}$	More growth/more Equity

Our analysis hopes to prove a general point that the joint analytical determination of inequality, growth, and a political equilibrium is not an intractable proposition. The specific model achieves tractability by assuming limited life time and an economy in which the identity of the median household does not change over time. Hopefully, for future research, this approach would suggest other ways to ensure tractability in similar models and at the same time offer more generality. For example, what happens when individuals vote on a tax schedule rather than a tax rate. Also, there are several sources of individual heterogeneity. We have considered innate-skill heterogeneity, so as to illustrate the contrast with the existing literature as sharply as possible. Other sources of heterogeneity such as various types individual preference shocks should be considered and their implications toward long-run distribution and growth be systematically studied.

APPENDIX 8A.1

We prove that in the model of Section 3, $y_m^*/\overline{y}^* = K_m^*/\overline{K}^*$, where y_t is the after-tax transfer income, equal to $(1-\alpha)T_t^{1-\alpha}\overline{L}^{-\alpha}\overline{K}_t L_h + [1+\alpha(T_t\overline{L})^{1-\alpha} - \tau_t]K_{ht} + \theta_t\overline{K}_t$. In section 3.1 where τ is political and θ is not, in the steady state,

$$\frac{y_m}{\overline{y}} = \frac{(1-\alpha)(T_m^*\overline{L})^{1-\alpha}\overline{K}L_m^*/\overline{L} + [1+\alpha(T_m^*\overline{L})^{1-\alpha} - \tau_m^*]K_m^* + \theta\overline{K}}{[(1-\alpha)(T_m^*\overline{L})^{1-\alpha} + 1 + \alpha(T_m^*\overline{L})^{1-\alpha} - \tau_m^* + \theta]\overline{K}}$$

$$= \frac{(1-\alpha)(T_m^*\overline{L})^{1-\alpha}L_m^*/\overline{L} + [1+\alpha(T_m^*\overline{L})^{1-\alpha} - \tau_m^*]n_m^* + \theta}{(1-\alpha)(T_m^*\overline{L})^{1-\alpha} + 1 + \alpha(T_m^*\overline{L})^{1-\alpha} - \tau_m^* + \theta}.$$

Thus

$$\frac{y_m}{\overline{y}} = n_m = \frac{(1-\alpha)(T_m^*\overline{L})^{1-\alpha}(L_m^*/\overline{L} - n_m^*) + \theta(1-n_m^*)}{(1-\alpha)(T_m^*\overline{L})^{1-\alpha} + 1 + \alpha(T_m^*\overline{L})^{1-\alpha} - \tau_m^* + \theta}$$

Substituting the steady state condition (29), it is readily seen that the numerator of the above term is zero. This proves that $y_m/\overline{y} = n_m$.

Eq. (29) also holds in section 3.2, wherein τ is not political and θ is political. Hence, in this case also, $y_m^*/\overline{y}^* = K_m^*/\overline{K}^*$

References

Aghion, P. and P. Bolton (1997), "A Theory of Trickle-Down Growth and Development", *Review of Economic Studies*, 64: 151-172.

Aghion, P. and P. Howitt (1998), *Endogenous Growth Theory*, MIT Press, Cambridge.

Aghion, P., E. Caroli and C. Garcia-Penalosa (1999), "Inequality and Economic Growth: The Perspective of the New Growth Theories", *Journal of Economic Literature*, 37: 1615-60.

Alesina, A. and D. Rodrik (1994), "Distributive Politics and Economic Growth", *Quarterly Journal of Economics*, 109: 465-490.

Banerjee, A. and A. Newmann (1993), "Occupational Choice and the Process of Development", *Journal of Political Economy*, 101: 274-98.

Barro, R. (1990), "Government Spending in a Simple Model of Endogenous Growth", *Journal of Political Economy*, 98 Part 2: S103-26.

Barro, R. and X. Sala-i-Martin, *Economic Growth*, Mc-Graw Hill.

Bertola, G. (1993), "Factor Shares and Savings in Endogenous Growth". *American Economic Review*, 83: 1184-1198.

Benabou, R. (1995), *Unequal Societies*, New York: New York University, April, Mimeo. Revised May 1996, Cambridge, MA: NBER Research Working Paper 5583.

Caselli, F. and J. Ventura (1999), "A Representative Consumer Theory of Distribution", *American Economic Review* 90: 909-926.

Das, S.P. (2000), "Trade Among Similar Countries and the Personal Distribution of Income and Wealth", *Economica*, 67, 265-281.

———. (2001), "Endogenous Distribution and the Political Economy of Trade Policy", *European Journal of Political Economy*, 17, 465-491.

Drazen, A. (2000), *Political Economy in Macroeconomics*, Princeton University Press, Princeton: New Jersey.

Forbes, K. (2000), "A Reassessment of the Relationship Between Inequality and Growth", *American Economic Review*, 90: 869-887.

Galor, O. and J. Zeira (1993), "Income Distribution and Macroeconomics", *Review of Economic Studies*, 60: 35-52.

Galor O., and O. Moav. (2002), "Das Human Kapital", *Brown University Working Paper.*

Jones, L. and R. Manuelli (1990), "A Convex Model of Equilibrium Growth: Theory and Policy Implications, *Journal of Political Economy*, 98(5): 1008-1038.

Li, H. and H. Zou (1998), "Income Inequality is not Harmful for Growth: Theory and Evidence, *Review of Development Economics*, Vol 2(3), 318-334.

Lundberg, M. and L. Squire (2003), "The Simultaneous Evolution of Growth and Inequality, *Economic Journal*, 113, 326-344.

Loury, G. (1981), "Intergenerational Transfers and the Distribution of Earnings", *Econometrica*, 49: 843-867.

Matsuyama, K. (2000), "Endogenous Inequality", *Review of Economic Studies*, 67: 743-759.

Perotti, R. (1993), "Political Equilibrium, Income Distribution, and Growth", *Review of Economic Studies*, 60: 755-776.

Persson, T. and G. Tabellini (1994), "Is Inequality Harmful for Growth? Theory and Evidence", *American Economic Review*, 48: 600-621.

Piketty, T. (1997), "The Dynamics of the Wealth Distribution and the Interest Rate with Credit Rationing", *Review of Economic Studies*, 64: 173-189.

Ranjan, P. (2001), "Credit Constraints and the Phenomenon of Child Labour", *Journal of Development Economics*, 64: 81-102.

Saint-Paul, G. and T. Verdier (1993), "Education, Democracy, and Growth", *Journal of Development Economics*, 42: 399-407.

The paper has benefited from seminar presentations at the Catholic University of Louvain, Hong Kong University of Science and Technology, Indian Statistical Institute - Delhi, Tilburg University, DIW Berlin, ZEI Bonn, the Econometrica Society Meetings in Atlanta (January 2002), the Conference for Business Cycle and Growth Research (June 2002), University of Wisconsin-Milwaukee, and the University of Konstanz. Chetan Ghate thanks the Chapman Fund at Colorado College for financial support. He also thanks the Department of Macro and Forecasting at DIW Berlin for financial support where part of this paper was written. Satya Das acknowledges financial support from the Belgian French Community's program, "Action de Recherches Concertee' 99/04-235". See DIW Berlin Discussion Paper 310 for an earlier working paper version of this paper, Discussion Papers in Economics, Discussion Paper 03-06, Indian Statistical Institute, Delhi, September 2003.

9

Measuring Benefits from Reduced Air Pollution in the Cities of Delhi and Kolkata in India Using Hedonic Property Prices Model

M.N. MURTY, S.C. GULATI
AVISHEK BANERJEE

1. Introduction

Commodities could be distinguished by the characteristics they possess and their prices are functions of these characteristics. From the point of view of the owner, land property could be distinguished in terms of its location, size, and local environmental quality, while from the worker's perspective, a job is a differentiated product in terms of the risk of an on job accident, working conditions, prestige, training and enhancement of skills, and the local environmental quality at the work place. Environmental characteristics like air or water quality affect the price of land either as a producer good or as a consumer good. Ridker (1967) and Ridker and Henning (1976) provided the first empirical evidence that air pollution affects the property values. Freeman (1974), and Rosen (1974) used the hedonic price theory to interpret the derivative of hedonic property price function with respect to air pollution as a marginal implicit price and therefore the marginal willingness-to-pay of individuals for air pollution reduction. Thaler and Rosen (1976) are the first to suggest that the labour market could be viewed as the hedonic market. The derivative of the hedonic wage function with respect to any job characteristic, say exposure to air pollution at work place, could be interpreted as the marginal implicit price or worker's marginal willingness to accept for increased exposure to pollution.

In a hedonic prices model therefore there are two equations to be estimated: The hedonic price function and the individual's marginal willingness-to-pay function for the improved environmental quality[1]. In the model of hedonic property prices estimated in this paper, the equations are given as:

$$P_{hi} = P_h (S_i, N_i, Q_i) \quad ...(1)$$

$$b_{ij} = b_{ij} (q_j, Q_i^*, S_i, N_i, G_i) \quad ...(2)$$

Equation (1) is the hedonic price equation where P_{hi} is the property price[2] of the ith house, S_i consists of the structural characteristics of the house, N_i contains the neighbourhood characteristics of the house and Q_i stands for the Environmental characteristics of the house. Equation (2) is the individual's marginal willingness to 'pay function where b_{ij} is the marginal willingness-to-pay for improved air quality for the jth household, while Q_i^* is the vector of other environmental characteristics and G_i stands for socio-economic characteristics. q_j is the particular environmental characteristic for which we want to derive the marginal willingness-to-pay function. There are a number of empirical studies[3], mainly in the developed country context, estimating the hedonic property value model for environmental values. The objective of these studies is to estimate the hedonic price and the individual's marginal willingness-to-pay functions with the required curvature properties. For example, one expects that property prices are an increasing function of the environmental quality given the characteristics of the house. Similarly, the individual's marginal willingness-to-pay is a decreasing function of environmental quality (inverse demand function for environmental quality)[4].

Obtaining estimates of these functions with the required properties depends upon: (a) Correctness of data used, and (b) Choice of appropriate functional forms. This paper, using the data collected through carefully designed household surveys in Delhi and Kolkata, the two important urban areas in India, explains the importance of

1. See Freeman (1974a) for the derivation of these equations using models explaining consumer choices of private goods, house property, jobs and environmental quality.
2. Here the monthly rental value of the house is taken as a proxy for the property price.
3. Ridker (1967) and Ridker and Henning (1976) provide the first empirical evidence that air pollution affects the property values. The early studies include Freeman (1974a; 1974b), Anderson and Crocker (1971; 1972), Lind (1973), Pines and Weiss (1976), Polinsky and Shavell (1976), Nelson (1978), Portney (1981), Horowitz (1986), Murdoch and Thayer (1988), and Kanemoto (1988). The most recent studies include the following: Michaels and Smith (1990), Parsons (1992), Lansford and Jones (1995), Kiel (1995), Kiel and McClain (1995), and Mahan, Polasky, and Adams (2000). Recent studies in India are: Parikh (1994), Sen (1994) and Murty, Gulati and Banerjee (2003).
4. Some studies have failed to obtain an inverse demand function for environmental quality for example, Mahan, Polasky, and Adams (2000).

choice of appropriate functional forms in the estimation of the hedonic property value model and provides estimates of consumer surplus benefits to households in both the cities from reducing air pollution to the safe level.

2. Choice of Functional Forms in Hedonic Price Models

The choice of functional form has usually been restricted both by theoretically unwarranted restrictions and by convenience in dealing with the problem at hand. As a result in most of the studies, a linear or a semi-log and at most a trans-log model has been widely used. Griliches (1967) suggested the use of the Box-Cox (1964) methodology for choosing among alternative functional forms under a relevant statistical framework. The early exception from the over restrictive theoretical framework was noted in Goodman (1978). The flexible functional form includes the quadratic, translog, square root quadratic, generalised square root and generalised Leontief. However, Halvorsen and Pollakowski (1981) provide a lucid discussion on the combination of the Box-Cox and the flexible functional form approaches. They specify a generalised functional form, namely the quadratic Box-Cox functional form, which yields all other functional forms as special cases. Blackley, James and Ondrich (1984) provide some evidence of the inappropriateness of using the iterative OLS technique and the Variance Bias, resulting there from, in the Box-Cox estimates and advocate the use of a method of modified scoring.

The Quadratic Box-Cox Model

The general quadratic Box-Cox functional form for the hedonic property price equation (1) incorporating all other functional forms as special cases is given by:

$$P^{(\theta)} = \alpha_0 + \sum_{i=1}^{m} \alpha_i X_i^{(\lambda)} + \frac{1}{2} \sum_{i=1}^{m} \sum_{j=1}^{m} \gamma_{ij} X_{i=1}^{(\lambda)} X_{j=1}^{(\lambda)} \qquad \ldots(3)$$

where P is the price of property, X_i's are the characteristics of the house including structural, neighbourhood and environmental features, α_i and Υ_{ij}'s are the regression coefficients with coefficients $\Upsilon_{ij} = \Upsilon_{ji,}$ for all i and j (i,j = 1,2,3,...m) and $P^{(\theta)}$ and $X^{(\lambda)}$ are Box-Cox transformations as given below:

$$P^{(\theta)} = \left(P^{\theta} - 1\right)/\theta, \qquad \text{for all } \theta \neq 0$$

$$= \text{Ln } P \quad \theta = 0$$

$$X_i^{(\lambda)} = \left(X_i^{\lambda} - 1\right)/\lambda \quad \text{For all } \lambda \neq 0$$

$$= \text{Ln } X_i \quad \lambda = 0$$

The transformations are continuous around $\theta = 0$ and $\lambda = 0$ since the limit for the $\theta \neq 0$ case as $\theta \rightarrow 0$ is Ln P and similarly the limit for $\lambda \neq 0$ case as $\lambda \rightarrow 0$ is Ln X_i. It can be easily found out that by imposing appropriate restrictions on θ and λ we can arrive at the more specific functional forms of interest. Imposing zero restrictions on θ and λ we can obtain the trans log form attributed to Christensen, Jorgenson and Lau (1971, 1973) given by:

$$\text{LnP} = \alpha_0 + \sum_{i=1}^{m} \alpha_i \text{LnX}_i + \frac{1}{2}\sum_{i=1}^{m}\sum_{j=1}^{m} \gamma_{ij} \text{LnX}_i \text{LnX} \qquad \ldots(4)$$

Similarly, imposing the restriction $\theta = \lambda = 1$ yields the quadratic form attributed to Lau (1974), imposing $\theta = 2$ and $\lambda = 1$ we obtain the square root form, (see Diewert, 1974) and with $\theta = 1$ and $\lambda = 1/2$ we can attain the generalised non-homogeneous version of the generalised Leontief form[5]. Adding a stochastic term to equation (3) we get: -

$$P^{(\theta)} = \alpha_0 + \sum_{i=1}^{m} \alpha_i X_i^{(\lambda)} + \frac{1}{2}\sum_{i=1}^{m}\sum_{j=1}^{m} \gamma_{ij} X_{i=1}^{(\lambda)} X_{j=1}^{(\lambda)} + \varepsilon_t \qquad \ldots(5)$$

It is assumed that the true values of θ and λ are distributed normally and independently with zero mean and constant variance. The values of θ, λ, α_0, $\alpha_{i's}$, Υ_{ij} and σ^2 (where σ is the standard error of the regression) are estimated jointly by the maximum likelihood technique. The choice of θ and λ are such that they maximise the log likelihood function for the sample observations[6]. Most of the econometric packages[7] have routine programme to compute these estimates. The significance of the θ and λ in the respective regressions has been tested by the Chi-Squared test of the Wald-statistics. The

---

5. For the derivation of these functional forms refer to Halvorsen and Pollakowski (1981).
6. It may be noted that the Box-Cox transformation increases the chances for obtaining normally distributed residuals even though the maximum likelihood estimate does not try to choose θ and λ that make the residuals normally distributed, Box-Cox (1966).
7. Stata 8 has been used for the current estimation and analysis.

same test of significance has been performed on the rest of the parameters of equation (3). The Likelihood ratio test is then employed to test the Null hypothesis of standard values of θ and λ (viz. $\theta = 0 = \lambda$, $\theta = 1 = \lambda$, and $\theta = -1 = \lambda$) separately against the alternative hypothesis of an unrestricted maximum likelihood estimate of θ and λ.

3. Data Sources and Design of Household Survey

Primary data on house characteristics and socio-economic conditions of 1250 respondents from the cities of Delhi and Kolkata were collected. The survey design was based on two stage stratified and circular systematic sampling procedures adopted in areas surrounding the functioning air pollution monitoring centres in the cities. The ambient air quality data of the study areas are collected from the publications of the Central Pollution Control Board (CPCB) and the West Bengal Pollution Control Board in India.

The information about socio-economic characteristics of the household members inclusive of educational levels of adult members, occupational status, size, sex and age composition of the family members, and incomes are collected.

Information was elicited on type of house, structural characteristics, locational/neighbourhood characteristics comprising distances from highways, bus stops, schools/colleges, industrial complexes, public parks, etc. was also elicited. Further, information on community characteristics like majority religion, dominant professional group, and crime rate in the locality was collected. Information on the respondent's perception of the environmental conditions/characteristics such as the air quality, water quality, extent of green cover, etc. was also collected.

Detailed information on prices of properties was also elicited from the respondents. To cross check, the property prices obtained from the respondents in the survey, data on property prices were also collected from the property dealers in the surveyed areas. We surveyed 1250 households from each city expecting that information could be obtained completely for at least 1000 households per city. The sample size was divided equally around the functioning air pollution monitoring stations in the two cities. For illustration, the sample size of 1250 in Delhi was divided into a sub-sample size of around 180 around each of the seven pollution-monitoring stations of the Central Pollution Control Board (CPCB). In Kolkata the sample size of around 65 was fixed around 19 air-pollution monitoring centres monitored by the West Bengal Pollution Control Boards (WBPCB). Ultimately, full information could be obtained only for 1187 households in Delhi and 1204 households in Kolkata. Thus, the first stage of stratification was geographic which was purposive in the sense that the localities around the monitoring stations were the selection criterion for the locality.

In the second stage, in each city the inhabited localities around the monitoring stations were stratified according to the type of locality adjudged by the standards of living of the inhabitants in terms of size of the houses, types of the houses such as bungalows/independent houses or flats, type of conveyances used in general, etc. through physical verification by visiting the areas. At this stage, three localities one each from the high, medium and low income category were identified to draw a sample comprising a whole range of households in terms of socio-economic status. The identification and mapping of localities selected for the survey has provided the necessary framework for selecting the households in the third stage. The selection of the targeted number of households was done by adopting a circular systematic sampling procedure in each selected locality nearer to the monitoring station.

4. Model for Estimation and Measurement of Variables

The hedonic property value model consists of a set of two equations one representing the hedonic price function (1), and another representing the marginal willingness-to-pay function (2) for estimation. The two equations of the hedonic property value model estimated in this paper with Box-Cox transformations of both dependent and independent variables are given below:

Hedonic Property Price Function

$$(Y_1)^{(\theta)} = \alpha_1 + \beta_1(X_1)^{(\lambda)} + \beta_2(X_2)^{(\lambda)} + \beta_3(X_3)^{(\lambda)} + \beta_4(X_4)^{(\lambda)} + \beta_5(X_5)^{(\lambda)} + \beta_6(X_6)^{(\lambda)} + \beta_7(X_7)^{(\lambda)} + \beta_8(X_8) + \beta_9(X_9) + \beta_{10}(X_{10})^{(\lambda)} + \beta_{11}(X_{11}) + \beta_{12}(X_{12})^{(\lambda)} + \beta_{13}(X_{13})^{(\lambda)} + \beta_{14}(X_{14})^{(\lambda)} + \beta_{15}(X_{15})^{(\lambda)} + \beta_{16}(X_{16})^{(\lambda)} + \beta_{17}(X_{17})^{(\lambda)} + u_1 \quad \ldots(6)$$

Inverse Demand Function[8] *or Individual Marginal Willingness-to-pay for Environmental Quality*

$$(Y_2)^{(\theta')} = \alpha_2 + \gamma_{19}(X_{19})^{(\lambda')} + \gamma_{20}(X_{20})^{(\lambda')} + \gamma_{13}(X_{13})^{(\lambda')} + \gamma_{21}(X_{23})^{(\lambda')} + \gamma_{10}(X_{10})^{(\lambda')} + u_2 \quad ...(7)$$

where θ and λ are the transformations used in the hedonic price equation and θ′ and λ′ are the transformations used in the marginal implicit price function. Since these transformations apply only to positive values of Y and X, the constant and the dummy variables are not transformed. The model used in the empirical estimation contains only those variables that have provided significant Wald statistics and only one cross[9] product term (X_{20}) has turned out to be significant and has been used in the above model. The variables used in an estimation of the above two equations are described as follows:

Monthly rent (Y_1): Information on the monthly rents, for the house is collected from each household. Imputed monthly rental values were used for the owner-occupied houses in Delhi and Kolkata. Data for monthly rents collected through the survey is compared with the information about the market rents and property prices collected from the interviews of property dealers from different localities in Delhi and Kolkata.

Structural Characteristics of the House

Covered area (X_1): Data for total covered area of the houses were collected directly from the households and the figures were reported

8. It might be noted that the literature on the hedonic property value model suggests the use of all the independent variables in the hedonic property price function also as independent variables in the willingness-to-pay function. We have two reasons for using the restricted functional form of the model reported in equation (7).

   Firstly, it is the only one that satisfies the required curvature property of the inverse demand function for the entire relevant range of the atmospheric quality, given by the current average concentration of SPM to the safe level prescribed by WHO and the MINAS. The unrestricted willingness-to-pay estimate also satisfies the curvature properties of the inverse demand function but at a very stringent range of the atmospheric quality.

   Secondly, the Box-Cox transformation, as evident from the chi-square test, is relevant only for the restricted model and not for the unrestricted model and the transformed unrestricted model is even rejected in favour of the double log model. But the unrestricted double log model also fails to provide the required curvature properties of the inverse demand function. Thus the transformed Box-Cox restricted model is the best fit in our search for an appropriate functional form for the willingness-to-pay function that renders all the properties of the inverse demand function and is also robust to all statistical tests of significance.

   The estimates of the unrestricted model (only for the pooled model) and the inverse demand function are shown also in Table 9.6 and Figure 9.4, respectively.

9. X_{20} is obtained as the square of X_{13}.

in square yards. In the case of independent owner occupied or rented houses care was taken to exclude any uncovered area. For the flats, of course no such problems was encountered. In the case of multistoried buildings, the covered area was scaled for the number of floors.

Number of rooms including drawing rooms (X_2): The total number of rooms including drawing room were considered as a control variable for the monthly rental value of the house.

Indoor sanitation (X_3): The index for indoor sanitation was constructed out of the following information: separate kitchen, separate bathrooms and toilets, and condition of indoor ventilation. The index ranges from 0 to 6. Whenever a facility was found separately in a house it scored a value of 1 otherwise 0, in this way it can take up to a maximum value of 3 where separate kitchen, toilet and bathroom facilities are available. For ventilation, a scale of 1 to 3 was used with a higher number denoting better ventilation. These values were then added to arrive at the composite scale of 0 to 6.

Distance Characteristics

Distance from business centre (X_4): The distance from any common business centre in the city was collected from each household.

Distance from national highways (X_5): The distance of the house from the national highways were collected and then an average distance was computed which proxies for the overall distance of the house from these national highways.

Distance from slums (X_6): Distance from the nearby slums was collected for area around each monitoring station in the cities separately.

Distance from industry (X_7): Distance from nearby industries for each monitoring station in each city was used to control for the extreme conditions of pollution in certain parts of the cities.

Distance from shopping centre (X_8): The distance from the nearest local shopping complex was collected for each monitoring station in the cities.

Environmental Variables

Perception about air quality (X_{10}): This is an ordered variable in the range of 1 to 3, which is used to rank the locality in terms of the air quality as perceived by the households, the higher the rank, the higher the air quality available.

Perception about water quality (X_{12}): This is also an ordered variable in the range of 1 to 3, which is used to rank the locality in terms of the water quality as perceived by the residents of that area, the higher being the rank, the higher the water quality.

Dummy for Adequacy of Green Cover (X_{11}): This is a 1, 0 binary dummy variable, which is used to ascertain the perception of a household in any locality about the adequacy of the green cover (tree cover) in its location.

SPM (X_{13}): The average concentration of SPM in μ gms/m^3 in the last six months from the month of survey for a particular locality is used as the pollution variable.

SO_2 (X_{14}): The average concentration of SO_2 in μ gms/m^3 in the last 6 months for a particular locality is used as the pollution variable.

NO_x (X_{15}): The average concentration of NO_x in μ gms/m^3 in the last six months for a particular locality is used as the pollution variable.

Water supply (X_{16}): The hours of water supply in the particular locality.

Other Variables:

Business or salaried class (X_9): A dummy variable assigning 1 to business communities and 0 to salaried class communities.

Variables for the Marginal Willingness-to-Pay Function:

Marginal willingness-to-pay (Y_2): The linear transformation of the marginal implicit prices for unit changes in the concentration of SPM or implicit marginal price for environmental quality is estimated using the following expression:

$$\frac{\partial Y_1}{\partial X_{13}} = \frac{X_{13}^{\lambda-1}}{Y_1^{\theta-1}}(\beta_{13}), \qquad \ldots(8)$$

where linear predicted household-specific values of Y_1 and the observed values of X_{13} have been used in the computation of the household-specific marginal implicit price. The modulus value of the above expression is used as the dependent variables in the marginal willingness-to-pay function.

Square of SPM (X_{20}): The square of SPM is used in the second equation keeping in mind the necessary curvature property of the willingness-to-pay function and its significance of Υ_{20} in the regression.

It is expected that the pollution, SPM, positively related to the marginal willingness-to-pay for reduction in pollution. Alternatively the environmental quality is expected to be inversely related to the marginal willingness-to-pay. The descriptive statistics of all the selected variables are presented in the Appendix (Tables A9.1, A9.2 and A9.3).

City Dummy (X_{23}): All the observations belonging to Delhi are marked as 1 and all observations belonging to Kolkata are marked as 0 in the pooled model.

Socio-economic Variables

Education in years (X_{18}): The education variable is constructed by adding the years of education undertaken by the first five adult members of the family and dividing by five.

Annual gross family income (X_{19}): This is based on the gross annual family income of the household. In the absence of any concrete figures for actual incomes for certain households it was necessary to offer certain income brackets to the respondents to choose from.

5. Estimates of Hedonic Property Value Model Under Alternative Functional Forms

Estimates of the hedonic property price function for Delhi under the general quadratic Box-Cox estimation and the trans log functional forms are provided in Table 9.1. In both the estimates the structural variables like Covered Area (X_1), Number of rooms (X_2), Indoor sanitation (X_3) show the correct sign and is significant at the 1 per cent level. Among the distance characteristics variables Distance from Business centre (X_4), Distance from industries (X_7) and Distance from national highway (X_5) are also significant at 1 per cent and bear the correct sign. Distance from slums (X_6) and the dummy for availability of slum (X_8) have proper signs and are significant at the 1 per cent level. The variables measuring the distance from shopping centre (X_{17}) has a positive coefficient and it is also significant in the unrestricted model.

It is also noted that the presence of business class (X_9) affects house rents significantly in both the model estimates. The Environmental variables like Perception about air quality (X_{10}), Adequacy of green cover (X_{11}) and Perception about water quality (X_{12}) have expected signs in both the models but they are not significant. Even hours of water supply (X_{16}) do not seem to affect

Table 9.1

Estimates of Hedonic Price Equation for Delhi.

Variables (Expected Signs)	*Dependent Variable Monthly House Rent*	
	Trans log Model $\theta = 0$ $\lambda = 0$	*Box-Cox Transformation* $\theta = 0.0765446$*** $\lambda = -0.1064827$*
	Coefficients (t-statistics)	*Coefficients (Chi^2 statistics)*
Constant	10.23759*** (11.37)	19.53819
Covered Area: X_1(+)	0.183950*** (3.95)	0.5438875*** (19.883)
No. of Rooms: X_2(+)	0.646681*** (9.30)	1.466924*** (167.047)
Indoor Sanitation: X_3(+)	0.464654*** (4.39)	1.023839*** (25.667)
Distance from Business Centre: X_4 (+)	0.143340*** (4.59)	0.2859844*** (16.481)
Distance from National Highways: X_5 (+)	0.051224*** (3.36)	0.0948012*** (16.481)
Distance from Slums: X_6(+)	0.202827*** (3.22)	0.4425801*** (13.032)
Distance from Industries: X_7 (+)	0.144710*** (3.03)	0.3456081*** (12.303)
Dummy for Slums: $^{\$}X_8$(-)	-0.257561*** (-4.17)	-0.5026985*** (16.009)
Dummy for Business or Salaried Class: $^{\$}X_9$ (+)	0.173580*** (3.43)	0.3713925*** (15.379)
Perception about Air Qlty: X_{10} (+)	0.089259 (1.22)	0.1493541 (1.040)
Adequacy of Green Cover: $^{\$}X_{11}$ (+)	0.044258 (0.89)	0.0933311 (1.213)
Perception about Water Qlty: X_{12} (+)	0.060599 (0.86)	0.1530054 (1.364)
SPM: X_{13}(-)	-0.658795*** (-5.59)	-2.644776*** (38.595)
SO_2: X_{14}(-)	0.142859* (1.62)	-0.922619*** (9.604)
NO_x: X_{15}(-)	-0.268090*** (-2.63)	0.446201** (4.034)
Water Supply in Hrs: X_{16} (+)	-0.033733 (-1.23)	-0.091236 (2.264)
Distance from Shopping Centre: X_{17} (-)	0.019048 (1.30)	0.0406528* (3.303)

Contd. ...

Contd. ...

	Coefficients (t-statistics)	Coefficients (Chi^2 statistics)
Uncentred R^2	0.4504	Sigma = 1.421134
Adjusted R^2	0.4424	LR Chi^2 (18) = 733.67
		Probability > Chi^2 = 0.000
		Uncentred R^2 = 0.618
		Log Likelihood = -11585.625

Likelihood Ratio Test

Test H_0	*Restricted Log Likelihood*	*Chi^2 Statistics*
$\theta = -1 = \lambda$	-14875.305	6579.36***
$\theta = 0 = \lambda$	-11599.854	28.46***
$\theta = 1 = \lambda$	-12809.207	2447.16***

Note: *(**) & (***) denotes significance at 10 (5) & (1) % levels. $ denotes variable without transformation.

house rents significantly. The coefficient of the pollution variable, SPM concentration (X_{13}) is highly significant and has the expected sign in both the models. Given that pollution concentrations of SO_2 and NO-x are quite within the safe limits we believe a further reduction or a slight increase in their concentration would not affect house rents significantly. The uncentred R^2 is computed for both the models and it is much higher in the unrestricted model. Other standard diagnostic tests were performed on these models and both the models are free from any serious problem[10]. The likelihood ratio test is also performed on each of the independent variables and there was no problem of convergence encountered in the process[11].

The Likelihood ratio test is employed to test the Null hypothesis of standard values of θ and λ (viz. $\theta = 0 = \lambda$, $\theta = 1 = \lambda$ and $\theta = -1 = \lambda$) separately against the alternative hypothesis of unrestricted maximum likelihood estimates of θ and λ. The tests reject the null hypothesis of θ and λ to be of any of the above standard form against the alternative of unrestricted θ and λ in all the models estimated in the paper. Thus the quadratic Box-Cox estimation is superior when compared to the parametric estimates of the trans log model (or any other restricted model) thereby highlighting the importance of the appropriate choice of the functional form for the hedonic price equation.

10. The White's heteroscedasticity corrected standard errors are reported.
11. For a detailed discussion in the estimation method consult Stata 8 Reference Manual (Vol. 1, A to F).

The linear predictions of the house rents $Y_{1,}$ were computed from the model estimates of the hedonic price equation using the appropriate reverse transformation and these were used to compute the house specific estimates of the marginal implicit prices as shown by equation (8) above. The expression for Delhi is given by[12]:

$$\left|\frac{\partial Y_1}{\partial X_{13}}\right| = \left|\frac{X_{13}^{\lambda-1}}{Y_1^{\theta-1}}(-2.644776)\right| \qquad ...(9)$$

The household marginal willingness-to-pay function for the reduction in SPM is estimated by regressing the implicit marginal prices on income, education and other socio-economic variables and the SPM concentration and its square. Table 9.2 provides the parametric estimates of the marginal willingness-to-pay function under the two models. For this function the standard Z test does not reject the null hypothesis that lambda is equal to zero even at the 10 per cent level of significance so the Box-Cox transformation has been employed only to the dependent variables for which the standard Z statistic is significant at the 5 per cent level.

For the marginal implicit price function[13] the socio-economic variables like Education (X_{18}), Gross annual household income (X_{19}) and the Perception for air quality variable (X_{10}) bear an expected positive sign and are significant at the 1 per cent level for both the model estimates. There is a notable distinction in the signs of X_{13} and X_{20} (pollution variables) in the two models. Only parametric estimates

---

12. For the trans log model theta and lambda are zero and hence equation (13) reduces to the ratio of X_{13} to Y_1 times the coefficient (-0.658).

13. The marginal implicit price for each household derived from the hedonic property price function using equation 9, is not an observed variable. In the context of regression on derived variables Feenstra and Hanson (1997, 1999), Haskel and Slaughter (2001, 2002) and Dumont *et al.* (2003) suggest different methods of correcting the standard errors of the parametric estimates. All the methods suggest a reduction of the standard error of the parametric estimate for gaining efficiency. Since our parametric estimates are highly significant with this enlarged standard error (uncorrected) bands, we can safely expect them to be significant with further reduction in the standard error. Thus this correction seems redundant in our case. On the other hand, Noboru Hidano (2002) suggests that the problem of identification in case of the marginal implicit price function can be avoided by using higher order functional forms for the hedonic price function than the marginal implicit price function. In this context it may be noted that since the Box-Cox transformation uses different functional forms for the two sets of equations this problem of identification is also overcome. Further, in the case of the hedonic price function, in all the cities and in the pooled model as well, a both side transformation with separate parametric values of theta and lambda has been found statistically suitable whereas in the marginal implicit price function only the right hand side transformation is statistically significant. So it is evident that a different functional form has been assumed for estimating the two equations and the problem of identification does not arise.

of the unrestricted Box-Cox estimation satisfy the required curvature property of the marginal willingness-to-pay function.

Table 9.2

Estimates of Marginal Willingness-to-pay Equation for Delhi

Log Values of Variables (Expected Signs)	*Dependent Variable Marginal Rent*	
	Trans Log Model $\theta = 0$	*Box-Cox Transformation* $\theta = 0.0736085^{**}$
	Coefficients (t-statistics)	*Coefficients (Chi^2 statistics)*
Constant	-43.17935*** (-3.61)	-0.5406424
Education X_{18} (+)	0.430238*** (5.87)	0.0316471*** (53.814)
Income X_{19} (+)	0.538860*** (13.76)	2.6e-06*** (294.164)
SPM X_{13} (+)	14.32783*** (3.51)	0.0117879*** (71.954)
Sq SPM X_{20} (-)	-1.336191*** (-3.89)	-0.0000166*** (90.493)
Perception about Air Quality X_{10} (+)	0.270875*** (3.46)	0.1780826*** (43.498)
		Sigma = 0.5686012
Uncentred R^2	0.357199	LR Chi ^{2} (5) = 658.27
Adjusted R^2	0.354477	Probability > Chi^2 = 0.000
		Uncentred R^2 = 0.555
		Log Likelihood = -3707.6189

Likelihood Ratio Test

Test H_0	*Restricted Log Likelihood*	*Chi^2 Statistics*
$\theta = -1$	-4350.042	1284.85***
$\theta = 0$	-3710.2565	5.28**
$\theta = 1$	-4070.3201	725.40***

Note: *(**) & (***) denotes significance at 10 (5) & (1) % levels.

Table 9.3 provides the parametric estimates of hedonic property price function for Kolkata. In the case of Kolkata, the Box-Cox transformation is given only to the dependent variable, as the transformation of the independent variables does not produce any significant change in the regression as is evident by the Chi^2 test. The likelihood ratio test rejects the H_0 for all the standard values of θ tested against the unrestricted value of θ.

In the unrestricted model the regression coefficient for (X_{13}) is quite small when compared to the same for the Delhi model.

Table 9.3

Estimates of Hedonic Price Equation for Kolkata

Variables (Expected Signs)	*Dependent Variable Monthly House Rent*	
	Trans Log Model $\theta = 0$ $\lambda = 0$	*Box-Cox Transformation* $\theta = 0.3681178$***
	Coefficients (t-statistics)	*Coefficients (Chi² statistics)*
Constant	10.58682*** (14.39)	35.29286
Covered Area: X_1(+)	-0.026117 (-1.06)	-0.000507* (2.716)
No. of Rooms: X_2(+)	0.955376*** (14.82)	2.488142*** (294.673)
Indoor Sanitation: X_3(+)	0.291560*** (3.12)	1.817918*** (29.506)
Distance from Business Centre: X_4 (+)	0.137361*** (5.57)	0.2563974*** (12.624)
Distance from National Highways: X_5 (+)	0.061320 (0.94)	0.974085** (6.240)
Distance from Slums: X_6(+)	0.150310 (1.34)	-0.0110185 (0.001)
Distance from Industries: X_7 (+)	0.051119 (0.70)	-0.1726866 (0.096)
Dummy for Slums: $^{\$}X_8$(-)	-0.379371*** (-5.59)	-4.930523*** (31.733)
Dummy for Business or Salaried Class: $^{\$}X_9$ (+)	0.056327* (1.62)	1.455582*** (7.164)
Perception about Air Qlty: X_{10} (+)	0.050404 (0.78)	0.5017189 (0.709)
Adequacy of Green Cover: $^{\$}X_{11}$ (+)	0.087828* (1.74)	2.303671** (5.546)
Perception about Water Qlty: X_{12} (+)	0.173977** (2.33)	-0.5017189 (0.823)
SPM: X_{13}(-)	-0.719903*** (-7.13)	-0.0587933*** (71.564)
SO_2: X_{14}(-)	0.174656 (1.13)	0.4905682** (5.461)
NO_x: X_{15}(-)	-0.177321* (-1.88)	0.014077 (0.738)
Water Supply in Hrs: X_{16} (+)	0.034463 (0.95)	0.1109009* (2.888)
Distance from Shopping Centre: X_{17} (-)	-0.044881 (-0.71)	0.9406537*** (7.249)

Contd. ...

Contd. ...

	Coefficients (t-statistics)	Coefficients (Chi^2 statistics)
Uncentred R^2	0.3873	Sigma = 13.44937
Adjusted R^2	0.3786	LR Chi ^{2} (17) = 526.88 Probability > Chi^2 = 0.000 Uncentred R^2 = 0.4376
		Log Likelihood = -10836.371

Likelihood Ratio Test

Test H_0	*Restricted Log likelihood*	*Chi^2 Statistics*
$\theta = -1$	-13365.004	5057.26***
$\theta = 0$	-11022.034	371.33***
$\theta = 1$	-11462.206	1251.67***

Note: *(**) & (***) denotes significance at 10 (5) & (1) % levels. $ denotes variables without transformation.

However it is highly significant and bears the correct negative sign. We are again indifferent to the signs picked up by the coefficients of (X_{14}) and (X_{15}) for the reasons stated above. Among the structural characteristics, the coefficients of (X_3) and (X_2) have required positive signs and are highly significant while the coefficient of (X_1) bears the opposite sign and is insignificant in the trans log model while in the unrestricted model it is significant. The dummy for Slums X_8 is significant and negative in both the models while the distance characteristics produce mixed results for Kolkata as a whole[14]. Similar to the model for Delhi, the linear predictions for (Y_1) are computed using expression (8) to get the household specific marginal implicit prices. In this case however exogenous variables are not transformed and so the expression for the marginal implicit price is:

$$\left|\frac{\partial Y_1}{\partial X_{13}}\right| = \left|\frac{1}{Y_1^{\theta-1}}(-0.0587933)\right| \qquad \ldots(10)$$

The estimates of marginal willingness-to-pay function for Kolkata are given in Table 9.4 below. The coefficients of all the explanatory variables except Income (X_{19}) bear the correct sign and are highly significant. Even in case of Kolkata the unrestricted model shows the household diminishing marginal willingness-to-pay for the atmospheric quality.

---

14. They are still more effective in case of the unrestricted model (e.g. X_5 and X_{17}).

Table 9.4

Estimates of Marginal Willingness-to-pay Equation for Kolkata

Log Values of Variables (Expected Signs)	*Dependent Variable Marginal Rent*	
	Trans Log Model $\theta = 0$	*Box-Cox Transformation* $\theta = 0.4792194^{**}$
	Coefficients (t-statistics)	*Coefficients (Chi^2 statistics)*
Constant	-22.96979** (-2.48)	3.069313
Education X_{18} (+)	0.796318*** (6.94)	0.0119188*** (22.779)
Income X_{19} (+)	0.571237*** (11.52)	-2.42e-07*** (9.191)
SPM X_{13} (+)	6.737927** (2.07)	0.0021936*** (10.354)
Sq SPM X_{20} (-)	-0.693091** (-2.42)	-3.63e-06*** (11.905)
Perception about Air Quality X_{10} (+)	0.173072*** (3.30)	0.0336502*** (10.415)
Uncentred R^2	0.333585	Sigma = 0.5686012
Adjusted R^2	0.330727	LR Chi ^{2} (5) = 61.23 Probability > Chi^2 = 0.000 Uncentred R^2 = 0.50
		Log Likelihood = -3707.6189

Likelihood Ratio Test

Test H_0	*Restricted Log likelihood*	*Chi^2 Statistics*
$\theta = -1$	-1421.3999	49.53***
$\theta = 0$	-1399.136	5.01**
$\theta = 1$	-1399.4891	5.71**

Note: *(**) & (***) denotes significance at 10 (5) & (1) % levels.

Two separate estimates of the marginal willingness-to-pay function are made using the pooled data for Delhi and Kolkata. One estimate is based on the hedonic property price functions estimated for the segmented house markets Delhi and Kolkata. The implicit marginal prices for SPM reductions are computed for each market and then pooled. The pooled implicit marginal prices are regressed on the SPM levels and the socio-economic characteristics of households along with a city specific dummy variable (X_{23}). This is one approach to deal with the econometric problem of identification in the estimation of the household marginal willingness-to-pay function in the hedonic property value model as discussed in

Table 9.5

Estimates of Marginal Willingness-to-pay Equation for the Pooled Model

Log Values of Variables (Expected Signs)	Dependent Variable Marginal Rent	
	Trans Log Model $\theta = 0$	Box-Cox Transformation $\theta = 0.4792194^{**}$
	Coefficients (t-statistics)	Coefficients (Chi^2 statistics)
Constant	-30.62877*** (-5.25)	0.4782014
Education X_{18} (+)	0.558753*** (9.23)	0.013794*** (88.590)
Income X_{19} (+)	0.554709*** (18.01)	8.87e-07*** (325.828)
SPM X_{13} (+)	9.689258*** (4.77)	0.0052934*** (228.374)
Sq SPM X_{20} (-)	-0.950415*** (-5.42)	-7.7e-06*** (258.450)
Perception about Air Quality X_{10} (+)	0.221595*** (5.05)	0.0477618*** (40.216)
City Dummy X_{23} (+)	0.790453*** (21.48)	0.214818*** (327.223)
		Sigma = 0.2530792
Uncentred R^2	0.42295	
Adjusted R^2	0.42148	LR Chi ^{2} (6) = 1096.25 Probability > Chi^2 = 0.000 Uncentred R^2 = 0.46372
		Log Likelihood = -6373.6493

Likelihood Ratio Test

Test H_0	Restricted Log Likelihood	Chi^2 Statistics
$\theta = -1$	-7116.5125	1485.73***
$\theta = 0$	-6400.8154	54.33**
$\theta = 1$	-7502.4537	2257.61**

Note: *(**) & (***) denotes significance at 10 (5) & (1) % levels.

Freeman (1993). Another estimate is based on the hedonic property price function estimated using the pooled data for Delhi and Kolkata. However, we are reporting the results of only the marginal willingness-to-pay function for the pooled model estimated by using the market segmentation approach[15].

The parametric estimates of the two models have the proper sign and are highly significant. In this case also, the curvature property is

15. The complete set of results of the pooled model is available on request from the authors.

satisfied by the unrestricted model only. The likelihood ratio test rejects H_0 for all standard forms of θ and thus the unrestricted model is unambiguously superior to the trans log counterparts[16] in the estimates for both the cities as well as the pooled model. Further, only by following the segmented market approach in the case of pooled model estimates, the required curvature property was satisfied.

Ideally, one could expect that the similar sets of structural and neighbourhood variables (as used in the estimation of the Hedonic price function) along with the environmental and socio-economic characteristics determine the marginal willingness-to-pay for environmental quality. However in the current study, it has been observed that the parametric estimates of the pollution variables remain unaffected with the inclusion of the structural and environmental characteristics in the marginal willingness-to-pay function. The robustness of the parametric estimates can be attributed to the weak separability between the Environmental variables with the Structural and Neighbourhood characteristics while determining the marginal willingness-to-pay for clean air. The parametric estimate of the unrestricted[17] marginal willingness-to-pay is provided in Table 9.6. The Likelihood ratio test rejects the double log model as well as all other standard functional forms of the marginal willingness-to-pay function in favour of the both sides transformed unrestricted model. Also in the both sides transformation model the individual z-test rejects the null hypothesis that the true value of λ and θ are zero. However all single-sided transformations or double-sided transformation with the same parameter of the unrestricted model are rejected in favour of the double log model and render insignificant parametric estimates of λ and θ as well. Thus it is easy to conclude that the both side transformation model is more appropriate than any other model in terms of statistical analysis. But unfortunately, even the both side transformation model fails to offer the required curvature property of the inverse demand function in the relevant range[18], just as any other functional form of the unrestricted model. Figure 9.4 represents the inverse demand function estimated from the

---

16. All standard transformations are rejected in favour of the unrestricted quadratic Box-Cox transformation.
17. Using all the independent variables that were used in the hedonic price function.
18. The relevant range is defined as the current average concentration of SPM to the WHO, MINAS prescribed safe level of 200 m gm/m^3.

Table 9.6

Estimates of Marginal Willingness-to-pay Equation for the Pooled Model (Unrestricted)

Dependent Variable Marginal Rent

Box-Cox Transformation Parameters
Theta = -0.0526165 ***
Lambda = -0.3364357***

Variables	*Coefficients (Chi^2 statistics)*	*Variables*	*Coefficients (Chi^2 statistics)*
Constant	-316.5959	Dummy for Business or salaried class: $^{\$}X_9$	0.3092857*** (26.029)
Covered Area: X_1	0.826*** (431.178)	Perception about Air Qlty: X_{10}	0.0274651*** (13.754)
No. of Rooms: X_2	0.0340558*** (332.138)	Adequacy of Green Cover: $^{\$}X_{11}$	0.0043971*** (0.187)
Indoor Sanitation: X_3	0.0495319*** (140.092)	Perception about water Qlty: X_{12}	0.0107325** (4.572)
Distance from Business Centre: X_4	0.0631395*** (129.693)	SPM: X_{13}	-42.17456*** (408.905)
Distance from National highways: X_5	0.0312554*** (331.616)	Sq SPM X_{20}	141.5829*** (404.324)
Distance from Slums: X_6	0.2264228*** (198.459)	Water Supply in Hrs: X_{16}	-0.0302438*** (8.623)
Distance from Industries: X_7	0.1892529*** (728.652)	Distance from Shopping Centre: X_{17}	0.0093668*** (35.112)
Dummy for Slums: $^{\$}X_8$	-0.2085701*** (858.672)	LR Chi^2 (20) = 2929.85 Probability > Chi^2 = 0.000 Uncentred R^2 = 0.78 Log Likelihood = -5268.4761	

Likelihood Ratio Test

Test H_0	*Restricted Log Likelihood*	*Chi^2 Statistics*	*Test H_0*
$\theta = -1$	-6449.8946	2362.84***	$\theta = -1$
$\theta = 0$	-5541.989	547.03***	$\theta = 0$
$\theta = 1$	-6674.0822	2811.21***	$\theta = 1$

Note: *(**) & (***) denotes significance at 10 (5) & (1) % levels.

unrestricted model. The market segmentation approach has been followed for all the pooled data estimates.

The unrestricted willingness-to-pay function fails to provide the required curvature properties in the individual city-specific[19] models as well. Thus the welfare gains obtained from a reduction of air pollution have been computed only from the restricted model of the marginal willingness-to-pay function.

6. Inverse Demand Functions for Environmental Quality and Welfare Gains from Reduced Air Pollution

By fixing variables X_{18}, X_{19} and X_{10} in the estimated[20] equations of marginal willingness-to-pay at their sample mean values, and treating pollution variables (X_{13}) and (X_{20}) as the only variable, the inverse demand function[21] for clean air was derived. After applying the appropriate reverse transformation, the linearised[22] predicted values of marginal willingness-to-pay (MWP) in the inverse demand functions for Delhi, Kolkata and the Pooled model are given by equations (11), (12) and (13). The reverse transformation is necessary in order to express the predicted values of marginal willingness-to-pay, out of the Box-Cox transformed variables, in the actual rupee values, given that Monthly rent (Y_1) is expressed in rupees.

$$MWP = [1.051322+0.0008677\ X_{13}-0.0000012\ X_{20}]^{13.585} \quad \text{[Delhi]} \quad \ldots(11)$$

$$MWP = [2.560514+0.0010512\ X_{13}-0.0000017\ X_{20}]^{2.0867} \quad \text{[Kolkata]} \quad \ldots(12)$$

$$MWP = [0.826114+0.0009079\ X_{13}-0.0000013\ X_{20}]^{13.585} \quad \text{[Pooled]} \quad \ldots(13)$$

From the above estimates of the inverse demand function the marginal willingness-to-pay, for a typical household, for a reduction in SPM concentration by one micro gram per metre cube from the current average level of pollution, is computed as Rs. 12.63 for Delhi, Rs. 8.06 for Kolkata and Rs. 10.21 for a representative household in the pooled model. By using suitable dummies for the cities and the city-specific SPM concentrations the willingness-to-pay for reduction in SPM

19. These estimates are not reported here.
20. Given in Tables 9.2, 9.4 and 9.6 for Delhi, Kolkata and the Pooled model, respectively.
21. This is also the marginal willingness-to-pay function for clean air.
22. The reverse linear transformation refers to the $Y = (1 + \theta\alpha_0 + \theta\Sigma\alpha_i X_i)^{1/\theta}$ in which anything other than X_{13} and X_{20} are set at their mean values.

concentration by one micro gram per meter cube from the current average level of pollution, is computed as Rs. 12.01 in Delhi and Rs. 8.74 in Kolkata from the pooled model. The marginal willingness-to-pay estimated from the individual estimates are thus very close to the estimates obtained from the pooled model. This shows that the pooled model may be used for extrapolation of consumer surpluses for any representative city in India using the benefit transfer method. The graphs of inverse demand functions are shown in Figures 9.1, 9.2 and 9.3, respectively for Delhi, Kolkata and the pooled model. The SPM concentration is shown in reversed scale on the X-axis to represent ambient air quality and MWP is shown on the Y-axis

Figure 9.1

Inverse Demand Function for Clean Air in Delhi

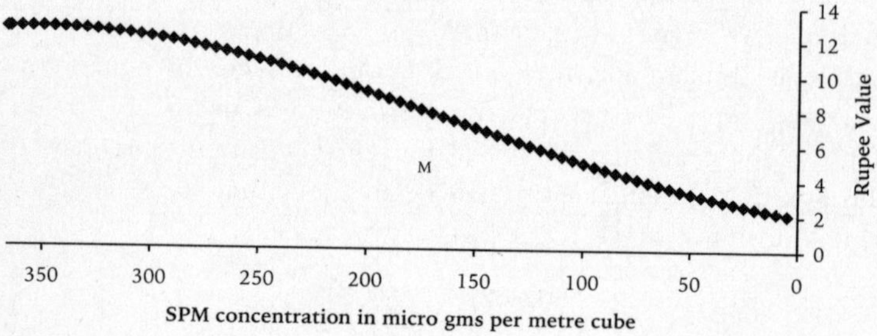

Note: The graph is generated from the Current average level of SPM of 366.31 μ gm/m³ to zero SPM, while the safe limit for SPM concentration is 200 μ gm/m³.

Figure 9.2

Inverse Demand Function for Clean Air in Kolkata

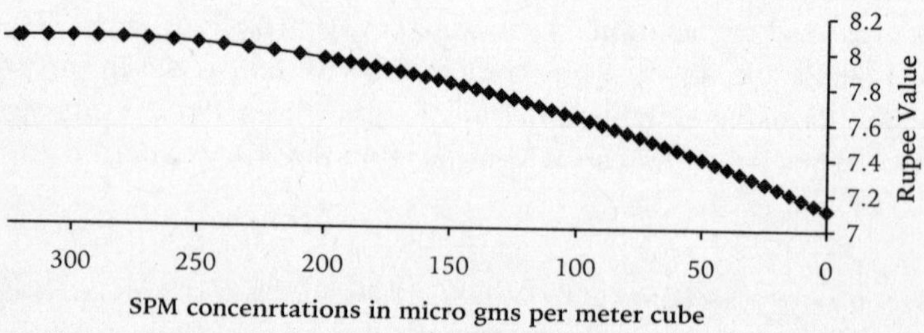

Note: The graph is generated from the Current average level of SPM of 321.39 μ gm/m³ to zero SPM, while the safe limit for SPM concentration is 200 μ gm/m³.

Figure 9.3

Inverse Demand Function for the Pooled Model of Delhi and Kolkata

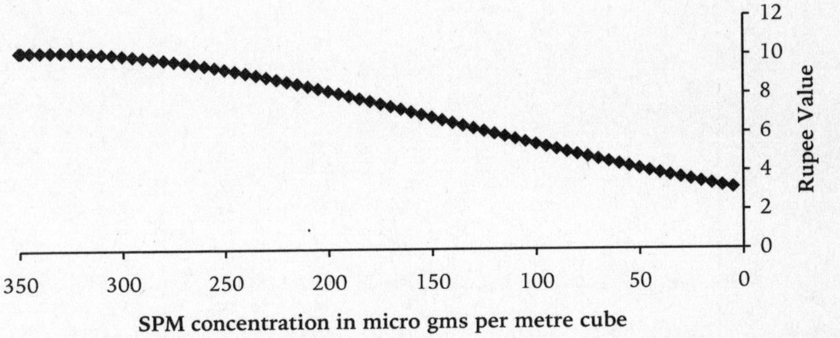

Note: The graph is generated from the Current average level of SPM of 349.09 μ gm/m³ to zero SPM, while the safe limit for SPM concentration is 200 μ gm/m³.

Figure 9.4

Inverse Demand Function for the Pooled Model (Unrestricted Model)

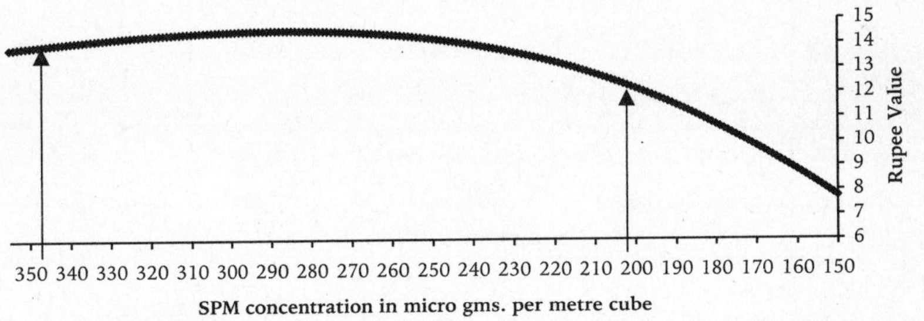

Note: The graph is generated from the Current average level of SPM of 349.09 μ gm/m³ to zero SPM, while the safe limit for SPM concentration is 200 μ gm/m³.

The consumer surplus generated by a reduction of SPM concentration from the current average to the safe level of 200 μ gm/m³ is computed by integrating the inverse demand function given by equations (11) to (13) within 200 μ gm/m³ as the lower limit[23] and the current average level of pollution in the respective cities as the

23. 200 μ gm/m³ is the safe WHO and MINAS standard for residential area in India.

Table 9.7

Estimates of Welfare Gains to Urban Households in Delhi, Kolkata and for the Pooled Model

Nature of Gains to Households	*Gains to Household Based on Individual Estimates from Cities*		*Gains to Household Using Market Segmentation Approach*[24]		
	Delhi	*Kolkata*	*Delhi*	*Kolkata*	*Pooled*
Monthly gains in Rental value due to reduction of SPM concentration by 1 μ gms/m³	Rs. 12.63	Rs. 8.06	Rs. 12.01	Rs. 8.74	Rs. 10.21
Monthly gains in Rental value due to reduction of SPM concentration from the current average to the safe level corresponding to 200 μ gms/m³	Rs. 1946.14	Rs. 977.22	Rs. 1887.65	Rs. 980.69	Rs. 1420.61
Annual gains in Rental value due to reduction of SPM concentration by 1 μ gms/m³	Rs. 151.56	Rs. 96.72	Rs. 144.12	Rs. 104.88	Rs. 122.52
Annual gains in Rental value due to reduction of SPM concentration from the current average to the safe level corresponding to 200 μ gms/m³	Rs. 23353.68	Rs. 11726.59	Rs. 22651.80	Rs. 11768.28	Rs. 17047.32
Annual gains in Rental value due to reduction of SPM concentration from the current average to the safe level corresponding to 200 μ gms/m³ to the total Urban Households[25].	Rs. 54833.08 Million	Rs. 37026.16 Million	Rs. 53185.10 Million	Rs. 37157.78 Million	Rs. 92612.69 Million[26]

24. The estimates of individual cities are calculated by using the city-specific dummy and the city's average level of pollution.
25. The total urban population is obtained from Census 2001 data and deflated by the average size of household in the respective cities which is 5.46 for Delhi and 4.56 for Kolkata.
26. The total urban population of Delhi and Kolkata is used to evaluate the total gains

upper limit. Integration of the inverse demand functions were carried out in Mathematica[27] 4.1 and the results of the consumer surpluses are provided in Table 9.7. The estimated consumer surplus also measures the average willingness-to-pay by a representative household for reduction in the ambient air pollution from the current average to the safe WHO or MINAS[28] standards. The annual welfare gains to a typical household from reducing SPM concentration from the current level to the MINAS standard of 200 μ gms/m^3 in Delhi, and Kolkata are respectively, Rs. 23353.68 and Rs. 11726.59. According to 2000 census, Delhi and Kolkata have urban populations of 12.8 millions, and 14.4 millions with sample average household sizes of 5.46 and 4.56 respectively. Thus there are 23,47,942, and 31,57,452 estimated urban households in Delhi and Kolkata. The annual benefits from reducing the SPM concentration to safe level in Delhi and Kolkata are respectively estimated as Rs. 54,833.08 million and Rs. 37,026.16 million. The estimates of welfare gains to the two cities as computed from the Pooled model are also given in Table 9.7. These estimates are very close to the individual estimates of gains in these cities. This shows the robustness of the pooled model that may be used in extrapolating welfare gains from a reduction in air pollution in some other metropolitan centres in India. The welfare gains are not computed from the trans log model, as the required curvature properties are not satisfied by the inverse demand function.

7. Conclusion

Empirical studies using the observed behavioral methods (household production function and hedonic prices models) look for the derivation of an inverse demand function or marginal willingness-to-pay function for the environmental quality with appropriate curvature properties for an estimation of the consumer surplus benefits from the improved environmental quality. The failure to obtain an inverse demand function in some empirical studies might arise either due to: (a) the poor quality of data used and (b) inappropriate functional form used for the estimation of hedonic price and willingness-to-pay functions. We have

27. Software for Mathematical Solutions.

28. MINAS: Minimum National Standards for Environmental Pollution in India.

shown that given the reliable data, the inverse demand function with the required properties could be derived with the choice of appropriate functional form for the hedonic property price and the marginal willingness-to-pay equations. Starting from a more general quadratic Box-Cox functional form for the hedonic price function a number of functional forms could be considered and tested for their appropriateness.

The hedonic property price function is estimated using the primary data collected for house characteristics through carefully designed household surveys in Delhi and Kolkata. Estimates of consumer surplus benefits to a representative household from each city are obtained by integrating the inverse demand function for air quality in the range of current average quality and the quality corresponding to safe level.

A representative household gets an annual benefit of Rs. 23,353.68 in Delhi and Rs. 11,726.59 in Kolkata. When the benefits are extrapolated to all the urban households in each city, the households in Delhi get benefits worth Rs. 54,833.08 million while those in Kolkata get benefits worth Rs. 37,026.16 million. Though these benefits appear to be high, they are not so in comparison to the cost to various economic agents like the Government and polluters to reduce the air pollution levels from the current level to the safe level. In fact these benefit estimates justify the cost of environmental policy changes like introducing CNG operated vehicles, and substituting the metro rail in place of road transport and the relocation of polluting industries in the cities.

APPENDICES

Table A 9.1

Descriptive Statistics of the Variables Used for Estimation of the Hedonic Property Value Model: Location Delhi

	Rent (Rs/month) (Y_1)	Covered Area (Sq yards) (X_1)	Number of Rooms (X_2)	Indoor Sanitation Index (X_3)	Distance from Business Centre (Km) (X_4)	Distance from National Highway (Km) (X_5)
Mean	9536.612	136.9534	4.096040	4.462511	4.992334	1.279174
Std. Dev.	13725.58	342.6036	2.527597	1.148752	4.975135	1.397169
Observations	1187	1187	1187	1187	1187	1187

	Distance from Slums (Km) (X_6)	Distance from Industry (Km) (X_7)	Dummy for Nearby Slums (X_8)	Dummy for Business Community (X_9)	Perception of Air Quality Index (X_{10})	Index for Adequacy of Green Cover (X_{11})
Mean	1.594302	1.330526	0.571188	0.541702	2.144903	0.622578
Std. Dev.	1.217707	1.317624	0.495115	0.498468	0.623511	0.547041
Observations	1187	1187	1187	1187	1187	1187

	Perception About Drinking Water (X_{11})	SPM (X_{13})	SO_2 (X_{14})	NO_2 (X_{15})	Water Supply (Hours/day) (X_{16})	Distance from Nearest Shopping Centre (Km) (X_{17})
Mean	2.127211	366.3136	12.96807	36.45013	5.998678	2.788031
Std. Dev.	1.113989	86.42897	4.088191	13.13383	5.958350	3.247169
Observations	1187	1187	1187	1187	1187	1187

	Education Index (Years) (X_{18})	Gross Annual Family Income (Rs) (X_{19})	SPM*SPM (X_{20})
Mean	12.29264	179565.3	141649.4
Std. Dev.	4.238082	127156.2	69776.29
Observations	1187	1187	1187

Table A 9.2

Descriptive Statistics of the Variables Used for Estimation of the Hedonic Property Value Model: Location Kolkata

	Rent (Rs/month) (Y_1)	*Covered Area (Sq ft.)* (X_1)	*Number of Rooms* (X_2)	*Indoor Sanitation Index* (X_3)	*Distance from Business Centre (Km)* (X_4)	*Distance from National Highway (Km)* (X_5)
Mean	3902.831	1169.304	4.324751	4.889535	5.157973	1.137949
Std. Dev.	4288.262	1284.462	3.041145	1.356095	6.775391	1.062752
Observations	1204	1204	1204	1204	1204	1204
	Distance from Slums (Km) (X_6)	*Distance from Industry (Km)* (X_7)	*Dummy for Nearby Slums* (X_8)	*Dummy for Business Community* (X_9)	*Perception of Air Quality Index* (X_{10})	*Index for Adequacy of Green Cover* (X_{11})
Mean	0.330133	0.627816	0.553156	2.095515	1.830565	0.347176
Std. Dev.	1.167176	0.789318	0.497373	0.761728	0.785062	0.483201
Observation	1204	1204	1204	1204	1204	1204
	Perception About Drinking Water (X_{12})	*SPM* (X_{13})	SO_2 (X_{14})	NO_2 (X_{15})	*Water Supply (Hours/day)* (X_{16})	*Distance from Nearest Shopping Centre (Km)* (X_{17})
Mean	2.182724	331.3123	8.892027	123.3310	8.711379	1.243937
Std. Dev.	0.807179	83.98949	2.018197	37.08074	6.359156	1.309642
Observation	1204	1204	1204	1204	1204	1204
	Education Index (Years) (X_{18})	*Gross Annual Family Income (Rs)* (X_{19})	*SPM*SPM* (X_{20})			
Mean	14.28763	158930.1	116816.2			
Std. Dev.	3.165503	102890.3	53862.82			
Observation	1204	1204	1204			

Table A 9.3

Descriptive Statistics of the Variables Used for Estimation of the Hedonic Property Value Model: Location Pooled Data of Delhi and Kolkata

	Rent (Rs/month) (Y_1)	*Covered Area (Sq Yards) (X_1)*	*Number of Rooms (X_2)*	*Indoor Sanitation Index (X_3)*	*Distance from Business Centre (Km) (X_4)*	*Distance from National Highway (Km) (X_5)*
Mean	6546.224	679.1058	4.194072	4.677541	4.973521	1.782558
Std. Dev.	10354.50	1146.499	2.783644	1.275187	5.904172	2.033789
Observations	2391	2391	2391	2391	2391	2391

	Distance from Slums (Km) (X_6)	*Distance from Industry (Km) (X_7)*	*Dummy for Nearby Slums (X_8)*	*Dummy for Business Community (X_9)*	*Perception of Air Quality Index (X_{10})*	*Index for Adequacy of Green Cover (X_{11})*
Mean	0.957724	0.976673	0.560484	1.328437	1.976979	0.486410
Std. Dev.	1.349522	1.139571	0.496428	1.009871	0.727994	0.548683
Observations	2391	2391	2391	2391	2391	2391

	Perception About Drinking water (X_{12})	*SPM (X_{13})*	*SO_2 (X_{14})*	*NO_2 (X_{15})*	*Water Supply (Hours/day) (X_{16})*	*Distance from Nearest Shopping Centre (Km) (X_{17})*
Mean	2.147190	349.0961	10.81923	82.08902	7.376280	2.533180
Std. Dev.	0.968021	86.66497	3.770856	52.22872	6.330675	2.637017
Observations	2391	2391	2391	2391	2391	2391

	Education Index (Years) (X_{18})	*Gross Annual Family Income (Rs) (X_{19})*	*SPM*SPM (X_{20})*	*Dummy Delhi=1, Kolkata=0 (X_{23})*
Mean	13.76080	167671.7	129375.9	0.477474
Std. Dev.	3.790868	115361.6	63181.19	0.499593
Observations	2391	2391	2391	2391

References

Anderson, Robert J., and Thomas D. Crocker (1971). "Air Pollution and Residential Property Values," *Urban Studies* 8: 171-80.

———. (1972). "Air Pollution and Property Values: A Reply" *Review of Economics and Statistics.* 54, 470-73.

Blackley, Paul., James, R. Follain, and Jr. Jan Ondrich (1984). "Box-Cox Estimation of Hedonic Models: How Serious is the Iterative OLS" *The Review of Economics and Statistics* 66: 348-53.

Box, G., and D. Cox (1964). "An Analysis of Transformations", *J. Roy. Statist. Soc. Ser. B.* 26: 211-52.

Christensen, L., D. Jorgenson, and L. Lau (1971). "Conjugate Duality and Transcendental Logarithmic Production Function", *Econometrica* 39: 255-56.

Dales. J.H. (1968). *Pollution, Property and Prices*. University of Toronto Press, Toronto.

Diewert, W. (1974). "Functional Forms for Revenue and Factor Requirement Functions", *International Economic Review* 15: 119-30.

Dumont, M., G. Rayp, P. Willeme, O. Thas, (2003). "Correcting Standard Error in Two-Stage Estimation Procedures with Generated Regressands", *Working paper No. D2003/7012/10,* Universitiet Gent.

Feenstra R.C., and G.H. Hanson (1997). "Productivity measurement and the impact of trade and technology on wages: estimates for the US 1972-1990, NBER Working Paper No. 6052.

———. (1999) "The Impact of Outsourcing and High-technology Capital on Wages: Estimates for the United States, 1979-1990, *Quarterly Journal of Economics* 114 (3): 907-40.

Freeman, A. Myrick, III, (1974a). "Air Pollution and Property Values: A Further Comment", *Review of Economics and Statistics* 56: 454-56.

———. (1974b). "On Estimating Air Pollution Control Benefits from Land Value Studies", *Journal of Environmental Economics and Management* 1: 74-83.

———. (1993). *The Measurement of Environmental and Resource Values Theory and Methods,* Washington D. C. Resources for the Future.

Goodman, C. Allen, (1978). "Hedonic Prices, Price Indices and Housing Markets", *Journal of Urban Economics*. 5: 471-84.

Griliches, Z. (1967). "Hedonic Price Index Revisited: Some Notes on the State of the Art", *1967 Proceedings of the Business and Economic Statistics Section*, pp.324-32, American Statistical Association.

Halvorsen, Robert, and H.O. Pollakowski (1981). "Choice of Functional Form for Hedonic Price Equation", *Journal of Urban Economics,* 10: 37-49.

Haskel, J., and M.J. Slaughter (2001). "Trade Technology and UK Wage Inequality" *The Economic Journal,* 111:163-87.

———. (2002). "Does the Sector bias of Skill-biased Technical Change Explain Changing Skill Premia? *European Economic Review* 46: 1757-83.

Hidano Noboru (2002). 'The Economic Valuation of the Environmental and Public Policy: A Hedonic Approach' Edward Elgar Publishing Limited, UK.

Horowitz, Joel L. (1986). "Bidding Models of Housing Markets," *Journal of Urban Economics,* 20: 168-90.

Kanemoto, Yoshitsugu (1988). "Hedonic Prices and the Benefits of Public Projects," *Econometrica,* 56: 981-89.

Kiel, K.A. (1995). "Measuring the Impact of the Discovery and Cleaning of Identified Hazardous Waste sites on House Values", *Land Economics,* 71: 428-35.

Kiel, K.A., and K.T. McClain (1995) "The Effect of an Incinerator Sitting on Housing Appreciation Rates", *Journal of Urban Economics*, 37, 311-23.

Lansford, N.H., and Lonnie Jones (1995). "Recreational and Aesthetic Value of Water via the Hedonic Price Analysis", *Journal of Agricultural and Resource Economics*, 20: 341-55.

Lau, L. (1974). 'Application of Duality Theory: A Comment', *Frontiers of Quantitative Economics* (M. Intriligator and D. Kendrick Eds.), Vol. 2, 176-199. North Holland, Amsterdam.

Lind, Robert C. (1973). "Spatial Equilibrium, the Theory of Rents, and the Measurement of Benefits from Public Program," *Quarterly Journal of Economics*. 87: 188-207.

Linneman, P. (1980). "Some Empirical Results on the Nature of Hedonic Property Functions for the Urban Housing Market", *Journal of Urban Economics* 8: 47-68.

Mahan, B.L., S. Polasky, and R.M. Adams (2000). "Valuing Urban Wetlands A Property Price Approach", *Land Economics*, 76: 100-13.

Markandya, A. and P. W. Abelson (1985). 'The Interpretation of Capitalised Hedonic Prices in a Dynamic Environment'. *Journal of Environmental Economics and Management* pp.12195-206.

Mendelsohn, R. (1987). "A Review of Identification of Hedonic Supply and Demand Functions", *Growth and Change*, 18: 82-92.

Michaels, G.R.and Smith, V.K. (1990). "Market Segmentation and Valuing Amenities with Hedonic Models: The Case of Hazardous Waste Sites". *Journal of Urban Economics* 28(2): 223-42.

Murdoch, James C., and Mark J. Thayer, (1988) "Hedonic Price Estimation of Variable Urban Air Quality," *Journal of Environmental Economics and Management* 15(2): 143-46.

Murty, M.N., S.C. Gulati, and A. Banerjee (2003). "Hedonic Property Prices and Valuation of Benefits from Reducing Urban Air Pollution in India", Working Paper No. E 237/2003, Institute of Economic Growth, Delhi.

Nelson, Jon P.(1978). "Residential Choices, Hedonic Prices and the Demand for Urban Air Quality", *Journal of Urban Economics* 5(3): 357-69.

Parikh, K.S. (1994). *Economic Valuation of Air Quality Degradation in Chembur*, IGIDR Project Report, Mumbai.

Parsons, G.R. (1992). "The Effect of Coastal Land Use Restrictions on Housing Prices: A Repeat Sale Prices", *Journal of Environmental Economics and Management* 22: 25-37.

Pines, David, and Yoram Weiss, (1976) "Land Improvement Projects and Land Values," *Journal of Urban Economics* 3: 1-13.

Polinsky, S, A. Mitchell, and Steven Shavell (1976). "Amenities and Property Values in a Model of an Urban Area," *Journal of Public Economics* 5: 119-29.

Portney, P.R. (1981). "Housing Prices, Health Effects and Valuing Reduction in Risk of Death", *Journal of Environmental Economics and Management* 8, 72-78.

Ridker, Ronald G. (1967). *Economic Costs of Air Pollution Studies in Measurement*, Praeger, New York.

Ridker, Ronald G. and John A. Henning (1976). "The Determinants of Residential Property Values with Special Reference to Air Pollution," *Review of Economics and Statistics* 49: 246-57.

Rosen, S. (1974). "Hedonic Prices and Implicit Markets, Product Differentiation in Pure Competition", *Journal of Political Economy* 82: 34-55.

Sen, Akshay (1994). *Determinants of Residential House Price: A Case Study of Delhi*, (M.Phil Dissertation, Delhi School of Economics) Delhi.

Thaler, R. and S Rosen (1976). "The Value of Life Savings", *Household Production and Consumption*, N. Terleckyi (ed), Columbia University Press: New York.

10

Dynamics of Rice Production in Kerala: A Cobweb Approach

K.P. MANI

1. Introduction

Agricultural policymakers, searching for long term economic projections certainly need the use of Cobweb models which describe the simultaneous adjustments in prices and outputs. The model can be used to examine the responsiveness of output of individual crops to price movements and other factors and also for inter-regional comparisons of output responses. Kerala is a typical agricultural economy, the important food crop being rice followed by coconut and rubber.

2. Cropping Pattern in Kerala

Shifts in cropping pattern in favour of cash crops in majority of the economies in recent years and the consequent reduction in area under food crops weakens the sustainability of food availability. The reduction in area under food crops in Kerala from 40.43 per cent in 1970-71 to 18.74 per cent in 1992-93 and 16.52 per cent in 1999-2000 is a phenomenon occurred very rarely in any country. The gravity of the problem is more severe when the state is 70 per cent short of foodgrains. The area index of foodgrains has lost considerably and continuously from 102.55 to 58.38, whereas the gain in the productivity was not adequate enough to make good this short fall. On the other hand, the index of area under non-food crops increased from 100.52 in 1976-79 to 159 in 1999-2000 (Economic Review, Government of Kerala, 2000 p. 33). It is also worthwhile to note that among the non-food categories, the growth of area expansion index is tremendous in the case of coconut and rubber.

Table 10.1

Gross Cropped Area Under Major Crops in Kerala (1960-61—1999-2000)

Crops	*1960-61*	*1970-71*	*1980-81*	*1985-86*	*1990-91*	*1999-00*
Rice	778.91	874.93	763	641	559.45	348.20
	(61.20)	(57.67)	(59.21)	(51.37)	(52.40)	(50.34)
Non-food Crops						
Coconut	500.76	719.14	651.37	704.68	870.02	1080.0
	(56.64)	(56.96)	(47.61)	(43.31)	(45.02)	(62.83)
Rubber	122.87	179.26	237.77	330.32	384.00	469.9
	(13.90)	(14.18)	(17.36)	(20.30)	(19.95)	(28.72)
Coffee	16.80	31.56	57.95	65.64	75.05	83.7
Tea	37.63	37.59	36.16	34.74	34.71	36.8
Other Plantations	205.91	295.90	385.88	491.35	560.35	NA

Source: 1. Government of Kerala (1975), Agricultural Statistics in Kerala, The Bureau of Economics and Statistics, Thiruvananthapuram.

2. Government of Kerala, Economic Review (for various years), State Planning Board, Thiruvananthapuram.

3. CMIE (1999), India's Agricultural Sector – A Compendium of Statistics, Bombay, July.

Table 10.1 provides a clear picture and trends of the cropping pattern in the state from 1960-61 to 1999-2000. Out of the gross cropped area of 2349 thousand hectares in 1960-61, rice occupied 778.91 hectares, forming 33.15 per cent of the gross cropped area. But the share of gross cropped area under rice consistently came down to 28 per cent in 1980-81 and 15.45 per cent in 1999-2000. In absolute terms, the area under rice declined from 778.91 thousand hectares in 1960-61 to 678.28 thousand hectares in 1980-81, the average annual fall being 0.68 per cent. Further between 1980-81 and 1999-2000, the area under rice declined by 30.53 per cent, absolute fall during the 15 year period being 207.13 thousand hectares. The fall in cumulative area in 1995-96, compared to 1960-61 being 307.76 thousand hectares. The area divided for all food crops together was about 46 per cent in 1960-61 but it came down to just 16.52 per cent in 1999-2000. The major reason is the domination of cash crops like coconut and rubber, which is evident from further examination. In the year 1960-61, coconut constituted 21.31 per cent and rubber constituted 5.23 per cent of the gross cropped area. These shares marginally improved to 22.77 per cent and 8.24 per cent respectively by 1980-81. But since 1980-81, there is a tremendous leap. The area under coconut reached 982.10 in 1995-96, almost double the area in 1990-91. Similarly, area under rubber reached 449.00 thousand hectares in 1995-96, an increase of 3.68 times compared to 1960-67. While the area under rice declined by 336.55 thousand hectares from 1980-81 to 1999-2000, area under coconut and rubber increased by 330.73 thousand and 211.23 thousand hectares during the same period. These three crops constituted 60 per cent of the gross cropped area in 1960-61 and 62 per cent in 1999-2000 and the trends clearly establish the claim that Kerala farmers are shifting the area under rice to coconut and rubber while the state is 70 per cent short in rice production compared to consumption requirements and when the state lacks linkages to absorb coconut and rubber.

Table 10.2

Gross Change in Area Between 1975-76 to 1999-2000

Districts	*Rice*	*Coconut*	*Rubber*	*Gap*	*Gap After 2% for Other Crops*
Thiruvananthapuram	-20.11	15.86	17.620	—	—
Kollam	-27.77	-18.98	0.450	46.3	37.04
Alapuzha	-41.45	-8.35	-0.371	50.17	40.14
Kottayam	-19.12	-16.63	52.30	—	—
Idukki	-11.18	4.90	21.15	—	—
Ernakulam	38.99	13.17	33.73	—	—
Thrissur	64.28	23.89	11.26	12.63	10.10
Palakkad	34.21	26.70	16.74	—	—
Malappuram	46.80	32.78	8.67	5.35	4.28
Kozhikode	52.65	22.16	0.34	30.15	24.12
Kannur	67.16	6.38	6.87	53.91	43.12
	382.27	102.06	169.13		158.80

Source: Computed from Table 10.1.

In the succeeding section an attempt is made to examine the inter district, intra-district and inter-temporal shifts in cropping pattern with reference to rice, coconut and rubber on production and yield.

3. Cropping Pattern - Inter District Analysis

Inter district analysis clearly shows that area under rice declined in all the districts between 1975-76 and 1999-2000. Maximum fall occurred in Trichur district (64.28 thousand hect.), followed by Kozhikode, Malappuram and Palakkad districts. There is fall in Kannur and Alappuzha districts also, but it is due to the division of these districts respectively to Kasaragod and Pathanamthitta. All the districts together made a decline of 382.27 thousand hectares during the time span. Decade wise, the fall is 242.97 thousand hectares between 1975-76—1985-86 and 139.30 thousand hectares between 1985-86 and 1990-91. Hence we may infer that the relative contribution of rice to the total cropped area consistently declined in all the districts in the state, the steep fall being in Northern parts.

Naturally, this fall should be reflected in an increase of the area of other crops particularly coconut and rubber felt "a priori". In the case of area under coconut, maximum increase is recorded in Northern districts, particularly Malappuram (32.78 thousand hect) and Kozhikode (22.16 thousand hect) between 1975-76 and 1999-2000. During the same period Thrissur district and Palakkad district respectively recorded an increase of 23.89 thousand hectares and 26.70 thousand hectares. It is important to note that Kollam and Kottayam districts record a fall in the area under coconut. During the period 1975-76 to 1990-2000 the net increase in the area under coconut in the state is 102.06 thousand hectares, decade wise split up being (-50.37) thousand hectares and 152.43 thousand hectares. Compared to the fall in the area under rice between 1985-86 and 1999-2000 (139.30 thousand hectares) it is seen that the spread in area under coconut which is higher than the spread in the case of staple food rice. Hence we may infer that, in the recent years, there is definitely a trend in favour of coconut plantations in northern Kerala.

Kerala state Contributes nearly 90 per cent of rubber production in the country. Inter district data reveal that since 1975-76, rubber plantations were extended to all the districts. It is also seen that over the last 25 years, area under rubber cumulatively increased by 169.13 thousand hectares.

In the succeeding paragraphs an attempt is also made to examine the variations in production and yield with respect to rice, coconut at the inter-district level during the period 1975-76 to 1999-2000. Rice production improved from 1067.53 thousand tonnes in 1960-61 to 1364.87 thousand tonnes in 1975-76. Since then it started to decline and the current production (1999-2000) is 1002.7 thousand tonnes. The productivity was 1558 Kg/hect in 1975-76 and 1920 Kg/hect in 1999-2000. The districts which recorded maximum in production are, Palakkad and Thrissur districts of which Palakkad district served as the "rice bowl" of Kerala immediately after the formation of the state in 1956.

The production of coconut increased from 3439 million nuts in 1975-76 to 5303 million nuts in 1999-2000, respective yield being 4962 and 5890. Among the districts, net addition was the highest in Kozhikode, Malappuram and Kannur districts followed by Thrissur, Palakkad, Ernakulam and Thiruvananthapuram districts. It is striking to observe that in Kollam district production came down.

Kerala has the virtual monopoly over production of rubber in the country. The state's rubber production increased by 3.14 times over the last 20 years, the improvement in yield being 1.63 times. In absolute terms, yield improved from 611Kg/hect in 1975-76 to 1000 Kg/hect in 1999-2000. Leaving home district Kottayam, the other districts made commendable performance of production of rubber are Ernakulam, Thrissur and Thiruvananthapuram. The good performance of production and yield is definitely due to the efforts taken by the Rubber Board. But the crucial question as raised earlier is whether the excess supply of rubber in relation to consumption "within state" will able to attract sufficient margins. It is true that still there is wide gap between present production and consumption. But whether the gap will be filled by domestic rubber or imported rubber?

The above discussion validates our hypothesis that the cropping pattern of Kerala State has turned in favour of cash crops particularly coconut and rubber at the cost of area under rice, the staple food of the state. Thus in this paper an attempt is made to assess the reasons behind this shift, with emphasis on instantaneous adjustment in prices.

4. Materials and Methods

The annual details on farm prices, and yield of rice over the years 1985-86 to 1999-00 published by the Directorate of Economics and Statistics, Kerala, were used for the study. Since published data on market prices are discontinuous, only farm price which is the important price factor of output response of primary producers has been considered.

In real life supply consumes time and the adjustment of supply to price changes is not instantaneous, although demand may adjust to price variations instantaneously and therefore requires no time lag. Cobweb theorem is the simplest model of these dynamics of demand, supply and price.

Taking the linear versions of lagged supply and current demand function as,

$D1 = a + bp_1$ where $a > 0$, $b = = 0$ ...(1.1)

And $S_1 = c + dp_1$ where $d > 0$ ...(1.2)

Where D_1=Demand for a commodity in

Period t; S_1=Supply of a commodity in

Period t; P_1 = Price of a commodity in

Period t and p_{1-1} = Price of a commodity in period t-1

In equilibrium,

$D_1 = S_1$ ...(1.3)

Hence $a + bp_1 = c + dp_{1-1}$

Or, $P_1 = (c-a)/b - d/bp_{1-1}$

Shifting the time period subscripts ahead by one period as done by Agarwal (1976) and Mehta (1991), the general equation of time path will be

$P_1 = [p_0 - (c-a)/(d-b)](d/b)^1 + (c-a)/(d-b)$ ...(1.4)

price in period t will be just equal to the price in the initial period i.e., $p_1 = p_0$ when t=0.

Table 10.3

Supply, Demand and Farm Price of Rice in Kerala (1985-86 to 1998-99)

Year	*Time Period*	*Supply Kg ha^{-1}*	*Demand, Kg ha^{-1}*	*Farm Price, Rs. Kg^{-1}*
1985-86	0	1520	1468	1.83
1986-87	1	1468	1541	1.07
1987-88	2	1541	1592	0.97
1988-89	3	1592	1638	1.29
1989-90	4	1638	1587	1.37
1990-91	5	1587	1660	1.52
1991-92	6	1660	1678	1.79
1992-93	7	1678	1632	2.08
1993-94	9	1720	1729	2.01
1994-95	10	1729	1708	2.41
1995-96	11	1708	1709	2.44
1996-97	12	1709	1753	1.62
1997-98	13	1753	1956	1.95
1998-99	14	1956	1942	1.90

Figure 10.1a

Demand, Kg ha-1

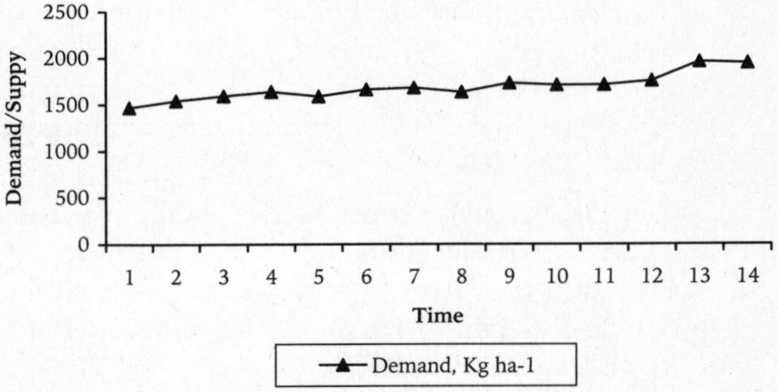

On the basis of equation (1.4) the following propositions have been derived.

Figure 10.1b

Supply, Kg ha-1

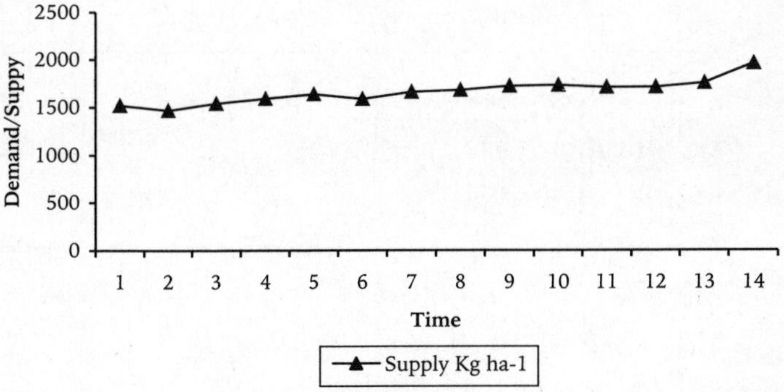

(1) The amount (c-a)/(d-b) of equation (1.4) can be taken as the equilibrium price of the model denoted by p = (c-a)/(d-b) substituting in (1.4), the equation can be rewritten as

$$P_1 = (p_0\text{-}p)\ (d/b)^1 + p \qquad \ldots(1.5)$$

(2) In equation (1.5) p_0-p shows the difference between the initial price and the equilibrium price and its sign will determine whether time path will commence above or below the equilibrium.

(3) The difference between b and d will determine the Cobweb phenomenon (or disequilibrium phenomenon).

In this case there will be oscillations: (i) if $d>b$ it is a diverging or explosive Cobweb; (ii) if $k<b$ it is a converging or damped Cobweb and (iii) if $d = b$ it is a regular Cobweb where b is the slope of the market demand curve of equation (1.1) and d is the slope of the market supply curve of equation (1.2).

The yield or production per hectare in any year has been considered as the quantity supplied in the corresponding year and it is considered to be the quantity demanded in the previous year. Table 10.1 shows the supply, demand and farm prices of rice in Kerala for the period (1985-86 to 1989-90). The demand side of rice estimated according to equation (1.3) is

$$D_1 = 1391.56 - 154.52\ p_1 \qquad \ldots(2.1)$$

Standard error: (126.51) (61.004)

t value: (2.533*)

And the equation (2.2) explaining the supply side of rice in Kerala which is estimated according to equation (1.7) is

$$S_1 = 1373.53 - 144.08\ p_{1-1} \qquad \ldots(2.2)$$

Std. Error: (112.988) (50.102)

t value: (2.876**)

At equilibrium, according to equation (1.5) the resulting equation of time path obtained is

$$P_1 = (1.83 - 1.73)\ (0.93)^1 + 1.73 \qquad \ldots(2.3)$$

Equation (2.3) reveals the following

(1) The equilibrium price (p) and equilibrium quantity (Q) of rice are 1.73 Rs. Kg^{-1} and 1382.23 kg ha^{-1} respectively.

(2) p_0-p which is the difference between initial price and equilibrium price is Rs. 0.10 per kg of rice and the positive sign indicates that the time path starts above the equilibrium price.

(3) Since slope of the supply curve (d) is less than slope of the demand curve (b), the price

Table 10.4

Projected Time Path of Farm Prices and Equilibrium Quantities of Rice in Kerala

Year	*Time Period*	*Time Path of Farm Prices, Rs. kg⁻¹*	*Equilibrium Quantities, kg ha⁻¹*
1985-86	0	1.73	1124.24
1986-87	1	2.75	966.63
1987-88	2	2.68	977.45
1988-89	3	2.53	1000.62
1989-90	4	2.55	997.53
1990-91	5	2.50	1005.26
1991-92	6	2.44	1014.53
1992-93	7	2.39	1022.26
1993-94	8	2.35	1028.44
1994-95	9	2.30	1036.16
1995-96	10	2.26	1543.82
1996-97	11	2.23	1046.98
1997-98	12	2.19	1053.16
1998-99	13	2.16	1057.80
1999-00	14	2.13	1062.43
2000-01	24	1.92	1094.88
2050-51*	75	1.73	1124.24

* Projections

Structure showed a converging or damped Cobweb with positive shift in demand and supply curves. Table 10.2 clearly explains the damped Cobweb price structure of rice in Kerala. The time path of prices of rice projected using equation (2.3) is shown in Table 10.2.

The price fluctuations tend to become smaller and smaller while moving towards equilibrium price with time. Farmer's reactions to movements in prices can be explained in a convergent Cobweb framework as follows.

The Cobweb is above the equilibrium price of Rs. 1.73 per kg of rice. The initial quantity of supply (S_0) is 1124.25 kg ha^{-1} and the corresponding initial price (P_0) is 1.73 Rs. Kg ha^{-1}. Consumer demand (D0) for rice is 1124.25 kg ha-1 and this quantity equals the initial market supply. The producers of rice induced by the higher price in period '0' (i.e. 1985-86) increase their supply to S_1 in the next period

'1' (ie 1986-87). Due to this initiation market supply has increased in the next year, but the price per kg of rice falls instantaneously to p_1. The quantity demanded per hectare at this lower price is D_1 and is equal to the supply in period 't', S_1. But this lower price P_1 induces producers to lower the supply of rice to S_1. This process continues indefinitely, producing a Cobweb pattern which is known as damped Cobweb. However, over time this gap between market demand and supply narrows down and the price coverage towards the equilibrium price level p = 1.73 Rs. kg ha^{-1}. The farmer output response to changes in prices, in a convergent framework, thus explained in Table 10.2 indicates how the present pattern of price and outputs are likely to affect the future movements. Hence, under the present conditions Cobweb will disappear only after 60 years.

Adjustment time is a factor affecting the stability of a market model. In order to reach the equilibrium position, an excess of price over equilibrium price must induce a decrease in price. To reduce the time lag in achieving the equilibrium price, the instability of supply to adjust immediately to change in price should be changed. Thus, a stable supply behavior can reform the price structure of rice in Kerala. In other words, the study of the system of price-quantity relationship of rice over the years reveals the need for a stable supply model for the farmers in order to achieve the equilibrium position at the earliest. This is in conformity with the relationships established by Waugh (1970).

References

Agarwal, K.S. (1976). *Introduction to Econometrics*, Lakshmi Narain Agarwal Educational Publishers, New Delhi, P. 197-203.

Mehta, B.C. (1991). *Mathematical Economics: Microeconomic Models*. Sultan Chand & Sons Publishers, New Delhi, P. 213.

Waugh, F.V. (1970). "Readings in the Economics of Agriculture", *AFA Series*, George Allen & Unwin Ltd.; London, p. 89-106.

Section II

Welfare

11

Rural Poverty and Rural Infrastructure: The Case of India

SIDDHARTHA MITRA
S.D. BRAHMANKAR
VISHAL HANDA

1. Introduction

It is now well accepted that infrastructure development leads to economic development. Binswanger (1987) showed on the basis of a cross-country study that a 10 per cent increase in the percentage of roads paved or the percentage of area under irrigation led to a nine per cent increase in aggregate output . Binswanger (1989) also did a village level study of India and found that increase in road length, primary schools and rural electrification per unit area contributed significantly to the growth in aggregate output. However, a positive effect of infrastructure development on economic development does not necessarily imply a positive effect on poverty. Nevertheless, analytically it is easy to argue that a growth in infrastructure stocks should lead to poverty reduction. For example, roads provide the poor with better access to employment opportunities. Education raises the human capital stock of the poor. Accessible drinking water facilities firstly keep the poor free of diseases and also help to economise on the time to fetch water. The former factor increases their productivity and the latter facilitates the attainment of literacy. The availability of telecommunication and electricity facilitates remunerative off-farm employment and increases the incomes of the rural poor.

The question is whether the positive effects of infrastructure on poverty alleviation are significant. Second, these effects of rural infrastructure are partial equilibrium effects and whether these contribute to decreases in poverty in a general equilibrium framework is something to be ascertained. There is, however, some empirical evidence that the link between the stock of infrastructure and poverty is negative. Bredie and Beehary (1998) show that easy acessibility to drinking water facilities might lead to an increase in school enrolment particularly among girls. According to their study for Madagascar, 83 per cent of the girls who did not go to school spent time collecting water while only 58 per cent of the girls who attended school spent time collecting water. It is apparent from these figures that availability of drinking water by reducing the need to go very far for water would promote literacy among girls. Hoque (1998) shows that there is a very strong link between fertility and fertility related issues and electrification. According to his study for Bangladesh, 46.6 per cent of women in electrified households practise family planning as opposed to only 25.5 percent of women in non-electrified households. The mean ideal family size for the former is 2.67 and for the latter is 3.06.

Perhaps the most comprehensive study of the effect of infrastructure on poverty reduction is by Fan *et al.* (2000). They estimate the effect of different types of government expenditure on poverty. The infrastructure stock variables accounted for are electrification (percentage of rural villages that are electrified), the literacy rate of rural population, irrigation facilities and road density in rural areas. The model is one of simultaneous equations and is for the period 1970-93. The results show that a million rupees (at 1993 prices) spent on roads would lift 123.8 people out of poverty. A similar effect on education would lift 41 people out of poverty.

Our paper is also concerned with the impact of infrastructure stock on poverty. However, it is different from Fan *et al.*'s analysis in several ways. First, we cover a more recent period. 1983-1997. Second, we use certain additional variables pertaining to infrastructure stock: percentage of villages with telecom facilities, percentage of villages with drinking water facilities and percentage of villages with medical facilities. Instead of road density we use the variable "percentage of villages with access to roads". Third, whereas Fan *et al.* use the percentage of rural households that are landless we use the proportion of the agricultural workforce that is composed of landless and marginal farmers. The latter variable excludes those individuals that have left the farm sector for the non-farm sector. These individuals are provided with the opportunity for a better livelihood and a chance to come out of poverty. Fourth, our main interest is in finding out how the percentage incidence of poverty in an Indian state is affected by the percentage of villages that have access to an infrastructure stock. Fifth, we use a single equation model, which is the reduced form of a simultaneous equation model.

2. The Model

Our objective is to determine the effect of deficiency of rural infrastructure on poverty using panel data for different Indian states corresponding to three time periods. The poverty in an Indian state is hypothesised to depend on the following factors relating to deprivation:

(a) **Marginal/landless farmers**: The proportion of agricultural labour force composed of landless and marginal farmers.

(b) **Drinking Water**: The proportion of villages that do not have full access to drinking water.

(c) **Illiteracy.**

(d) **Roads**: The proportion of villages, which do not have access to roads.

(e) **Electricity**: The proportion of villages, which are not electrified.

(f) **Telecom**: The proportion of villages with no access to telecom services (no access to Village Public Telephones).

(g) **Medical Facilities**: The proportion of villages without access to medical facilities.

Due to the fragility of the Indian database it is not possible to find three points of time (each separated from the other by a fair number of years) in the recent past for which data for all three points of time on all variables are available. Table 11.1 sums up the availability of data and Table 11.2 explains the data sources.

Table 11.1

Availability of Data

Variable	*Period 1*	*Period 2*	*Period 3*
Drinking Water	1980	1985	1990
Telecom	1987	1991	1999
Electricity	1981	1991	1997,2000
Medical Facilities	1981	1991	Not Available
Poverty	1983	1993-94	1999-2000
Roads	1982	1987	1997
Cultivators	1981	1991	Not Available
Literacy	1981	1991	1997

Table 11.2

Data Sources

Variables	*Data Sources*
Cultivators	A Note on Operational Land Holdings in India 1991-92, NSS 48th Round: *Sarvekshana* Jan-Mar. Vol. 20, No. 3, 1997
(Landless + Marginal)	A Note on Some Aspects of Operational Holdings, NSS 37th Round: *Sarvekshana* Jan-Mar. Vol. 12, No. 1-2, 1988(B)
	Census of India: State Profile 1991, India; Census of India: A Hand Book of Population Statistics, 1981, India
Roads	Basic Road Statistics (various issues), Ministry of Surface Transport (GoI)
Telecom	Indian Telecom Statistics (various issues), Ministry of Communication (GoI)
Rural Poverty	NSS 43rd, 50th Rounds and Angus Deaton's (2003) adjusted estimates based on NSS 55th Round
Drinking Water	Ministry of Agriculture (www.indiastat.com)
Medical Facilities and	Census of India (1981): States Profile of Availability of Infrastructural Facilities in Rural areas
Electricity	Census of India (1991): Availability of Infrastructural Facilities in Rural Areas of India
Literacy	Manpower Profile of India, Yearbook 2000 (IAMR)

In order to make up for the deficiency of not having a complete set of data for three points of time we had to resort to interpolation and extrapolation. In our final choice of time points for the panel regression we used the criteria of incorporating as much original (as opposed to interpolated/extrapolated) data as possible and of maximising the recentness of the time periods. We finally settled for the time periods 1983, 1993 and 1997.

The impact of rural infrastructure on rural poverty reduction has been estimated earlier by Fan, Hazell and Thorat (2000). Their effort is commendable. Here we again model the same phenomenon but think of rural poverty as the outcome of deficiency of rural infrastructure at the village level.[1] This point will become clearer later. Second, we allow for interaction between different types of infrastructure in reducing poverty. Thus, the poverty alleviating effects of provision of a road in a rural area are enhanced if there is provision of clean drinking water.

1. If the village does not have access to a road then that will increase the chances of every body in the living in poverty.

It is assumed that an increase in any of the above factors, (a)-(g), leads to an increase in the incidence of poverty. Two relationships between poverty and the above factors can be hypothesised:

(1) Poverty can be estimated to be additively separable in these factors (linear model)[2]. The coefficients on each of these factors have to be estimated.

(2) We assume that these factors interact to determine the incidence of poverty in the following sense: the increase in poverty resulting from an increase in the incidence of one of these factors will be greater when the incidence of the other factors is higher. In this case we assume poverty to be a multiplicative function of these factors with the effect of a factor captured by the size of its exponent. This corresponds to a log-linear model.

3. Results

Regression results of our analysis are given in Table 11.3.

Table 11.3

Linear Regression Results

	Regression 1	*Regression 2*	*Regression 3*	*Regression 4*
R-square	.652	.630	.588	.554
Electricity	.052			
Medical Facilities	-.035			
Illiteracy	.250	.549*		
Marginal/Landless Farmers	.439*	.482*	.392*	
Roads	- .092			
Telecom	.021			.073**
Drinking Water	.149		.314*	.298*

Note: (a)* denotes significance at 10 per cent level and ** denotes significance at 15 per cent level, (b) The first row gives the values of R-square in the individual regressions whereas the others give the coefficients on the mentioned variables.

In the first regression all the infrastructure variables are insignificant. Moreover "medical facilities" and "roads" have the

2. $Poverty_{jt} = \alpha j + \Sigma\beta_i X_{ijt}$ where i refers to the ith dependant variable (dependant variables are mentioned in Table 11.3, j subscripts states and t subscripts time periods). When the model is log-linear then we estimate $Ln\ (Poverty)_{jt} = \theta + \Sigma\beta_i\ Ln(Xijt)$

opposite of the expected signs. Only the proportion of farmers that are landless and marginal is significant. Stepwise weeding out of the more insignificant infrastructure variables leaves us only with illiteracy. In regression 2 we use only "marginal/landless farmers" and "illiteracy" as independent variables. Both variables are significant with coefficients of .482 and .549 respectively. Moreover, we have a good fit with a R-square of .630. The coefficients imply that a 10 percentage point increase in literacy would reduce poverty by 5.49 percentage points. An identical decline in the other significant variable would reduce poverty by 4.82 percentage points. An interesting finding which should be noted is that whenever we include both "illiteracy" and "water" in the regression not more than one turns out to be significant. It seems from our findings that availability of water impacts on poverty through its effect on illiteracy. This conclusion is further supported by the fact that the two variables are highly correlated. In regression 3 the only change we make from regression 2 is replace illiteracy with "water". Both "marginal/landless farmers" and "water" are again significant with coefficients of .392 and .314 respectively. Our coefficients imply that a 10 per cent decrease in "marginal/landless farmers" would reduce poverty by 3.92 percentage points. Similarly a decrease in "water" by 10 per cent would reduce poverty by 3.14 per cent.

It is quite possible that the variable "marginal/landless farmers" captures the impact of variables such as electricity, telecom etc. This is because of the opportunities for off-farm employment that are provided by the spread of electricity and telecom facilities and roads. We did run regressions of "marginal/landless farmers" on the variables measuring deficiency in the relevant types of infrastructure. "Telecom" and "Roads" had a significant positive effect on the dependant variable confirming our suspicions.[3] As we understand it, roads and telecommunication facilities, by facilitating non-farm employment opportunities for landless agricultural labour and marginal farmers, help to shrink the proportion of these in the non-agricultural labour force. Keeping this in mind we ran a set of regression excluding "marginal/landless farmers" but including its

3. The regression had an R-square of 0.28. "Roads" was significant at the 10 per cent level with a coefficient of .16. "Telecom" was significant at the 20 per cent level with a coefficient of .05.

determining infrastructure variables. After leaving out the insignificant variables we ran regression 4 which had water and telecom as the independent variables. The coefficients of these two variables were .298 and .073 respectively. The fit was reasonable with a R-square of .554. The coefficients implied that a reduction in water by 10 per cent would increase poverty by 2.98 percentage points. A similar reduction in telecom would reduce poverty by 0.73 percentage points. The log-linear version of the model did not have a good fit and was therefore discarded.

4. Lessons

If we go by the results then providing access to drinking water, education and land is a good way of reducing poverty. A lot of Indian economists and sociologists say that we have missed the bus as far as land reforms go. However, we can still eradicate a fair amount of poverty if we provide good drinking water and education as well as incentives to the non-farm sector. We take the case of Uttar Pradesh, the largest state in India with a population of 166 million. In 1997 Uttar Pradesh had an incidence of poverty of 37.15 per cent. It had a literacy of 56 per cent and 2.18 per cent villages lacked access to water. Around 69.61 per cent farmers were marginal or landless. Going by our results (regression 2), if Uttar Pradesh attains complete literacy poverty will go down by 24 percentage points. Note that it is possible to effect a reduction of the number of marginal/landless farmers through expansion of the non-farm sector. If the proportion of farmers that are marginal/landless in Uttar Pradesh is reduced by twenty percentage points then there would be an additional reduction of poverty by 9.6 per cent. Thus, if Uttar Pradesh was made 100 per cent literate and the proportion of farmers that are landless/marginal went down by 20 per cent then poverty would be reduced to 3.55 per cent. For Andhra Pradesh, a large Southern state an increase in literacy by 30 percentage points will wipe out poverty. What about Bihar, the state with the highest incidence of poverty? Currently the incidence of poverty in Bihar is 52.87 per cent. The literacy level is 49 per cent and the share of marginal/landless farmers in total workforce is 76.18 per cent. Surprisingly, only 1.17 per cent of its villages are without access to proper drinking water. If the share of marginal/landless farmers in the agricultural workforce is reduced by

30 percentage points and the state's literacy is increased by 30 percentage points then the incidence of poverty in Bihar would go down to around 22.3 per cent - a net decline of around 30.6 per cent percentage points.

How costly is it to provide our villages with drinking water and education facilities? Here are some estimates.

5. Conclusions

The basic conclusion that emerges from this paper is that there are two significant factors determining rural poverty – (a) the proportion of the agricultural labour force that is accounted for by landless labour and marginal farmers and (b) literacy rates. It is the landless labour and marginal farmers that characterise the bulk of the supply of rural labour in Indian states.

We have seen that till now providing access to water has been a major means of increasing literacy. This is also supported by the results of a fixed effects regression of illiteracy on deficiency in water. As the proportion of villages with access to water nears 100 per cent this channel of increasing literacy is fast becoming exhausted. Alternative channels need to be explored such as economic incentives, better sanitation in schools, better functioning of schools, participation of the community in schooling etc.

References

Binswanger H. *et al.* (1987). "On the Determinants of Cross-country Aggregate Agricultural Supply", *Journal of Econometrics*, 36, No.1

Binswanger, H., Khander, S., and Rozenzweig, M. (1989). "How Infrastructure and Financial Institutions Affect Agricultural Output and Investment in India", *World Bank Working Paper Series 163*.

Bredie, J., & Beehary, G. (1998). "School Enrolment Decline in Sub-Saharan Africa", *World Bank Discussion Paper* No. 395.

Deaton, A. (2003). "Prices and Poverty, 1987-2000", *Economic and Political Weekly*, Vol.38 (4), pp: 362-368.

Eswaran, M. and E. Kotwal (1994). *Why Poverty Persists in India*, Oxford University Press.

Gupta, D.B. and S. Mitra (2003). "Water and its Sustainable Pricing", *Margin*, Vol. 36, No.1, pp: 99-112.

Hoque, N. (1988) *Rural Electrification and its Impact on Fertility: Evidence from Bangladesh* PhD dissertation, The Pennsylvania State University.

Fan, S., Hazell, P. and S. Thorat (2000). "Government Spending, Growth and Poverty in Rural India", *American Journal of Agricultural Economics*, 82(4), pp:1038-1051.

12

Public Policy Stance and Human Development: A Panel Analysis

LEKHA S. CHAKRABORTY

1. Introduction

Human development is broadly defined as a process of enlarging people's choices, as well as raising the level of well being. Theoretically, these choices can be infinite and vary intertemporally and across regions[1]. From among these, the choice to lead a long and healthy life; the choice to acquire knowledge and be educated; and to have access to resources needed for a decent level of living are identified as three most critical and socially valuable (UNDP, Human Development Reports). A range of social outcomes can reflect these choices in the well being of people, most important being the life expectancy, literacy and the per capita income. The Human Development Reports noted that life expectancy and educational attainments are valued ends in themselves; and per capita income is to incorporate other aspects of well being not captured by indicators on the social attainments on education, health and longevity of people.

What promotes human development? Growth of per capita income has been considered as a measure of improving human development. However, empirical literature revealed that per capita income can not be a sole determinant of achieving human development; public spending on social sectors also has a significant role to play (Streeten, 1979; Isenman, 1980, Sen, 1981, Bhalla, S S and Glewwe, 1986; Kanbur, R, 1991; Anand and Ravallion, 1993).

The aim of the paper is to analyse the impact of public policy stance, in terms of the public expenditure incurred on health and

---

1. For details, refer Human Development Reports, UNDP.

education, and human development. This paper does not refute the widely explored link between growth of per capita income and the human development, rather to emphasise that it does substantially through higher public expenditure, particularly through health care and education. The crucial question thus is that *does public policy stance make an impact on human development*. Since there is a contemporaneous transformation of many socio-economic and policy variables that result in the human development, it is a difficult task to establish a bivariate link between the two. However, an analysis of macrolink between public policy stance - proxied by the public expenditure - and human development would enable us to realise whether the money spent by government, especially on human resource development, is transformed to the end results of better human development indicators.

The paper is divided into four sections. Apart from the introduction, Section 2 deals with some theoretical issues related to public policy stance and human development while Section 3 interprets the data. Section 4 deals with the specification of the model and econometric estimation. Section 5 interprets the results and draws conclusions.

2. Theoretical Issues Related to Public Policy Stance and Human Development: A Synoptic View

Theoretically, there are six reasons why public policy stance should promote human development. First and above all, human development is an end itself, which needs no further justification. Second, it is a means to higher productivity. Third, it reduces human reproductivity, by lowering the desired family size. Fourth, human development is good for the physical environment; that the impact of population growth and population density is detrimental for environment due to deforestation, desertification and soil erosion. Fifth, reduced poverty contributes to a healthy civil society, democracy and greater social stability. Sixth, it has political appeal, for it may reduce civil disturbances and increase political stability (Streeten, 1994).

The arguments for public policy stance, in terms of expenditure as the key policy instrument, rest on the fact the functioning of the market cannot, by itself, activate the signaling, response and mobility of economic agents to achieve efficiency in both static (allocative efficiency) and dynamic (shift in the production frontier) terms (Arndt, 1998).

The case of public expenditure proceeds from market failures of one kind or another. Markets fail to secure appropriate signals, responses and mobility because: (i) not all goods and services are traded. Markets cannot determine the prices of public goods; (ii) goods exhibiting externalities in consumption and production force a wedge between market prices and social valuation and the market will not ensure a socially desired supply; (iii) some goods are characterised by increasing returns to scale. In case of such natural monopolies, society can gain from lower prices and higher output when the public sector is the producer or a subsidy is paid to the private sector to cover the losses of producing optimal output; (iv) information asymmetry between the providers and consumers of services such as social insurance can give rise to the problems of moral hazard and adverse selection; and (v) state intervention is necessary also for securing income redistribution (Rao, M.G., 1998).

The theoretical and empirical advancement towards public policy intervention in providing human development reflect the community's growing concern with social aspects of development; steel mills, dams and machine building industries have now been displaced from the commanding heights of development strategy, instead so-called soft sectors such as education and health have occupied the centre stage (Mundle, 1998). Certain public goods such as defence, administration, a clean environment etc. that cannot be provided by market, because no consumer can be excluded once these services are provided and hence consumers will not 'buy' these services (Mundle, S., 1998).

In assessing human development, the orthodox measures of well being, such as growth of GDP per head or by some distribution-corrected value of GNP per head, used in empirical literature have inherent limitations in capturing wider aspects of well being and the contingent process of development. The genesis of critique of the use of GNP per capita for measuring the level of development in various countries can be traced back to the United Nations Report, 1954, in which specific recommendations were made against the use of this indicator as a measure of human development (Noorbakhsh, 1998). Subsequently, a formidable array of literature followed since 1970s in support of this proposition and argued for construction of indices based on socio-economic indicators for measuring development (Hicks and Streeten, 1979; Morris, 1967, Adelman and Morris, 1967, UNRISD, 1972). In the seventies, the concept of "basic needs" became the central core of the debate on human development policies (Hicks and Streeten, 1979). The array of literature in favour of social indicators to measure human development has resulted in the collation of data on a spectrum of socio-economic indicators across countries, which has inevitably resulted in the attempts to construct the composite indices of human development.

There can be little doubt about the value of higher real income in opening up possibilities of living worthwhile lives that are not available at lower levels of income[2]. Empirical evidence showed that in a semi-logarithmic framework of regressing proportionate shortfalls of life expectancy against per capita GDP, revealed that nearly half of the variations in the life expectancy could be attributed to differences in GNP per head (Anand and Ravallion, 1993). In this context, it is important to note that the substantial impact of higher GDP per head on life expectancy and other social outcomes of better literacy level, low mortality rates among children and better schooling among children seems to work via factors in which public policy stance play a significant part.

3. Interpreting Data

Apart from the four major countries in South Asia, namely Bangladesh, India, Pakistan and Sri Lanka, the sample includes Australia, Canada, Norway, Sweden, United Kingdom and United States to represent countries with high HDI and GDI; China, Indonesia, Malaysia, and South Korea to represent Asian countries outside South Asia, and Gambia to represent countries with low HDI and GDI outside South Asia. The data used are for 1993, 1994 and 1995. The data on Human Development Index and Gender-related Development Index was compiled from the UNDP Human Development Reports, while data on GDP, public spending on health and education in US dollar terms (in '000) and relevant population figures are compiled from World Development Indicators electronic database. The public expenditure on education for Bangladesh is taken

2. Dreze and Sen, 1995

from *Key Indicators of Developing Asian and Pacific Countries, 1999* of Asian Development Bank.

The available macro statistics that best reflect human development is Human Development Index (HDI). It is a composite index based on life expectancy at birth, gross enrolment ratio, adult literacy rate and real GDP per capita. However, HDI has been criticised for a first-world bias; that the use of GDP, longevity and literacy levels in the base of the HDI can result in these measures producing high rankings for developed countries even when there is significant gender inequality in a country. It is also criticised on the grounds that the multi-dimensions of human development cannot be measured by conceptually limited composite index and some others criticised it as being limited in measuring human development by the quality and limitation of data (Murray, 1993; Srinivasan, 1994). The technical properties of the HDI has also been under criticism (McGrillivray, 1991; McGillivray and White, 1993; Dossel and Gounder, 1994; Chowdhury, 2004).

HDI has been favoured in the empirical literature on the ground that it reflects the inadequacy of other indices like GNP to capture human development (Streeten, 1994 and Streeten, 1995). It is argued that HDI gives a less skewed picture of distribution than that presented by the GNP per capita. It has been preferred to per capita income as the latter neglects the distributional aspects (Desai, 1991). Broadly, the constituent indicators of the HDI are favoured by researchers as it is at best a summary index at a very aggregate level (Dasgupta and Weale, 1992; Streeten, 1995, Haq, 1995).

The gender sensitive adjustment of human development index is Gender Development Index (GDI). In other words, GDI adjusts the average achievement of each country in life expectancy, educational attainment [better literacy levels and gross enrolment ratio] and income in accordance with the gender disparity. The values for HDI and GDI range between 0 and 1. The values closer to zero indicate acute deprivation. The values closer to one indicate attainable levels of development. The developed countries including .the Nordic countries, Sweden and Norway top the GDI scale. While the GDI of below 0.5 for Gambia, Mozambique, Pakistan, Bangladesh, India etc showed that women suffer the double deprivation of overall achievement in human development.

Table 12.1

Human Development Index of Selected Developed and Developing Countries

Country	*1993*	*1994*	*1995*
Canada	0.951	0.96	0.93
Australia	0.929	0.931	0.926
Bangladesh	0.365	0.368	0.443
China	0.609	0.626	0.679
India	**0.436**	**0.446**	**0.544**
Indonesia	0.641	0.668	0.662
Malaysia	0.937	0.943	0.924
Norway	0.937	0.943	0.924
Sri Lanka	0.698	0.711	0.717
Sweden	0.933	0.936	0.924
United Kingdom	0.924	0.931	0.914
United States	0.94	0.942	0.923
Gambia, The	0.292	0.281	0.374
Pakistan	0.442	0.445	0.476
Korea, Rep.	0.886	0.765	0.851

Source: UNDP, Human Development Reports, 1995-2000

India's overall ranking on gender-related development is poor, even in comparison with the country's human development levels. India's Gender Development Index (GDI) (Box 12.1) is lower than that for all developing countries as well as the GDI for all countries except Pakistan in the medium human development group to which India belongs (Table 12.2).

Low GDI reflects gender disparity in basic capabilities because of lack of education and health standards. The gender development index of Canada and the Nordic countries like Sweden and Norway showed the highest in the world and the index is nearing unity.

Table 12.3 showed that public expenditure on health in Canada and Sweden are at similar levels with respect to their ratio of GDP, which hovered around 7 per cent of GDP, though a marginal declining trend is noted over the years. This allocation is higher than that of other developed countries and out of alignment with the developing countries. Canada has a predominantly publicly-financed, privately-delivered health care system. It provides universal accessibility and a comprehensive coverage for medically necessary hospital, in-patient and out-patient physician services[3].

Table 12.2

Gender Development Index of Selected Developed and Developing Countries

Country	*1993*	*1994*	*1995*
Canada	0.927	0.939	0.94
Australia	0.912	0.917	0.918
Bangladesh	0.336	0.339	0.342
China	0.601	0.617	0.641
India	**0.410**	**0.419**	**0.424**
Indonesia	0.616	0.642	0.651
Malaysia	0.772	0.782	0.785
Norway	0.926	0.934	0.935
Sri Lanka	0.679	0.694	0.700
Sweden	0.929	0.932	0.932
United Kingdom	0.886	0.896	0.907
United States	0.923	0.928	0.927
Gambia, The	0.275	0.263	0.277
Pakistan	0.383	0.392	0.399
Korea, Rep.	0.816	0.826	0.826

Source: UNDP, Human Development Reports, 1995-2000

The allocation on health in developing countries in general is much lower than that of developed countries. Among the developing countries, India's public expenditure on health is as low as less than 1 per cent of GDP, which is the lower than that of Bangladesh, Pakistan, China, Malaysia and Sri Lanka. The public health expenditure in India is mainly spent on the communicable disease control programmes, family welfare schemes and nutrition schemes. It is to be noted that Sri Lanka's social indicators are high relative to income, which threw a hypothesis that social spending can have an impact on improvements in social indicators. At the sametime, Pakistan's social indicators are by any standard poor, especially taking into account of its relatively rapid income growth.

3. The Federal and Provincial Government have shared responsibility in health care in Canada. The federal government is responsible for setting and administering national principles or standards for the health care system, assisting in the financing of provincial health care services through fiscal transfers while governments are responsible for managing and delivering health services; planning, financing, and evaluating the provision of hospital care, physician and allied health care services; managing some aspects of prescription care and public health (www.hc-sc.gc.ca).

Table 12.3

Public Expenditure on Health of Selected Developed and Developing Countries

(As per cent of GDP)

Country	*1993*	*1994*	*1995*
Canada	7.34	7.05	6.70
Australia	5.66	5.64	5.65
Bangladesh	1.13	1.16	1.15
China	2.05	2.06	1.92
India	**0.71**	**0.69**	**0.65**
Indonesia	0.67	0.66	0.63
Malaysia	1.45	1.31	1.26
Norway	6.71	6.62	6.66
Sri Lanka	1.41	1.59	1.64
Sweden	7.66	7.39	7.08
United Kingdom	5.85	5.81	5.83
United States	6.08	6.29	6.47
Gambia, The	1.83	1.81	1.72
Pakistan	0.98	0.96	1.02
Korea, Rep.	2.06	2.01	2.14

Source: World Development Indicators Database & *Key Indicators of Developing Asian and Pacific Countries, 1999*, Asian Development Bank.

Table 12.4

Public Expenditure on Education Selected Developed and Developing Countries

(As per cent of GDP)

Country	*1993*	*1994*	*1995*
Canada	7.22	6.91	—
Australia	5.56	5.38	5.45
Bangladesh	—	—	—
China	1.86	2.40	2.27
India	**3.58**	**3.54**	**3.31**
Indonesia	1.78	1.42	1.40
Malaysia	5.15	5.18	4.68
Norway	8.17	8.25	8.08
Sri Lanka	3.14	3.20	3.04
Sweden	—	7.96	8.07
United Kingdom	5.48	5.42	5.33
United States	5.26	5.36	—
Gambia, The	5.06	5.35	5.61
Pakistan	2.60	2.79	2.80
Korea, Rep.	4.43	3.70	3.68

Source: Same as Table 12.2.

The trends in public expenditure on education showed that the Nordic countries like Sweden and Norway top in the world at 8 per cent of GDP on education.

Contrary to the trends in public expenditure on health, India showed a better status in relation to the public expenditure on education at around 3 per cent of GDP, which is higher than that of other developing countries like Indonesia, Sri Lanka, Pakistan and China. In India, elementary education has been given greater priority relative to secondary and higher education.

Box 12.1

Gender Development Index

The Human Development Index [HDI] is a gender-neutral measurement of the average achievements in a country in three basic dimensions of human development: longevity, knowledge and a decent standard of living. Longevity is measured by life expectancy at birth, knowledge by adult literacy and the combined gross primary, secondary and tertiary enrolment ratio, and standard of living by Gross Domestic Product (GDP) per capita in US dollars in purchasing power parity (PPP) terms.

Let L denote life expectancy at birth in years, A adult literacy as per cent, E combined gross primary, secondary and tertiary enrolment ratio in per cent, and Y per capita GDP in PPP US dollar terms. The value of each variable for a country is transformed into its deviation from the minimum possible value of the variable expressed as a proportion of the maximum deviation possible, i.e. maximum less minimum. Thus, after transformation we have

$$L^* = (L-25)/(85-25),\ A^* = A/100,\ E^* = E/100, \text{ and } Y^* = (Y - \min Y)\ (\max Y - \min Y).$$

Given the minimum life expectancy for women and men of 27.5 years and 22.5 years, respectively, the average minimum life expectancy is taken as 25 [= (27.5 + 22.5)/2]. Similarly, maximum life expectancy is taken as 85. The maximum and minimum of both adult literacy and enrollment are taken as 100 and 0, respectively. The maximum and minimum for Y are exogenously fixed. HDI is computed as

$$\{L^* + (2/3 \times A^* + 1/3 \times E^*) + Y^*\}/3.$$

The Gender Development Index (GDI) uses the same variables as HDI, but adjusts for the degree of disparity in achievement across genders. The average value of each of the component variables is substituted by "equally distributed equivalent achievements". The equally distributed equivalent achievement for a variable is taken as that level of achievement that if attained equally by women and men would be judged to be exactly as valuable socially as the actually observed disparate achievements. Taking an additively separable, symmetric and constant elasticity marginal valuation function with elasticity 2, the equally distributed equivalent achievement X_{ede} for any variable X turns out to be

$$X_{ede} = [\, n_f\ (1/X_f) + n_m\ (1/X_m)]^{-1}$$

where X_f and X_m are the values of the variable for females and males, and n_f and n_m are the population shares of females and males. X_{ede} is a 'gender-equity-sensitive indicator'(GESI).

Thus, for this chosen value of 2 for constant elasticity marginal valuation function, GDI is computed as

$$\{L_{ede} + (2/3 \text{ x } A_{ede} + 1/3 \text{ x } E_{ede}) + Y_{ede}\}/3.$$

Source: Lahiri, A; Chakraborty, L S and Bhattacharrya (2002).

The prima facie orienting data exploration strongly suggest that growth of per capita income, while important, is not the primary determinant of improvement in human development. The next section econometrically delve deep into the question of effectiveness of public policy intervention versus 'growth mediated' human development.

4. Specification of the Model and Econometric Results

The model is specified with per capita expenditure on health and education and per capita income as regressors. It is generally observed that the human development is positively correlated to the income levels of a country. However, the question we are interested in is how effective the expenditure by government on social sectors like education and health in attaining better levels of human development. The model thus is specified in the following form:

Model 1

$$HDI_{it} = \alpha_i + \beta_1\, PUB\_H_{it} + \beta_2\, PUB\_E_{it} + \beta_3\, PC_{it} + u_{it}$$

where HDI_{it} = Human Development Index

α_i = country-specific intercepts

PUB_H_{it} = per capita expenditure on health in US $

PUB_E_{it} = per capita expenditure on education in US $

PC_{it} = per capita income in US $

Table 12.5

Effect of Public Expenditure on Education and Health and Per Capita Income on HDI: Fixed Effects Model

Variable	*Coefficient*	*Std. Error*	*t-Statistic*	*Prob.*
PUB_Health	4.38E-05	0.000297	0.147385	0.8841
PUB_Education	0.000215	0.000233	0.922748	0.3653
Per Capita Income	9.64E-06	1.63E-05	0.590350	0.5605
Fixed Effects				
CAN—C	0.775481			
AUS—C	0.845657			
BAN—C	0.393477			
INDIA—C	0.476017			
INDO—C	0.662845			
CHIN—C	0.639940			
MAL—C	0.801753			
KOR—C	0.839328			
SWE—C	0.675639			
USA—C	0.822650			
UK—C	0.833708			
NOR—C	0.605086			
PAK—C	0.455921			
GAM—C	0.314740			
SRI—C	0.710185			
Adjusted R-squared	0.98			

The results showed that public expenditure on health and education and per capita income have positive relationship with human development index, but found insignificant (Table 12.5).

Model 2

$$GDI_{it} = \alpha_i + \beta_1 PUB\_H_{it} + \beta_2 PUB\_E_{it} + \beta_3 PC_{it} + u_{it}$$

where GDI_{it} = Gender Development Index

α_i = country-specific intercepts

PUB_H_{it} = per capita expenditure on health in US $

PUB_E_{it} = per capita expenditure on education in US $

PC_{it} = per capita income in US $

Table 12.6

Effect of Public Expenditure on Education and Health and Per Capita Income on GDI: Fixed Effects Model

Variable	*Coefficient*	*Std. Error*	*t-Statistic*	*Prob.*
PUB_Health	0.000109	4.72E-05	2.305947	0.0301
PUB_Education	7.64E-06	4.20E-05	0.182016	0.8571
Per Capita Income	8.47E-06	2.54E-06	3.329001	0.0028
Fixed Effects				
CAN—C	0.931689			
AUS—C	0.880259			
BAN—C	0.336920			
INDIA—C	0.415018			
INDO—C	0.629168			
CHIN—C	0.616800			
MAL—C	0.754983			
KOR—C	0.767843			
SWE—C	0.931877			
USA—C	0.892128			
UK—C	0.866726			
NOR—C	0.914376			
PAK—C	0.388021			
GAM—C	0.269561			
SRI—C	0.686724			
Adjusted R-squared	0.998			

When the relationship between per capita expenditure on education and health is regressed on gender development index in a panel framework, per capita expenditure on health is found positive and significant, while per capita expenditure on education is found positive, but insignificant. However, per capita income is found positive and significantly related to GDI.

The results from the link between HDI and GDI with the per capita expenditure on health and education and per capita income (Table 12.5 and 12.6) have not been in tandem with the *a-priori* expectations that all the three regressors will be positively related to HDI and GDI and also will be significant. This may be due to the multicollinearity problem between per capita expenditure on health and per capita expenditure on education.

Table 12.7

Per Capita Expenditure on Health and Education: Results from Pooled Least Square Estimation

Variable	*Coefficient*	*Std. Error*	*t-Statistic*	*Prob.*
PUB_Education	2.030696	0.341273	5.950357	0.0000
Fixed Effects				
CAN—C	-1496.913			
AUS—C	-991.9845			
BAN—C	-8.073305			
INDIA—C	-22.45062			
INDO—C	-21.50143			
CHIN—C	-11.06980			
MAL—C	-301.5005			
KOR—C	-521.5585			
SWE—C	-2132.156			
USA—C	-1209.125			
UK—C	-994.7487			
NOR—C	-3020.148			
PAK—C	-20.54165			
GAM—C	-31.41797			
SRI—C	-30.83554			
Adjusted R-squared	0.99			

The multicolinearity between per capita expenditure on health and per capita expenditure on education is revealed from the pooled least square estimates of regressing per capita expenditure of health on education (Table 12.7). We have re-specified the models 1 and 2 to avoid multicolinearity problems between per capita expenditure on health and education as follows.

Model 3

$$HDI_{it} = \alpha_i + \beta\, PUB_{it} + \gamma\, PC_{it} + u_{it}$$

where HDI_{it} = Human Development Index

α_i = country-specific intercepts

PUB_{it} = per capita combined expenditure on education and health in US $

PC_{it} = per capita income in US $

The estimation of the fixed effects model (Models 3) of pooled least squares with white heteroskedasticity-consistent standard errors of regressing between HDI and per capita combined expenditure on health and education showed a significant positive relationship between the two (Table 12.8). Further, the results showed that increase in public expenditure on human resource development by 1000 US dollars could increase the HDI to 0.5 percentage points. The coefficient of per capita income is 0.019; which translate that rise in per capita income by 1000 US dollars in a country can lead to 0.019 percentage point rise in HDI. Thus the results showed that social spending has stronger impact on human development than economic growth *per se*.

Table 12.8

Effect of Public Expenditure on Education and Health and Per Capita Income on HDI: Fixed Effects Model

Variable	*Coefficient*	*Std. Error*	*t-Statistic*	*Prob.*
Per Capita Income	0.019244	0.005136	3.747160	0.0009
Pub Exp. on H & E	0.506417	0.058633	8.637080	0.0000
Fixed Effects				
CAN—C	-405.0515			
AUS—C	-348.5907			
BAN—C	-6.850728			
INDIA—C	-11.83919			
INDO—C	-21.90376			
KOR—C	-261.3866			
USA—C	-405.9201			
UK—C	-335.7900			
NOR—C	-841.3220			
GAM—C	-12.96152			
PAK—C	-12.88181			
SRI—C	-17.79179			
SWE—C	-570.7858			
MAL—C	-134.4510			
CHIN—C	-9.481227			
Adjusted R-squared	0.999868			

Now we turn to attempt the impact of per capita income and per capita combined expenditure on health and education on Gender Development Index (GDI).

Model 4

$$GDI_{it} = \alpha_i + \beta\, PUB_{it} + \gamma\, PC_{it} + u_{it}$$

where GDI_{it} = Gender Development Index

α_i = country-specific intercepts

PUB_{it} = per capita expenditure on education and health in US $

PC_{it} = per capita income in US $

The results revealed that combined public expenditure on education and health in per capita terms has a significant positive effect on GDI. An increase in per capita combined expenditure on health and education by US$1,000 tend to raise GDI more than the increase led by per capita income (Table 12.9).

Table 12.9

Effect of Per Capita Combined Public Expenditure on Education and Health and Per Capita Income on GDI

Variable	*Coefficient*	*Std. Error*	*t-Statistic*	*Prob.*
Per Capita Income	6.52E-06	1.55E-06	4.217243	0.0003
Pub Exp. on H & E	5.89E-05	1.76E-05	3.335489	0.0027
Fixed Effects				
CAN—C	0.972663			
AUS—C	0.915521			
BAN—C	0.337613			
INDIA—C	0.416216			
INDO—C	0.631384			
KOR—C	0.794284			
USA—C	0.933189			
UK—C	0.900694			
NOR—C	0.999481			
GAM—C	0.270872			
PAK—C	0.389324			
SRI—C	0.688524			
SWE—C	0.989616			
MAL—C	0.768584			
CHIN—C	0.617759			
Adjusted R-squared	0.998			

Public expenditure on health and education thus can be expected to influence HDI and GDI over a period of time more effectively than 'growth-led' human development. The specified models by abstracting from the lagged effect of such expenditure on HDI and GDI may have a downward bias in the estimated effect, but the dynamics of the impact could not be estimated because of data problems.

5. Conclusion

The paper examined the impact of public policy stance on human development across countries in a multivariate framework. Using fixed effects model of pooled least squares for the early 1990s, the analysis of link between per capita expenditure on health and education and Human Development Index (HDI) revealed that there is a positive functional relationship between the two. The per capita income, though found significant in determining human development, is not a sole factor, which leads to human development. Also, the estimated coefficients of pooled least squares revealed that per capita spending on education and health has relatively stronger impact on human development than growth in per capita income *per se*. The same results were obtained when HDI is replaced for GDI in model specifications. This result is in confirmation with the trend that public expenditure on human capital formation gets transformed to the end results of better human development indicators and gender-sensitive indicators in particular, despite the constraints of intra-household disparities in resource allocation. In other words, the public policy stance plays a crucial role in human development.

References

Adelman, I. and Morris, C.T. (1967). *Society, Politics and Economic Development*, John Hopkins University Press, Baltimore.

Anand, S. and Kanbur, R. (1991). "Public Policy and Basic Needs Provision: Intervention and Achievement in Sri Lanka", in Dreze, J. and Sen, A., eds., *The Political Economy of Hunger*, Volume 3, Oxford;Clarendon.

Anand, S. and Ravallion, M. (1993). "Human Development in Poor Countries: On the Role of Private Incomes and Public Services", *Journal of Economic Perspectives*, 7 (Winter).

Ardndt, Heinz W. (1998). "Market Failure and Underdevelopment", *World Development*, 16 (2).

Aturupane, H., Glewwe, P. and Isenman, P. (1994). 'Poverty, Human Development and Growth: An Emerging Consensus?', *American Economic Review*, Vol 84(2), 244-249.

Chowdhury, Samik (2004). *Human Development Index: Some Methodological Issues*, Unpublished M. Phil Thesis, Jawaharlal Nehru University.

Chu Ke , Y. and Hemming, R. ed. (1991). *Public Expenditure Handbook: A Guide to Public Expenditure Policy Issues in Developing Countries*, International Monetary Fund, Washington D C.

Dasgupta, P. and Weale, M. (1992). "On Measuring the Quality of Life", *World Development*, 20, 119-131.

Desai, M. (1991). "Human Development: Concept and Measurement", *European Economic Review*, 35 (350-357).

Diamond J. (1989). "Government Expenditure and Economic Growth: An Empirical Investigation", *IMF Working Paper*, No.89/45, Washington D C.

Dossel, D.P. and Gounder, R. (1994). "Theory and Measurement of living levels: Some empirical results for Human Development Index", *Journal of International Development*, 6 (415-435).

Dreze, J. and Sen, A. (1995). *India: Economic Development and Social Opportunity*, Oxford India Paperbacks.

Easterly, W. and Rebelo, Sergio (1993). "Fiscal Policy and Economic Growth: An Empirical Investigation, *Journal of Monetary Economics*, 57, 255-292.

Government of India (2001). *National Human Development Report*, Planning Commission.

Griffin, C. (1992). *Health Care in Asia: A Comparative Study on Cost and Financing*, The World Bank, Washington D C.

Grossman, G.M. and Helpman, E. (1994). "Endogenous Innovation in the Theory of Growth", *Journal of Economic Perspective* 8(1), 23-43.

Grossman, P.J. (1988). "Government and Economic Growth: a Non-linear Relationship", *Public Choice*, 56(2), 193-200.

Haq, M.U. (1995). *Reflections on Human Development*, Oxford University Press, New York.

Hicks and Streeten, P. (1979). "Indicators of Development: The Search for a Basic Needs Yardstick", *World Development*, 7, 567-580

Isenman, P. (1980). "Basic Needs: The Case of Sri Lanka", *World Development*, 8(3), 237-58.

Lahiri, A.; Chakraborty, Lekha S. and Bhattacharrya (2002): "Gender Budgeting In India", *NIPFP Study*, New Delhi.

Landau, D. (1983). "Government Expenditure and Economic Growth: A Cross Country Study", *Southern Economic Journal*, 49(3), 783-792.

McGillivray, M. (1991). "The Human Development Index: Yet Another Redundant Composite Development Indicator?", *World Development*, 19, 1461-1468.

McGillivray, M. and White, H. (1993). "Measuring development? The UNDP's Human Development Index", *Journal of International Development* 5, 183-192.

Morris, M.D. (1979). *"Measuring the Condition of the World's Poor: The Physical Quality of Life Index"*, Pergamon, New York.

Mundle, S. (1998). "Financing Human Development: Some Lessons from Advanced Asian Countries", *World Development*, 26(4), 659-672.

Noorbakhsh, F. (1998). "A Modified Human Development Index", *World Development*, 26 (3), 517-528.

Pack, H. (1994). "Endogenous Growth Theory: Intellectual Appeal and Empirical Shortcomings", *Journal of Economic Perspectives*, 8 (1), 55-77.

Psacharapoulas, G. (1994). "Returns to Investment in Education: A Global Update", *World Development*, 22(9).

Rao, M.G. (1998). "Accomodating Public Expenditure Policies: The Case of Fast Growing Asian Economies", *World Development*, 26(4), 673-694.

Sen, A. (1981). "Public Action and the Quality of Life in Developing Countries", *Oxford Bulletin of Economics and Statistics*, 43(4), 287-319.

Sen, A. (1988). "The Concept of Development", *Handbook of Development Economics*, Volume I, ed., H. Chenery and T.N. Srinivasan, pp 9-26, Elsevier Science Publishers, Amsterdam.

Sen, A. (1998). "Human Development and Financial Conservatism", *World Development*, Vol 26 (4), 733-742

Srinivasan, T.N. (1994). "Human Development: A New Paradigm or Reinvention of the wheel?", *American Economic Review*, Papers and Proceedings, 84, 238-243.

Streeten, P. (1979). "From Growth to Basic Needs", *Finance and Development*, 16(3), 28-31.

Streeten, P. (1995). *"In Reflections on Human Development"*, ed. M.ul Haq, Oxford University Press, New York.

Summers, L. (1992). "Investing in All the People", *Policy Research Working Paper No. 905*, The World Bank, Washington D C.

United Nations (1954). *Report on International Definition and and Measurement of Standards and Levels of Living*, United Nations, New York.

United Nations Development Programme (various issues): *Human Development Reports*, various issues.

United Nations Research Institute for Social Development (UNRISD) (1972). *"Contents and Measurement of Socio-economic Development"*, Praeger Publishers, New York.

Van de walle, D. (1998). "Assessing the Welfare Impacts of Public Spending", *World Development*, 26(3): 365-379.

World Bank (2000). *World Development Data Base*, electronic version.

The author acknowledge Professor Ashok Lahiri, Professor Diane Elson, Professor Swapna Mukhopadhyay, Dr Hiranya Mukhopadhyay and Dr Pinaki Chakraborty for their valuable comments. The usual disclaimer applies.

13

Maternal Health Care Utilisation: An Empirical Analysis Based on Rural India

ANINDITA CHAKRABARTI

1. Introduction

The efficacy of the health system in developing countries is undermined by lack of utilisation of existing facilities. For example, it has been widely acknowledged that better use of maternal health care facilities in less developed countries will reduce maternal as well as child mortality. The problem is exacerbated for India where, "more than 100,000 women...die every year from causes related to pregnancy and childbirth".[1] Under such circumstances, it becomes vital to identify the factors responsible for non-use of modern maternal health facilities. In India there exists considerable variation in terms of utilisation of institutional health facilities by pregnant women. In 1995, the south Indian states of Kerala (96.8 per cent) and Tamil Nadu (64.2 per cent) recorded high percentage of "births in institutions". The corresponding figures for the relatively backward northern states of Rajasthan (7.6 per cent) and Uttar Pradesh (7.2 per cent) and also the economically well off Punjab (12.4 per cent) were quite low.[2] The objective of our study is to determine how much of this inter-state variation (in use of formal care for delivery) can be explained by differences in socio-economic and cultural factors.

The remainder of this paper is divided into several sections. The next section outlines the ongoing research on determinants of maternity service use and also elaborates on how our study departs from the current literature. Section 3 gives details on the data used

1. See National Family Health Survey (NFHS-2), 1998-99, Page 196, India.
2. Statistics on Children in India, Hand Book 1998, National Institute of Public Cooperation and Child Development.

for the purpose of our analysis and the mechanism used to design the requisite variables. Section 4 presents the empirical methodology while the results are discussed in Section 5. Section 6 concludes.

2. Literature Review

There has been considerable research, particularly in developing countries, exploring the economic and socio-cultural barriers that deter women from seeking maternal health services. A partial list of these studies, based primarily on south Asian countries, includes Wolfe *et al.* (1984), Basu (1992), Bhatia *et al.* (1995), Raghupathy (1996), Pebley *et al.* (1996), Kumar (1999), Acharya *et al.* (2000), Shariff *et al.* (2002), Bloom *et al.* (2001), Matsumura *et al.* (2001), Navaneetham *et al.* (2002), and Paul *et al.* (2002). Amongst the maternal attributes, education was found to have the strongest association with use of delivery facilities at time of birth. Education improves utilisation by a) increasing awareness b) empowering women to take decisions on her own health risks c) increasing her ability to communicate with health personnel in an environment alien to her own world. However consensus was not reached on the level of education required to have a significant impact on utilisation. Estimates from some studies revealed that the women educated only till primary level did not behave significantly differently from those who are illiterate (Raghupathy, Navaneetham *et al.*). Women's status, captured in terms of her working status, has produced dubious results: odds of using modern maternal health services were found to be lower for employed women in Nepal (Matsumura *et al.*) and in South-India (Navaneetham *et al.*). This was rationalised on the ground that in developing countries women are compelled to work outside their home due to poverty. The predominant use of socio-economic variables (such as education and employment status) to proxy for women's status have been questioned on the grounds that consistent relationship was not obtained between these variables and the health outcomes across cultures (Bloom *et al.*, Jejeebhoy *et al.* (2001)). A limited number of studies, based on regional Indian data, have also explored the role played by women's status in promoting the use of maternal health services (Basu, Bhatia *et al.*, Bloom *et al.*). They have constructed direct measures of women's autonomy on the basis of her decision-making power, control of resources and freedom of movement within her household. Autonomy was found to significantly enhance institutional births amongst women in Varanasi, a city located in Uttar Pradesh (U.P.) (Bloom *et al.*) and immigrant workers in U.P (Basu). On the other hand, it had no impact on the health seeking behaviour of women located in a sub-district near Bangalore (Bhatia *et al.*). The existing literature also hypothesised that birth history of the mother will affect utilisation apart from these individual dimensions. Hence, variables such as respondent's age, birth order, number of living children etc. were used to control for parity. Amongst these variables, only birth order was unequivocally found to influence choice of delivery care. Birth order is expected to work in two ways. Firstly, as the number of children the respondent has borne increases, she may tend to rely more on her past experiences and depend less on formal care. Secondly, a higher birth order suggests a greater family size and hence lower resources (both time and money) available to seek formal healthcare.

In orthodox and traditional social systems, an individual's demand for (maternal) health services is influenced by her cultural and socio-economic environment. Hence, in all of the above-mentioned studies household profile is also assumed to have considerable impact on utilisation pattern. We have briefly enlisted the results obtained for only those variables that have been commonly used to quantify the household effect. In all cases, women belonging to prosperous households and those with educated husband prefer facility based delivery care. Note, odds of using institutional facility is expected to be higher in the latter case because better educated husbands are expected to earn more and also spread information/knowledge. However none of the previous studies have used any control for husband's work status. In addition to these factors, studies pertaining to India have also accounted for religion and caste of the household. It is generally believed that Muslim women are less prone to use formal care because of restriction placed on their freedom of movement and overall lower autonomy. On the other hand some authors are of the opinion that women's behavioral pattern depends more on the different kinship structure prevalent over the various regions in India (North *vis-à-vis* South). Consequently after controlling for frequency of contact with natal kin (Basu) and regional location (Jejeebhoy), no significant difference was found to exist between the status of Hindu and Muslim women. This may be the underlying reason why consistent result was not obtained for variable controlling for religion in the literature.[3] As far as the caste structure is concerned, women from Scheduled Caste/Scheduled Tribe (SC/ST) background were found to have significantly higher probability of delivering at home. This can be explained by the fact that the former are economically poorer and often faces social discrimination.

This paper departs from the present literature on certain aspects. All of the above mentioned papers (Shariff *et al.* being the only exception) on India have only looked into specific sub-regions. However, in our case all the fourteen major States were taken into consideration while estimating the determinants of use of formal delivery care. The previous literature also makes no distinction between giving birth at a public health institute vis-à-vis that in a private institute and treats the outcome as a binary variable (use of delivery facilities *versus* non-use). However, in India, in addition to public health system, there is a strong private medical sector. So far as maternity care is concerned, private maternity homes and clinics are at least as popular as public facilities because of easy accessibility and perceived higher quality. Consequently, we have examined the demographic, social and economic barriers to the use of public and private care separately.

None of the prior studies on India have examined the specific importance of availability/accessibility of health care institutions. Studies that have used both rural and urban data (Bhatia *et al.*, Navaneetham *et al.*) have used only dummies to control for current residence (rural or urban) to account for accessibility of health services. However, we have estimated the importance of availability of health facilities *per se* in determining an individual's choice of institutional birth. Moreover, we have also looked into the role played by other community level facilities[4] that have not been considered previously. Since our data included details on only village level infrastructure we have based our analysis on the rural data. Two of these village level variables deserve special mention. In developing countries, particularly in rural areas, where the access to health services is limited, mother's ability to command social resources may make an important difference. Social resources include her capacity to

3. In fact Bhatia *et al.* found that Muslim women have significantly higher odds of giving births in institutions compared to the Hindu women in a sub-district near Bangalore in South India.

4. The definition and construction of these variables have been discussed in details later.

mobilise emotional and cognitive support (in terms of advice and information) from other community members. In absence of direct data, we have controlled for community-level facilities, which helps in evolvement of supportive social network. This was the rationale behind incorporating "community facility" and Information Education Communication (IEC).[5] The latter is a programme launched to promote information, education and communication.

3. Data and Variables Used in the Analysis

To analyse the factors governing the utilisation of delivery facilities in rural India we have used the 1998-99 Indian National Family Health Survey (NFHS) data. The NFHS, using ever-married women in the age group of 15-49 as respondents, gives a comprehensive account of contraceptive use, maternal and child health and the associated socio-cultural-economic factors both at the individual and household level. In addition, for its rural sample, it also provides detailed information on various village level characteristics for example infrastructure and facilities available in the village.

The NFHS explores the usage of delivery and child health facilities for the last two births since January 1995. We have looked into the details of the most recent birth only. This was done because the data can be expected to be more accurate for the most recent birth because of better recall on part of the respondent. The place of birth has been grouped as "*home*" (includes all births at own, parents or others home) "*government facility*" (includes all births at government hospitals or dispensaries, family welfare clinics, community health centres, primary health centres, sub-centres, rural hospitals and other public sector health facilities) and "*private facilities*" (includes all deliveries at private hospitals or clinics or maternity homes and other private facilities).[6] In total 16,671 respondents confirmed that they had a birth during the above-mentioned period. As seen from Table 13.2, the majority of those births took place at home (76.53 per cent) with the

---

5. Adams (2002) has estimated the significance of women's social networks, within and outside her household, in reducing health hazards of children. However, the impact of the former on women's choice of maternity care has not been studied.

6. In addition to the above categories, NFHS also has another category for place of birth namely "others". This has been dropped from our sample related to delivery. Since the latter has only 39 observations (0.23 per cent) this omission is assumed not to cause sample selection bias.

rest being divided equally between government and private facility respectively (approximately 11 per cent in each case). Table 13.1 provides information on the various variables used in our analysis where as Table 13.2 reports the descriptive statistics of the corresponding variables.

Amongst the household level variables, the factor that foremost comes to mind is the household's economic condition. Unfortunately,

Table 13.1

Variables and Description

Variables	*Description*
	Outcome Variables
	Place of Delivery
Home	All deliveries at home (code is 1)
Government Facility	All deliveries at a public facility (code is 2)
Private Facility	All deliveries at a private facility (code is 3)
	Household Characteristics
Muslim	Dummy =1 if household head is Muslim (Reference group is Hindu)
Religmisc	Dummy =1 if household head is Christian or Sikh or Buddhist or Jain or Jewish or Parsi or Others (Reference group is Hindu)
Caste1	Dummy =1 if household head is Scheduled Caste
Caste2	Dummy =1 if household head is Scheduled Tribe
Members	Ever married women in the age group of 15-49
Femhead	Dummy =1 if household head is female
Agriland	Dummy =1 if household owns any agricultural land
Goodsn	Dummy =1 if household owns any one of the non-luxury goods
Goodsnl	Dummy =1 if household owns any one of the non-luxury goods and any one of the luxury goods as well
Husbandedu1	Dummy =1 if husband is primary educated (base group is no education)
Husbanduhigh	Dummy =1 if husband is secondary or higher educated (base group is no education)
Husbandoccu	Dummy =1 if husband's occupation is non-agricultural, non-manual and non-domestic
	Respondent Characteristics
Media	Dummy =1 if respondent reads newspaper or watches television or listens to radio once a week
Respedu1	Dummy =1 if respondent is primary educated (base group is no education)

Contd...

...Contd...

Variables	*Description*
	Outcome Variables
	Place of Delivery
Respeduhigh	Dummy =1 if respondent is secondary or higher educated (base group is no education)
Respoccu	Dummy =1 if respondent's occupation is non-agricultural, non-manual and non-domestic
Sons	Dummy =1 if respondent has at least one living son
Bord	Birth Order
Freedom	Index to freedom of movement
Decision	Index to decision making power
Autonomy	Index to autonomy
	Village Characteristics
Railway	Distance to the nearest railway station
Road	Distance to all weather road
Electricity	Dummy =1 if village has electricity
Govhlth	Dummy =1 if village has a government health facility
Pvthlth	Dummy =1 if village has a private health facility
Comfacl	Dummy =1 if village has a community centre or a community television
IEC	Dummy =1 if village has any one of the community level IEC activities for health and family welfare
Statedum	State Dummies (base group is Kerala)

the NFHS does not include questions on household's income or expenditure. However, it does provide data on household ownership of various items for example furniture, consumer durables, means of transportation etc. Previous studies have used different methods to assuage the level of household's prosperity on the basis of its ownership of such goods. We have adopted the methodology used by Pandey (2000) and have constructed two dummies "*Goodsn*" and "*Goodsnl*" respectively (see Table 13.1) to capture household's economic status.[7] Although classification of the goods into "non-luxury" and "luxury" is discretionary but the descriptive statistics (see Table 13.2)

7. The goods chosen to be non-luxury are pressure cooker, clock, fan, bicycle, sewing machine, radio while luxury items included telephone, refrigerator, colour television, black & white television, car and motorcycle.

indicate that the division is not entirely unfounded. Around 75 per cent of the household belonging to the rural sample was found to own at least one of the non-luxury items. However, only 22 per cent of the households were found to have one of the luxury items as well. In addition to this we have also controlled for household's landholding (see "*Agriland*" in Table 13.1). This was included not only to reflect upon its economic status but also because the propertied class may be more orthodox in terms of traditional practices and rituals. "*Agriland*" was included to estimate whether this behavioral difference (if any) gets reflected in the pattern of utilisation of institutional facilities for births. Sixty-Five per cent of the rural households reported that they own some agricultural land. A woman's maternity choice is strongly influenced by her husband's views and socio-economic background. "*Husbanndedu1*", "*Husbandeduhigh*" and "*Husbandoccu*" described in Table 13.1 were included to control for the respondent's husband's characteristics[8]. Social and cultural norms differ across households belonging to different caste and religious groups. We have introduced "*Muslim*", "*Religionmisc*", "*Caste1*" and "*Caste2*" (Table 13.1 elaborates on these variables) to capture the impact of the latter on respondent's utilisation pattern. Only eleven per cent of the rural sample included Muslim households while approximately four per cent comprised of other miscellaneous religious groups. Two other household level variables enlisted in Table 13.1 are "*Members*" and "*Femhead*". The latter was used to decipher whether female-headed households behave differently from the male counterparts. Around six per cent of the rural households had a female member as its head.

The basic profile of the respondent, namely her level of education and her occupation is expected to be associated with her choice of institution for delivery. Dummy variables designed to capture the respondent's level of education and her profession (see "*Respedu1*", "*Respeduhigh*" and "*Respoccu*" depicted in Table 13.1) was thus

8. DHS broadly classifies husband occupation as (a) not working (b) professional/ technical/managerial (c) clerical (d) sales (e) agricultural-employee (f) household & domestic (g) services (h) skilled manual (i) unskilled manual. "Husbandoccu1" has been generated by clubbing categories (b), (c), (d) and (g) together. This is why "Husbandoccu" in Table 13.1 has been described as non-agricultural, non-manual and non-domestic. The reason behind this kind of categorisation is that these professions are the least most likely ones amongst the rural households. In fact only 16 per cent of the husbands were employed in these occupations in the rural sector.

Table 13.2

Descriptive Statistics of Variables

Variables	*Observations*	*Mean/Proportion*	*Std. Dev*
	Household Characteristics		
Muslim	16735	0.110	0.312
Religmisc	16735	0.043	0.204
Caste1	16036	0.225	0.418
Caste2	16036	0.120	0.325
Members	16746	1.558	0.852
Femhead	16746	0.057	0.232
Agriland	16744	0.650	0.477
Goodsn	16656	0.750	0.430
Goodsnl	16656	0.220	0.420
Husbandedu1	16703	0.179	0.384
Husbeduhigh	16703	0.484	0.500
Husbandoccu	16610	0.164	0.371
	Respondent Characteristics		
Media	16732	0.420	0.494
Respedu1	16741	0.145	0.352
Respeduhigh	16741	0.217	0.412
Respoccu	16727	0.015	0.122
Sons	16746	0.754	0.431
Bord	16746	3.042	2.012
Freedom	16740	0.341	0.696
Decision	16708	0.711	0.752
Autonomy	16704	1.052	1.166
	Village Characteristics		
Railway	16606	24.497	24.495
Road	16542	14.103	28.739
Electricity	16709	0.804	0.397
Govhlth	15822	0.449	0.497
Pvthlth	16644	0.292	0.455
Comfacl	16704	0.286	0.452
IEC	16637	0.392	0.488

Outcome Variables

Place of Delivery

Variable	*Frequency*	*Per cent*	*Cumulative Frequency*
Home	12759	76.53	76.53
Government Facility	1978	11.86	88.40
Private Facility	1934	11.60	100
Total	16671	100	...

Note: We are aware of the fact that the standard deviation makes less sense in case of binary variable.

incorporated as explanatory variables.[9] The descriptive statistics in Table 13.2 reveal that approximately 14 per cent of the respondents had primary education and 22 per cent were educated till secondary or higher level[10]. Only one per cent of the respondents were engaged in non-agricultural, non-domestic and non-manual activities. In addition to the respondent's education, her exposure to media can potentially increase her access to information and hence is included as part of respondent's characteristics (see "*Media*" in Table 13.1). A relatively high proportion of the respondents (42 per cent) in the rural sample were found to read newspaper, or watch television or listen to radio once a week.

Apart from these fundamental characteristics, the literature suggests that birth history of the mother can exert significant impact on her use of maternal health care. The two variables introduced for this purpose are "*Bord*" and "*Sons*" (details are available in Table 13.1). A dummy variable has been generated to ascertain whether the respondent will behave differently if she has at least one living son *vis-à-vis* a mother who has none.[11] A large section of the literature (Dasgupta, M., L.C. Chen, and T.N. Krishnan (1998)) has postulated that the potential worth of a male child to a household is perceived to be greater than in the case of a female. "*Sons*" was designed to assuage whether this preference also influences choice of maternity care. If the respondent has no living son, she will probably be more inclined towards giving birth at a formal health care institution to reduce risk of complications during delivery because of her comparatively higher expectations (to have a son!) from the current delivery. The existing literature has largely relied on women's education and status of employment to account for her economic and social autonomy within the household. The advantage of using the NFHS data is that it enables us to explicitly control for the respondents autonomy. Three sets of variables ("*Freedom*", "*Decision*" and "*Autonomy*") have been created for this purpose.

---

9. The dummy for the respondent's occupation namely "Respoccu" has been designed exactly in the same manner as "Husbandoccu".

10. It is interesting to note that for both levels, the respondents were considerable less educated than the husbands. As seen from Table 13.2, approximately 18 per cent of the husbands had acquired primary education and 49 per cent were educated even further to secondary and higher level.

11. Although she might have at least one living daughter.

The degree of women's autonomy was captured in two different areas: her decision-making power and freedom of movement. The NFHS questions the respondent on the following issues. Firstly, who decides on obtaining health care for herself? Secondly, who decides on purchasing jewellery or other major household items? Thirdly, whether she is allowed to set aside money for her own use. Three separate binary variables were created for each of the above-mentioned cases. For the first two cases the corresponding dummy variable was assigned a value of one if the respondent was the sole decision-maker. In the third case the dummy took the value of one if the respondent replied in affirmative. The variable *"Decision"* (see Table 13.1) was composed by adding up these three binary variables and has a score from 0 to 3. The underlying assumption is that equal weights can be given to these household decisions.[12] The index of *"Freedom"* was generated in a similar fashion. The NFHS includes questions on whether the respondent requires permission to (a) go to the market or (b) to visit a friend. Two separate binary variables were created for each of (a) and (b) with a value of one assigned to those cases where the respondent did not require any permission. The variable *"Freedom"* (see Table 13.1) was created by adding up these two binary variables and has a score from 0 to 2. The underlying assumption in this case also is that equal importance can be given to these indicators of freedom of movement. The index of *"Autonomy"* was computed by adding up *"Decision"* and *"Freedom"* and has a score of 0 to 5. It is a reflection of the overall independence and status enjoyed by the respondent within her household.

The existing literature (Dyson *et al.* (1983), Basu, Jejeebhoy) reiterates that there exists a clear distinction in the kin-ship structure prevalent in the northern and southern states of India. The former are more patriarchal and male-centred than the latter. Consequently women's autonomy can be expected to be lower for the northern states as compared to the southern ones. Our indices, designed to quantify the extent of autonomy exercised by our respondents, also capture this phenomenon. The weighted[13] average values of *"Decision"*

12. The NFHS also enquires if the respondent has any authority regarding items cooked in the household. However, this component has not been used to construct the index of decision. It appears unreasonable to attach equal importance to this aspect vis-à-vis other aspects considered for constructing "Decision".
13. Weight for the ith state = Number of observations for the ith state/Total number of observations in the sample.

"Freedom" and *"Autonomy"* for the northern states were found to be 0.29, 0.70 and 0.99 respectively. The corresponding values for the southern states, equivalent to 0.62, 0.88 and 1.49 respectively, were much higher.[14]

Village level characteristics were included in this study to control for infrastructure, availability of health and other community level facilities. *"Electricity" "Railway"* and *"Road"* were incorporated as indicators of overall development of the village (described in details in Table 13.1). The latter two also assumes significance because health facilities are sparsely located in the rural sector and in this case availability of transport facilities can become important factors controlling the individuals' utilisation pattern. Table 13.2 shows that approximately 80 per cent of the villages belonging to the rural sample were electrified and on an average a village was located around 25 Kilometers from a railway station and 14 Kilometers from all weather road condition. The village was deemed to have a government facility (see *"Govhlth"* in Table 13.1) if a government hospital or a government dispensary or a community health centre/rural hospital, or a primary health centre or a sub-centre is located within the village. Presence of a private hospital or private clinic within the village was taken as a measure of availability of private health facility (see *"Pvthlth"* in Table 13.1). Around 45 per cent of the villages were found to have at least one of the above-mentioned government health institutions and 29 per cent of the villages had a private health care facility.

As discussed earlier, variables instrumental in developing social network, namely *"Comfacl"* and *"IEC"*, were introduced to quantify the impact of community participation on individual behaviour. Presence of a community centre within the village may promote exchange of ideas and spill over of knowledge (or prejudices?) amongst its members. Similarly, a community television located in the village can be instrumental in spreading information to a wider set of people. *"Comfacl"* (see Table 13.1) was included to estimate whether such community level facilities have any impact on individual choice. The

14. The northern states are Bihar, Gujarat, Haryana, M.P., Punjab, Rajasthan and U.P. The southern states comprises of A.P., Karnataka, Kerala, Maharashtra and Tamil Nadu. This division is adopted from Kishor, S. (1998).

NFHS village questionnaire provides detailed information on the community level IEC activities for health and family welfare during the last one year. The binary variable "*IEC*" (enlisted in Table 13.1) assumes a value of one if the village has a film show, exhibition, drama/song/dance performance, puppet show and group meeting as part of its IEC activities. It is important to estimate the significance and impact of such organised community based activities on the respondent's choice between seeking formal care *vis-à-vis* abstaining from it. The summary statistics reveal considerable heterogeneity amongst villages in terms of "*Comfacl*" and "*IEC*". Only 49 per cent of the villages covered in the rural sample confirmed that they had a community centre or a community television set. The figure for IEC activities was higher and equivalent to approximately 39 per cent.

4. Empirical Methodology

We have used a multinomial logit model to estimate the determinants of delivery choices in rural India. Multinomial logistic regression estimates the following probabilities

$$P(y = j) = \exp(\beta j * x) / \sum_{j=1}^{3} \exp(\beta j * x)$$

P(y=j) denotes the probability of choosing outcome "*j*" for all *j=1*, 2 and *3*. Note outcome1 indicates "*Home*", outcome2 indicate "*Government Facility*" and outcome3 denotes "*Private Facility*". The vector *x* includes all the independent variables included in the model and discussed in the preceding section and β_j is the corresponding coefficient vector for each of the outcome "*j*". To make the system identifiable, in the multinomial logit framework, one of the coefficients is set to 0.[15] In our case we have set β_1 to *0* or in other words "*Home*" is treated as the base category. Consequently

$$P(y = 1) = 1/(1 + \exp(\beta_2 * x) + \exp(\beta_3 * x)) \quad ...(1)$$

$$P(y = 2) = \exp(\beta_2 * x)/(1 + \exp(\beta_2 * x) + \exp(\beta_3 * x)) \quad ...(2)$$

$$P(y = 3) = \exp(\beta_3 * x)/(1 + \exp(\beta_2 * x) + \exp(\beta_3 * x)) \quad ...(3)$$

---

15. It doesn't matter which one since they each yield the same probabilities.

This, in turn, leads to the following odds relative to the reference group namely "*Home*"

$$P(y = 2) / P(y = 1) = \exp(\beta_2^* x) \qquad \ldots(4)$$

$$P(y = 3) / P(y = 1) = \exp(\beta_3^* x) \qquad \ldots(5)$$

Hence,

$$\text{Log}((P(y = 2) / P(y = 1)) = (\beta_2^* x) \qquad \ldots(6)$$

$$\text{Log}((P(y = 3) / P(y = 1)) = (\beta_3^* x) \qquad \ldots(7)$$

The coefficient vector $\beta_2(\beta_3)$ estimates the impact of the independent variables on the log of odds (logit) of choosing to deliver at a government facility (private) facility in contrast to delivering at home.

5. Results

The multinomial logit (log of the odds) models, corresponding to equations 6 and 7, quantifying the impact of the individual, family and community level factors, on delivery choices are presented in Table 13.3 and in Table 13.4 respectively. Model A of Table 13.3 looks into only the respondent's profile while Model B inculcates her other household features. Model A indicates that the respondent's exposure to media and her educational attainment significantly increase her odds[16] of using government facility or private facilities vis-à-vis home. On the other hand, her occupation pattern does not significantly affect her institutional choice for the delivery of her most recent child. The two variables, namely "*Sons*" and "*Bord*" were included to see whether her birth history matters. The estimates reveal, *ceteris paribus*, a unit increase in the respondent's pregnancy order decreases her odds of using government facility by approximately 17 per cent (P(y=2)/P(y=1)= exp(-0.182)=0.834) and private facility by around 19 per cent (P(y=3)/P(y=1)= exp (-0.212)=0.809. The other variable of interest i.e. "*Sons*" has a negative significant impact on the (log of) odds of delivering at a private institution relative to home. Respondents with at least one living son has around 17 per cent lower odds of delivering at a private facility than a woman with none (P(y=3)/P(y=1)= exp(-0.19)=0.827).

16. Also known as "relative risks".

This confirms our conjecture that if the respondent has no living son then she is more willing to seek institutional care because she is more averse to risks of complications at the time of delivery. It is interesting to note that this phenomenon is true only in the case of private facilities and not for government facilities. The underlying reason behind this might be that the perceived quality of the former is higher than the latter.

Table 13.3

Multivariate Results for Births at Institutions (Respondent and Household Characteristics Only)

Variables	*Coeff.*	*S.E.*	*P>|z|*	*Coeff.*	*S.E.*	*P>|z|*
	Outcome=Government Facility					
	Model A			*Model B*		
	Household Characteristics					
Muslim	...	...	...	–0.617	0.162	0.000
Religmisc	...	...	...	0.018	0.158	0.910
Caste1	...	...	...	–0.215	0.081	0.008
Caste2	...	...	...	–0.479	0.118	0.000
Members	...	...	...	0.100	0.034	0.004
Femhead	...	...	...	0.209	0.117	0.073
Agriland	...	...	...	–0.219	0.072	0.002
Goodsn	...	...	...	0.347	0.079	0.000
Goodsnl	...	...	...	0.244	0.075	0.001
Husbandedu1	...	...	...	0.264	0.097	0.007
Husbanduhigh	...	...	...	0.346	0.081	0.000
Husbandoccu	...	...	...	0.144	0.074	0.050
	Respondent Characteristics					
Media	0.432	0.066	0.000	0.198	0.074	0.007
Respedu1	0.447	0.082	0.000	0.276	0.089	0.002
Respeduhigh	0.945	0.084	0.000	0.670	0.087	0.000
Respoccu	–0.132	0.196	0.501	–0.089	0.201	0.659
Sons	–0.078	0.068	0.247	–0.092	0.068	0.176
Bord	–0.182	0.021	0.000	–0.153	0.021	0.000
Freedom	0.052	0.039	0.191	0.043	0.042	0.310
Decision	0.107	0.042	0.010	0.094	0.044	0.033
Constant	0.842	0.286	0.003	0.661	0.291	0.023

Contd...

...Contd...

Variables	*Coeff.*	*S.E.*	*P>|z|*	*Coeff.*	*S.E.*	*P>|z|*
	Outcome = Private Facility					
	Model A			*Model B*		
	Household Characteristics					
Muslim	...	...	...	–0.049	0.144	0.733
Religmisc	...	...	...	0.808	0.132	0.000
Caste1	...	...	...	–0.430	0.097	0.000
Caste2	...	...	...	–0.726	0.164	0.000
Members	...	...	...	–0.050	0.035	0.152
Femhead	...	...	...	0.193	0.119	0.104
Agriland	...	...	...	–0.031	0.076	0.685
Goodsn	...	...	...	0.417	0.095	0.000
Goodsnl	...	...	...	0.817	0.076	0.000
Husbandedu1	...	...	...	0.137	0.104	0.188
Husbanduhigh	...	...	...	0.360	0.093	0.000
Husbandoccu	...	...	...	0.425	0.078	0.000
	Respondent Characteristics					
Media	0.560	0.072	0.000	0.084	0.082	0.305
Respedu1	0.534	0.085	0.000	0.299	0.091	0.001
Respeduhigh	1.410	0.075	0.000	0.873	0.079	0.000
Respoccu	–0.121	0.200	0.545	–0.201	0.216	0.351
Sons	–0.190	0.074	0.010	–0.229	0.077	0.003
Board	–0.212	0.026	0.000	–0.224	0.029	0.000
Freedom	0.012	0.038	0.757	0.031	0.038	0.419
Decision	0.137	0.041	0.001	0.093	0.041	0.024
Constant	0.921	0.282	0.001	0.725	0.303	0.017
Pseudo $-R^2$	0.22			0.24		
Log Likelihood Statistic	–9183.5			–8438.8		
Number of Observations	16591			15714		

Note: Standard Errors (S.E.) are robust to clustering at the village level.

The autonomy enjoyed by the respondent plays an important role. Even after controlling for the fundamental characteristics of the respondent, in terms of educational qualification and professional pattern, her right to make decisions of her own cast a significant impact on the relative odds. An unit increase in her decision-making power, everything else being held constant, enhances the chances of delivery at a public facility *vis-à-vis* home by around five per cent

(P(y=2)/P(y=1)=exp(0.052)=1.053). The corresponding change in odds of delivery at a private institution in contrast to home is approximately one per cent (P(y=3)/P(y=1)=exp(0.012)=1.012).

Model B of Table 13.3, in addition to the respondent's characteristics also features the household characteristics. Inclusion of the latter does not change any of the results (in terms of sign and significance) for all of the respondent-specific variables except for "*Media*". The latter loses its significance for the private outcome. To get a clearer notion about how the respondent's family, the infrastructure and development of her village influences her utilisation pattern one has to see Table 13.4 where we have also included state dummies Kerala serving as the reference state.[17]

As mentioned earlier, the results from the most general models have been tabulated in Table 13.4. Model C and Model D of Table 13.4 differ in respect to how the respondent's autonomy has been characterised. Similar to the previous Table 13.3, in Model C, "*Freedom*" and "*Decision*" has been incorporated separately. In Model D, these two components have been combined to define "*Autonomy*".

In keeping with the earlier quantitative estimates, in Model C and in Model D, a respondent with at least primary education or higher education chooses significantly differently than women with no education at all. In all of the three models the magnitude of impact of higher education is larger than that of primary education. For Model C (P(y=2)/P(y=1)=exp(0.661)= 1.937) and Model D (P(y=2)/P(y=1)=exp(0.663)= 1.941), the odds of selecting a public facility over delivering at home is around 94 per cent higher for respondents who have been educated beyond the primary level as compared to those who has none. However, the odds of utilising a public facility in contrast to giving birth at home increase by approximately 34 per cent (for Model C and Model D) if the respondent is just primary educated. The multinomial logit estimates of giving birth at a private facility *vis-à-vis* at home show a similar pattern. In each of these three models, the odds of utilising the former over the latter is highest if the respondent has been educated at a higher level. A significant impact of "*Media*" was recorded only if the

17. It is noteworthy that each of these state dummies had a negative and significant coefficient for all the reported cases. Although we do not report the estimated coefficients, but the results are available on request.

respondent chooses to deliver her most recent child at a public institution *vis-à-vis* home. A respondent who reads newspaper, or watches television or listens to radio once a week, *ceteris paribus*, is 9 to 10 per cent more likely to deliver at a public place than one who does not ((P(y=2)/P(y=1) is equal to exp(0.096)=1.101 for Model C, and exp(0.097)= 1.102 for Model D. The impact exerted by "*Bord*" and "*Sons*" in governing the respondent's choices closely resemble the pattern depicted in the previous section and hence is not elucidated further. The autonomy enjoyed by the respondent within her household and how it influences her choices is of primary interest.

It is worthwhile to note that no matter how the impact of autonomy is captured, it continues to exert a significant impact, even after accounting for her other basic features and including a host of household and village characteristics[18]. Estimates from Model C (conforming with previous results), reveal that a woman who has greater authority to make her own decisions regarding obtaining health care for herself, buying expensive household items and/or setting aside money for her own use, behave significantly differently from one who is deprived from this right.

The magnitude of the impact of "*Decision*" is higher for the odds of birth at a public facility *vis-à-vis* home as compared to that of a delivery in a private institute over home. Results enlisted in Table 13.4 show that a unit increase in "*Decision*", *ceteris paribus*, increases the odds of delivering at a government facility by around 13 per cent (P(y=2)/P(y=1)=exp(0.124) = 1.132) and that in a private institution by approximately eight per cent (P(y=3)/P(y=1)=exp(0.075)= 1.078). "*Freedom*" on the other hand is found to exert no significant impact on the respondent's choices. The variable "*Autonomy*" that captures the respondent's overall right of self-government yields interesting result. Holding every other factor constant, if the autonomy exercised by a respondent increases by one unit then her odds of choosing a public institution for delivery of her child rises by around ten per cent (P(y=2)/P(y=1)=exp(0.094)= 1.099 in Model D of Table 13.4) and that of delivering at a private institution increases by approximately six per cent (P(y=3)/P(y=1)=exp(0.056)= 1.058 in Model D of Table 13.4).

---

18. The manner in which autonomy is denoted does not have any impact on the sign and significance of the other variables describing the respondent's characteristics. This is evident from the result discussed in the previous paragraph.

Table 13.4

Multivariate Results for Births at Institutions (General Model)

Variables	Coeff.	S.E.	P>|z|	Coeff.	S.E.	P>|z|
	Outcome=Government Facility					
		Model C			Model D	
	Household Characteristics					
Muslim	–0.634	0.178	0.000	–0.633	0.178	0.000
Religmisc	0.081	0.174	0.641	0.083	0.174	0.634
Caste1	–0.248	0.088	0.005	–0.250	0.088	0.004
Caste2	–0.408	0.135	0.003	–0.410	0.135	0.002
Members	0.111	0.036	0.002	0.110	0.036	0.002
Femhead	0.285	0.124	0.021	0.286	0.124	0.021
Agriland	–0.179	0.078	0.022	–0.180	0.078	0.021
Goodsn	0.341	0.080	0.000	0.342	0.080	0.000
Goodsnl	0.208	0.083	0.012	0.210	0.082	0.011
Husbandedu1	0.294	0.100	0.003	0.294	0.100	0.003
Husbanduhigh	0.328	0.089	0.000	0.327	0.089	0.000
Husbandoccu	0.161	0.077	0.037	0.162	0.077	0.036
	Respondent Characteristics					
Media	0.204	0.080	0.011	0.206	0.080	0.010
Respedu1	0.294	0.087	0.001	0.296	0.087	0.001
Respeduhigh	0.661	0.090	0.000	0.663	0.090	0.000
Respoccu	–0.071	0.212	0.737	–0.068	0.213	0.749
Sons	–0.079	0.070	0.255	–0.080	0.069	0.252
Bord	–0.154	0.023	0.000	–0.154	0.023	0.000
Freedom	0.062	0.044	0.163	...	...	....
Decision	0.124	0.047	0.008	...	...	....
Autonomy	...	...	....	0.094	0.027	0.001
	Village Characteristics					
Railway	–0.004	0.002	0.038	–0.004	0.002	0.036
Road	0.000	0.001	0.815	0.000	0.001	0.801
Electricity	0.443	0.132	0.001	0.442	0.132	0.001
Govhlth	–0.109	0.089	0.218	–0.110	0.089	0.214
Pvthlth	0.031	0.096	0.743	0.029	0.095	0.762
Comfacl	0.103	0.093	0.266	0.104	0.093	0.263
IEC	–0.014	0.087	0.869	–0.016	0.087	0.855
Cons	0.285	0.363	0.432	0.300	0.363	0.408

Contd...

Contd...

Variables	*Coeff.*	*S.E.*	*P>|z|*	*Coeff.*	*S.E.*	*P>|z|*
	Outcome = Private Facility					
	Model C			*Model D*		
	Household Characteristics					
Muslim	0.010	0.143	0.942	0.012	0.143	0.936
Religmisc	0.814	0.136	0.000	0.814	0.136	0.000
Caste1	–0.389	0.099	0.000	–0.390	0.099	0.000
Caste2	–0.515	0.170	0.003	–0.517	0.170	0.002
Members	–0.060	0.038	0.112	–0.060	0.038	0.110
Femhead	0.194	0.122	0.110	0.195	0.121	0.108
Agriland	0.049	0.074	0.511	0.048	0.074	0.516
Goodsn	0.414	0.097	0.000	0.415	0.097	0.000
Goodsnl	0.747	0.082	0.000	0.748	0.082	0.000
Husbandedu1	0.126	0.109	0.248	0.126	0.109	0.249
Husbanduhigh	0.351	0.099	0.000	0.351	0.100	0.000
Husbandoccu	0.442	0.080	0.000	0.443	0.080	0.000
Media	0.312	0.077	0.000	0.309	0.077	0.312
Respedu1	0.441	0.080	0.000	0.440	0.080	0.441
Respeduhigh	0.889	0.089	0.000	0.886	0.089	0.889
Respoccu	0.080	0.200	0.689	0.075	0.199	0.080
Sons	–0.092	0.068	0.178	–0.091	0.068	–0.092
Board	–0.179	0.023	0.000	–0.179	0.023	–0.179
Freedom	0.165	0.040	0.000	...	...	...
Decision	0.078	0.044	0.080	...	...	...
Autonomy	...	...	...	0.120	0.024	0.004
	Village Characteristics					
Railway	–0.007	0.002	0.001	–0.007	0.002	0.001
Road	–0.002	0.001	0.222	–0.002	0.001	0.219
Electricity	0.456	0.184	0.013	0.456	0.184	0.013
Govhlth	–0.007	0.100	0.942	–0.007	0.100	0.942
Pvthlth	0.207	0.103	0.044	0.206	0.103	0.045
Comfacl	0.253	0.104	0.015	0.254	0.104	0.015
IEC	0.254	0.094	0.007	0.252	0.094	0.007
Cons	–0.195	0.387	0.614	–0.188	0.388	0.627
Pseudo $-R^2$	0.23			0.24		
Log Likelihood Statistic	–7580.3			–7580.8		
Number of Observations	14534			14534		

Note: Standard Errors (S.E.) are robust to clustering at the village level.

Now let us examine how the respondent's social background, her household's economic condition and other characteristics, the overall infrastructure present in her village, and community level facilities and programmes directed to generate awareness influences her pattern of utilisation of institutional care. Estimates enlisted in Table 13.4 shows that respondents of different religions and castes choose differently. In both models (Model C and D) respondents residing in a household where the head is "*Muslim*" have a significantly lower (log of) odd of choosing public facility as compared to where the head is of Hindu origin. This is not true for the private outcome. On the other hand, respondents coming from a miscellaneous religious background (see Table 13.1 for details) favour private institution in contrast to delivering at a home.

Households belonging to the Scheduled Caste (*Caste1*) and Scheduled Tribe (*Caste2*) have a significantly lower inclination to avail the facilities of a public or a private institution for child-delivery. The total number of ever-married women in the age group of 15 to 49 ("*Members*") was included because of the following reason. In large parts of rural India, especially where exogamy is practiced and the joint family system prevail; the women find themselves as members of large households where the opinion of the elder women of the families (mother-in-law, sister-in-law) is what matters. Under the circumstances one might expect traditional and orthodox methods will be adopted more in households where the number of "*Members*" are large and the respondent is likely to be prejudiced by the experiences and the beliefs of the former.

Contrary to our conjectures, the multinomial logit models estimates a significant positive coefficient for "*Members*" when we look into the utilisation of public facility in contrast to home. For the delivery at a private institution *vis-à-vis* home all three models yield the expected negative sign but is not significant. One plausible reason might be that "*Members*" is actually computing the impact of the overall household size on utilisation pattern. If the respondent belongs to a household with more family members, (particularly dependants such as children as higher number of "*Members*" indicate) then because of scarcity of resources she may not be able to use the private facilities. The constraint may not be as strong for public facilities since they are largely free.

In our study, we have re-estimated the Models enlisted in Table 13.4 by replacing "*Members*" with the total size of the household and all of the other variables.[19] The signs and significance of all of the other explanatory variables exactly match with that reported in Table 13.4. In case of utilisation of public facility, the estimated coefficient for household size is once again positive and significant. However, *ceteris paribus*, an additional family member, was found to significantly reduce the odds of giving birth at a private facility *vis-à-vis* home by around three per cent $(P(y=3)/P(y=1)=\exp(-0.027)=0.974)$ irrespective of how respondent's autonomy was modeled in this re-estimation.

We have also attempted to look into the importance of the kinship structure by controlling for matriarchal households. If the head of household is female then this was found to significantly enhance the utilisation of institutional public care. The odds of delivering at a government institution in contrast to home was found to be approximately 33 to 35 per cent higher if the head of the household is female as compared to a patriarchal system $(P(y=2)/P(y=1)=\exp(0.285)=1.330$ for Model C, and $P(y=2)/P(y=1)=\exp(0.286)=1.331$ for Model D. The multinomial logit estimates for the private outcome is positive but is insignificant.[20]

The economic condition of the respondent's household will of course play a decisive role in determining her pattern of consumption of health services. "*Goodsn*" and "*Goodsnl*" throw light on the assets owned by the household. Both have a significant positive impact on the (log of) odds of seeking the services offered by either a public institution or private facility *vis-à-vis* giving birth at home. Moreover, the magnitude of impact of the relevant variables is substantially higher in case of private facilities as compared to public facility. This stems from the fact that affordability is a bigger issue for the latter because the monetary cost (for e.g. fees) attached to private facilities is comparatively higher. Moreover, as seen from the estimated figures, improvement in economic condition (in terms of acquiring additional luxury assets) more than doubles the odds of selecting a private facility for birth of the most recent child in contrast to home.

19. Results are not reported here but available on request

20. Although it becomes significant in a one tailed test.

"*Agriland*" not only reflects upon the economic status of the household but also enables us to capture the differences in preference between the rural land-holding classes with respect to the others. Existing literature points out that the former is more traditional and orthodox in their outlook than the latter. This is also substantiated by our estimates compiled in Table 13.4. Households possessing agricultural land were found to have significantly lower odds of using public or private facility for child-delivery.

Finally, the respondent's husband's profile was measured in terms of his educational qualification and nature of occupation. Respondent's whose husband's are educated at least till primary level or beyond are found to prefer formal care, either public or private, as compared to delivering at home (see "*Husbandedu1*" and "*Husbanduhigh*" in Model C and in Model D of Table 13.4). In this case also, we see that irrespective of the outcomes (i.e. government facility or private facility), the magnitude of impact is larger if the husband has attained higher education relative to those who has been educated only till primary school. However, unlike the case of the respondent, the nature of occupation of the husband is found to be a significant determinant of the pattern of utilisation of health services.

Now let us look into the role played by village level characteristics in governing respondent's choices. No clear picture emerges when we look into the existing literature (Kishor (1998)) analysing the impact of economic development on health outcomes (particularly in the context of gender differences). Whether the former has any role in formulating individual preferences remains to be seen. "*Railway*", "*Road*" and "*Electricity*" were incorporated as measures of overall level of development and infrastructure prevalent in the village. The first two variables, quantifying the distance of the village from the nearest railway station and all weather condition roads, also shed light on the accessibility of health facilities. As the proximity of the village from the railway station declines, the (log of) odds of using either a government facility or a private facility *vis-à-vis* home significantly declines (*albeit* by a small magnitude) for all of both the Models enlisted in Table 13.4.

Incorporating "*Govhlth*" and "*Pvthlth*" controlled for availability of health services. Surprisingly, availability of a government facility was found to have no bearing on the respondent's odds of using the former for the delivery of her most recent child. The importance of "*Govhlth*" maybe undermined by the fact that even if the public facility is available, this *per se*, might not induce the respondent to avail its services because of poor quality. Since, given the data, it was not possible to specifically control for the quality of services at the time of the relevant delivery, the problem persist. On the contrary, presence of a private facility in the village was found to propagate the utilisation of a private health facility in contrast to delivering at home. The odd of using a private institution was found to increase by 23 per cent in Model C ($P(y=3)/P(y=1) = \exp(0.207) = 1.230$) and in Model D ($P(y=3)/P(y=1) = \exp(0.206) = 1.229$).[21] As discussed earlier, rural communities are close knit and perceptions, practices and knowledge shared by an entire commune may percolate down to an individual level and can act as a guiding force in the respondent's decision-making process. This was the rationale behind including facilities and programmes aimed at creating greater awareness amongst the village community, namely "*Comfacl*" and "*IEC*". The former is of no significance if the choice is in between a public institution *vis-à-vis* home. However, if the village has a community centre and/or a community television set then the odds of delivering at a private institution is significantly enhanced. The latter increases by approximately 29 per cent in Model C ($P(y=3)/P(y=1) = \exp(0.253) = 1.288$) and in Model D ($P(y=3)/P(y=1) = \exp(0.254) = 1.289$). Multinomial logit estimates for "*IEC*" exhibit a similar pattern and is significant only if the outcome is private facility *versus* births at home. Note, such facilities and programmes are orchestrated as part of the government policies to generate information and felicitate utilisation of institutional care. However, our estimates reveal that such mechanisms exert a substantial impact only if the odds are between delivering at a private institution in reference to home. The reason underlining this phenomenon remains to be explored.

21. The accessibility of health facilities may also be captured in terms of its proximity. This was also taken care of (results reported in Model I of Table A.1) and availability was measured by distance to the nearest government facility ("govnear") and that of the nearest private facility ("pvtnear"). Change of definition does not affect our basic result. An unit increase in the distance to private facility, *ceteris paribus*, significantly decreases the (log of) odds of using private health facility. A similar association is present between "govnear" and (log of) odds of using public health facility, but is significant only under a one tailed test.

Our results are robust to inclusion/exclusion of other explanatory variables and changes in definitions of autonomy variables. Finally, we look into some other tests to justify our model specifications (see Table 13.5 and Table 13.6). The multinomial logit framework has been subject to criticism because the former assumes the existence of Independence of Irrelevant Alternatives (hence forth IIA). Note the relative odds of choosing a government facility over home (or private facility over home) is the same no matter what other alternatives are available or what the attributes of other alternatives are (see equation 4 and 5). Since the ratio is independent from alternatives other than those taken under consideration, it is said to be independent of irrelevant alternatives. Table 13.5 presents the Hausman Test and the Small – Hsiao tests conducted to ascertain whether IIA holds for our analysis. Note for each of these models both of the above-mentioned tests validate that IIA property models. Another series of tests were conducted to confirm that the outcome variables are distinct or in

Table 13.5

IIA Tests for Multinomial Logit Models of Utilisation of Delivery Facilities

Hausman Tests of IIA Assumption (H_0: Odds are IIA)					*Small-Hsiao Tests of IIA Assumption (H_0: Odds are IIA)*				
Omit	*Chi2*	*df*	*P>Chi2*	*Evidence*	*Omit*	*Chi2*	*df*	*P>Chi2*	*Evidence*
		Model A					*Model A*		
2	–7.61	22	...	FOR H_0	2	18.245	22	0.691	FOR H_0
3	2.333	22	1.000	FOR H_0	3	24.988	22	0.298	FOR H_0
		Model B					*Model B*		
2	–20.335	34	...	FOR H_0	2	19.962	34	0.973	FOR H_0
3	0.092	34	1.000	FOR H_0	3	43.630	34	0.125	FOR H_0
		Model C					*Model C*		
2	–3.134	41	...	FOR H_0	2	47.857	41	0.214	FOR H_0
3	–108.93	41	...	FOR H_0	3	43.002	41	0.386	FOR H_0
		Model D					*Model D*		
2	–3.684	40	...	FOR H_0	2	31.582	40	0.827	FOR H_0
3	21.019	40	0.994	FOR H_0	3	27.302	40	0.937	FOR H_0

Table 13.6

Specification Tests for Multinomial Logit Models of Utilisation of Delivery Facilities

	Wald Tests for Combining Outcome Categories		
Categories Tested	*Chi-Square*	*df*	*P>Chi2*
		Model A	
2 – 3	609.048	21	0.000
2 – 1	1253.261	21	0.000
3 – 1	1666.395	21	0.000
		Model B	
2 – 3	758.027	33	0.000
2 – 1	1521.425	33	0.000
3 – 1	1738.593	33	0.000
		Model C	
2 – 3	723.337	40	0.000
2 – 1	1600.171	40	0.000
3 – 1	1610.327	40	0.000
		Model D	
2 – 3	720.207	39	0.000
2 – 1	1579.204	39	0.000
3 – 1	1575.554	39	0.000

other words they cannot be combined with each other[22]. Results from the Wald test show that none of these categories (i.e. "Home", "Government Facility" and "Private Facility") can be combined with each other for each of these models (see Table 13.6).

6. Conclusion

Our empirical results show that education particularly that of the respondent plays a vital role in modulating the utilisation of delivery care. Unlike some of the previous studies, even primary education makes a difference in terms of usage of public or private facility but the magnitude of impact increases substantially if the respondent (mother) is educated to a higher level. As pointed out earlier, one of

22. "If none of the xk's significantly affects the odds of outcome m *versus* outcome n, we say that m and n are indistinguishable with respect to the variables in the model (Long (1997) page 162).

the channels through which husband's education enhances utilisation is by improving his work status and hence the economic condition of the household. Apart from education, the other variable instrumental in spreading awareness i.e. "*Media*" has a beneficial impact by facilitating births at a public institution *vis-à-vis* home. Analysis of health seeking behaviour during childbirth also suggest that autonomy enjoyed by women, particularly her ability to make her own decisions, have a significant impact even after controlling for other attributes particularly education. These results suggest that policies directed towards improving the health status of women must go beyond merely enhancing her educational opportunities. Also, policies should be designed to target the vulnerable group i.e. women who had comparatively higher number of births, particularly if they already have a living son because they are more averse to seeking institutional care. The other group of women who needs special attention is those who belong to the SC/ST background. In rural India, the latter are often forced to reside in isolated locations away from the main village settlement reserved for the higher caste people. Since health facilities are closer to the main settlement this acts as an additional constraint. So far as religion is concerned, Muslim women do not behave significantly different from Hindus in terms of delivering at a private institution *vis-à-vis* at home. However, they show a comparatively lower inclination to use the public facilities as compared to the Hindus. Public health policies designed to address the specific needs of these groups will obviously bear fruitful results. Apart from these socio-cultural factors, the other household feature that was found to have a strong influence on the respondent's utilisation pattern is the household's economic condition measured in terms of its possession of durable goods. Unfortunately this is also true when we analyse the choice of giving birth at a public institution *vis-à-vis* at home although public health services is provided at zero or negligible fee. However, in reality such services involve hidden cost because of opportunity cost of time spent on travelling and also waiting for such services, corruption induced bribery etc. Dearth of data on the physical attributes, quality etc. of the health service used deters us from measuring the impact of the above mentioned factors.

Unlike the previously mentioned literature we have also studied the importance of a host of village level characteristics. First and foremost we would like to point out that in spite of controlling for availability (and even proximity) of both public as well as private health facility, other variables capturing the over all development of the village for instance *"Road"*, *"Railway"*, *"Electricity"* significantly influences the odds of delivering at a public or private facility *vis-à-vis* home. This indicates that studies that have controlled for health care availability by just using a dummy for current location (i.e. rural or urban) grossly over-estimates the magnitude of impact of the former on the utilisation of maternal health facilities. So far as the health infrastructure is concerned, availability of a government facility was found to have no bearing on the respondent's utilisation choice but presence of a private facility in the village was found to propagate the utilisation of a private health facility in contrast to delivering at home. To get a clearer picture it is imperative that we analyse the role played by the quality of the specific health service used by the respondent at the time of birth. However, we are handicapped by the lack of data. Our study also explores the benefits of community level facilities and programmes directed at creating general awareness and promoting communication. Surprisingly, although such infrastructures are provided by the government, they have a significant impact only on the probability of seeking private institutional facilities as compared to home. In fact the magnitude of impact of the former on the odds of using a private facility marginally exceeds that of availability of private health facility.

To conclude, health policies should be oriented towards meeting the specific needs of individuals particularly those belonging to the vulnerable groups i.e. SC/ST, Muslims and also women with higher number of pregnancies. Also overall rural development, in terms of better infrastructure, health facilities and other informative community level programmes are required to mitigate the cultural and economic barriers that deter the use of maternal services.

References

Acharya L.B. and J. Cleland (2000), "Maternal and Child Health Services in Rural Nepal: Does Access or Quality Matter More?", *Health Policy and Planning*, 15, 223-229.

Adams A.M. and S. Madhavan and D. Simon (2002), "Women's Social Networks and Child Survival in Mali", *Social Science and Medicine*, 54, 165-178.

Basu, A.M. (1992), *Culture, the Status of Women and Demographic Behavior*, Oxford: Calrendon.

Bhatia, J.C. and Cleland, J. (1995), "Determinants of Maternal Care in a Region of South India", *Health Transition Review*, 5, 127-142.

Bloom, S. and D. Wypij and M. Das Gupta (2001), "Dimensions of Women's Autonomy and the Influence on Maternal Health Care Utilisation in a North Indian City", *Demography*, 38, 67-78.

Dasgupta, M. and L.C. Chen and T.N. Krishnan (1998), *Women's Health in India: Risk and Vulnerability*, Oxford University Press, Delhi, India.

Dyson, T. and M. Moore (1983), "On Kinship Structure, Female Autonomy, and Demographic Behaviour in India", *Population and Development Review*, 9, 35-60.

Jejeebhoy, S. and Z.A. Sathar (2001), "Women's Autonomy in India and Pakistan: Influence of Religion and Region", *Population and Development Review*, 27, 687-712.

Kishor, S. (1998), "Gender Differentials in Child Mortality: A Review of the Evidence", 19-54, in M. Dasgupta, L.C. Chen and T. N. Krishnan edited *Women's Health in India: Risk and Vulnerability*, Oxford University Press, Delhi, India.

Long, J.S. (1997), *Regression Models for Categorical and Limited Dependent Variables*, Thousand Oaks, CA: Sage Publications.

Matsumura, M. and B. Gubhaju (2001), "Women's Status, Household Structure and The Utilisation of Maternal Health Services in Nepal", *Asia-Pacific Population Journal*, 16, 23-44.

National Family Health Survey (1998-99), India, International Institute for Population Sciences, Mumbai, India and Measure DHS +, ORC Macro, Maryland, U.S.A.

Navaneetham, K. and A. Dharmalingam (2002), "Utilisation of Maternal Health Care Services in Southern India", *Social Science and Medicine*, 55, 1849-1869.

Pande, R.P. (2000), "Family Composition Effects on Gender Differentials in Nutrition and Immunization in Rural India", *Hopkins Population Center Papers on Population*, Working Paper 00-01, 1-29.

Paul, B.K. and D.J. Rumsey, (2002), "Utilisation of Health Facilities and Trained Birth Attendants for Childbirth in Rural Bangladesh: An Empirical Study", *Social Science and Medicine*, 54, 1755-1765.

Pebley, A.R. and N. Goldman and G. Rodriguez (1996), "Prenatal and Delivery Care and Childhood Immunization in Guatemala: Do Family and Community Matter?", *Demography*, 33, 231-247.

Raghupathy, S. (1996), "Education and the Use of Maternal Health Care in Thailand", *Social Science and Medicine*, 43, 459-471.

Shariff A. and G. Singh (2002), "Determinants of Maternal Health Care Utilisation in India: Evidence from a Recent Household Survey", *National Council of Applied Economic Research Working Paper*, 85, 1-38.

Wolfe, B.L. and J.R. Behrman (1984), "Determinants of Women's Health Status and Health Care Utilisation in a Developing Country: A Latent Variable Approach", *Review of Economics and Statistics*, 66, 696-703.

14

Quality of Health Care and Household Choice

Evidence from NSS and NFHS Data for the State of West Bengal

SUBRATA MUKHERJEE

1. Introduction

In a developing country, like India, there is an obvious imperative to allocate scarce fiscal resources in the health sector based on a clear understanding of how allocation of resources is going to affect the demand. It has been documented in a few studies that given the individual-level characteristics, the important determinant in the choice of health care provider, other than cost of health care, is the quality of health care. In the context of health sector reforms, the price hike (by means of user fees and cost recovery) of health care is often justified as a mean to generate additional revenues for quality improvement. The implicit assumption is that price hike associated with quality improvement would not have negative impact on utilisation.

Despite its importance, studies examining the role of quality on demand for health care are lacking in the context of developing countries because of conceptual ambiguity associated with the definitions of quality, lack of appropriate measures of quality and non-existence of appropriate data sets. The present study is an attempt to reduce the information gap. Drawing on public health and standard of living literature, we attempt to define and measure health care quality from consumer's point of view and present some evidence from NSS (52nd Round) and NFHS (2) unit-record data for the state of West Bengal.

The Sections of the paper are arranged in the following way: Section 2 deals with the conceptual and measurement issues of health care quality. It critically reviews the existing approaches and suggests a modified one, which suits the purpose at hand better than the existing approaches. Section 3 attempts to show how perceived quality and choice are linked in a theoretical framework of representative consumer. Section 4 describes the data sources. Section 5 presents the empirical evidence from NSS 52 and NFHS 2 data. Section 6 makes a few concluding remarks.

2. Concept and Measurement of Health Care Quality

The idea of quality assessment is new neither in general industry nor in health care. Focus on outcome measurement in health care dates back more than eighty years (Codman 1920). Individual opinion dates back almost forty years (Bushur, Metzern and Worder 1967). In public health literature several definitions of quality of health care have been offered. The most frequently cited definitions of health care quality are by Donabedian (1966, 1980) and Institute of Medicine (1990).

Donabedian, probably for the first time, proposed a systematic approach to define and assess quality of health care. His characterisation of the approach to quality assessment includes elements of the structure of the health care delivery system, the process of care and the outcomes of care. Structure refers to the resources available, including characteristics of the providers and settings of care. Process refers to provider's performance including normative behaviour. Outcomes refer to any change in patient's current and future health status that can be attributed to antecedent health care, including patient's satisfaction. The structure, process and outcome measures are causally linked so that structure affects the probability of good process of care, which in turn can affect outcomes such as health status and quality of life. According to him, quality is a property of the health care process and is complex and multidimensional in nature. He defines quality as the expected ability of care to achieve the highest possible net benefits according to the valuations of individuals and society (Donabedian 1980).

IOM (1990) has defined quality of care as the degree to which health services for individuals and populations increase the likelihood of desired health outcomes and are consistent with current professional knowledge.

There are other approaches as well (for example, Roemer and Aguilar 1988; Anderson and Zwelling 1996; Cambell and others 1997 and so on), but the basic concepts remain the same. A review of literature shows that the notions of quality embodied in theses approaches are basically two: quality defined purely from biomedical perspective and quality defined purely from patient's satisfaction with the care. When defined purely from biomedical perspective, quality of care is interpreted as the degree to which the actual performance or achievement of health facility or health care provider correspond to the established medical standard (Wouter, Adeyi and Morrow 1993). In this notion, quality shows the capacity of the health care to perform certain specific health interventions combined with some indicators on how well these interventions are carried out (Roemer and Montoya Aguilar 1988). This approach mainly relies on the technical or quantifiable components such as compliance with the standardised process infection or hospitalisation rates. On the other hand, patient's satisfaction with the care captures patient's perception about the quality of service received.

Both Donabedian's and IOM's definitions suffer from the limitations of one kind or other which prevent us to use them in explaining consumer's behavior. Firstly, controversy exists over the relative value of Donabedian's three types of measures. The data on structural features might fail to reflect the potential level of quality because of three reasons: (a) Better structural features is a necessary and not sufficient condition for better quality. (b) The official data (or data provided by the facility) on structural features are often exaggerated and does not show the reality (Thomas, Lavy, and Strauss 1991)[1]. (c) Since every transaction of health care is different from each other, quality has only to be assessed at the individual-care level. In other words, quality of a provider is reflected on the quality of care it produces and therefore, it can only be assessed at the individual care level[2]. Although process measures of quality are well developed

1. This problem can be more rampant in assessing government health care facilities.
2. It does not matter to an individual what facilities a provider or health facility has, what individuals receive (as perceived by them) matters to them and influence their behaviour.

in comparison to other measures, they are good measures of quality of care only to the extent that they can be linked to actions on the part of the health care provider or system that can be changed. The process measures have their own limitations. However, they have been also criticised on two accounts. (a) They do not address the individual's benefit. An individual's ultimate concern is the net benefit of care and he may not be interested in the process as such. (b) It is not possible to observe various components of process and monitor them. The frustration with the limitations of structural and process measures has led to a push for more outcome measures. But the pitfalls of outcome measures are many. Long time periods required for many outcomes to develop and the difficulty in identifying the components of health outcomes that are attributable to the health care. To use outcome measures for assessing quality it must be adjusted for severity and risks.

Secondly, Donabedian suggested that the structural measures have to be combined with process and outcome measures in order to assess the quality of care. His approach takes into account both technical and interpersonal aspects of quality. But no clear method is suggested how to use in a unified manner, on the one hand, the structural, process and outcome measures and on the other hand, technical and interpersonal aspect of quality. (Koran 1975a, 1975b). Some observers question the relationship of structural measures of standards to either process or outcome measures because of little empirical evidence of direct connections (Donaldson 1999). IOM's approach basically reflects biomedical perspective.

Thirdly, one of the major limitations of Donabedian and IOM's definition of quality is that they are very broad and they try to be all-purposive. The notion of quality can be different depending on the perspective and depending on the perspective, the elements of quality assessment may be different. For example, the essential elements of quality may be understood in a quite different ways among various individuals and professional groups. While health professionals are more concerned with objective and technical measures of quality (such as statistical measures of clinical performance), the lay individuals of health services may base quality on less technically complex and more subjective notions (such as measures of overall satisfaction). Further, within individual group the rank of different elements of quality may vary from individual to individual. It is necessary to distinguish the possible perspective from which the quality of health care can be viewed. There are three perspectives which appear to be important: (a) consumers; (b) providers; and (c) State. The State (which is a collection of different interest groups like politicians, bureaucrats etc.) can have a different priorities over the elements of quality.

Fourthly, in assessing the quality of a provider, we must decide the boundary of services that the provider is supposed to provide. This means quality of a provider should be assessed on the basis of quality of health care the provider is supposed to provide.

Fifthly, it is also important to clearly define the object whose quality has to be assessed. The object can be individual provider, health care institution, or health care system a whole and so on.

Sixthly, a distinction on the time point of assessment is also important. We need to make a difference between *ex ante* assessment and *ex post* assessment. As far as individual's choice of health care providers is concerned, the individuals have to assess quality of the health care provider prior to the treatment. His judgement may be based on the available information on the characteristics of the provider or facility. The source of such information could be his personal experience or experience of others. This notion of perceived quality can be termed as *ex ante* assessment of quality. The *ex ante* assessment of quality is different from *ex post* assessment, as the latter is assessment of heath care quality after the individual has received the service. Sufficient time should also be allowed to make such assessment. The *ex ante* assessment of current period is expected to be influenced by the *ex post* assessment of the previous period.

Economists also have been concerned with the quality of goods and services for a long time. However, in economics the discussions on quality have mainly been concentrated in the construction of price indices. In economics, the study of quality has mainly been to figure out quantity. In economic approach to quality measurement, four definitions of quality are found: (1) user value; (2) user component; (3) cost component; and (4) total cost (Payson 1994). Among these four definitions, the user value definition seems to be close to the notion of quality if the purpose is to explain consumer's behaviour.

But the straightforward approach of user value definition is not possible because the health care shares some peculiar characteristics which are generally not found in other goods and services. (1) In a seminal paper Arrow (1963) rigorously pointed out that uncertainty as the quality of product is more intense in health care than any other important commodity. In most of the commodities the possibility of learning from one's own experience or that of others is strong because there is an adequate number of trials. But in case of health care it is not true, particularly in case of severe illness. (2) Health care services is intangible because it is not possible to count and measure and cannot be stored or inventoried or tested for quality. Consumer experience either directly or vicariously from outside sources, is frequently the only means of verifying whether health care services meets the desirable quality. (3) Each transaction of health care is different from one another. This heterogeneity occurs because the services are delivered by different physicians, nurses and others to a variety of patients with varying needs. Patients' needs frequently vary from person to person and from visit to visit depending on the health and other conditions. Interaction among physicians, other health staff, patients and timing factors combine in an infinite number of ways to affect the quality of the health care services rendered. (4) In health care the production and consumption are inseparable. The services are consumed when they are produced which makes quality control difficult.

Our search for an appropriate approach to define and measure health care quality is guided by the following two important criteria: Firstly, it must meet the motivation that makes us interested in the concept of the health care quality, doing justice to the trickiness of the idea. Secondly, the approach must be practical in the sense of being usable for actual assessments of the quality of care. Our basic purpose is to explain individual's choice of health care using quality as an argument. So we attempt to understand the notion of quality that individuals are guided by in choosing health care providers. In doing so we draw analogy from Sen's contribution to standard of living literature (Sen 1987).

Essentially there are two pure perspectives from which the quality of health care can be viewed. One can view quality of care as looking into the process of health care an individual succeeds in getting from a health care provider, purely from a biomedical perspective[3]. Others can view just looking at individuals' satisfaction with the care. The first notion of quality is important when we are interested in standardising the delivery of care by different providers for efficient utilisation of resources (i.e. maximising the impact of health care on health status) given the current state of medical knowledge. The second notion of quality is important when our interest is to explain individuals' choice of health care provider. We call this notion of quality as perceived quality of care. At the conceptual level we should treat these two notions of quality separately. Since the purpose of the present study is to explain the role that quality plays in explaining individual's choice of health care providers, it is the second notion of quality, which is important to us. The second notion of quality is also important for the first notion of quality to be operational in achieving its objective. The health care quality which complies with notion of quality purely from biomedical perspective cannot achieve efficiency in improving the health status of people unless it affects people's utilisation in a positive way, because effectiveness depends not only on what services are provided but also on what services are utilised.

We accept a part of Donabedian's definition, in principle, that health care quality is the expected ability of care to achieve the highest possible net benefit according to the valuations of individual. But we differ on Donabedian's approach of simultaneous use of structure, process and outcome indicators.

Whether it is physician's notion of health care quality purely from a biomedical perspective or health care quality as perceived by individuals, assessing quality of care is an evaluative exercise. Since perceived quality of care is the quality of care evaluated by individual himself, it is similar to - what Sen calls - self evaluation (Sen 1987). On the other hand, in evaluating the quality of care from biomedical perspective, a group of medical experts, on the basis of agreed upon standard, decides what should be the efficient process of care in a given context (including the current stage of medical knowledge). This is equivalent to Sen's concept of standard evaluation, since it is shared notion of a group of medical experts. Any evaluative exercise

3. This is not same as health professionals' view of health care quality. In the public health literature, health professional's notion of quality also includes individual's satisfaction with care.

involves two basic questions (a) what are the objects of value; and (b) how valuable are the objects (Sen 1987).

Consider, for example, the perceived quality of care. The perceived quality of care does have one-to-one correspondence with individual's overall satisfaction with the care. Better the quality of care as perceived by the individual, higher is the satisfaction. If increase in the value of one characteristic of a provider gives an individual higher overall satisfaction, then that characteristic of the provider can be called an object of value in the evaluation of perceived quality. The sources of satisfaction can be of two types: satisfaction due to expected improvement in health status and satisfaction due to the reasons which are not purely related to expected improvement in health. Depending on sources of satisfaction, the observable characteristics of a health care provider can be divided into two categories: (a) characteristics, which the individual thinks, do have bearing on the technical competence of the provider; and (b) characteristics which show provider's inter-personal and environmental aspects (as assessed by the individual).

We can roughly call these two characteristics as technical characteristics and functional characteristics.[4] Better technical characteristics indicate higher expected health outcome. So better technical characteristics of the provider give higher satisfaction to the individual, as it increases the expectation of better health outcome. On the other hand, better functional characteristics may have impact on individual's satisfaction but they do not contribute to the overall satisfaction through increase in expected health outcome.[5] For example, if an individual thinks that doctors with higher qualification, longer experience or doctors who spend more time with the patients give higher expected health status, then these characteristics contribute to better quality through better technical competence. Similarly the behaviour of the doctor (e.g. politeness, respect to the patient, maintaining dignity, respecting privacy etc.), comfort and cleanliness at the facility indicate better functional characteristics and gives higher satisfaction to the individual. Needless to say, this

4. They might not be the perfect terms to describe.
5. It is true that inter personal components and environment can have positive impact on the health status.

satisfaction is completely different from satisfaction due to higher expected health status.[6] However, in reality it is very difficult to isolate these two components in overall satisfaction. Physical illness creates in the patient a variety of psychological needs that he expects to be satisfied in the patient-physician interaction (Donabedian 2000).

If two providers have same functional characteristics, it is reasonable to assume that the individual will get higher overall satisfaction from that provider whose technical characteristics are, according to his evaluation, are better. Similarly, if two providers have same technical characteristics (as assessed by the individual), individual's overall satisfaction will be higher with the provider with better functional characteristics (as evaluated by the individual). If one provider has better technical characteristics and other has better functional characteristics, then it is reasonable to argue that the individual will always have a lexicographic preference for technical competence. This means he will get higher overall satisfaction from the provider with better technical characteristics.

In assessing the quality of care, different individuals can have different list of objects and different priorities among the objects depending on their perception about technical and functional aspects of health care. To an individual, for instance, the objects of technical aspect of quality can be the duration of consultation time, doctor's qualification or doctor's experience etc. The relative importance of these components will be evaluated differently by different individuals. Depending on the evaluation, same health care provider may yield different level of satisfaction to different individuals and same individual may get different level of satisfaction from competing health care providers.

In evaluating the quality of health care we consider those characteristics of care which contribute to individual's overall satisfaction from care and which are distinct from the elements of price/cost.

Donaldson (1999) argued that quality of care should not be defined on a sliding scale in which judgements about quality vary according to what can or cannot be afforded. We do consider access as elements of cost and not quality, because poor access just increases

6. Strictly speaking a few items affecting two types of satisfaction are difficult to separate out in reality.

the monetary and non-monetary cost of care. Moreover, most of the factors that influence individuals' access to health care are beyond the scope of health sector (Haddad *et al.*, 1998). For example, connectivity, mode of transport, bridge, etc. determine the time to reach the health care facility. On the other hand, the factors which determine the individual's per unit cost of time are wage rate, type of employment[7] etc. Similarly, we do not consider non-availability of drug as a dimension of quality. Those components of care which can be compensated by incurring higher cost without affecting the expected health outcome essentially increases the total cost of treatment. Non-availability of the medicine at facilities does not matter if the individuals have option and ability to procure medicines from outside the facility without affecting the probable health outcome[8].

3. Theoretical Framework: A Representative Individual

The theoretical literature on health care demand modelling has undergone a major evolution since the early-1960s, when economists first became interested in estimating the demand for health services. Early health care demand models were simple reduced form equations derived from the assumptions of utility maximisation. In the 1970s the major contributions have been made in health care modelling by Grossman (1972), Acton (1975) and Christianson (1976). Since late-1980s a number of studies have been done with more richness and sophistication (Gertler, Locay and Sanderson 1987; Gertler and van der Gaag 1990; Mwabu, Ainsworth and Nyamete 1993; Gupta and Dasgupta 2000; Sahn, Younger and Genicot 2002). These studies basically model health care demand in a short-run static discrete choice framework. Our theoretical framework of utility maximisation of a representative individual draws on these theoretical models but we differ from them mainly on two points. (1) Instead of assuming utility as a function of health status (and consumption of non-medical goods), we assume the utility of an ill individual as a function of

7. Timing of the facility also determines the opportunity cost of time. If the timing of the facility coincides with the working hours of the informal workers, they will have to incur higher access cost to utilise that facility.

8. Of course, the loss of health outcome due to non-availability of life-saving essential drugs may not be compensated. In such case such non-availability can be considered as quality dimension.

improvement in health status due to treatment (and consumption of non-medical goods). (2) We incorporate the notion of quality which we developed in the previous section (Section 2).

Let's the utility function of an ill individual conditional on treatment from provider j be defined as

$U_j = U(H_j, C_j)$

Where H_j = improvement in perceived health status if he seeks health care from provider j; C_j = consumption of non-medical goods if he seeks care from provider j.

We assume that improvement in perceived health status depends on quality of provider j as perceived by the individual. This means, higher is the quality as perceived by the individual, higher will be the improvement in expected health status and *vice versa*.

$H_j = Q(Q_j)$

Let Z_j be the vector of all possible dimensions/characteristics of a provider that the individual thinks do have positive bearing on quality of care. Z can be split into two sub-vectors; vector of technical characteristics (Z^t) and vector of functional characteristics (Z^f).

Therefore, $Z = (Z^t, Z^f)$

For the individual Q_j can then be expressed as

$Q_j = f(Z_j, X')$

Where X' is individual's characteristics which affect perception of Q_j, given Z_j. In other words, X' determines what should be the elements of Z and how much weights should be attached to them.

The budget line of the individual can be expressed as

$Y = P_j^* + C_j$

Where Y = permanent income of the individual including the value of time; and P_j^* = price of health care.

The price of health care is the sum of the direct price of health care (P_j^D) and the access costs an individual incur in accessing care (P_j^A). Access cost is the sum of monetary and non-monetary costs that an individual incur in accessing care.

$P_j^* = P_j^A + P_j^D$

While the direct price is not expected to vary across individuals with the same illness characteristics in a same facility, access costs can vary to a considerable extent depending on the total time taken to access the care and opportunity cost of time.

Therefore the budget line can be rewritten as $Y = C_j + P_j^A + P_j^D$

For an individual each j represents a particular combination of perceived quality, direct price and access cost (i.e. Q_j, P_j^D, P_j^A).

An ill individual, in maximising utility subject to the budget constraint, chooses that provider j, which gives him maximum utility.

The indirect utility function can be written as $V_j = U(Q(f(Z_j, X'), Y-(P_j^A + P_j^D) = V(Z_j, P_j^A, P_j^D, X)$[9]. Suppose there are three options to an individual j = 0 (no care), G (care from government provider) and P (care from private provider). The individual will choose self care if $V_0 > \text{Max}(V_G, V_P)$, otherwise he chooses care from government or private providers. The individual will choose care from government or private provider depending upon $V_G > V_P$.

Figure 14.1

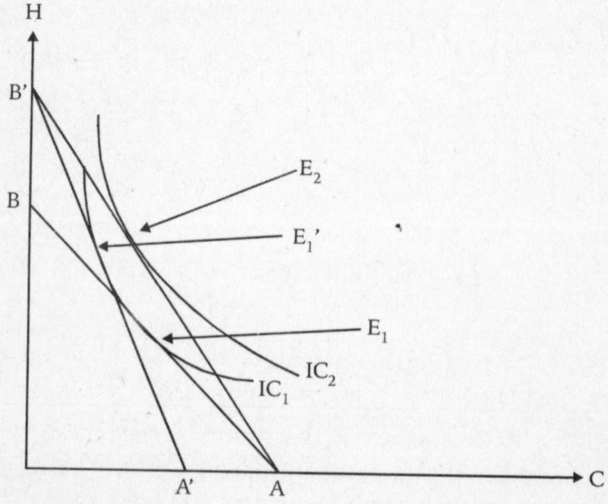

Note: C = Consumption of non-medical goods;
H = Improvement in expected (perceived) health status

9. X = X' U Y

An improvement in quality for an individual, in this framework, implies change in the Z vector from Z to Z' such that Q(Z', X) > Q(Z, X). If the improvement in quality is associated with increase in price, should we call it quality improvement? We have made a clear distinction between price and quality of health care and argue that the notion of quality improvement is independent of change in price of health care. A hypothetical example can make out intuition clear. For example, if the price of care from provider A is much higher than that from provider B, an individual may still consider quality of A is much better than that of B, irrespective of whether he can afford it or not. Now the important question is if improvement in quality is associated with increase in price of health care, will it be acceptable? It can be argued that it depends on the individual's trade off between quality and price of health care. Suppose quality-price attributes of a provider changes from (Z, P^D, P^A) to $(Z', P^{D'}, P^{A'})$, it will be acceptable to the individual if $V(Z', P^{D'}, P^{A'} \mid X) > V(Z, P^D, P^A \mid X)$.

Figure 14.1 shows the representative individual's indifference map. Consumption of non-medical goods and improvement in the expected (perceived) health status[10] of the individual are measured along the horizontal and vertical axes respectively. The linear budget line is drawn on the assumption that price of per unit improvement in health is constant[11] and price of non-medical goods is adjusted to unity. Given the budget line AB, the equilibrium is at point E_1 on the indifference curve IC_1. The quality improvement (without any change in the price), is shown by the rightward rotation of the budget line (to AB'). This means that at each level of C the individual can higher improvement in health status compared he used to get before the quality improvement. The new equilibrium after the quality improvement is at point E_2 on a higher level indifference curve IC_2. Generally quality improvement is coupled with price hike. This implies that the new budget line will rotate leftward keeping B' fixed. Any rotation between B'A and B'A' is acceptable to the individual. The budget line B'A' returns the individual to the original level of utility.

10. It is assumed that improvement in expected (perceived) health status can be measured by some unit.
11. In reality it may not be constant and expected to increase with the increase in expected improvement in perceived health status.

4. Data Sources

We have used unit-record data from two household surveys, namely, National Health Survey 52nd (NSS 52) Round and National Family Health Survey 2 (NFHS 2) for the State of West Bengal. NSS 52 was carried out during 1995-96, while NFHS 2 was carried out during 1998-99.

We have used the NSS 52 Data (Central sample) under the Schedule 25.0. NSS 52 divided all illness into two categories depending on the treatment they required. (1) Illness which required hospitalised or in-patient care. (2) Illness which required out-patient care. The reference period for first and second kinds of illness were 365 and 15 days respectively preceding the date of survey. Our analysis is based on illness of the second kind. NSS 52 Sample for West Bengal includes 41606 individuals (in 8249 households). Our analysis is based on 2772 illness episodes reported by 2741 individuals.

Depending on whether formally treated or not all illness can be divided into two categories. Formal treatment includes treatment from (1) public hospital; (2) primary health centre; (3) public dispensary; (4) ESI doctor, AMA etc; (5) private hospital; (6) nursing home; (7) charitable institution run by public trust; (8) private doctors; and (9) others. It excludes treatment from medicine shop and non-medical professional practitioners. While the first four sources of treatment can be considered as government, the rest may roughly be considered as private. All formally treated illness can be divided into two categories: (1) any measure taken from non-government sources; and (2) no measure taken from non-government sources. NSS 52 Data does not provide information on quality directly for the health care facilities utilised. But for treated illness which took any measure from non-government sources, it provides data on reasons for not utilising the government facilities. The reasons are classified into nine categories: (1) government doctor/facility is too far; (2) not satisfied with the treatment; (3) long waiting; (4) lacks personal attention; (5) bad treatment; (6) doctor/staff corrupt or charge money; (7) medicine not available or ineffective if available; (8) private doctor is easily available; and (9) others. In addition to utilisation and quality related data, data on household consumption expenditure and household occupational categories are used. NSS 52 divides all rural and urban households into 5 and 4 occupational categories respectively.

The rural categories are (1) self-employed in non-agriculture; (2) agricultural labour; (3) other labour; (4) self-employed in agriculture; and (5) others. The urban categories are (1) self employed; (2) regular wage or salaried; (3) causal labour; and (4) others.

The NFHS 2 Sample for West Bengal covers 4408 ever married women (of age group 15-49) from 4725 households. Section 3A of NFHS 2 Women's questionnaire covers a few questions about the quality of the recently visited health care facility. The care covers family planning, child birth related care, immunisation and other curative care. The facilities cover government, NGO, private and others. Four types of questions are asked which can be considered as different dimensions of quality: (1) During this visit did the staff spend enough time with you? (2) Did the staff talk to you nicely/somewhat nicely/not nicely? (3) Did the staff respect your need for privacy? (4) Would you say the health facility was very clean/somewhat clean/not clean? The unit-record data set of NFHS 2 also contains a variable - called standard of living index - which are constructed from the information on household asset holdings (The detail of index formulation is given in the Appendix 14A.1 (A1)).

It must be noted that NFHS 2 Data is not used as a complement to NSS 52 Data. The NFHS 2 Data reflects the opinion of women (aged 15-49) and the data covers all kinds of health care including care related to family planning, child birth and immunisation. Another important point is while NSS 52 Data gives the *ex ante* opinion about quality, NFHS 2 Data presents *ex post* opinion about the quality.

5. Evidence from NSS 52 and NFHS 2 Data

The data on household consumption expenditure provided by NSS 52 can be used as a proxy for the economic status of the household the individual belongs to. To examine the variations in choice of individuals belonging to different economic status, we have selected bottom 30 per cent and top 10 per cent of the population (following ranking by per capita consumption expenditure, starting from the poorest) separately for rural and urban, as groups for comparison. Throughout this paper bottom 30 per cent and top 10 per cent are roughly referred as rich and poor, in the context of NSS 52 Data. In case of NFHS 2 Data poor stands for women with lowest standard of living and rich stands for women with highest standard of living (See Appendix 14A.1 (A1)).

The mean and median based summary statistics of household consumption expenditure by household occupational categories are presented in Table 14.1. If we exclude the category *others*, the Table shows that in the rural sector *agricultural labour* is the poorest group followed by *other labour*, *self-employed in non-agriculture* and *self-employed in agriculture* is the richest group. In the urban sector, *casual labour* is the poorest group followed by *self-employed* and *regular wage or salaried* is the richest group. The similar order of mean and median household consumption expenditure across household categories and our intuitive understanding about the nature of work help us to develop a new combined classification by putting together both rural and urban households.

The new classification has three categories apart from the category *others*. The categories are *labour*, *self-employed* and *regular wage or salaried*. The objective of this reclassification is to use household occupational category as a proxy for opportunity cost of time rather than economic status. The absolute and proportionate loss of household income can be taken as proxy for opportunity cost of time.

We assume that the opportunity cost of time is highest for the *labour* category (which shows lowest economic status) and lowest for the regular wage or salaried category (which shows the highest economic status). The basis of our assumption is the flexibility a household generally does enjoy in allocating its working hours. It is reasonable to argue that *labour* class does have less bargaining power in deciding about its working hours and their income is strongly dependent on the duration of the time they work. So a sudden reduction in their working hours (even if it is of short duration) may reduce their earnings. The *regular wage or salaried* class also does not have flexibility in allocating their working hours, but it is less likely that they do sacrifice income due to temporary reduction in working hours. The case of *self-employed* is a complicated one, since it covers a wide range of households (very high income and very low income). We assume that they have more flexibility in allocating their working hours and have lower opportunity cost of time compared to labour class. This is our assumption and subject to empirical verification. The mean and median household consumption expenditure and average loss of household income due to illness across (reclassified) household occupational categories are presented in Table 14.2.

Table 14.1

Summary Measures of Household Consumption Expenditure (in Rs.) by Household Occupational Categories

Household Occupational Categories	*Mean*	*Standard Deviation*	*Median*	*Inter Quartile Range (IQR)*
Rural				
Self-employed in non-agriculture	1579.54	36.35	1456	779
Agricultural labour	1202.38	22.56	1089	581.5
Other labour	1251.31	66.43	1122.50	928
Self-employed in agriculture	1660.68	33.31	1458.50	949.5
Others	1619.89	65.51	1481.5	1110.2
Urban				
Self-employed	2157.32	48.50	1851	1296.5
Regular wage/salaried	2290.45	43.11	2096	1743
Casual labour	1427.19	50.25	1310.50	941.5
Others	1642.45	96.07	1299.50	1407.5

Source: NSS 52

Table 14.2

Mean and Median Household Consumption Expenditure by Occupational Categories (Reclassified)

Household Occupational Categories	*Mean*	*Median*	*Average Loss of Household Income*	*Loss as a Percentage of Household Consumption Expenditure*
Labour	1231.27	1107	33.80	2.75
Self-employed	1743.00	1518	31.45	1.80
Regular wage/salaried	2290.45	2096	11.06	0.48
Others	1625.61	1404	19.62	1.21

Source: NSS 52

Now we consider an individual's choice problem between different health care providers. Our problem and available NSS 52 Data allows us to divide all health care providers into two mutually exclusive categories, namely government and others (which can roughly be called private). But this categorisation excludes medicine shop, non-medical professional practitioners and other similar kind of providers. The percentage of treated illness by sources is presented in Table 14.3. It shows that private is the major source of treatment for both the rich and the poor. The figures after adjusting for missing values show that utilisation of government facilities are around 20-23 per cent for the poor and around 9-10 per cent for the rich. Given the higher incidence of rural poverty (40.48 per cent according to 1993-94 estimates by Planning Commission), it is clear that many of the people below the poverty line are forced to visit the private providers. A normative look at the Table suggests that dependence of the poor in general and rural poor in particular on government facilities is much lower than what is desirable.

Table 14.3

Percentage of Treated Illness Not Taken Any Measure from Non-government Sources and Percentage of Treatment from Government Sources

	Rural		*Urban*	
	Poor	*Rich*	*Poor*	*Rich*
Percentage of treated illness not taken any measure from non-government sources (level 8)	20.37	9.45	20.66	8.68
Percentage of treatment from government sources (level 9)	22.61	10.24	22.31	9.09

Source: NSS 52

NSS 52 Data provides us information on the reasons for non-utilisation of government facilities. The reasons can be reclassified based on our new approach to quality assessment. Consider, for example, the first reason 'government facility is too far'. The far off government facility indicates long distance. The long distance can be coupled with absence of suitable mode of transport or high opportunity cost of time or both. Long waiting increases total time spent on seeking medical care and if that leads a sacrifice of income on the part of household where the individual belongs to, it is an indication of high access cost to care. Similarly corruption at medical facility just increases the cost of accessing care and, therefore, can be added to the access cost. 'Private facility easily accessible' means the access cost of private care is lower than the access cost of government care. All these reasons indicate that the access cost of government care is higher compared to care from private facilities.

The reasons like 'not satisfied with the treatment', 'lacks personal attention' and 'bad treatment' show lower quality of care at the government facilities as perceived by the individuals. This perception may be based on the information available to the individuals. The sources of such information can range from personal experience to report by media.

Non-availability of medicine increases the direct cost of treatment if there is a provision to procure the medicine from outside the facility without having any negative impact on individual's expected health status. It is difficult to attribute ineffectiveness of medicine as a quality dimension since it is individuals' judgement about the effectiveness of medicine. If an individual takes longer time to get cured than what is expected, then whether it is because of wrong diagnosis, bad medicine or fault on the part of the individual is difficult to say without any clinical examination.

So we can reclassify the reasons for non-utilisation of government facilities into three categories, namely, 'higher access cost', 'lower perceived quality' and 'others' (which includes the reason 'non-availability of medicine or good medicine' and 'others'). Data on the reasons (reclassified) for non-utilisation of government facilities is presented in Table 14.4. It shows that it is the higher access cost, which turns out to be the major reason for lower utilisation of government facilities for all four groups. The lower perceived quality accounts for the second major reason for non-utilisation of government facilities. The results also show that the relative importance of quality compared to access cost is much higher for the rich compared to the poor and *vice versa*.

The percentage distribution of reasons for non-utilisation of government facilities by household occupational categories

Table 14.4

Percentage Distribution of Treated Illness (which have taken any measure from non-government sources) by Reasons for Utilisation of Non-government Facilities

Reasons	*Rural*		*Urban*	
	Poor	*Rich*	*Poor*	*Rich*
Access cost	77.4	47.18	53.59	53.19
Quality	8.75	39.66	6.5	31.75
Others	7.2	9.0	19.28	10.29

Source: NSS 52

(reclassified) gives us some interesting findings (Table 14.5). In the labour class, 69.1 per cent of the illness reported higher access cost as reason for utilisation of non-government facilities. This was followed by self-employed (59.2 per cent) and then regular wage or salaried (46 per cent). This evidence is in line with our assumption that opportunity cost of time is highest for the labour class and lowest for the regular wage or salaried class.

Table 14.5

Percentage Distribution of Treated Illness Which Have Taken At Least One Treatment from Non-government Sources by Reasons (Reclassified)

Reasons	*Labourer*	*Self-employed*	*Wage or Salaried*
Access cost	69.1	59.2	46.0
Perceived quality	19.7	30.9	30.4
Others	11.2	10.0	23.7

Source: NSS 52

We have one more evidence to support our assumption. NSS 52 provides data on average loss of household income due to illness. A household may incur financial loss when some earning member of the household fall sick and the nature of employment does not provide any safeguard to compensate the loss. The average loss of household income can be taken as an indicator of household's opportunity cost of time. The data shows (Table 14.2) that both absolute average loss of household income and loss as a percentage of average household consumption expenditure is highest for the labour class and lowest for the regular wage or salaried class.

We have argued in Section 2 that choice of health care provider is a complex process where a set of individual-level and provider-level factors interact with each other in the determination of final outcome. Now we examine the association between choice of health care provider and a few factors with the help of multinomial logit model.[12] Our dependent variable takes on multiple values: *no treatment, treatment*

12. When the dependent variable's categories have no natural ordering, multinomial/polytomous logistic regression can be applied.

from govt. facility and *treatment from private facility*. The independent variables, we have considered are, *log of household consumption expenditure, household occupational categories, sex, place of residence* (rural or urban) and *nature of illness*. Household consumption expenditure is an indicator of economic status and log is taken to remove the asymmetry. Household occupational categories are proxies for opportunity cost of time (and thereby that of access cost of treatment). Sex is included to examine whether there exists any gender discrimination in choice. Place of residence is basically an indicator of access to health care. Urban sector does have better access to health care in general and private health care in particular. (The detailed variable definitions are given in Appendix 14A.1 (A2)). The results of the multinomial logistic regression are presented in Table 14.6.

Table 14.6

Results of Multinomial Logistic Regression

Number of obs = *2653*
F (14,2639) = *5.05*
Prob > *F* = *0.0000*

Dmchoice	*rrr*	*Std. Err.*	*t*	*P>t*
Dmchoice = 1 (government facility is chosen)				
Lnhhmce	1.075977	0.206233	0.38	0.702
Dhhtype1	1.516985	0.416235	1.52	0.129
Dhhtype2	2.392326	0.934853	2.23	0.026
Dhhtype3	2.666778	1.211844	2.16	0.031
Dillnat	0.882373	0.215463	–0.51	0.608
Dsector	1.960227	0.557828	2.37	0.018
Dsex	1.215412	0.272495	0.87	0.384
Dmchoice = 2 (private facility is chosen)				
Lnhhmce	1.997851	0.320922	4.31	0
Dhhtype1	1.154225	0.223603	0.74	0.459
Dhhtype2	1.088525	0.333076	0.28	0.782
Dhhtype3	1.62291	0.550762	1.43	0.154
Dillnat	0.678784	0.130812	–2.01	0.044
Dsector	1.707041	0.359759	2.54	0.011
Dsex	0.969492	0.161988	–0.19	0.853

Note: Dmchoice = 0 (the ill individual did not seek any formal treatment) is the base for comparison.

Source: Estimated from NSS 52

No (formal) treatment has been considered as a base for comparison. The relative risk ratio (rrr along with significance values are reported in the Table (see Appendix 14A.1 (A3) for a note on 'rrr'). When the choice is government, the variables *Dhhtype2*, *Dhhtype3* and *Dsector* and when the choice is private the variables *lnhhmce*, *Dillnat* and *Dsector* are turned out to be significant. For example, the odds favouring choice is *government* over choice *is no care* are 2.39 times higher for individuals belonging to household occupational category *regular wage or salaried* than for others. This is consistent with the fact that time element of access cost is higher for *government care* and *regular wage or salaried* have lower opportunity cost of time. Similar explanation holds for the other categorical variables. The variable *lnhhmce* is not significant when the choice is *government care* but significant when the choice is *private care*.

If we assume that the direct price of government care is lower than that of private care, then an individual utilises a private facility either on better quality ground or on lower access cost ground. While an individual's preference for quality is expected to intensify with increase in economic status, the access cost is expected to be more sensitive to the occupational categories. This hypothesis is also tested with the help of multinomial logit model. Our dependent variable *Dmchoice1* takes on three values *chosen government facility*; *chosen private facility on lower access cost ground* and *chosen private facility on better quality ground* (see Appendix 14A.1 (A-4)). The same set of independent variables has been used. The results of the multinomial logit regression are presented in Table 14.7. Two important observations are worth mentioning. **(1)** the 'rrr' of *lnhhmce* is higher when the choice of private is on better quality grounds compared to when the choice of private is on lower access cost ground. This shows as economic status improves people's rejection of government is more on quality ground than access cost ground. **(2)** The odds favouring *private is chosen on lower access cost ground* over *government is chosen* are 2.99 (=1/0.334292) times higher for *non-regular wage/salaried* class than *other* class. This points out that it is higher access cost (and not lower quality) which is responsible for the rejection of government facilities by the non-*regular wage/salaried* class.

In our discussion on the concept and measurement of health care quality in Section 2, we proposed that all possible dimensions of

Table 14.7

Results of Multinomial Logistic Regression

Number of obs = 1858
F (14,1844) = 5.82
Prob > F = 0.0000

Dmchoice1	rrr	Std. Err.	t	P>t
Dmchoice1 = 1 (private is chosen on lower access cost ground)				
Lnhhmce	1.806651	0.321487	3.32	0.001
Dhhtype1	0.695645	0.178207	–1.42	0.157
Dhhtype2	0.334292	0.108566	–3.37	0.001
Dhhtype3	0.573634	0.230244	–1.38	0.166
Dillnat	0.593083	0.130788	–2.37	0.018
Dsector	0.851274	0.203156	–0.67	0.5
Dsex	0.845636	0.171039	–0.83	0.407
Dmchoice1 = 2 (private is chosen on better quality ground)				
Lnhhmce	2.622054	0.565871	4.47	0
Dhhtype1	1.155649	0.356547	0.47	0.639
Dhhtype2	0.683452	0.261943	–0.99	0.321
Dhhtype3	0.924659	0.421607	–0.17	0.864
Dillnat	1.461851	0.357928	1.55	0.121
Dsector	0.76786	0.217286	–0.93	0.351
Dsex	0.633171	0.145972	–1.98	0.048

Note: Dmchoice1 = 0 (the ill individual sought treatment from government facility is the base for comparison).
Source: Estimated from NSS 52

quality can be reduced to two broad dimensions/aspects: the technical dimension and the functional dimension. NSS 52 Data does not allow us to examine individual's response to these two types of components separately. The recent National Family Health Survey (NFHS 2) gives us some information about these two dimensions of quality. The Data shows that 49.95 per cent of the women in rural areas and 45.72 per cent of the women in urban areas have visited a health facility in last 12 months. The data also shows that the share of government sector in total care are 49.58 per cent and 42.35 per cent for the rural and urban sectors respectively (IIPS 2001). As expected and observed in case of NSS 52 Data utilisation of government facility comes down when we move from lower economic status to higher economic status (Table 14.8). We have taken the standard of living index constructed by NFHS 2 as measures of economic status (See Appendix 14A.1 (A1)).[13] The NFHS 2 estimates of government utilisation is much higher compared to the NSS 52 estimates. This does not necessarily inconsistency in comparison to NSS 52 Data, since NFHS 2 covers care related to family planning, immunisation and child birth and people's dependence on government for these types of care may be higher compared to other types of care.

Table 14.8

Utilisation of Government and Private Facilities

	Rural		*Urban*	
	Poor	*Rich*	*Poor*	*Rich*
Government	53.04	35.96	65.12	31.59
Private	46.96	74.04	34.88	68.41

Source: NFHS 2

Based on the information collected on four quality-related questions, we have created four categorical variables depending upon the questions asked. They are *time, talk, privacy and clean*. The variable *time* shows whether the respondent feels that the health staff spent sufficient time with her. The variable *Talk* shows whether the respondent feels that health staff talked to her nicely or somewhat nicely. *Privacy* shows whether the respondent feels that her need for privacy was respected, in case privacy was needed. The variable *clean* shows whether the individual feels the facility was clean or somewhat clean. According to our classification of dimensions of perceived quality, *time* belongs to the technical dimension and *talk, privacy* and *clean* belong to the functional dimension. Sufficient time spent by the health staff could make the individual confident about the technical competence of the health staff. Higher technical competence gives expectation of better outcome. The functional dimensions like *talk, privacy* and *clean* do not generally contribute to expected health outcome, but they contribute to the individual's satisfaction with the care.

---

13. By rich and poor women we mean women with high and low values of standard of living index respectively.

The figures on the percentage of women who have reported positive responses on these four dimensions of quality are presented in Table 14.9. Data shows that the percentage of women who reported that the health staff at the government facilities had spent sufficient time is substantially higher for the higher economic status compared to the lower economic status. In case of private care, the percentage of women who reported that the health staff had spent sufficient time with them does not vary much across economic status.

Table 14.9

Percentage of Women Reported Positive Responses on Four Dimensions of Quality

Dimensions of Quality	*Rural*				*Urban*			
	Poor		*Rich*		*Poor*		*Rich*	
	Govt.	*Private*	*Govt.*	*Private*	*Govt.*	*Private*	*Govt.*	*Private*
Time	75.01	93.96	88.01	96.72	68.98	92.19	89.25	95.01
Talk	95.89	99.35	100	100	92.77	100	97.94	99.048
Privacy	12.22	27.17	24.39	33.76	13.05	18.04	22.27	52.17
Clean	97.66	99.01	94.07	98.33	98.21	100	100	97.88

Note: Time = percentage of women who reported that the health staff spent sufficient time; Talk = percentage of women who reported that health staff talked to them nicely or somewhat nicely; Privacy = percentage of women who reported that their need for privacy was respected in case it was required; and Clean = the percentage of women who reported.

Source: NFHS 2.

An individual's judgement about whether a health staff had spent sufficient time depends on her perception of sufficient time and obviously subjective in nature because it is affected by her characteristics. For example, an educated or rich women's expectation about consultation time can be quite different from that of a poor or less educated women. Expectations also vary depending on the facility one uses. A woman may expect lengthier consultation time if she visits a private facility compared to a situation when she visits a government facility. In other words, expectation also varies depending upon the type of the facility, the women's level of awareness, economic status etc. We have estimated a logit model to examine how the responses on sufficiency of time vary across economic status and type of providers after controlling for education and sector (see Appendix 14A.1 (A5) for variable definitions). The results of the logit regression are presented in Table 14.10. The results show that the variables *Dedu2*, *Dedu3* and *Dfacility* are significant at less than 1 per cent less than 5 per cent and less than 1 levels respectively. The odd ratios for the higher educated women are significantly higher than one. The possibility of stronger correlation between standard of living and education level of women warns us not to give much emphasise on the sign and magnitude of the respective coefficients. But the coefficient of *Dfacility* is expected and noteworthy. The odds favouring 'health staff spent sufficient time' are 5.27 time higher for private facilities than other facilities.

Table 14.10

Results of Logistic Regression

Number of obs = 2095
F (7,2088) = 18.54
Prob > F = 0.0000

Dtime	*Coeff.*	*Odd ratio*	*Std. Err.*	*t*	*P>t*	*Mean*
Dssli1	–0.06339	0.9386	0.166126	–0.38	0.703	0.4740
Dssli2	0.390277	1.4774	0.336536	1.16	0.246	0.1656
Dedu1	–1.65E-01	0.8479	0.174774	–0.95	0.344	0.2425
Dedu2	0.542921	1.7210	0.203336	2.67	0.008	0.3041
Dedu3	0.840159	2.3167	0.402985	2.08	0.037	0.0945
Dfacility	1.662215	5.2710	0.168666	9.86	0	0.5575
Dsector	–0.18897	0.8278	0.159847	–1.18	0.237	0.4267
_cons	1.05789	2.8803	0.122829	8.61	0	1

Source: Estimated from NFHS 2

Let us again consider the functional aspect of quality (presented in Table 14.9). As far as the variable talk is concerned, the percentage of women who reported that health staff had talked to them nicely or somewhat nicely, varies considerably across economic status for government care. In case of government care, the percentage of women who reported that health staff had talked to them nicely or somewhat nicely is lower for lower economic status compared to the higher economic status. This kinds of variations is not of considerable magnitude in case of private care.

In case of 'privacy', percentage of women who reported that their need for privacy was respected (in case privacy was required) is highest for the private compared to the government for women of both lower and higher economic status. There is also evidence of higher discrimination at government facility on privacy ground against the women of lower economic status.

If cleanliness of the facility is an important element of functional quality, a richer women are expected to choose a health facility (preferably in private) with better cleanliness. Since richer are expected to choose high cost private facilities with better cleanliness, a comparison between lower and higher economic status is not possible for private care. But the comparison can be, to some extent, meaningful in case of government care, if we assume that government facilities are more-or-less homogeneous on cleanliness aspect if it is measured in an objective manner. In that case a rich woman's satisfaction with the cleanliness of government facilities is expected to lower than that of a poor woman. In other words, the percentage of women reported that government facility was clean is expected to be lower for the women belonging to the higher economic status compared to the women belonging to the lower economic status. While rural areas shows the expected pattern, in case of urban areas the evidence is just the opposite.

Throughout our analysis we have assumed that direct price does not play any significant role in the choice of out-patient health care and tried to explain the difference in choice in terms of differences in access cost and perception about the quality of care. Although most of the studies found (Akin and others 1984; Schwartz, Akin and Popkin 1988; Birdsall and Chuhan 1986; Heller 1982) the effect of direct price on choice either insignificant or very weak, there are a few studies (Mwabu 1986, 1988; Gertler, Locay and Sanderson 1987; Alderman and Gertler 1988; Cretin and others 1988) which show that direct price has significant effect on choice. However, most of the studies show that distance and/or time price is an important factor as far as choice of care is concerned. It is reasonable to argue that direct price is not important when it constitutes a small proportion of income, but it becomes more and more important as the share of direct price in total income becomes large and large (for example in-patient care).

6. Conclusion

Our findings question the argument put forward by proponents of health sector reforms that price hike associated with quality improvement would not have negative impact on utilisation of health care. Based on our approach to quality measurement, the evidence from NSS 52 Data shows that it is the higher access cost and not poor quality which is responsible for lower utilisation of government facilities for individuals from all economic status. The evidence shows that the relative importance of quality over access costs gets stronger as one moves from lower to higher economic status. The evidence also shows that access cost is higher for the people who are poor or in the unorganised sector, because the major determinant of access cost is the nature of employment which is beyond scope of health sector reforms. Regarding functional aspect of quality, NFHS 2 Data indicates evidence of discrimination on the basis of economic status in the government facilities. As far as consultation time element of technical quality is concerned, NFHS 2 shows that private facilities are better than government facilities.

APPENDIX 14A.1

A1: Construction of Standard of Living Index in NFHS 2

The standard of living index is calculated by adding up the following scores: (a) Household type: 4 for *pucca*, 2 for semi-*pucca*, 0 for *Kachha*. (b) Toilet facility: 4 for own flush toilet, 2 for public or shared flush toilet or own pit toilet, 1 for shared or public pit toilet, 0 for no facility. (c) Source of lighting: 2 for electricity, 1 for kerosene, gas or oil, 0 for other source of lighting. (d) Main fuel for cooking: 2 for electricity, liquid petroleum gas, or biogas, 1 for coal, charcoal, or kerosene, 0 for other fuel. (d) Source of drinking water: 2 for pipe, hand pump or well in residence/yard/plot, 1 for public tap, hand pump, or well, 0 for other water source. (e) Ownership of house: 2 for yes, 0 for no. (f) Ownership of agricultural land: 4 for 5 acres or more, 3 for 2.0-4.9, 2 for less than 2 acres or acreage not known, 0 for no agricultural land. (g) Ownership of irrigated land: 2 if owns at least some irrigated land, 0 for no irrigated land. (h) Ownership of livestock: 2 if owns live stock, 0 if does not own livestock. (I) ownership of durable goods: 4 for each car or tractor, 3 each for a moped/scooter/motorcycle, telephone, refrigerator, or colour television, 2 each for a bicycle, electric fan, radio/transistor, sewing machine, black and white television, water pump, bullock cart, or thresher, 1 each for mattress, pressure cooker, chair, cot/bed, table, or clock/watch.

Index score ranges from 0-14 for a low SLI to 15-24 for a medium SLI to 25-67 for a high SLI. (International Institute for Population Sciences 2001, p29).

A2: Dmchoice = 0 if the ill individual did not seek any care; = 1 if the ill individual sought treatment from government facility; = 2 if the ill individual sought treatment from private facility. Dhhtype1 = 1 if the individual belongs to a self-employed household category; = 0 if otherwise. Dhhtype2 = 1 if the individual belongs to a regular wage or salaried household category; = 0 otherwise. Dhhtype3 = 1 if the individual belongs to 'others' household category; = 0 if otherwise. Dsex = 1 if male; = 0 if female. Dsector = 1 if urban; = 0 if rural. Dnatill = 1 if the illness is of chronic type; = 0 if the illness is of acute type.

A3: The relative risk ratio (rrr) resembles the odds ratios of the logistic regression. The relative risk ratio for category j of y and predictor X_k (rrr_{jk}) equals the amount by which the predicted odds favouring y = j (compared with y = base) are multiplied per 1 unit increase in x_k, other things being equal. In other words, the relative risk ratio rrr_{jk} is such that if all x variables except x_k stay the same,

rrr_{jk} * P(y = j | x_k) / P(y = base | x_k) = P(y = j | x_{k+1}) / P(y = base | x_{k+1}) [Hamilton 2003].

A4: Dmchoice2 = 0 if the ill individual sought treatment from government facility; = 1 if the ill individual sought treatment from private facility on lower access cost ground; = 2 if the ill individual sought treatment from private facility on better quality ground.

A5: Dtime = 1 if the health staff had spent sufficient time; = 0 if the health staff did not spend sufficient time. Dsslil = 1 if the standard of living index is medium; = 0 if otherwise. Dssli2 = 1 if standard of living index is high; = 0 otherwise. Dedu1 = 1 if education is primary; = 0 otherwise. Dedu2 = 1 if education is secondary; = 0 otherwise. Dedu3 = 1 if education is higher; = 0 otherwise

Dfacility = 1 if private facility was utilised; = 0 if government facility was utilised. Dsector = 1 if the sector is urban; = 0 if the sector is rural.

References

Acton (1975). "Non-monetary Factors in the Demand for Medical Services: Some Empirical Evidence", *Journal of Political Economy*, 83(3): 595- 614.

Akin, J., C. Griffin, D. Guilkey and B. Popkin (1986). "The Demand for Primary Health Care Services in the Bicol Region of Philippines", *Economic Development and Cultural Change*, 34(4): 755-82.

Akin, J.S., C. Griffin, D.K. Guilkey and B.M. Popkin (1984). *The Demand for Primary Health Care in the Third World*, Totowa, NJ Littlefield, Adams.

Alderman, H. and P. Gertler (1988). *The Substitutability of Public and Private Medical Providers for the Treatment of Children's Illnesses in Urban Pakistan*, International Food Policy Research Institute, Washington DC.

Anderson, E. and L. Zwelling (1996). "Strategic Service Quality Management for Health Care", *American Journal of Medical Quality*, Spring.

Arrow, K.J. (1963). "Uncertainty and the Welfare Economics of Medical Care", *The American Economic Review*, 53(5): 941-73.

Birdsall N. and P. Chuhan (1986). *Client Choice of Health Treatment in Rural Mali*, World Bank, Washington DC.

Bushshur, R., C. Metzern and C. Worder, (1967). "Consumer Satisfaction with Group Practice", *American Journal of Public Health*, 57: 1991-1999.

Cambell, S.M., M.O. Roland and S.A. Buetow (2000). "Defining Quality of Care", *Social Science and Medicine*, 51: 1611-1625.

Christianson, J.B. (1976). "Evaluating Location for Outpatient Medical Facilities", *Land Economics*, 52 (3): 299-313.

Codman, E. (1920). *A Study of Hospital Efficiency*, Moston Mass: Thomas Todd Co.

Cretin, K. and E.B. Keeler, A.P. Williams and Y. Shi (1988). *Factors Affecting Town-Countryside Differences in the Use of Health Services in Two Rural Countries in Sichuan*, Rand Corporation, Santa Monica, Calif.

Donabedian A. (1966). "Evaluating the Quality of Medical Care", *Milbank Memorial Quarterly*, 44, 166-203.

Donabedian A. (1980). *Exploration in Quality Assessment and Monitoring, Vol 1: Definition of Quality and Approaches to its Assessment*, Ann Arbor, MI: Health Administration Press.

Donabedian, A. (2000). "Evaluating Physician Competence", *Bulletin of the World Health Organisation*, 78(6): 857 – 860.

Donaldson, M.S. (1999). *Measuring the Quality of Health Care*, National Academy Press.

Gertler, P. and J. van der Gaag (1988). "Measuring the Willingness to Pay for Social Services in Developing Countries", *Living Standard Measurement Working Paper* 45, World Bank, Washington D.C.

Gertler, P., L. Locay and W. Sanderson (1987). "Are User Fees Regressive? The Welfare Implications of Health Care Financing Proposal in Peru", *Journal of Econometrics*, 36 (Supp.): 67-88.

Grossman, M. (1972). "On the Concept of Health Capital and the Demand for Health", *Journal of Political Economy*, 80: 223-255.

Gupta, I. and P. Dasgupta (2000). "Demand for Curative Health Care in Rural India: Choosing Between Private, Public and No Care", *Working Paper*, Institute of Economic Growth, New Delhi.

Haddad, S., P. Fournier, N. Machouf and F. Yatara (1998). "What Does Quality Mean to Lay People? Community Perceptions of Primary Heath Care Services in Guinea", *Social Science and Medicine*, 47(3): 381-94.

Hamilton, L.C. (2003). *Statistics with STATA*, Wodsworth Group/Thomson Learning, Belmont, USA.

Heller, P. (1982). "A Model on the Demand for Medical and Health Services in Peninsular Malaysia", *Social Science and Medicine*, 16: 267-84.

Institute of Medicine (1990). *A Strategy for Quality Assurance* (editor K N Lohr), National Academy Press, Washington DC.

International Institute for Population Sciences (2001). *National Family Health Survey 1998-99: West Bengal*, IIPS, Mumbai

Koran, L.M. (1975a). "The Reliability of Clinical Methods, Data and Judgements: Part I", *New England Journal of Medicine*, 293: 642 – 646.

Koran, L.M. (1975b). "The Reliability of Clinical Methods, Data and Judgements: Part I", *New England Journal of Medicine*, 293: 695 – 701.

Mwabu, G., M. Ainsworth and A. Nyamete (1993). "Quality of Medical Care and Choice of Medical Treatment in Kenya: An Empirical Analysis", *Journal of Human Resources*, 28(4): 838-62.

Mwabu, G. (1986). "Health Care Decisions at the Household Level: Results of Health Survey in Kenya", *Social Science and Medicine*, 22 (3):313-19.

Mwabu, G. (1988). *Conditional Logit Analysis of Household Choice of Medical Treatments in Rural Villages in Kenya*, Kenyatta University, Department of Economics, Nairobi.

Payson, S. (1994). *Quality Measurement in Economics: New Perspective on the Evolution of Goods and Services*, Edward Elger, Aldershot.

Roemer, M.I. and C. Montoya-Aguilar (1988). *Definition of Quality*, World Health Organisation, Geneva.

Sahn, D.E., S.D., Younger and G. Genicot (2002). "The Demand for Health Care Services in Rural Tanzania." (Source: http://www. Aris.ss.uci.edu/ggenicot/Tanzania.pdf. Forthcoming in *Oxford Bulletin of Economics and Statistics* with a new title "Demand Elasticities for Health Service Providers in Tanzania")

Schwartz, J.B., J.S. Akin, and B.M. Popkin (1988). "Price and Income Elasticities of Demand for Modern Health Care: The Case of Infant Delivery in Phillipines", *The World Bank Economic Review* 2(1): 49-76.

Sen, A. (1987). *The Standard of Living*, Cambridge University Press, Cambridge.

Thomas, D., V. Lavy and J. Strauss (1991). "Public Policy and Anthropometric Outcome in the Cote d'Ivoire", *Centre Discussion Paper No 643*, Economic Growth Centre, Yale University.

Wouters, A., O. Adeyi and R. Morrow (1993). *Quality of Health Care and its Role in Cost Recovery*, UG Agency for International Development, Washington DC.

15

Economic and Social Benefits of Micro-Finance Programmes

An Econometric Analysis

D. RAJASEKHAR
S. MADHESWARAN

1. Introduction

Micro-finance implies providing poor people in rural and urban areas, especially women, with savings and credit facilities for setting up or expanding business, for investing in self-employment activities and for increasing household security. In India, micro-finance programmes are becoming increasingly popular. The popularity of these programmes[1] has been, in part, because of the belief that they will lead to economic and social benefits in the following manner:

- Lending to the poor is considered to be costly and risky because of their low savings propensities and inability to provide collateral. Micro-finance groups, however, can target the poor better as the joint liability compels these groups to be small and homogenous[2] so that the members have

1. Since the early 1990s, NABARD has been linking SHGs formed by the NGOs, banks and government to formal banking institutions through Bank-SHG linkage programme. Rashtriya Mahila Kosh was set up in 1993 as part of the Department of Women and Child Development to provide credit facility to the NGOs working with micro-finance groups. Between 1993 and 1999, it provided 57.62 crore to 349,752 women in micro-finance groups formed by 688 NGOs and other organisations (DWCD 2000). Commercial banks, Regional Rural Banks and co-operatives also started to form the SHGs (consisting mostly of women) and channel the credit under priority sector lending to members in these groups. Although the aggregate picture on the efforts by the formal banks is not available, the indications are that the banks have found micro-finance groups as viable instruments for lending to the poor and meeting the priority sector lending targets.
2. Important requirements to ensure that the group members undertake collective action to further the interest of members as a whole (Olsen 1965). However, larger and heterogeneous groups can do well if the incentive system is not distorted (Rajasekhar 1996).

incentives to participate in selection, monitoring and ensuring the repayment of loans (Stiglitz 1990). This implies that the groups can be formed for the poorest as the households with similar characteristics (savings capacity, credit needs, etc.) actually contribute to their success.

- Micro-finance programmes enable the poor to save. Until about the late-1980s, savings mobilisation had not been given emphasis on the assumption that the poor could not save. The studies, however, argue that if the institutions provide demand-oriented (conveniently located facilities and flexible accounts) savings products, the poor will contribute savings (Vogel 1994; Fiebig *et al.* 1999 and Rutherford 1999). Savings mobilisation (focusing on voluntary savings as well) has been emphasised in micro-finance programmes (Morduch 1999). The growing amount of savings improves the confidence among members in investing and expanding the existing Income Generating Activities (IGAs), and household income security.
- As the amount of members' savings at the disposal of the group increases, the member households can withdraw savings or take credit for consumption, which leads to reduced dependence on the moneylenders, food security, and enhanced access to health and education. This helps the poor to have confidence in investing on IGAs as the access to consumption credit frees them from uncertainties of how to meet the consumption emergencies.
- Micro-finance groups improve access of the poor to credit. Lending to a group member is less risky because of peer selection, which, in turn, takes care of problems posed by adverse selection (Ghatak 1999).
- Access to production credit enables them to undertake IGAs through which poverty can be reduced (Rajasekhar 2000 and 2002). The credit to the poor households in a group is considered to be less risky because of peer monitoring. The borrowers in each group have the ability to enforce contracts between each other, and they jointly decide which type of activities to undertake (Stiglitz 1990). Through exploiting the ability of the neighbours to enforce contracts and monitor

each other, the micro-finance groups can offer low interest rates on loans and raise repayment rates.

- Credit for women to undertake IGAs enables them to have access to resources and income. This may lead to enhanced decision-making within the household, and thereby, enable them to spend the income on health, education, consumption, etc. Women involved in IGAs have to interact with markets (for both buying and selling) located near and far from their homes. This implies improved mobility for women. Such mobility gradually enables them to play an active role in social, political and economic issues affecting self, household and community. In this, people's institutions promoted by NGOs would give them a helping hand. Thus, micro-finance leading to income generating activities would contribute to women's empowerment.
- Repayment rates are expected to be high in micro-finance groups having dynamic incentives such as each successful repayment leads to larger loan amount (Besley 1995). This improves the information between the group and members (thus screening out the worst borrowers before the loan size is increased), and contributes larger loan amounts and higher repayment. Repayment is also expected to be higher because group lending programmes influence the members to commit weekly or monthly repayment immediately after a loan is disbursed. Regular repayments give early warnings on emerging problems, screen out undisciplined borrowers, and allow the group to get hold of cash flows before they are consumed or otherwise diverted. Repayment rates are known to be high despite that no explicit collateral exists in the group. These groups go for collateral substitutes such as savings linked to credit and group assurance on repayment. High repayment in micro-finance groups implies higher potential for financial sustainability and ability to serve the poor in the long run.
- It is believed that the micro-finance programmes will help the rural poor to address the problems of the poor in undertaking IGAs such as inadequate access to skills, raw-materials and marketing. Since these groups consist of people with similar

characteristics, they realise the need to pressurise the system for changes in policies and delivery mechanisms through lobbying and advocacy (Olsen 1965). The federations of micro-finance groups (at *gram panchayat*, *taluk* and project levels) help the poor not only in negotiating with the market and other suppliers of the critical inputs but also in accessing them at reduced costs. Through appropriate inputs aimed at building the capacity, such groups can access the services (extension, subsidised inputs, etc.) from other development actors such as line departments. The rural poor also learn how to select viable and feasible IGAs, and acquire skills on business operations.

- The IGAs enable women to have access to income, and enhanced decision-making on health, education, consumption, etc. Women also interact with outside markets and the community, and this process gradually enables them to play an active role in social, political and economic issues affecting self, household and the community (Mayoux 1998).
- The organisations (SHGs, etc.) promoted for the people, especially poor women, enable them to develop leadership qualities, enhance self-management, and facilitate them to be self-reliant. These also strengthen the individual and collective decision-making, and bargaining.
- Regular savings by enabling the people to develop confidence and introducing them to local banks contribute to the improved creditworthiness of the poor. This enables an improved interface between banks and people's institutions.

However, the studies on micro-finance question this optimism. While one group of studies (Hashemi, Schuler and Riley 1996; Puhazhendi and Badatya 2002) argues that micro-finance has very beneficial social and economic impact, others caution against such optimism (Montgomery *et al.* 1996; Goetz and Sen Gupta 1996; Buckley 1997; Rogaly 1996; Mayoux 1998; Rajasekhar 2002a; Kropp and Suran 2002). Other studies suggest beneficial impact of micro-finance programmes, but argue that micro-finance does not assist the poorest (Hulme and Mosley 1996) thus questioning the ability of the programmes to target the poor, to sustain the services provided and to reduce poverty. The studies also note that there are only limited data available on the impact of NGO programmes on poverty and that NGOs' comparative advantage over other service agencies needs to be investigated rather than assumed (Kabeer and Murthy 1996).

In this context, the paper seeks to examine the functioning of micro-finance programmes, and analyse economic benefits (improvement in livelihoods and access to resources) and social benefits (improvement in education levels) of the micro-finance programmes on members in the specific context of two NGO programmes in Karnataka and Andhra Pradesh.

The organisation of the paper is as follows. Section 2 describes sources of data, which consists of profile of the selected districts and NGO's considered in the study. Section 3 deals with empirical results followed by the conclusion and policy implication in the last section.

2. Sources of Data

The data sources for the study were primary data collected from the project areas of two NGOs in Karnataka and Andhra Pradesh, namely, *Grama Vikas* and Sanghamitra Service Society (*Sanghamitra,* hereafter), respectively, with the help of survey method, focus group discussions and semi-structured discussions. In all, 106 households having varying period of membership in micro-finance groups formed the sample. The study considered new entrants into SHGs as a comparison group. Accordingly, the study was conducted in four villages in the two project areas of NGOs. T.N. Halli was selected from the project area of *Grama Vikas,* which had two SHGs, one about 10 year old and the other, formed in 1999. The former was considered as member group, while the latter as the comparison group. Three villages - Bathinapadu, Kothapeta and S. Amaravaram - were selected from the project area of Sanghamitra. Two SHGs in each of the villages of Bathinapadu and Kothapeta were more than nine-year old. Thus, the members in these four groups were considered as belonging to member group. Since these two villages did not have relatively new groups, S. Amaravaram was selected, where two groups had been formed in 1998. The members in these two groups were considered as the comparison group.

2.1 The Profile of the Selected Districts

An important factor contributing to the success of micro-finance is the context in which these programmes are operating. The selected project areas are proximate to the cities. In terms of size, both the districts are more or less similar. The growth rate of population was almost similar and both the districts recorded lower growth rates than the State during the last two decades. There was no significant difference between the districts in the levels of illiteracy excepting that female illiteracy was more in Kolar district. Higher education was also less in Kolar district. A finding common to both the districts was that the youth accounted for larger proportion of the literate as well as highly educated population.

The rainfall is more uneven and uncertain in Kolar district compared to Krishna district. Irrigation facilities have been well developed in Krishna as compared to Kolar. Further, Krishna district has assured irrigation facilities through canals. In Kolar, wells account for over 86 per cent of the total irrigated area. This implies that farmers in Kolar depend on private and expensive form of irrigation. The project areas of both the NGOs are similar in terms of irrigation facilities, and grow dry and rain-fed crops such as groundnut, vegetables, cotton, etc. In both the districts, plantation and horticulture crops are significant.

The agrarian structure in both the districts is characterised by the presence of marginal holdings with concomitant implications for the viability of small farming, and the need for subsidiary occupation.

In general, and also for both males and females, the workforce participation rates were lower in Kolar as compared to Krishna. In both the districts, the youth accounted for a larger proportion of the non-workers. Thus, unemployment was higher among the youth. There were significant differences between the districts as far as the occupational distribution was concerned. The proportion of cultivators was higher in Kolar. On the other hand, agricultural labour and non-farm activities provided employment to a bulk of workforce in Krishna. In both the districts, the feminisation of agricultural labour market was taking place, and non-farm activities were more confined to urban areas, and among men in rural areas. In both the districts, services, small business and small manufacturing were significant non-farm activities.

Banking network was relatively more developed in Krishna with larger bank-branch network and higher level of advances, and, bulk of the credit went for crop production. On the other hand, although a significant proportion of credit went to crop production in Kolar, plantation and horticulture, dairy and other priority sectors were important. Interestingly, these activities were also important in Krishna district although the level was not the same as in Kolar district. A detailed discussion on the factors contributing to the rapid flow of credit to these activities suggests that financial institutions preferred these activities as the infrastructure and marketing facilities were developed for these activities. An added dimension was that these were land based activities, and preferred by the affluent sections in the rural areas, and better off among the poor. As a consequence, the institutional credit agencies did not deliver much credit for start-up enterprises and for those activities, which were needed for the very poor.

Thus, the agrarian structure in both the districts was characterised by the presence of marginal holdings with concomitant implications for the viability of small farming, and the need for subsidiary occupation. This was particularly important since the primary data suggested that it was the households belonging to SC categories in both the districts who were landless and owned tiny landholdings. They were pursuing subsistence agriculture. Though illiteracy was high in these households, one or two persons had completed either school or some college education and were unemployed. The need to provide formal credit to such households for both improving the land productivity and undertaking alternative occupations should have received priority given that these were poor and belonged to depressed castes. However, as the discussion shows the formal banks preferred those activities which were land-based, profitable and offered collateral to the banks. Further, there was no adequate provision for consumption credit. It was because of these reasons that the micro-finance services delivered by the NGOs became very important to the poor.

2.2 The Selected NGOs

The savings and credit programmes of *Grama Vikas* and *Sanghamitra* were evolving over a period of time. The notable changes in the programmes in both the project areas were as follows: (i) The earlier large groups were divided on to small SHGs consisting of about 10-15 members in accordance with changes in the development perspective of the organisation. (ii) In both the project areas, the initial programme was essentially a small savings programme but, it was gradually transformed into somewhat larger savings and credit programme.

In both the programmes, incentives were provided for participating in the programme. Facility to contribute small savings to the group, savings linked to credit, taking attendance into consideration in so far as disbursal of loan and disallowing defaulters to borrow from the group were the same as institutional regulations formulated for running the programme.

The savings programme of *Grama Vikas* was larger than that of *Sanghamitra*. The amount of savings per member was higher in the former as compared to the latter. The lending programme of *Grama Vikas* was also comparatively larger. This was mainly because of the linkages with banks under NABARD's Bank-SHG linkage programme which had been started as early as in 1992 in the district. *Grama Vikas* was one of the first NGOs to participate in the programme. This contributed to an increase in the amount of credit available for the target group.

There were also differences between the NGOs in so far as the management of credit funds was concerned. The systems and procedures relating to people's management of credit operations were more developed in the case of *Grama Vikas*. On the other hand, while people participated in so far as operation of revolving credit fund of SHGs at the village level in the project area of *Sanghamitra* was concerned, the NGO retained decision-making power in the case of fund operated at the NGO level.

The federation of SHGs was developed by *Grama Vikas* and it continued to function in the case of the project area. The federation has been participating in the administration of savings and credit programme, and lobbying/advocating the cause of poor at cluster and project levels. This contributed to the members accessing loans from banks under the Bank-SHG linkage programme and other resources from the government. *Sanghamitra* was planning to form a federation at the time of the survey.

The group members in both the project areas were having access to more than one revolving credit fund, and a particular type of credit need was met by a particular source. While savings fund at the village level was meeting the consumption needs of members (especially in the case of *Grama Vikas*), the federation/banks in the case of *Grama Vikas*, and the NGO in the project area of *Sanghamitra* were meeting the production credit needs.

Another interesting feature was that, at the time of survey, members were showing interest in borrowing for land purchase and house construction and repairs. One can, thus, suggest that the members now have credit sources to meet their survival needs. With loans from savings fund, members are able to access services relating to education and health. With loans from federation and banks, member households are able to stabilise or improve agricultural production and/or start income generation activities. After meeting the survival needs, they are now focusing their attention on reducing the vulnerability through loans obtained for land purchase and house construction/repairs.

3. Empirical Results

The study covered 106 member households of micro-finance groups from the project areas of both the NGOs. Of them, 68 received micro-finance benefits for about eight years, while 38 joined in the micro-finance groups only a year prior to fieldwork. Throughout this paper, the former is referred as member group and the latter as comparison group.

Most of the sample members belonged to SC/ST and backward caste households. Further, they belonged to either landless or marginal farmer categories. All of them were women and illiterate. The proportion of widows and separated ranged across the project areas; overall, they formed 10 per cent of the total members. Most of them belonged to the age group of 30 to 40 years.

The sample members have been contributing savings to their group. In both the project areas, the monthly amount of savings contributed was Rs. 40. The average amount of savings in the project area of *Grama Vikas* was higher at Rs. 2,547 as compared to *Sanghamitra* at Rs. 2,239. There were substantial differences in the average amount of savings between member and comparison groups. Further, those in the comparison group had used only SHG as the source of savings, while those in the member group used a wide variety of savings sources such as SHGs, banks, insurance companies.

The sample member households in both the project areas have been accessing credit from their groups. In *Grama Vikas* project area, the average number of loans to a member was four during the period 1992-1999. There was no size class-wise difference in the access to credit from the SHG. The landless household in the member group accessed the maximum number of loans. The average amount obtained by each member was Rs. 17,893 during the reference period. The household, which accessed the maximum amount of loan, belonged to small farmer category. In the project area of *Sanghamitra*, members, on an average, obtained four loans and Rs. 11,490 during the period 1994 to 1999. Thus, the members in the project area of *Sanghamitra* obtained less loan amount as compared to those in *Grama Vikas* due to the following. The amount of loanable funds available in the programme of the latter was high due to linkages established between SHGs and banks under NABARD linkage banking programme.

The purpose-wise distribution of loans and loan amount shows that the activities of livestock and agriculture accounted for most of the loan amount in the project area of *Grama Vikas*. In the project area of *Sanghamitra*, the consumption and income generation activities accounted for most of the loan amount. While income generation activities were livestock and agriculture, and consumption loans were taken for construction of toilets, purchase of gas stoves, etc.

Table 15.1

Mean Total Income (in Rs.)

Grama Vikas	34,069
Sanghamitra	26,454
Memgroup	30,979
Compgroup	23,567
Non SC/ST	34,688
SC/ST	26,842
One occupation	19,198
Two occupations	30,245
Three occupations	27,665

The access to credit from SHGs enabled the members to undertake income generation activities and diversify the occupational base. This also enabled them to have higher income. Table 15.1 shows that the average income of households in the member group was higher at Rs. 30,979 as compared to that in the case of comparison group (Rs. 23,566). The qualitative evidence shows that the households which were suffering from problems of survival when they joined in the micro-finance group passed through this phase, and were having security (Box 15.1).

Box 15.1

From Survival to Security

Magbulbee, a 35-year old illiterate woman, was separated from her husband and was living in a small hut with her daughter, mother, sister (also separated) and niece. She was married at a young age to an agricultural labourer. After the birth of a female child, her husband became interested in his niece, and ran away with her. Outraged by this incident, Magbulbee lodged a complaint. Her husband, who was angry, returned to the village, and frequently quarrelled and tortured her. Village leaders intervened, and thrashed him. After this incident, her husband left the village and did not return. Magbulbee stayed with her mother-in-law, and was receiving financial support from maternal home. The village leaders advised her to stay with her parents since they found that there was no security for her in her husband's house. She came to her native place with her daughter. She could not stay there for a long time due to lack of house, and migrated to T.N. Halli in search of work. Magbulbee passed through a phase of vulnerability until she joined the SHG in 1992. She contributed small sums of Rs. 10 to 20 per month from the wage income. She made use of the opportunities available in the SHG. She took a loan of Rs. 600 in 1993 to purchase two sheep and undertook sheep rearing as supplementary activity. She gradually increased the number of sheep as she was earning profits. In 2000, she had 20 sheep. She also constructed a hut in 1994. In 1996, she purchased a cow with the help of loan taken from the bank under NABARD's bank-SHG linkage programme. She earned Rs. 18,720 from milk selling in 2000. The main source of income for the family is livestock, followed by income from sheep and wages.

The qualitative evidence also shows that the members with increased income have been sending their children including girls to schools. The proportion of literate to total members was higher in the case of households belonging to the member group. There were instances where members fought with their spouses to admit girl children in the college (Box 15.2).

Box 15.2

Augustine's Fight to Educate Her Daughter

Augustine, aged around 45 years, is an illiterate member of the oldest SHG in Bathinapadu village. She could not get education because of poverty of her parents, and was married at an early age. She learnt how to put her signature in the group. She stated that the importance of education became very evident after joining the group. As she was holding a leadership position in the group, she was required to travel to government offices to obtain resources for the group. She could not read the destination of buses, felt very handicapped in her interactions with officials (who would often say what do you illiterate know of government rules and regulations) and in undertaking leadership responsibilities. She, therefore, harboured the idea of providing good education to her daughter. When her daughter completed school education, her husband started to suggest that she be discontinued from studies and married off. Augustine put her foot down, and declared that she would provide education whatever may be the consequences. Her husband also became adamant and declared that he would not support her (both financially and in other respects) in admitting the daughter into the college. Augustine discussed the matter with group members, obtained a loan to admit her in the college and has been supporting her in education only through her own earnings. When this was being discussed, Augustine's husband was also there, and was still defending his position.

Notwithstanding this qualitative information, Table 15.1 shows that the average income differed across the project areas and among SC/ST and non-SC/ST categories. Further, the membership in micro-finance groups did not always result in members having larger number of occupations. A few of the members have had as many as five occupations while others had only one. Depending on the number of occupations, the income also differed. As noted in the introductory section, the literature notes that micro-finance benefits are not always equal to all the members in a group.

In this context, the determinants of household income, household savings, proportion of literate to total members in the household and diversification of occupation are analysed. The main variables along with details on measurement and descriptive statistics are listed in Table 15.2.

3.1 Determinants of Household Income

We found that the semi-log functional form was better than non-log form to estimate the determinants of household income. In order to justify the semi-log specification, we have tested the distribution of residuals for normality. The validity of the t-test and F-test also depended upon a normal distribution. The histogram of the distribution of the residuals for both semi-logarithmic and linear specifications was standardised by standard error of regression. If we look at Figure 15.1, the residuals are more close to normal probability curve in the case of semi-logarithmic specification. The results support the assumption that the appropriate regress and is natural logarithm of total household income.

Figure 15.1

Normal P-P Plot of Regression Standardised Residual Dependent Variable: Total Income of Households

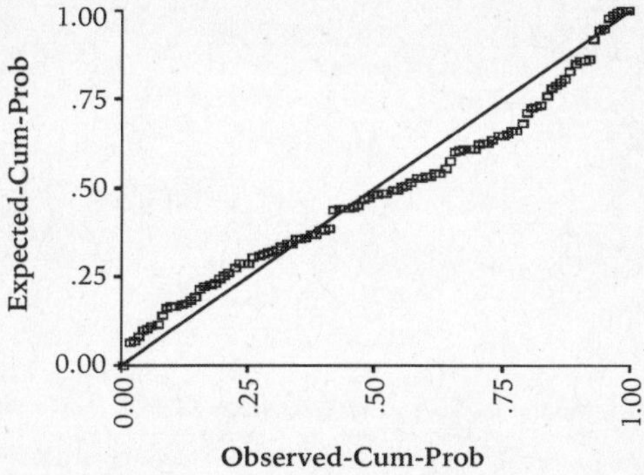

Figure 15.2

Normal P-P Plot Regression Standarised Residual Dependent Variable: LNINC

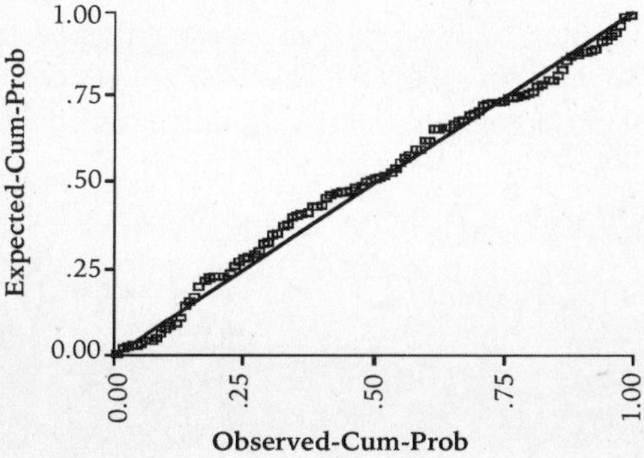

Table 15.2

Measurement and Descriptive Statistics of Main Variables

Variable	*Description*	*Mean*	*Standard Deviation*
TINC	Total Annual Household Income	28322.14	2875.18
LOAN	Loan obtained	8254.94	8909.08
LHOLD	Land holdings (in acres)	1.77	3.22
EDN	Education (in years)	1.64	1.91
PROJECT	1=Grama Vikas; 0 otherwise	0.25	0.43
MEMGROUP	1=Member group; 0 otherwise	0.64	0.48
SCST	1=Individual belongs to SC/ST; 0 otherwise	0.81	0.39
OCC2	1=Individuals having two occupations; 0 otherwise	0.42	0.50
OCC3	1=Individuals having three or more occupations; 0 otherwise	0.18	0.38
N = Number of observations		106	

In this model, the total income of household is the dependent variable and project area, member group, caste, occupation, loan obtained, land holding and education are the explanatory variables. The estimated equation is as follows:

$$\ln Y = \beta_1 + \beta_2 \text{project} + \beta_3 \text{Memgroup} + \beta_4 \text{scst} + \beta_5 \text{Occ2} + \beta_6 \text{Occ3}$$
$$+ \beta_7 \text{Loan} + \beta_8 \text{Lhold} + \beta_9 \text{Edn} + U$$

The results on determinants of household income are reported in Table 15.3.

The results show that the variable PROJECT is positive and significant at 5 per cent level. This indicates that the households from *Grama Vikas* project area were having 61 per cent of more income as compared to those from *Sanghamitra*. The coefficient of MEMGROUP is positive and significant. This suggests that membership in a group is likely to increase the household income by 3 per cent. As expected, the coefficient of caste variable negatively influenced the household income. One can infer from this result that non-SC/ST members were favourably placed in so far as obtaining economic benefits from the micro-finance programme was concerned. The members with more than one occupation obtained income higher than those having just one occupation. Hence, number of occupations and the level of income are positively related, which is supported by the regression result. We also found that about 60 per cent of the households in the

Table 15.3

Determinants of Income: OLS Estimates

Dependent Variable = Total Annual Household Income

(in Rupees)

Variable	*Semi-Log Form*		*Non-Log Form*	
	Co-efficient	*t values*	*Co-efficient*	*t values*
PROJECT	0.607	2.174	8326.45	1.99
MEMGROUP	0.0293	1.85	3548.25	1.65
SCST	- 0.513	- 1.848	-6287.00	- 1.72
OCC2	· 0.0822	1.65	1122.12	1.66
OCC3	0.130	1.75	1075.75	1.69
LOAN	0.00026	2.697	0.707	2.39
LHOLD	0.0660	3.26	3247.48	5.39
EDN	0.0443	1.68	613.53	1.65
CONSTANT	10.159		21887.23	
R^2	0.33		0.37	
F	5.98		4.91	
DW	2.00		1.83	
N	106		106	

Note: (1) 1% level of significance 2.58; 5% level of significance 1.96; 10% level of significance 1.65.

(2) Condition index number is less than 10 for all explanatory variables.

member group had access to more than one-livelihood sources. This implies that micro-finance programme enables the households to go for occupational diversification. Since LOAN provides control over the resources and technology, this variable was expected to influence the household income positively. This *a priori* expectation corroborates with the result obtained in this model. *Ceteris Paribus,* higher the size of land holding, higher will be the income of the households. This coincides with our result. It can be, thus, argued that the micro-finance benefits are not significant in the case of members belonging to SC/ST categories even if they have larger landholding. This further implies the prevalence of social exclusion even in the micro-finance programme. The result shows that education also positively influenced the household income. This can be attributed to the fact that education provides better information about the programme to access the livelihoods and other benefits. The R-square value is 0.33, which means 33 per cent of the variations in household's income were explained by the included variables. Further, the whole model is highly significant at 1 per cent level, which rejects the hypothesis that all the slope parameters are zero. Further the DW statistics in the cross-section data shows that there is no specification error in the model.

3.2 Determinants of Total Savings

It is often mentioned in the literature that with increased income, the members of micro-finance groups graduate from the phase of survival to security. The total savings of a household (in monetary terms) has been taken as a variable to indicate the security. In this context, the determinants of total household savings seem to be important. However, since the total income normally corresponds with the total savings, it leads to simultaneity bias. In order to overcome this problem, predicted income has been estimated in the first step and is included as one of explanatory variables (instrumental variable) in the savings equation. The estimated two stage least squares equation is as follows and the results are presented in Table 15.4.

$$\ln Y = \beta_1 + \beta_2 \text{project} + \beta_3 \text{Memgroup} + \beta_4 \text{scst} + \beta_5 \text{Occ2} + \beta_6 \text{Occ3}$$

$$+ \beta_7 Loan + \beta_8 Lhold + \beta_9 Edn + \beta_{10} Pincome + U$$

The results indicate that membership in micro-finance group significantly influenced the total amount of savings. This was possible in two different ways. First, longer the membership more will be the savings. Second, larger the loan amount from SHGs higher would be the savings amount. The latter indicates reciprocity. In other words, if members were confident that they would have reliable credit facility, they did not mind putting their surplus income as savings. The coefficients of occupation, education and income were positively and significantly associated with household savings. As expected, the caste had negative influence on total household savings. Interestingly, although the landholding positively influenced the household savings, lack of statistical significance suggests that this variable was not as significant a variable in determining savings as it was in the case of household income. This also suggests that the landless households also contributed larger amounts of savings.

Table 15.4

Determinants of Savings: Two Stage Least Square Estimates

Dependent Variable = Annual Savings

(in Rupees)

Variable	*Semi-Log Form*		*Non-Log Form*	
	Co-efficient	*t values*	*Co-efficient*	*t values*
PROJECT	0.528	2.25	178.19	1.95
MEMGROUP	2.085	13.45	1917.37	4.12
SCST	- 0.309	- 1.65	- 155.96	- 1.81
OCC2	0.228	2.06	759.40	2.28
OCC3	0.231	1.69	1041.78	2.39
LOAN	0.0003	3.08	0.0980	3.82
LHOLD	0.0211	1.60	20.652	0.357
EDN	0.0165	1.66	54.997	1.68
PREDICTED INCOME	0.0005	1.96	0.0186	2.18
CONSTANT (Pincome)	5.90		424.50	
R^2	0.85		0.60	
F	64.82		16.12	
DW	1.91		2.01	
N	106		106	

Note: (1) 1% level of significance 2.58; 5% level of significance 1.96 10% level of significance 1.65

(2) Condition index number is less than 10 for all explanatory variables

3.3 *Determinants of Social Benefits*

In the literature, it is often mentioned that with years of membership in micro-finance groups and increased income the member households give high priority to education, especially, girl education. Thus, micro-finance programmes contribute to social benefits. The proportion of literate to total number in a household is taken as an indicator of social benefits. Table 15.5, which provides the results on determinants of social benefits, shows that the education of the member significantly and positively influenced the importance given to the education of children in a household. The membership in a group also influenced the literacy levels. However, this was not statistically significant. This suggests that public expenditure on education is far more important than mere membership in micro-finance groups. As was the case in the other regression outputs, loan amount and landholding positively influenced the literacy levels in a household. Finally, the literacy levels were negatively and significantly associated with the caste status of a household.

Table 15.5

Determinants of Social Benefits

Dependent Variable = (Proportion of Literates to Total Number in Household)

Variable	*Co-efficient*	*t values*
PROJECT	4.694	2.41
MEMGROUP	2.186	1.39
SCST	- 15.40	- 1.76
EDN	5.36	4.18
LOAN	0.0004	1.44
LHOLD	0.0800	1.100
CONSTANT	48.55	
R^2	0.299	
F	4.095	
DW	1.924	
N	106	

Note: (1) 1% level of significance 2.58; 5% level of significance 1.96; 10% level of significance 1.65.

(2) Condition index number is less than 10 for all explanatory variables.

3.4 Choice of Diversification of Occupation

The use of probability models is conceptually preferable to conventional linear regression models when the dependent variable is dichotomous, because parameter estimates from the former overcome most weakness of linear probability models, namely, they provide parameter estimates which are asymptotically consistent and efficient. In this paper, a Probit model has been employed to study the determinants of diversified occupation. The general model is a binary choice model involving estimation of the probability of individual having more than one occupation (y) as a function of a vector of explanatory variables (x). It is assumed that there is an underlying response variable y^*_i defined by the regression relationship

$$y_i^* = \beta' x_i + u_i \qquad \ldots(1)$$

In practice, y^*_i is unobservable, what we observe is a dummy variable y defined by

$y = 1$ if $y^*_i > 0$ (having more than one occupation)

$= 0$ *otherwise (having one occupation)* ...(2)

From the above relations, we get

Prob (y_i = having more than one occupation) = Prob ($u_i > -\beta' x_i$)

$= 1 - F(-\beta' x_i)$ ...(3)

Where, F is the cumulative distribution function for u. In this case the observed values of y are just realisations of a binomial process with probabilities given by equation (3) and varying from trial to trail (depending on x_i). Hence, the likelihood function is

$$L = \prod_{y=0} F(-\beta' x_i) \prod_{y=1} [1 - F(-\beta' x_i)] \quad ...(4)$$

Taking the logarithm of L and maximising with respect to β, which gives the ML estimator of slope coefficient. The marginal effect of the slope parameter has been calculated as $\beta\phi(X_i)$ to interpret analogous to that of OLS result.

Table 15.6

Determinants of Diversification of Occupation: Probit Results

Dependent Variable= 1 (if members having more than one occupation); 0 otherwise

Variables	*Coefficient*	*t-values*	*Marginal Effect*
LHOLD	-0.1363*	2.26	0.01888
EDN	0.1766*	-1.96	-0.02445
LOAN	0.6896*	2.07	0.000001
PROJECT	13.2424*	2.03	0.18339
MEMGROUP	1.3331*	2.58	0.1846
SCST	-0.8077*	-1.96	-0.1118
Constant	0.1063		
Log-likelihood		-43.10959	
Restricted log-likelihood			
Chi square (7 df)			
Pseudo R-square			
Number of Observations		106	

Note: *5% level significance

The probit results have been reported in Table 15.6. The results show that an increase in the size of landholding decreases the probability of more diversified sources of income. This can be attributed to the fact that larger landholding reduces the uncertainty of household income. Coefficient of Education is positive and significant at 5 per cent level. This implies that increase in the level of education in terms of years of schooling increases the probability of alternative livelihoods. Since education provides better information about alternative occupations and existing market condition, it helps the members to have choices to undertake alternative occupation with which they can maximise their income to support their households. The coefficients of loan obtained from micro-finance groups, project area and membership are positive and significant, and all of them increase the likelihood of diversified occupation. It is assumed that loan provides the needed liquidity for investment to start the project. Therefore, our results also show that the amount of loan obtained increases the likelihood of diversification of occupation. Since the *Gram Vikas* project area has been implementing integrated programmes, it is helping the members to go for more than one occupation to improve their livelihoods. The results confirm that the micro-finance programmes improve the socio-economic status of the members. Like our previous result, the Non-SC/ST member has more livelihood options than the SC/ST. This conforms that not only in terms of income and saving but also the opportunity of alternative occupation is less for the hitherto neglected SC/ST members.

The highly significant Chi-square and Pseudo R-square (33 per cent) clearly shows that the estimated model is having good fit. The model predicts a high degree of occupational choice. Evaluating the probability of alternative occupation at the mean levels of the explanatory variables, 60 per cent of the households are having more than one livelihood.

4. Conclusions and Policy Implications

Micro-finance programmes are implemented all over the country with the assumption that these programmes would lead to poverty alleviation and empowerment of women members. This paper questions this assumption.

The economic benefits of micro-finance programmes are region specific. The programme did not result in larger amount of loans and income in the project area of *Sanghamitra* for the following reasons.

First, *Sanghamitra* could not facilitate the linkages between SHGs and banks under the NABARD Bank-SHG linkage programme as the policy environment was not favourable. In contrast, *Grama Vikas* facilitated linkages between banks and SHGs, and this resulted in substantial economic benefits to the members. Second, most of the members from the project area of *Sanghamitra* are agricultural labourers having fairly stable employment opportunities all through the year. Consequently, the opportunity cost faced by the agricultural labour households to switch to other occupations was high. Further, those who had undertaken milch animal rearing could not succeed in this activity largely on account of lack of marketing facilities for milk. This discussion leads to the policy conclusion that public investment on marketing facilities and government programmes such as linkage banking are essential if micro-finance programmes are to have significant anti-poverty impact.

The study results show that the loan amount, size of landholding, the number of occupations and education have positively and significantly influenced the economic and social benefits. On the other hand, the caste had negative influence. The results that the micro-finance benefits are not significant in the case of members belonging to landless and SC/ST categories lead to policy implication that micro-finance alone will not lead to poverty alleviation. In addition to micro-finance, other interventions relating to improvement in basic communities, marketing, etc., are important.

Interestingly, the educational level of the mother largely influences the proportion of literate to total members in a household. The membership in a group also influences the literacy levels; but the results are not significant. This suggests that public expenditure on education is far more important than mere membership in micro-finance.

The micro-finance programmes do provide access to credit for the poor and enable them to undertake income generation programmes. Given that the formal banks have not very well succeeded in the past in improving the access to credit for the rural households, the strategy of supporting the formation and nurturing of micro-finance groups is to be supported. However, the responsibilities such as development of marketing infrastructure and providing bank finance to micro-finance groups must be undertaken by the government as the micro-finance programmes cannot alone alleviate poverty.

References

Besley, Timothy (1995). "Savings, Credit and Insurance". In T.N. Srinivasan and Jere Behrman (eds.), *Handbook of Development Economics*, Vol. 3A. Amsterdam: Elsevier.

Buckley, Graeme (1997). "Micro-Finance in Africa: Is it Either the Problem or the Solution?" *World Development*, 25(7).

DWCD (2000). *Annual Report*, 1999-2000. New Delhi: DWCD.

Fiebig, Michael, Alfred Hannig and Sylvia Wisniwski (1999). *Savings in the Context of Micro-Finance – State of Knowledge*. Eschborn: CGAP-BMZ-GTZ.

Ghatak, Maitreesh (1999). "Group Lending, Local Information and Peer Selection". *Journal of Development Economics*, 60.

Goetz, Anne Marie and Rina Sen Gupta (1996). "Who Takes the Credit? Gender, Power and Control Over Loan Use in Rural Credit Programs in Bangladesh". *World Development*, 24(1).

Hashemi, Syed M., Sidney Ruth Schuler and Ann P. Riley (1996). "Rural Credit Programs and Women's Empowerment in Bangladesh". *World Development* 24(4).

Hulme, David and Paul Mosley (1996). *Finance Against Poverty*. London: Routledge.

Kabeer, Naila and R.K. Murthy (1996). "Compensating for Institutional Reclusion? Lessons from Indian Government and Non-Government Credit Interventions for the Poor". *IDS Discussion Paper* No. 356. Brighton: IDS.

Kropp, Erhard W. and B.S. Suran (2002). *Linking Banks and Self Help Groups in India: An Assessment*. Bombay: NABARD.

Mayoux, Linda (1998). "Women's Empowerment and Micro-Finance Programs: Approaches, Evidence and Ways Forward". *Discussion Paper.* Milton Keynes: The Open University.

Montgomery, R., D. Bhattacharya and D. Hulme (1996). "Credit for Poor in Bangladesh: The BRAC Rural Development Program and the Government Thana Resource Development and Employment Program". In Hulme and Mosley (1996).

Morduch, Jonathan (1999). "The Micro-Finance Promise". *Journal of Economic Literature*, XXXVII.

Olsen, Mancur (1965). *The Logic of Collective Action: Public Goods and the Theory of Groups*. Cambridge, MA: Harvard University Press.

Puhazhendi, V. and K.C. Badatya (2002). *Self-Help Group Bank Linkage Program for Rural Poor in India: An Impact Assessment*. Bombay: NABARD.

Rajasekhar, D. (1996). "Problems and Prospects of Group Lending in NGO Credit Programmes in India". *Savings and Development*, 20(1): 79-104.

———. (2000). "Non-Governmental Organisations (NGOs) in India: Opportunities and Challenges". *Working Paper No. 66*. Bangalore: Institute for Social and Economic Change.

———. (2002a). "Impact of Micro-Finance Programs on Poverty and Gender Equality: Some Evidence from Indian NGOs". In Shahra Razavi (ed.) *Shifting Burdens: Gender and Agrarian Change under Neoliberalism*. Blomfield: Kumarian Press, Inc.

Rogaly, Ben (1996). "Micro-finance Evangelism, Destitute Women' and the Hard Selling of New Anti-Poverty Formula". *Development in Practice*, 6 (2).

Rutherford, Stuart (1999). "The Poor and Their Money - An Essay about Financial Services for Poor People". *Finance and Development Research Project*. Manchester: University of Manchester, Institute for Development Policy and Management.

Stiglitz, J.E. (1990). 'Peer Monitoring and Credit Markets'. *The World Bank Economic Review*, 4 (3).

Vogel, R.C. (1994). "Savings Mobilisation: The Forgotten Half of Rural Finance". In D.W. Adams, D. Graham and J.D. Von Pischke (eds.), *Undermining Rural Development with Cheap Credit*. Boulder: Westview Press.

16

Repayment Performance of a Random Rosca in West Bengal

SAMAPTI GUHA
GAUTAM GUPTA

1. Introduction

Lending to the poor through peer groups has become an increasingly popular mode of poverty alleviation and income generation. The success of the Grameen Bank in providing credit to rural poor in Bangladesh through group lending has fostered numerous *Grameen*-style replications around the world. Theory emphasises that Micro-Credit programmes have overcome screening, monitoring and repayment problems faced by formal sector banking institutions through the process of joint liability lending. The success of Micro-Credit programmes depends on the repayment performance of the group. Several stylised models have been developed to capture some of the dynamics that prevail within these groups. Besley and Coate (1995) investigate the impact of group lending on repayment rates, where the members are made jointly liable for repayment. Their analysis suggests that one (positive) effect of these schemes is that successful borrowers may repay the loans on behalf of peers who obtain sufficiently poor returns. A negative effect arises if the entire group (or a substantially large section) defaults. It would be the case that some members of the group would have repaid their loan had they not been saddled with the weight of the liability for their peers' loans. Khandekar, Samad and Khan (1998) showed that the three[1] most important Micro-Credit programmes of Bangladesh have had positive impacts on income, production and employment, particularly in the rural non-farm sector that use traditional technology.

1. Three Micro-Credit programmes of Bangladesh are Grameen Bank, Bangladesh Rural Advancement Committee (BRAC) and Bangladesh Rural Development Board's (BRDB) RD-12 project.

In this paper four models attempting to explain repayment behaviour of members *vis-á-vis* loans taken from a Rosca group is proposed. The objective is to econometrically estimate the parameters attached to variables that can possibly explain the members' decision to repay or default. The data for the empirical study is obtained from an exhaustive survey (described in previous chapter) of a large Rosca programme in West Bengal, India facilitated by Jeevika Development Society (JDS). The survey covers 1074 member-households belonging to 111 groups. Two members are chosen to act as signatories (leaders) and an account is opened in a local bank for the group fund. In each of the four proposed models the dependent variable is the member's decision to repay or default. Thus the dependent variable is categorical in nature and a logit estimation method is used.

This paper is divided into five sections. Section 2 analyses some factors that may be important in the formation of a Rosca group. Section 3 examines the repayment performance of the Rosca groups. This section is divided into two sub-sections, 3(a) and 3(b). Section 3(a) examines the impact of group specific variables on repayment performance. Section 3(b) examines the mixed impact of group and individual specific variables on repayment performance. Section 4 compares the results of these two impacts. Section 5 concludes the paper.

Table 16.1

Analysis of Variance

Model	*Sum of Squares*	*df*	*Mean squares*	*F*	*Sig.*
Regression	40638.453	1	40638.453	.023	.880
Residual	1907286564.580	1072	1779185.228		
Total	**1907327203.033**	**1073**			

Note: a) Predictors: (Constant), GROUP
b) Dependent Variable: INCOME.

2. Factors Leading to Formation of Rosca

Theory suggests that the random Rosca is effective if a group is formed by homogeneous members (Besley *et al.*, 1993). Homogeneity has been defined by them as groups, which are formed with members who come from the same income class. In the present sample, it is hypothesised that there is no variation in income within a group. It is obtained from the F test given in the Table 16.1 that the variation in income within a group is not significant. Therefore we cannot reject our hypothesis. This strengthens the presupposition that the appropriate institutional design (Random Rosca) is being used here.

In these groups set up by JDS, there are two signatories to the bank account maintained on behalf of the group. These two signatories are also responsible for maintaining the book of accounts for the group. They also act as conveners of group meetings. It is presumed here that there may be one or two members in the group who led the movement towards forming a group and who motivate others to join. Presumably these leaders naturally act as the signatories for the group. It is hypothesised here that financial hardship faced by the women leading the groups may have been a motive force in formation of groups. There was a question in the study relating to financial difficulties faced by a member at the time of group formation. It is next calculated how many group leaders (signatories) faced such difficulties when their group was formed. From the Table 16.2 it is seen that 58.44 per cent of group signatories faced financial problems and 61.69 per cent of them had outstanding loans outside Rosca at the time of group formation. These two factors provide some insight into the dynamics that leads to the formation of a Rosca group.

Table 16.2

Motivating Factors of Group Formation

Factor Leading to the Formation of Group	*(%)*
Percentage of signatories (leaders) who faced financial hardship at the time of group formation	58.44
Percentage of signatories who had outstanding loan at the time of group formation	61.69

3. Repayment Performance of Group Members

The repayment performance of group-based credit schemes is examined in this section. Section 3(a) analyses the impact of group specific variables on the repayment performance of members in the group. Section 3(b) examines how the individual *and* group specific variables affect the repayment performance of members in the group. The name of variables and their explanations are given below:

Table 16.3

Description of Variables

Variable Name	*Explanation*
Repaglon	= 1, if the member repays her group loan; = 0, otherwise.
Occu1	= 1, if the member is an agricultural labour. = 0, otherwise.
Occu2	= 1, if the member is in service. = 0, otherwise.
Occu3	= 1, if the member is a businesswoman. = 0, otherwise.
Shareten	= 1, if the member or her spouse is a share tenant; = 0, otherwise.
Resland	= Value of residential land that is owned by the member (Rs.).
Futrlon	= Amount Demanded for future loan by the member (Rs.).
MD	= 1, if member does not wish to change the size of group. = 0, otherwise.
Finaprob	= 1, if member has financial problem when she joins the group; = 0, otherwise.
Groupage	= Length of time for which the group has been in existence.
Grosize	= Size of the group (number of members in a group).
Peelonre	= 1, if member generally repays her peer's loan. Borrower borrows this loan from her peers to repay the group loan; = 0, otherwise.
SS1	= 1, if the defaulter is allowed to repay loan and interest by her peers. = 0, otherwise.
SS2	= 1, if the defaulter is allowed to continue to contribute her savings; = 0, otherwise.
SH	= 1, if the borrower does not get any loan in future in case of delayed repayment of group loan; = 0, otherwise.
V1	= 1, if village=Bhasa; = 0, otherwise
V3	= 1, if village=Khariberia; = 0, otherwise
V4	= 1, if village=Parbatipur; = 0, otherwise
V5	= 1, if village=Bojberia; = 0, otherwise
V7	= 1, if village=Chakrajumullah; = 0, otherwise

Contd. ...

Contd. ...

Variable Name	*Explanation*
V10	= 1, if village=Samali; = 0, otherwise
V11	= 1, if village=Angarberia; = 0, otherwise
V12	= 1, if village=Nandabhanga; = 0, otherwise
V13	= 1, if village=Gazipur; = 0, otherwise
V17	= 1, if village=Daulatpur; = 0, otherwise.
V18	= 1, if village=Amgachhia; = 0, otherwise.

3(a) Impact of Group Specific Variables on Repayment Performance

The impact of group specific variables on the repayment performance is analysed in this section. The objective is to check the following hypotheses.

i) the age of the group does not affect the repayment performance;

ii) the size of the group does not affect the repayment performance;

iii) the repayment of peer's loan by the defaulting member does not affect the repayment performance;

iv) the level of social sanction imposed by members on the defaulter does not affect the repayment performance;

v) the loan recovery process has no impact on repayment performance;

vi) the desirable group size according to members does not affect the repayment performance.

The dependent variable Repaglon is binary for which the Limited Dependent Variable (LOGIT) method is used to check the impacts of group specific variables on the dependent variable. It was observed in the survey that Rosca members have faced different types of social sanctions when they defaulted. Once a default occurs in the group, it was found during the survey that members try to devise various ways to recover the amount. Other members of a group often resort to some informal arrangements to recover this loan and interest from the defaulter. These arrangements vary among groups. Two dummies SS1 and SS2 are considered to understand the effects of these informal arrangements on repayment performance of the Rosca members. SH is considered to examine the effect of social sanction on repayment performance of members. In this section two models are considered to assess the impact of group specific variables on repayment performance. The loan recovery processes are different in these two models.

Model I

A regression equation for repayment of group loan (Repagloan) on size of the group, age of the group, repayment of peer's loan, one of the processes of loan recovery (defaulter is pressurised to repay loan and interest within the lifetime of Rosca), social sanction and desirable group size is constructed. The model is as follows:

$$\text{Repaglon} = \alpha + \beta_1\text{Groupage} + \beta_2\text{Grosize} + \beta_3\text{Peelonre} + \beta_4\text{SS1} + \beta_5\text{SH} + \beta_6\text{MD} + u$$

The theoretical justifications of introducing these explanatory variables are as follows:

- *Groupage*: Groupage is considered as an explanatory variable. Groups, which exist for a long period, continue their savings and lending activities successfully over many rotations. Each member therefore becomes a borrower several times and such members are more convinced of the benefits of keeping a Rosca alive. These groups may achieve sustainability within the lifetime of Rosca. It is expected that the age of the group is likely to positively influence repayment rates.
- *Grosize:* Grosize is considered as an explanatory variable. Most of the theoretical literature suggests that the group, which contains large number of members, may fail to achieve sustainability. The strength of peer monitoring is generally very low in large group as informational requirements for effective peer monitoring is very high. So it is important to find the impact of group size on repayment performance.
- *Peelonre*: When faced with a possibility of default, some groups attempt to have an informal arrangement amongst members. In this case, the defaulting member may borrow the sum from another member and repay her loan to the Rosca. This happens when her peers insist upon repayment

of the loan to the group in order to continue the group activities. It is expected that peer pressure is very strong in these groups. A negative sign for the coefficient to Peelonre is expected because repayment of group loan implies that loan from the peer is not repaid at the same time.

- *SS1, SS2*: Often members of a group realise that a borrower is about to default. In such case discussions with the concerned member may ensue resulting in the group allowing the defaulting member some latitude in repayment. They may allow partial repayment of a kind that amounts to rescheduling of the defaulters obligations. In the present survey two such arrangements were observed. These are:
    - i) Defaulter is allowed to only repay loan and interest, but is allowed more time to contribute her savings (SS1).
    - ii) Defaulter is allowed to only contribute her savings but is given more time to repay the loan and interest (SS2).
- *SH*: It was found in the survey that some groups imposed a threat of exclusion from loans in the future in case of delays in repaying loan. That is a borrower member was debarred from future loans even if she repaid her loan and interest after a delay. In the survey members were asked whether the defaulter got any future loan after their delayed repayment of previous loans or not. SH is a dummy variable that captures the impact of such threats on repayment performance. It is also expected that SH has a positive impact on repayment performance.
- *MD*: MD captures the discomfort with current size of the group. It was observed that members, who were comfortable with the existing group size, did not want to change the group size. It is expected that they have good repayment performance.

Results of the Regression Analysis

The regression equation for estimation is given as:

$$\underset{}{\text{Repaglon}} = \underset{(0.04218)}{-1.2348} + \underset{(0.0556704)}{0.0979686}\ \text{Groupage} + \underset{(0.0873238)}{0.146741}\ \text{Grosize}$$

$$\underset{(0.277149)}{-3.88947}\ \text{Peelonre} + \underset{(0.209713)}{0.173151}\text{SS1} + \underset{(0.230307)}{3.04391}\text{SH} + \underset{(0.41808)}{1.43827}\text{MD} + u$$

Mc Fadden $R^2 = 0.48$ (Standard Errors are in the Parentheses).

Table 16.4

Impact of Group Variables on Repayment Performance-I

Variable	*Marginal Value*	*t-ratio*	*P-value*
Constant	-0.1301314496	-1.18482	0.2361
Groupage	0.01032461411	1.7598	0.0784
Grosize	0.01546462232	1.68043	0.0929
Peelonre	-0.4098999888	-14.0339	0.000
SS1	0.01824788336	0.825658	0.4090
SH	0.3207885597	13.2168	0.0000
MD	0.1515749883	3.44018	0.0006

Results of testing of hypotheses are given in the Table 16.4. It is observed that

- Groupage is significant at 92 per cent level. The sign of the marginal value shows that repayment performances of older groups are better.
- It may be recalled that in this sample Grosize lies between 8 and 13. This variable is significant at 91 per cent level. The sign of the marginal value indicates that groups with larger size (number of members nearer to 13) have good repayment performance.
- Peelonre is significant at 99 per cent level. It is concluded from the sign of the marginal value that the member has good repayment performance when she repays the loan to the group even by borrowing from other members of the group. Naturally, she does not repay her peer's loan at the same time. As mentioned earlier, this is via discussions within the group that other members arrange it such that a borrower in difficulty may repay group loan first in order to continue the group activities.
- SS1 is insignificant.
- SH is significant at 99 per cent level. The sign of the marginal value suggests that threat of exclusion from future loan has positive impact on repayment performance.
- MD is significant at 99 per cent level. The sign of the marginal value indicates that the group has good repayment

performance if members do not want to change their group size.

Model II

In Model II a dummy variable SS2 is introduced to capture the impact of one of the loan recovery processes on repayment performance and SS1 is dropped in this model. A regression equation of repayment of group loan on size of the group, age of the group, repayment of peer's loan, loan recovery process (defaulter is compelled to contribute her savings but allowed more time to make good the principle and interest), social sanction and desirable group size is constructed.

$$\text{Repaglon} = \alpha + \beta_1\text{Groupage} + \beta_2\text{Grosize} + \beta_3\text{Peelonre} + \beta_4\text{SS2} + \beta_5\text{SH} + \beta_6\text{MD} + u$$

Results of the Regression Analysis

The regression equation for estimation is given as:

$$\text{Repaglon} = \underset{(1.04088)}{-1.405797} + \underset{(0.054587717)}{0.108982168}\text{Groupage} + \underset{(0.087216045)}{0.153641432}\text{ Grosize}$$

$$\underset{(0.272244)}{-3.851217}\text{Peelonre} + \underset{(0.53427439)}{1.561833}\text{ SS2} + \underset{(0.233314)}{3.076704}\text{SH} + \underset{(0.42189)}{1.449531}\text{MD} + u$$

Mc Fadden $R^2 = 0.49$ (Standard Errors are in the Parentheses).

Table 16.5

Impact of Group Variables on Repayment Performance-II

Variable	*Marginal Value*	*t-ratio*	*P-value*
Constant	-0.1439725459	-1.35058	0.1768
Groupage	0.01116124394	1.99646	0.0459
Grosize	0.0157349548	1.76162	0.0781
Peelonre	-0.3944165669	-14.1462	0.000
SS2	0.1599527991	2.92328	0.0035
SH	0.3150960324	13.187	0.0000
MD	0.1484514816	3.43581	0.0006

Results of testing of hypotheses are given in the Table 16.5.

This model differs from the earlier one only in the sense that SS2 has been introduced and SS1 dropped. We find that SS2 is significant at 99 per cent level. The sign of the marginal value suggests that repayment performance is positively affected by an informal institutional arrangement of debt rescheduling whereby the borrower continue with her savings activities but is allowed more time to repay her principle and interest. Other results in the model are very similar to Model I.

3(b) *Impact of Individual and Village Specific Characteristics on Repayment Performance*

The combined effects of individual *and* group specific variables on repayment performance of group-members are examined in this section. Repayment performance for loan to group (which is a binary variable) is still the dependent variable. Eight additional explanatory variables are introduced in Models III and IV. Three dummy variables are included to capture the impact of occupation of members on their repayment performance. The objective is to check some hypotheses in addition to those tested in Model I and II. The additional hypotheses are

i) occupation of a member does not affect the repayment performance;

ii) incidence of share tenancy does not affect the repayment performance;

iii) financial problems faced by the member at the time of group formation does not affect the repayment performance;

iv) value of residential land of the member does not affect repayment performance;

v) demand for loan in the future does not affect repayment performance.

Table 16.6 shows that in nine villages all members had repaid their loans to their respective groups and in two villages all members had defaulted. Dummy variables are not included for these villages as there is no intra-village variation for repayment. In the other 11 villages repayment performance was found to be mixed. For these 11 villages 11 dummy variables were used to check the impact of villages on repayment. These models are estimated using the Maximum Likelihood Technique (LOGIT), as the dependent variable is binary.

Table 16.6

Repayment Performance of Members Across Villages

Name of the Village	*Repaid (number of members)*	*Default (number of members)*
Bhasa	43	106
Kajirhat	22	0
Khariberia	57	5
Parbatipur	27	1
Bojberia	27	3
Chandpur	40	0
Chakrajumullah	18	11
Nawbad	11	0
Rasapunja	50	0
Samali	11	20
Angarberia	46	15
Nandabhanga	26	5
Gazipur	78	2
Bagi	0	28
Abjakhali	49	0
Chhitbagi	39	0
Daulatpur	26	81
Amgachhia	94	1
Kastomahal	82	0
Gandhabaduli	20	0
Rajarampur	0	10
Bardeuli	20	0

Two models are considered to assess the impact of group *and* individual specific variables jointly on repayment performance. The informal institutional arrangements created by groups when faced with the possibility of default in these two models are different.

Model III

A regression equation for repayment of group loan on occupation, incidence of share tenancy, financial problems faced by a member at the time of group formation, value of residential land and demand for loan from the group in future are considered. These independent variables are in addition to those included in Model I and II. SS1 is also included in this model and it is replaced in the next model with

SS2. Dummy variables for each relevant village in which the group is located is included. The model is specified as follows:

$$\text{Repaglon} = \alpha + \beta_1 \text{ Occu1} + \beta_2 \text{ Occu2} + \beta_3\text{Occu3} + \beta_4 \text{ Shareten} + \beta_5 \text{ Finaprob} + \beta_6 \text{ Resland} + \beta_7 \text{ Futrlon} + \beta_8 \text{ Groupage} + \beta_9\text{Grosize} + \beta_{10}\text{Peelonre} + \beta_{11}\text{SS1} + \beta_{12}\text{SH} + \beta_{13}\text{MD} + \beta_{14} v_1 + \beta_{15} v_3 + \beta_{16}v_4 + \beta_{17}v_5 + \beta_{18} v_7 + \beta_{19} v_{10} + \beta_{21}v_{11} + \beta_{22} v_{12} + \beta_{23} v_{13} + \beta_{24} v_{17} + \beta_{25} v_{18} + u$$

The theoretical justifications for including the individual specific explanatory variables are as follows:

- *Occu1, Occu2, Occu3:* Occupation reflects the socio-economic status of members. Three dummy variables Occu1, Occu2, Occu3 are considered here. The description of these three dummies is given in Table 16.3. It has been seen previously that members forming these groups, by and large, come from the same income class so one would expect that occupational differences do not have significant influence on repayment performance.
- *Shareten:* Shareten reflects the financial status and condition of a member. Generally, share tenants are poor and are largely debarred from the formal credit market, as they have little or no collateral to offer. Joining Rosca may alleviate their financial hardship. It is expected that the motivation to repay will be high in groups that have a high proportion of share tenants.
- *Finaprob*: It was seen that about 60 per cent members were facing financial hardship at the time of group formation. It may be the case that this is a major motivation to form such groups. It may be expected that members, faced with financial problems, take extreme caution so that they do not default in the lifetime of the Rosca. The repayment rate of these members is expected to be high.
- *Resland*: It was noted that a member with high proportion of own residential land has poor repayment performance. This variable is now included in the next regression model to observe its impact on repayment performance in the presence of other variables. It may be the case that persons with high amount of own residential land join a Rosca in the face of some temporary financial hardship but do not have a long

term need for the Rosca. It is expected that Resland has negative impact on repayment.

- *Futrlon*: It was seen in the survey that some members felt a long term need to remain in a Rosca. This is because the nature of activities undertaken by her generates a need for credit on a regular basis. In the survey members were asked whether or not they would require a Rosca loan in future. Futrlon is included in this model to observe its impact on repayment performance. The important point is that it is uncertain whether the Rosca will continue its activities in future. It is expected that Futrlon positive impact on repayment performance.
- *Dummy Variables*: It was seen in the survey that in 11 villages repayment performance was mixed. 11 village dummies are used in the present model to identify the impact of each village on repayment performance. It is expected that repayment performance is different for different villages.

Results of the Regression Analysis

The regression equation for estimation is given as:

$$\begin{aligned}
\text{Repaglon} = {} & \underset{(1.19495)}{-2.85226} - \underset{(0.80373)}{0.491715}\text{Occu1} - \underset{(0.499064)}{0.130455}\text{Occu2} - \underset{(0.340904)}{0.060085}\text{Occu3} \\
& + \underset{(0.521651)}{0.134241}\text{Shareten} + \underset{(0.28253)}{0.54888}\text{Finaprob} - \underset{(0.00000006)}{0.00000007}\text{ Resland} \\
& + \underset{(0.000002)}{0.0000394}\text{ Futrlon} + \underset{(0.0701677)}{0.07452}\text{ Groupage} + \underset{(0.0966117)}{0.372217}\text{Grosize} \\
& - \underset{(0.374127)}{3.39195}\text{Peelonre} + \underset{(0.291668)}{0.510421}\text{SS1} + \underset{(0.366434)}{3.67409}\text{SH} + \underset{(1.22909)}{1.22909}\text{MD} \\
& - \underset{(0.42773)}{2.55464}V_1 - \underset{(0.68982)}{0.602463}V_3 + \underset{(1.11987)}{0.725658}V_4 - \underset{(0.81825)}{0.359307}V_5 - \underset{(0.6091)}{1.875}V_7 \\
& - \underset{(0.575522)}{3.74547}V_{10} - \underset{(0.55576)}{3.09618}V_{11} - \underset{(0.77120)}{4.6927}V_{12} + \underset{(0.81735)}{0.391147}V_{13} - \underset{(0.48725)}{2.58068}V_{17} \\
& + \underset{(1.30406)}{3.41015}V_{18} + u
\end{aligned}$$

Mc Fadden $R^2 = 0.54$ (Standard errors are in the parentheses).

Table 16.7

Impacts of Individual and Group Variables on Repayment

Performance-I

Variable	*Marginal Value*	*t-ratio*	*P-value*
Constant	-0.1799131465	-2.38693	0.0169
Occu1	-0.03101609601	-0.611791	0.5406
Occu2	-0.0082287940	-0.2614	0.7937
Occu3	-0.0041004591	-0.190689	0.8487
Shareten	0.0084675501	0.257338	0.7969
Finaprob	0.0346219675	1.94273	0.0520
Resland	-0.00000004	-1.02159	0.3069
Futrlon	0.0000019516	1.23132	0.2182
Groupage	0.0047009196	1.06212	0.2881
Grosize	0.0234785026	3.85271	0.0001
Peelonre	-.2139557572	-9.06631	0.0000
SS1	0.0321960266	1.75	0.0801
SH	.2317523682	10.0266	0.0000
MD	0.0775279730	2.32122	0.0202
Bhasa	-.1611400345	-5.9725	0.0000
Khariberia	-0.038001848	-0.87336	0.3824
Parbatipur	0.0457726378	0.647987	0.5169
Bojberia	-0.0226641430	-0.439117	0.6605
Chakrajumullah	-0.1182699588	-3.07851	0.0020
Samali	-0.2362549198	-6.50796	0.0000
Angarberia	-0.1952992803	-5.57112	0.0000
Nandabhanga	-0.2960036607	-6.0849	0.0000
Gazipur	0.02467251905	0.478555	0.6322
Daulatpur	-0.1627827007	-5.29647	0.0000
Amgachhia	0.2151033755	2.61503	0.0089

Results of testing of hypotheses are given in the Table 16.7. It is observed that

- Occu1, Occu2 and Occu3 are not significant. It was observed earlier that members belong to the same income class. It may be the case that due to lack of sufficient variation of this variable within a group the difference in occupational structure has little impact on repayment performance.

- Finaprob is significant at 95 per cent level. It is obtained from the sign of the marginal value that it positively influences the repayment rate. This indicates that members faced with financial hardship take every precaution not to lose the opportunity of Rosca credit by defaulting on their group-loans.
- Shareten, Resland, Futrlon and Groupage are not significant.
- Grosize is significant at 99 per cent level. This indicates that groups with larger size (number of members nearer to 13) have good repayment performance. It is noticed that this variable plays a significant role not only in the present model but also in the previous two Models I and II when only group specific variables are included.
- Peelonre is significant at 99 per cent level. It has negative impact on repayment performance. This result is very similar to that is obtained in Model I and II.
- SS1 is significant at 92 per cent level. The sign of the marginal value suggests that repayment performance is positively affected by SS1. The informal arrangement of debt rescheduling, where borrowers are allowed to repay their loans and interest and allowed to more time to contribute their savings, has positive impact on repayment performance of members. It is important to note that this variable plays a significant role in this model but insignificant role in the model I where only group specific variables are included. It may be said that individual characters of members have high influence on this arrangement of debt rescheduling.
- SH is significant at 99 per cent level. The sign of the marginal value suggests that repayment performance is positively affected by SH. This indicates that members repay their loans timely in order to get the opportunity of getting Rosca credit in future.
- MD is significant at 98 per cent level. The sign of marginal values shows that members, who are comfortable with the present group size, have good repayment performance. This finding is also similar to the one in Models I and II.

- Village Dummies are significant at 99 per cent level for seven villages. These are Bhasa, Chakrajumullah, Samali, Angarberia, Nandabhanga, Daulatpur and Amgachhia. The sign of the marginal values of these dummies suggests that repayment performance is not satisfactory in Bhasa, Chakrajumullah, Samali, Nandabhanga and Daulatpur.

Model IV

In model IV, SS2 is introduced and SS1 is dropped. A regression equation for repayment of group loan on all independent variables, which are included in Model III (except SS1) is considered.

$$\text{Repaglon} = \alpha + \beta_1 \text{ Occul} + \beta_2 \text{ Occu2} + \beta_3\text{Occu3} + \beta_4 \text{ Shareten} + \beta_5 \text{ Finaprob} + \beta_6 \text{ Resland} + \beta_7 \text{ Futrlon} + \beta_8 \text{ Groupage} + \beta_9\text{Grosize} + \beta_{10}\text{Peelonre} + \beta_{11}\text{SS2} + \beta_{12}\text{SH} + \beta_{13}\text{MD} + \beta_{14} v_1 + \beta_{15} v_3 + \beta_{16} v_4 + \beta_{17} v_5 + \beta_{18} v_7 + \beta_{19} v_{10} + \beta_{21} v_{11} + \beta_{22} v_{12} + \beta_{23} v_{13} + \beta_{24} v_{17} + \beta_{25} v_{18} + u$$

Results of the Regression Analysis

The regression equation for estimation is given as:

$$\begin{array}{l}
\text{Repaglon} = \underset{(1.1866)}{-2.51143} \underset{(0.801034)}{-0.491715\text{Occu1}} \underset{(0.50083)}{-0.0068254\text{Occu2}} \underset{(0.342574)}{-0.185275\text{Occu3}} \\
\underset{(0.523015)}{+0.134241\text{Shareten}} \underset{(0.285536)}{+0.54888\text{Finaprob}} \underset{(0.00000006)}{-0.00000007\text{ Resland}} \\
\underset{(0.000002)}{+0.000003\text{Futrlon}} \underset{(0.0692782)}{+0.0852427\text{ Groupage}} \underset{(0.0967721)}{+0.341941\text{Grosize}} \\
\underset{(0.367635)}{-3.40334\text{Peelonre}} \underset{(0.63844)}{+1.66239\text{SS2}} \underset{(0.36937)}{+3.8599\text{SH}} \underset{(0.530611)}{+1.16307\text{MD}} \\
\underset{(0.432356)}{-2.38184V_1} \underset{(0.67345)}{-0.546528V_3} \underset{(1.1036)}{+1.28663V_4} \underset{(0.79568)}{+0.218985V_5} \underset{(0.65339)}{-2.451941.875V_7} \\
\underset{(0.574357)}{-3.71495V_{10}} \underset{(0.54820)}{-3.00649V_{11}} \underset{(0.758455)}{-4.3924V_{12}} \underset{(0.817563)}{+0.30247347V_{13}} \\
\underset{(0.48109)}{-2.32546V_{17}} \underset{(1.3661)}{+3.78024V_{18}} + u
\end{array}$$

Mc Fadden $R^2 = 0.65$ (Standard errors are in the Parentheses).

The difference between Model III and Model IV is that SS2 has been introduced and SS1 (which is included in Model III) dropped in

Model IV. It is found that SS2 is significant at 99 per cent level. The sign of the marginal value suggests that repayment performance is positively affected by an informal institutional arrangement of debt rescheduling whereby the borrower continue with her savings activities but is allowed more time to repay her principle and interest. Other results in the model are very similar to Model III.

Table 16.8

Impacts of Individual and Group Variables on Repayment

Performance-II

Variable	*Marginal Values*	*t-ratio*	*P-value*
Constant	-.1521181132	-2.11645	0.03430
Occu1	-0.0212147706	-0.437248	0.66193
Occu2	-0.000413416386	-0.0136282	0.98912
Occu3	-0.0112221843	-0.540834	0.58862
Shareten	0.0009183964595	0.0289906	0.97687
Finaprob	0.02780101866	1.60746	0.10795
Resland	-0.00000004476	-1.10719	0.26821
Futrlon	0.000002192975	1.42347	0.15459
Groupage	0.0000021929752	1.23044	0.21853
Grosize	0.02071147611	3.53347	0.00041
Peelonre	-0.2061414459	-9.2574	0.00000
SS2	0.1006912294	2.60383	0.00921
SH	0.2337954529	10.45	0.00000
MD	0.07044738797	2.19194	0.02838
Bhasa	-0.1442686409	-5.50897	0.00000
Khariberia	-0.0331033435	-0.811539	0.41705
Parbatipur	0.07793161967	1.16584	0.24367
Bojberia	0.01326397163	0.275216	0.78315
Chakrajumullah	-0.1485146204	-3.75262	0.00017
Samali	-0.2250158043	-6.46802	0.00000
Angarberia	-0.1821037892	-5.48431	0.00000
Nandabhanga	-0.2660489995	-5.79125	0.00000
Gazipur	0.01832089791	0.369969	0.71140
Daulatpur	-0.1408537172	-4.83377	0.00000
Amgachhia	0.2289703240	2.76711	0.00565

4. The Comparison Between Models

The first two models analyse the impact of group specific variables on repayment performance. The Model III and IV analyse the mixed impact of group and individual specific variables on the repayment performance. The Mc Fadden R^2 of these models can be compared. It is obtained that the introduction of group *and* individual specific variables explained 54 per cent to 65 per cent of the variation whereas group specific variables explained only 48 per cent to 49 per cent. It implies that repayment performance of a Rosca depends not only on group activities but also on individual characteristics of group members.

5. Conclusion

Theory suggests that random Rosca performs well if members from homogeneous backgrounds form groups. From the ANOVA table it was seen that there is no significant variation in income among the members i.e., they came from the same income class. It was seen that two important factors lead to the formation of Rosca. These are i) financial hardship faced by members at the time of group formation and ii) outstanding loans that members borrow from informal lenders other than Rosca at a usurious rate of interest. Members who are facing financial hardship often do not overcome their problems by borrowing only once from Rosca. Those who need loans in the future repay their loans in time to continue the group activities of the Rosca. It is seen from the tabulated result that most of the group specific variables are significant. This indicates that these Rosca groups have performed well. The strength of social sanction has positive effect on repayment performance, which supports the theoretical finding.

References

Besley, T., S. Coate and G. Loury (1993). "The Economics of Rotating Savings and Credit Associations", *American Economic Review,* 83(4), 792-810.

Besley , T. and S. Coate (1995). "Group Lending, Repayment Incentives and Social Collateral", *Journal of Development Economics,* 46(1), 1-18.

Besley, T. and R.A. Levenson (1996). "The Anatomy of an Informal Financial Market: ROSCA Participation in Taiwan", *Journal of Development Economics,* 51(1), 45-68.

Handa, S. and C. Kirton (1999). "The Economics of Rotating Savings and Credit Associations: Evidence from the Jamaican Partner", *Journal of Development Economics,* 60(6), 173-194.

Khandekar, S.R., A.S. Hussain and H.K. Zahed (1998). "Income and Employment Effects of Micro-Credit Programmes: Village Level Evidence from Bangladesh" *The Journal of Development Studies,* 35(2), 96-124.

Mosley, P. (2001). "Micro-Credit and Poverty in Bolivia", *The Journal of Development Studies,* 37(4), 101-132.

Stiglitz, J. (1990). "Peer Monitoring and Credit Markets", *World Bank Economic Review,* 4(3), 351-366.

Wenner, M.D. (1995). "Group Credit: A Means to Improve Information Transfer and Loan Repayment Performance", *The Journal of Development Studies,* 32(2), 263-281.

Zeller, M. (1998). "Determinants of Repayment Performance in Credit Groups: The Role of Program Design, Intragroup Risk Pooling and Social Cohesion", *Economic Development and Cultural Change,* 46(3), 599-620.